REA

ACPL ITEM DISCARDED

W9-AEM-251

CIRCULATING WITH THE LISTED PROBLEMS(S):
Pencil markings throughout book. 11-16-2020

6·26·78

Cambridge Studies in Social Anthropology

GENERAL EDITOR: JACK GOODY

16

OUTLINE OF
A THEORY OF PRACTICE

OTHER TITLES IN THE SERIES

OUTLINE OF
A THEORY OF PRACTICE

PIERRE BOURDIEU

Translated by
RICHARD NICE

CAMBRIDGE UNIVERSITY PRESS

CAMBRIDGE

LONDON · NEW YORK · MELBOURNE

Published by the Syndics of the Cambridge University Press
The Pitt Building, Trumpington Street, Cambridge CB2 1RP
Bentley House, 200 Euston Road, London NW1 2DB
32 East 57th Street, New York, NY 10022, USA
296 Beaconsfield Parade, Middle Park, Melbourne 3206, Australia

© In the English language edition Cambridge University Press 1977
The original edition, entitled *Esquisse d'une théorie de la pratique, précédé de trois
études d'ethnologie kabyle*, was published by Librairie Droz S.A. in Switzerland
© Librairie Droz, 1972

First published in English translation 1977

Printed in Great Britain at the
University Press, Cambridge

Library of Congress Cataloguing in Publication Data
Bourdieu, Pierre.
Outline of a theory of practice.
(Cambridge studies in social anthropology; 16)
Translation with revisions of Esquisse d'une
théorie de la pratique.
Includes bibliographical references and index.
1. Kabyles – Addresses, essays, lectures.
2. Ethnology. I. Title.
DT298.K2B6913   301.2   76-11073
ISBN 0 521 21178 6 hard covers
ISBN 0 521 29164 X paperback

Contents

2013083

"The principal defect of all materialism up to now – including that of Feuerbach – is that the external object, reality, the sensible world, is grasped in the form of *an object or an intuition*; but not as *concrete human activity*, as *practice*, in a subjective way. This is why the active aspect was developed by idealism, in opposition to materialism – but only in an abstract way, since idealism naturally does not know real concrete activity as such."

K. Marx, *Theses on Feuerbach*

Translator's foreword

Outline of a Theory of Practice was first published in French in 1972 (*Esquisse d'une théorie de la pratique*). However, this English text incorporates most of the changes which Pierre Bourdieu has made since then. The argument is carried further, particularly as regards the concepts of practical logic and symbolic capital, the order of exposition is recast, and, partly for reasons of space, the ethnographic chapters with which the French edition opens have been curtailed.

This text is the cornerstone of an oeuvre which encompasses numerous major works in both anthropology and sociology – which crosses and challenges the boundary dividing their objects, tasks, and theories, and forces attention to the social conditions in which such sciences are possible.

The fieldwork in Kabylia which provided the ethnographic basis for this text and the starting-point for its reflections was carried out amid the tragic circumstances of the Algerian war, which brought to a head the contradictions inherent in the ethnologist's position. This was one factor in Bourdieu's subsequent move into the field of sociology, where the *separation* which is the hidden condition of all academic activity – most insidiously so in the behavioural sciences – could itself be grasped scientifically in the course of inquiry into the social functions of scholarship and the mechanisms of cultural and social reproduction.

The *Outline*, a "reflection on scientific practice which will disconcert both those who reflect on the social sciences without practising them and those who practise them without reflecting on them", seeks to define the prerequisites for a truly scientific discourse about human behaviour, that is, an adequate theory of practice which must include a theory of scientific practice.

The stages through which Bourdieu's work has passed, the problems he has set himself, are of course partly determined by the accidents of a biography; but also by the configurations of the intellectual field in France over a certain period. The commonplaces a translator might feel required to adduce in order to extenuate the visible loss entailed in extracting a text from its context touch only the surface of processes which the explicit thrust of Bourdieu's argument, here and elsewhere, enables us to grasp more profoundly as involving more than questions of "translatability". Bourdieu would be the last to regret the shedding of all that the text was immediately and tacitly granted, inasmuch as it bore the social marks which signal a product conforming to the local standards: the signs of recognition eliciting the recognition of already converted readers, the dignifying references, theoretical allusions, stylistic effects, have indeed every likelihood of remaining dead letters once outside the magic circle of belief.

But much more besides the value set on the text is at stake when it circulates beyond its field of production. The most autonomous work contains implicit reference to an intellectual universe whose cardinal points are scientific (and political) positions symbolized, in a given state of the field, by the names of authors or schools of thought or by "isms" which may cover totally different realities in different national traditions. These are the structures of the field of production, its divisions into antagonistic groups and rival schools, which, internalized, function as unexamined principles of perception and appreciation. When these bearings are removed the text becomes open to misreading.

Thus nothing guarantees that, for some readers, this work, written *against* the currents at present dominant in France, "structuralism" or "structural-Marxism", will not be merged with the very tendencies it combats. Less pessimistically, there is still reason to fear that the frequent references made to the Anglo-American philosophical tradition – a heaven-sent weapon against the theoreticism which so strongly characterizes French social science, from Durkheim to Lévi-Strauss – may, when returned to their original universe, take on a significance very different from the one they were given in a context in which that tradition is disdained or unknown, and be seen as a sign of allegiance to positivism (if not as an ingratiating gesture towards the intellectual establishment).

The fact remains that a text which seeks to break out of a scheme of thought as deeply embedded as the opposition between subjectivism and objectivism is fated to be perceived through the categories which it seeks to transcend, and to appear contradictory or eclectic (except when forcibly reduced to one or the other alternative). The provisional eclecticism which can juxtapose Wittgenstein with the young Marx finds its justification in the fact that all the resources of a tradition which from the beginning has made practice the negative obverse of theory are needed in order to think the unthinkable.

R. N.

I

The objective limits of objectivism

The practical privilege in which all scientific activity arises never more subtly governs that activity (insofar as science presupposes not only an epistemological break but also a *social* separation) than when, unrecognised as privilege, it leads to an implicit theory of practice which is the corollary of neglect of the social conditions in which science is possible. The anthropologist's particular relation to the object of his study contains the makings of a theoretical distortion inasmuch as his situation as an observer, excluded from the real play of social activities by the fact that he has no place (except by choice or by way of a game) in the system observed and has no need to make a place for himself there, inclines him to a hermeneutic representation of practices, leading him to reduce all social relations to communicative relations and, more precisely, to decoding operations. Charles Bally remarked that linguistic research takes different directions according to whether it deals with the researcher's mother tongue or with a foreign language, emphasizing in particular the tendency to *intellectualism* implied in observing language from the standpoint of the listening subject rather than that of the speaking subject, that is, as a "means of action and expression": "the listener is on the side of the language, it is with the language that he interprets speech".[1] And exaltation of the virtues of the distance secured by externality simply transmutes into an epistemological choice the anthropologist's objective situation, that of the "impartial spectator", as Husserl puts it, condemned to see all practice as a spectacle.

It is instructive to glance at the case of art history, which, never having really broken with the tradition of the *amateur*, gives free rein to celebratory contemplation and finds in the sacred character of its object every pretext for a hagiographic hermeneutics superbly indifferent to the question of the social conditions in which works are produced and circulate. Panofsky, for example, writing on Abbot Suger and the "invention" of Gothic architecture, only exceptionally and almost accidentally abandons the point of view of the interpreter who, more concerned with the *opus operatum* than the *modus operandi*, represses the question of artistic production under the concept of the "objective intention" of the work and reduces immediate comprehension to a decoding that is unaware that it *is* a decoding. To treat a work of plastic art as a discourse intended to be interpreted, decoded, by reference to a transcendent code analogous to the Saussurian "*langue*" is to forget that artistic production is always *also* – to different degrees depending on the art and on the historically variable styles

[1]

of practising it – the product of an "art", "pure practice without theory", as Durkheim says,[2] or to put it another way, a *mimesis*, a sort of symbolic gymnastics, like the rite or the dance; and it is also to forget that the work of art always contains something *ineffable*, not by excess, as hagiography would have it, but by default, something which communicates, so to speak, from body to body, i.e. on the hither side of words or concepts, and which pleases (or displeases) without concepts.

So long as he remains unaware of the limits inherent in his point of view on the object, the anthropologist is condemned to adopt unwittingly for his own use the representation of action which is forced on agents or groups when they lack practical mastery of a highly valued competence and have to provide themselves with an explicit and at least semi-formalized substitute for it in the form of a *repertoire of rules*, or of what sociologists consider, at best, as a "rôle", i.e. a predetermined set of discourses and actions appropriate to a particular "stage-part".[3] It is significant that "culture" is sometimes described as a *map*; it is the analogy which occurs to an outsider who has to find his way around in a foreign landscape and who compensates for his lack of practical mastery, the prerogative of the native, by the use of a model of all possible routes. The gulf between this potential, abstract space, devoid of landmarks or any privileged centre – like genealogies, in which the ego is as unreal as the starting-point in a Cartesian space – and the practical space of journeys actually made, or rather of journeys actually being made, can be seen from the difficulty we have in recognizing familiar routes on a map or town-plan until we are able to bring together the axes of the field of potentialities and the "system of axes linked unalterably to our bodies, and carried about with us wherever we go", as Poincaré puts it, which structures practical space into right and left, up and down, in front and behind.

Hence it is not sufficient for anthropology to break with native experience and the native representation of that experience: it has to make a second break and question the presuppositions inherent in the position of an outside observer, who, in his preoccupation with *interpreting* practices, is inclined to introduce into the object the principles of his relation to the object, as is attested by the special importance he assigns to communicative functions (whether in language, myth, or marriage). Knowledge does not merely depend, as an elementary relativism teaches, on the particular standpoint an observer "situated in space and time" takes up on the object. The "knowing subject", as the idealist tradition rightly calls him, inflicts on practice a much more fundamental and pernicious alteration which, being a constituent condition of the cognitive operation, is bound to pass unnoticed: in taking up a point of view on the action, withdrawing from it in order to observe it from above and from a distance, he constitutes practical activity as an *object of observation and analysis*, a *representation*.

From the mechanics of the model to the dialectic of strategies

The social world may be the object of three modes of theoretical knowledge, each of which implies a set of (usually tacit) anthropological theses. Although these modes of knowledge are strictly speaking in no way exclusive, and may be described as moments in a dialectical advance towards adequate knowledge, they have only one thing in common, the fact that they are opposed to practical knowledge. The knowledge we shall call *phenomenological* (or, to speak in terms of currently active schools, "ethnomethodological") sets out to make explicit the truth of primary experience of the social world, i.e. all that is inscribed in the relationship of *familiarity* with the familiar environment, the unquestioning apprehension of the social world which, by definition, does not reflect on itself and excludes the question of the conditions of its own possibility. The knowledge we shall term *objectivist* (of which structuralist hermeneutics is a particular case) constructs the objective relations (e.g. economic or linguistic) which structure practice and representations of practice, i.e., in particular, primary knowledge, practical and tacit, of the familiar world. This construction presupposes a break with primary knowledge, whose tacitly assumed presuppositions give the social world its self-evident, natural character.[4] It is only on condition that it poses the question which the *doxic* experience of the social world excludes by definition – the question of the (particular) conditions making that experience possible – that objectivist knowledge can establish both the structures of the social world and the objective truth of primary experience as experience denied *explicit* knowledge of those structures.

Finally, it is only by means of a second break, which is needed in order to grasp the limits of objectivist knowledge – an inevitable moment in scientific knowledge – and to bring to light the theory of theory and the theory of practice inscribed (in its practical state) in this mode of knowledge, that we can integrate the gains from it into an adequate science of practices. The critical break with objectivist abstraction ensuing from inquiry into the conditions of possibility, and thereby, into the limits of the objective and objectifying standpoint which grasps practices from outside, as a *fait accompli*, instead of constructing their generative principle by situating itself within the very movement of their accomplishment, has no other aim than to make possible a science of the *dialectical* relations between the objective structures to which the objectivist mode of knowledge gives access and the structured dispositions within which those structures are actualized and which tend to reproduce them.

This questioning of objectivism is liable to be understood at first as a rehabilitation of subjectivism and to be merged with the critique that naive humanism levels at scientific objectification in the name of "lived experience" and the rights of "subjectivity". In reality, the theory of practice and of the practical mode of knowledge inherent in all practice which is the precondition for a rigorous science of practices carries out a new reversal of the problematic which objectivism has to construct in order to constitute the social world as a system of objective relations independent of individual consciousnesses and wills. Just as objectivist knowledge poses the question of the conditions of the possibility of primary experience, thereby revealing that this experience (or the phenomenological analysis of it) is fundamentally defined as *not* posing this question, so the theory of practice puts objectivist knowledge back on its feet by posing the question of the (theoretical and also social) conditions which make such knowledge possible. Because it produces its science of the social world against the implicit presuppositions of practical knowledge of the social world, objectivist knowledge is diverted from construction of the theory of practical knowledge of the social world, of which it at least produces the lack.

Objective analysis of practical apprehension of the familiar world is not a new form of sacrificial offering to the mysteries of subjectivity, but a means of exploring the limits of all objective exploration. It teaches us that we shall escape from the ritual either/or choice between objectivism and subjectivism in which the social sciences have so far allowed themselves to be trapped only if we are prepared to inquire into the mode of production and functioning of the practical mastery which makes possible both an objectively intelligible practice and also an objectively enchanted experience of that practice; more precisely, that we shall do so only if we subordinate all operations of scientific practice to a theory of practice and of practical knowledge (which has nothing to do with phenomenological reconstitution of lived experience), and inseparably from this, to a theory of the theoretical and social conditions of the possibility of objective apprehension – and thereby to a theory of the limits of this mode of knowledge.

A single example will suffice to show how this sort of third-order knowledge does not cancel out the gains from objectivist knowledge but conserves and transcends them by integrating the truth of practical experience and of the practical mode of knowledge which this learned knowledge had to be constructed against, that is to say, inseparably, the truth of all learned knowledge. It will be remembered that Lévi-Strauss, criticizing Mauss's "phenomenological" approach to gift exchange, makes a complete break with native experience and the native theory of that experience, positing that it is the exchange as a constructed object which "constitutes the primary phenomenon, and not the individual operations into which social life breaks it down",[5] or, in other words, that the "mechanical laws" of the cycle of reciprocity are the unconscious principle of the obligation to give, the obligation to give in return, and the obligation to receive.[6] "Phenomenological" analysis and objectivist analysis bring to light two antagonistic principles of gift exchange: the gift as experienced, or, at least, meant to be experienced, and the gift as seen from outside. To stop short at the "objective" truth of the gift, i.e. the model, is to set aside the question of the relationship between so-called objective truth, i.e. that of the observer, and the truth that can scarcely be called subjective, since it represents the official definition of the subjective experience of the exchange; it is to ignore the fact that the agents practise as irreversible a sequence of actions that the observer constitutes as reversible. The observer's totalizing apprehension substitutes an objective structure fundamentally defined by its *reversibility* for an equally objectively *irreversible* succession of gifts which are not mechanically linked to the gifts they respond to or insistently call for: any really objective analysis of the exchange of gifts, words, challenges, or even women must allow for the fact that each of these inaugural acts may misfire, and that it receives its meaning, in any case, from the response it triggers off, even if the response is a failure to reply that retrospectively removes its intended meaning. To say that the meaning the gift has for the donor is recognized and consecrated only when the counter-gift has been made does not amount to restoring the structure of the cycle of reciprocity in different words. It means that even if reversibility is the objective truth of the discrete acts which ordinary experience knows in discrete form and calls gift exchanges, it is not the whole truth of a practice which could not exist if it were consciously perceived in accordance with the model. The temporal structure of gift exchange, which objectivism ignores, is what makes possible the coexistence of two opposing truths, which defines the full truth of the gift.

In every society it may be observed that, if it is not to constitute an insult, the counter-gift must be *deferred* and *different*, because the immediate return of an exactly identical object clearly amounts to a refusal (i.e. the return of the same object). Thus gift exchange is opposed on the one hand to *swapping*, which, like the theoretical model of the cycle of reciprocity, telescopes gift and counter-gift into the same instant, and on the other hand, to *lending*, in which the return of the loan is explicitly guaranteed by a juridical act and is thus *already accomplished* at the very moment of the drawing up of a contract capable of ensuring that the acts it prescribes are predictable and calculable. The difference and delay which the monothetic model obliterates must be brought into the model not, as Lévi-Strauss suggests, out of a "phenomenological" desire to restore the subjective experience of the practice of the exchange, but because the operation of gift exchange presupposes (individual and collective) misrecognition (*méconnaissance*) of the reality of the objective "mechanism" of the exchange, a reality which an immediate response brutally exposes: the *interval* between gift and counter-gift is what allows a pattern of exchange that is always liable to strike the observer and also the participants as *reversible*, i.e. both forced and interested, to be experienced as irreversible. "Overmuch eagerness to discharge one's obligations is a form of ingratitude", said La Rochefoucauld. To betray one's haste to be free of an obligation one has incurred, and thus to reveal too overtly one's desire to pay off services rendered or gifts received, so as to be quits, is to denounce the initial gift retrospectively as motivated by the intention of obliging one. It is all a question of style, which means in this case timing and choice of occasion, for the same act – giving, giving in return, offering one's services, paying a visit, etc. – can have completely different meanings at different times, coming as it may at the right or the wrong moment, while almost all important exchanges – gifts to the mother of a new-born child, or on the occasion of a wedding, etc. – have their own particular moments; the reason is that the lapse of time *separating* the gift from the counter-gift is what authorizes the deliberate oversight, the collectively maintained and approved self-deception without which symbolic exchange, a fake circulation of fake coin, could not operate. If the system is to work, the agents must not be entirely unaware of the truth of their exchanges, which is made explicit in the anthropologist's model, while at the same time they must refuse to know and above all to recognize it.[7] In short, everything takes place as if agents' practice, and in particular their manipulation of *time*, were organized exclusively with a view to concealing from themselves and from others the truth of their practice, which the anthropologist and his models bring to light simply by substituting the timeless model for a scheme which works itself out only in and through time.

To abolish the interval is also to abolish strategy. The period interposed, which must be neither too short (as is clearly seen in gift exchange) nor too long (especially in the exchange of revenge-murders), is quite the opposite of the inert gap of time, the time-lag which the objectivist model makes of it. Until he has given in return, the receiver is "*obliged*", expected to show his gratitude towards his benefactor, or, at least, to have regard for him, to refrain from using against him all the weapons he otherwise might, to pull his punches, lest he be accused of ingratitude and stand condemned by "what people say", which is what gives his actions their social meaning. The man who has not avenged a murder, not bought back his land from a rival family, not married off his daughters in time, sees his capital diminished from day to day by passing time – unless he is capable of transforming forced delay into strategic deferment, the space of time into deliberate spacing out: putting off revenge or the return of a gift can be a way of keeping one's partner-opponent in the dark about one's intentions; the moment for the comeback becomes impossible to pinpoint, like the really evil moment in the ill-omened periods of the ritual calendar, just before the upturn. After a certain point lack of response ceases to be an oversight and becomes disdainful refusal. Delay is also a way of exacting from him the deferential conduct that is required as long as relations are not broken off. It is understandable within this logic that a man whose daughter is asked for in marriage should feel he has to reply as soon as possible if the answer is no, lest he seem to be taking advantage of the situation, and offend the suitor, whereas if he intends to say yes, he may put off the reply for as long as he likes, so as to make the most of the temporary advantage of his position, which he will lose as soon as he gives his consent. Everything takes place as if the ritualization of interactions had the paradoxical effect of giving time its full social efficacy, never more potent than when nothing *but* time is going on. "Time", we say, "is on his side"; time can also work against one. In other words, time derives its efficacy from the state of the structure of relations within which it comes into play; which does not imply that the model of that structure can leave it out of account. When the unfolding of the action is heavily ritualized, as in the dialectic of offence and vengeance, there is still room for strategies which consist of playing on the time, or rather the *tempo*, of the action, by delaying revenge so as to prolong the threat of revenge. And this is true, *a fortiori*, of all the less strictly regulated occasions which offer unlimited scope for strategies exploiting the possibilities offered by manipulation of the tempo of the action – holding back or putting off, maintaining suspense or expectation, or on the other hand, hurrying, hustling, surprising, and stealing a march, not to mention the art of ostentatiously giving time ("devoting one's time to someone") or withholding it ("no time to spare"). We know, for example, how much advantage the holder of a transmissible power can derive from the art of delaying transmission and keeping others in the dark as to his ultimate intentions. Then there are all the strategies intended simply to neutralize the action of time and ensure the continuity of interpersonal relations, drawing the continuous out of the discontinuous, as mathematicians do, through infinite multiplication of the infinitely small, in the form, for example, of the "little presents" said to "keep friendship going" ("O present – *thunticht* – you won't make me rich but you are the bond of friendship").

Little presents, which are halfway between "gratuitous" gifts (*elma'tar*, unreturned gift, "like a mother's milk", or *thikchi*, a thing given without recompense) and the most rigorously "forced" gifts, must be of modest value and hence easy to give and easy to match; but they must be *frequent*, and in a sense continuous, which implies that they must function within the logic of "surprises" or "kind thoughts" rather than according to the mechanisms of ritual. These presents intended to maintain the everyday order of social intercourse almost always consist of a dish of cooked food, couscous (with a piece of cheese, when they mark a cow's first milk) and follow the course of minor family celebrations – the third or seventh day after a birth, a baby's first tooth or first steps, a boy's first haircut, first visit to the market, or first fast; linked to events in the life-cycle of men or the earth, they involve those wishing to *impart* their joy, and those invited to *take part* in that joy, in what is nothing less than a fertility rite: when the dish which contained the present is taken back, it always contains, "for good luck" (*el fal*), what is sometimes called *thiririth* (from *er*, to give back), that is to say, a little corn, a little semolina (never barley, a female plant and symbol of fragility), or, preferably, some dried vegetables, chick peas, lentils, etc., called *ajedjig* "flower", given "so that the boy [the reason for the exchange] will flourish", so that he will grow tall and be fruitful. These ordinary gifts (which include some of those they call *tharzefth*, which are visiting-presents) are sharply opposed to extraordinary gifts, *lkhir* or *lehna*, given for the major festivals called *thimeghriwin* (sing. *thameghra*) – weddings, births, and circumcisions – and *a fortiori* to *lw'ada*, the obligatory gift to a saint. And indeed, the little gifts between relatives and friends are opposed to the present of money and eggs which is given by affines remote both in space and in the genealogy, and also in time – since they are seen only intermittently, on the "great occasions" – and whose importance and solemnity make them a sort of controlled challenge in the same way that marriages within the lineage or neighbour-hood, so frequent and so closely woven into the fabric of ordinary exchanges that they pass unnoticed, are opposed to the more prestigious but infinitely more hazardous extraordinary marriages between different villages or tribes, sometimes intended to set the seal on alliances or reconciliations and always marked by solemn ceremonies.

This takes us a long way from the objectivist model of the mechanical interlocking of preregulated actions that is commonly associated with the notion of ritual: only a virtuoso with a perfect command of his "art of living" can play on all the resources inherent in the ambiguities and uncertainties of behaviour and situation in order to produce the actions appropriate to each case, to do that of which people will say "There was nothing else to be done", and do it the right way. We are a long way, too, from norms and rules: doubtless there are slips, mistakes, and moments of clumsiness to be observed here as elsewhere; and also grammarians of decorum able to state (and elegantly, too) what it is right to do and say, but never presuming to encompass in a catalogue of recurrent situations and appropriate conduct, still less in a fatalistic model, the "art" of the *necessary improvisation* which defines excellence.

To restore to practice its practical truth, we must therefore reintroduce time into the theoretical representation of a practice which, being temporally structured, is intrinsically defined by its *tempo*. The generative, organizing scheme which gives a discussion its unity or an improvised speech its "argu-ment", and attains conscious expression in order to work itself out, is an often imprecise but systematic principle of selection and realization, tending, through steadily directed adjustments and corrections, to eliminate accidents when they can be put to use, and to conserve even fortuitous successes. It is therefore practice, in its most specific aspect, which is annihilated when the scheme is identified with the model: retrospective necessity becomes prospective necessity, the product a project; and things which have happened, and can no longer not happen, become the irresistible future of the acts which made them happen. This amounts to positing, with Diodorus, that if it is true to say of a thing that it will be, then it must one day be true to say that it is, or, in the words of another paradox, that "Today is tomorrow, because yesterday tomorrow was today."[8] All experience of practice contradicts these paradoxes, and affirms that cycles of reciprocity are not the irresistible gearing of obligatory practices found only in ancient tragedy: a gift may remain unrequited, if it meets with ingratitude; it may be spurned as an insult.[9] Once the possibility is admitted that the "mechanical law" of the "cycle of reciprocity" may not apply, the whole logic of practice is transformed. Even in cases in which the agents' habitus are perfectly harmonized and the interlocking of actions and reactions is totally predictable *from outside*, uncertainty remains as to the outcome of the interaction as long as the sequence has not been completed: the passage from the highest probability to absolute certainty is a qualitative leap which is not proportionate to the numerical gap. This uncertainty, which finds its objective basis in the probabilist logic of social laws, is sufficient to modify not only the experience of practice (which phenomenological analysis describes, being more attentive than objectivism to the temporality of action) but practice itself, in giving an objective foundation to strategies aimed at avoiding the most probable outcome.

To substitute *strategy* for the *rule* is to reintroduce time, with its rhythm, its orientation, its irreversibility. Science has a time which is not that of practice. For the analyst, time no longer counts: not only because – as has often been repeated since Max Weber – arriving *post festum*, he cannot be in any uncertainty as to what may happen, but also because he has the time to totalize, i.e. to overcome the effects of time. Scientific practice is so "detemporalized" that it tends to exclude even the idea of what it excludes: because science is possible only in a relation to time which is opposed to that of practice, it tends to ignore time and, in doing so, to reify practices. (Which is to say, once again, that epistemological reflection is constitutive of scientific practice itself: in order to understand what practice is – and in particular the properties it owes to the fact that it unfolds in time – it is therefore necessary to know what science is – and in particular what is implied in the specific temporality of scientific practice.) The detemporalizing effect (visible in the synoptic apprehension that diagrams make possible) that science produces when it forgets the transformation it imposes on practices inscribed in the current of time, i.e. detotalized, simply by totalizing them, is never more pernicious than when exerted on practices defined by the fact that their temporal structure, direction, and rhythm are *constitutive* of their meaning.

From the "rules" of honour to the sense of honour

There are ways of avoiding ethnocentrism which are perhaps no more than so many devices for keeping one's distance and, at all events, for making a virtue out of necessity by converting a *de facto* exclusion into a choice of method. Thus, there would be less danger of locking the exchange of honour or the seemingly most ritualized gift exchange in reified, reifying models, if one were able to procure a theoretical mastery of social practices of the same class as those of which one may have a practical mastery. There is nothing, for example, more likely to inspire in an outside observer the illusion of mechanical necessity than *"forced" conversation*, which, to perpetuate itself, must endlessly create and recreate, often *ex nihilo*, the relationship between the interlocutors, moving them apart and bringing them together, constraining them to seek out points of agreement and disagreement, with the same earnestness at once sincere and feigned, making them by turns triumph and retreat, arousing mock quarrels that are always on the verge of becoming real ones, but quickly settled by a compromise or a return to the safe ground of shared convictions. But, by a radical change in point of view, one can equally apprehend this mechanical sequence of gestures and words "from a subjective point of view", as the Marx of the *Theses on Feuerbach* somewhat rashly puts it, or, preferably, from the standpoint of an adequate theory of practice: the unceasing vigilance one needs to exert so as to be "carried along" by the game, without being "carried away" *beyond* the game, as happens when a mock fight gets the better of the fighters, is evidence that practices as visibly constrained as these rest on the same principle as conduct more likely to give an equally misleading impression of free improvisation, such as *bluff* or *seduction*, which play on the equivocations, innuendos, and unspoken implications of verbal or gestural symbolism to produce ambiguous conduct that can be disowned at the slightest sign of withdrawal or refusal, and to maintain uncertainty about intentions that always hesitate between playfulness and seriousness, abandon and reserve, eagerness and indifference.

The language of rules and models, which seems tolerable when applied to "alien" practices, ceases to convince as soon as one considers the practical mastery of the symbolism of social interaction – tact, dexterity, or savoir-faire – presupposed by the most everyday games of sociability and accompanied by the application of a spontaneous semiology, i.e. a mass of precepts, formulae, and codified cues. This practical knowledge, based on the continuous decoding of the perceived – but not consciously noticed – indices of the welcome given to actions already accomplished, continuously carries out the checks and corrections intended to ensure the adjustment of practices and expressions to the reactions and expectations of the other agents. It functions like a self-regulating device programmed to redefine courses of action in accordance with information received on the reception of information transmitted and on the effects produced by that information. It can be seen that the typical hermeneutic paradigm of the exchange of words is perhaps less appropriate than the paradigm of the exchange of blows used by George H. Mead.[10] In dog-fights, as in the fighting of children or boxers, each move triggers off a counter-move, every stance of the body becomes a sign pregnant with a meaning that the opponent has to grasp while it is still incipient, reading in the beginnings of a stroke or a sidestep the imminent future, i.e. the blow or the dummy. And the dummy itself, in boxing as in conversation, in exchanges of honour as in matrimonial transactions, presupposes an opponent capable of preparing a riposte to a movement that has barely begun and who can thus be tricked into faulty anticipation.

It is sufficient to carry out a similar reversal of perspective in order to see that one can, for example, produce practically or reproduce theoretically all the honour conducts actually observed (or potentially observable), remarkable at once for their inexhaustible diversity and their quasi-mechanical necessity, without possessing the "filing-cabinet of prefabricated representations", as Jakobson puts it,[11] that would enable the agent to "select" the conduct appropriate to each situation, and without having to construct at great expense of effort a "mechanical" model which would at best be to the man of honour's regulated improvisation what an etiquette handbook is to the art of living or a harmony treatise to musical composition. The science of practice has to construct the principle which makes it possible to account for all the cases observed, and only those, without forgetting that this construction, and the generative operation of which it is the basis, are only the theoretical equivalent of the practical scheme which enables every correctly trained agent to produce all the practices and judgments of honour called for by the challenges of existence.

To make someone a challenge is to credit him with the dignity of a man of honour, since the challenge, as such, requires a riposte and therefore is addressed to a man deemed capable of playing the game of honour, and of playing it well. From the principle of mutual recognition of equality in honour there follows a first corollary: the challenge confers honour. "The man who has no enemies", say the Kabyles, "is a donkey" (the symbol of passivity). There is nothing worse than to pass unnoticed: thus, not to salute someone is to treat him like a thing, an animal, or a woman. The challenge, conversely, is "a high point in the life of the man who receives it". It is the chance to prove one's manliness (*thirugza*) to others and to oneself. A second corollary is this: he who challenges a man incapable of taking up the challenge, that is, incapable of pursuing the exchange, dishonours himself. Thus *elbahadla*, extreme humiliation publicly inflicted, recoils on the man who provokes it (*amahbul*): even the man who merits *elbahadla* possesses an honour; that is why *elbahadla* boomerangs. Hence the man who finds himself in a strong position must refrain from pushing his advantage too far, and should temper his accusation with a certain moderation, so as to let his adversary put *himself* to shame. "Better that he should strip himself", says the proverb, "than that I should unclothe him." His opponent, for his part, can always try to turn the tables by leading him on to overstep the permitted limits. This is done in the hope of rallying public opinion, which cannot but disapprove of the accuser's lack of moderation. The third corollary is that only a challenge (or offence) coming from an equal in honour deserves to be taken up; in other words, for there to be a challenge, the man who receives it must consider the man who makes it worthy of making it. An affront from a presumptuous inferior rebounds on its author. "The prudent, circumspect man [*amahdhuq*] does not get involved with an *amahbul*." *Elbahadla* would fall on the wise man who ventured to take up the *amahbul*'s senseless challenge; whereas in abstaining from all reply, he leaves him to bear the weight of his arbitrary acts. Likewise, dishonour would fall on the man who dirtied his hands in an unworthy revenge (hence, in certain cases, recourse to the hired killer, *amekri*). It is therefore the nature of the riposte which makes the challenge a challenge, as opposed to mere aggression.[12]

In game theory, the good player is the one who always supposes his opponent will discern the best strategy and who directs his own play accordingly; similarly, in the game of honour, challenge and riposte alike imply that each player chooses to play the game as well as he can while assuming that his adversary is capable of making the same choice. The gift is a challenge which honours the man to whom it is addressed, at the same time putting his point of honour (*nif*) to the test; consequently, just as to insult a man incapable of riposting dishonours oneself, so to make a present so great that it cannot be matched merely dishonours the giver. A gift or challenge is a provocation, a provocation to reply. "He has shamed him", the Moroccan Berbers used to say, according to Marcy, apropos of the challenge-gift (*tawsa*) which marked the great ceremonies.[13] The receiver of a gift is caught in the toils of exchange and has to choose a line of conduct which, whatever he does, will be a response (even if only by default) to the provocation of the initial act. He can choose to prolong the exchange or to break it off. If, obedient to the point of honour, he opts for exchange, his choice is identical with his opponent's initial choice: he agrees to play the game, which can go on for ever, for the riposte is in itself a new challenge. Formerly, it is said, as soon as vengeance had been taken, the whole family rejoiced at the ending of dishonour: the men let off rifle shots and the women uttered cries of '*you-you*', proclaiming that revenge was accomplished, so that all might see how a family of honour promptly restores its prestige and so that the opposing family should be left in no doubt as to the source of its misfortune.

Choosing the other alternative may take on different and even opposed meanings. The offender may, in terms of his physical strength, his prestige, or the importance and authority of the group to which he belongs, be superior, equal, or inferior to the person offended. While the logic of honour presupposes the recognition of an ideal equality in honour, the popular consciousness is nonetheless aware of actual inequalities. The man who declares "I've got a moustache, too" is answered with the proverb "The moustache of the hare is not that of the lion..." This is the basis of a whole spontaneous casuistry. Let us take the case where the offended party has, at least ideally, the means to riposte; if he proves incapable of taking up the challenge (whether a gift or an offence), if from pusillanimity or weakness he sidesteps it and renounces the chance of riposting, he is in a sense choosing to be the author of his own dishonour, which is then irremediable. He confesses himself defeated in the game that he ought to have played despite everything. But non-reply can also express the refusal to reply: the man who has suffered an offence refuses to regard it as such, and through his disdain, which he may manifest by calling in a hired killer, he causes the offence to recoil on its perpetrator, who is thereby dishonoured. Similarly in the case of the gift, the recipient may indicate that he chooses to refuse the exchange, either by rejecting the gift or by presenting an immediate or subsequent counter-gift identical to the original gift. Here, too, the exchange stops. In short, within this logic, only escalation, challenge answering challenge, can signify the option of playing the game.

In the case where the offender is clearly superior to the offended, only the fact of avoiding the challenge is held to be blameworthy, and the offended party is not required to triumph over the offender in order to be rehabilitated in the eyes of public opinion: the defeated man who has done his duty incurs no blame. The offended party is even able to throw back *elbahadla* on his offender without resorting to a riposte. He only has to adopt an attitude of humility which, by emphasizing his weakness, highlights the arbitrary and immoderate character of the offence. This strategy is, of course, only admissible so long as, in the eyes of the group, the disparity between the two antagonists is unequivocal; it is a natural course for those individuals socially recognized as weak, clients (*yadh itsumuthen*, those who lean on), or members of a small family.

Finally, in the case where the offender is inferior to the offended, the latter may riposte (thus transgressing the third corollary) but if he unfairly exploits his advantage, he exposes himself to the dishonour which would otherwise have rebounded on to the presumptuous offender. Wisdom advises him rather to abstain from any reply and to play the "contempt" gambit: since failure to riposte cannot be imputed to cowardice or weakness, the dishonour recoils on to the attacker. Although each of these "theoretical" cases could be illustrated with a host of observations and stories, the fact remains that the differences between the two parties are never clear-cut, so that each can play on the ambiguities and equivocations which this indeterminacy lends to the conduct. The distance between failure to riposte owing to fear and non-reply bespeaking contempt is often infinitesimal, with the result that disdain can always serve as a mask for pusillanimity.

Every exchange contains a more or less dissimulated challenge, and the logic of challenge and riposte is but the limit towards which every act of communication tends. Generous exchange tends towards overwhelming generosity; the greatest gift is at the same time the gift most likely to throw its recipient into dishonour by prohibiting any counter-gift. To reduce to the function of communication – albeit by the transfer of borrowed concepts – phenomena such as the dialectic of challenge and riposte and, more generally, the exchange of gifts, words, or women, is to ignore the structural ambivalence which predisposes them to fulfil a political function of domination in and through performance of the communication function.

If the offence does not necessarily bear within it dishonour, the reason is that it allows the possibility of riposte, which is recognized by the very act of giving offence.[14] But potential dishonour becomes more and more real the longer vengeance is delayed. Therefore the time-lag between the offence and the reparation must be as short as possible; a large family has indeed sufficient fighting men not to have to wait long. The reputation of its *nif*, its sensitivity and determination, lead it to appear as capable of riposting the very instant an offence is committed. The respect inspired by a good family is expressed in the saying that it can "sleep and leave the door open". The man of honour, of whom people say that he fulfils "his rôle as a man" (*thirugza*), is always on his guard; hence he is immune from even the most reckless attack, and "even when he is away, there is someone in his house". But things are not so simple. It is said that Djeha, a legendary figure, asked when he had avenged his father, replied, "After a hundred years had gone by." The story is also told of the lion who always walks with measured paces: "I don't know where my prey is", he said. "If it's in front of me, one day I'll reach it; if it's behind me, it'll catch up with me."

However close it may come to the logic of practices (and to the extent that it does), the abstract diagram which has to be constructed in order to account for that logic is liable to obscure the fact that the driving force of the whole mechanism is not some abstract principle (the principle of isotimy, equality in honour), still less the set of *rules* which can be derived from it, but the sense of honour, a disposition inculcated in the earliest years of life and constantly reinforced by calls to order from the group, that is to say, from the aggregate of the individuals endowed with the same dispositions, to whom each is linked by his dispositions and interests. *Nif*, literally the nose, is very closely associated with virility and with all the dispositions, incorporated in the form of bodily schemes, which are held to manifest virility; the verb *qabel*, commonly used to designate the fundamental virtues of the man of honour, the man who faces, outfaces, stands up to others, looks them in the eyes, knows how to receive as a host and to do his guest honour, also means to face the east (*elqibla*) and the future (*qabel*), the male orientation par excellence. This is sufficient to remind us that the point of honour is a permanent disposition, embedded in the agents' very bodies in the form of mental dispositions, schemes of perception and thought, extremely general in their application, such as those which divide up the world in accordance with the oppositions between the male and the female, east and west, future and past, top and bottom, right and left, etc., and also, at a deeper level, in the form of bodily postures and stances, ways of standing, sitting, looking, speaking, or walking. What is called the *sense of honour* is nothing other than the cultivated disposition, inscribed in the body schema and in the schemes of thought, which enables each agent to engender all the practices consistent with the logic of challenge and riposte, and only such practices, by means of countless inventions, which the stereotyped unfolding of a ritual would in no way demand. The fact that there is no "choice" that cannot be accounted for, retrospectively at least, does not imply that such practice is perfectly predictable, like the acts inserted in the rigorously stereotyped sequences of a rite; and this is true not only for the observer but also for the agents, who find in the relative predictability and unpredictability of the possible ripostes the opportunity to put their strategies to work. But even the most strictly ritualized exchanges, in which all the moments of the action, and their unfolding, are rigorously foreseen, have room for strategies: the agents remain in command of the *interval* between the obligatory moments and can therefore act on their opponents by playing with the *tempo* of the exchange. We know that returning a gift at once, i.e. doing away with the interval, amounts to breaking off the exchange. Likewise the lesson contained in the parables of Djeha and the lion must be taken seriously; the mastery which defines excellence finds expression in the play made with time which transforms ritualized exchange into a confrontation of strategies. The skilled strategist can turn a capital of provocations received or conflicts suspended, with the potential ripostes, vengeances, or conflicts it contains, into an instrument of power, by reserving the capacity to reopen or cease hostilities in his own good time.

Practice and discourse about practice

It would thus be possible to move on to the ground where talk of rules seems least misplaced, that of custom or "pre-law", and show that the "customary rules" preserved by the group memory are themselves the product of a small batch of schemes enabling agents to generate an infinity of practices adapted to endlessly changing situations, without those schemes ever being constituted as explicit principles. This is why, like Weber's Kadi-justice, customary law always seems to pass from particular case to particular case, from the specific misdeed to the specific sanction, never expressly formulating the fundamental principles which "rational" law spells out explicitly (e.g. all men are equal in honour).[15] The appropriate acts of jurisprudence concerning a particular offence, for example, those making it possible to assess the gravity of a theft according to the circumstances in which it was committed, can all be produced from a small number of schemes that are continuously applied in all domains of practice, such as the oppositions between the house (or mosque) and other places, between night and day, between feast days and ordinary days, the first member of each pair always corresponding to the severer penalty. It is clear that it is sufficient to combine the corresponding principles to produce the sanction appropriate to each case, real or imaginary – from, for example, theft committed by night from a dwelling house, the most heinous, to theft by day in a distant field, the least heinous, other things being equal, of course.[16] The generative schemes are so generally and automatically applicable that they are converted into explicit principles, formally stated, only in the very case in which the value of the object stolen is such as to sweep aside all extenuating or aggravating circumstances. Thus the *qanun* of Ighil Imoula, for example, reported by Hanoteau and Letourneux, provides that "he who steals a mule, ox or cow, by force or trickery shall pay 50 reals to the djemâa and pay the owner the value of the stolen animal, whether the theft was *by night or by day, from inside a house or outside, and whether the animals belong to the householder or to someone else*".[17] The same basic schemes, always functioning in the implicit state, apply in the case of brawls, which together with thefts normally occupy a considerable place in custom; there are the same oppositions, but sometimes with new implications, between the house and other places (the murder of a person caught in one's home, for example, entailing no sanction), night-time and daytime, feast days and ordinary days; and there are also variations according to the social status of the aggressor and the victim (man/woman, adult/child) and the weapons or methods used (whether it was by treachery – if, for example, the victim was asleep – or in man-to-man combat) and the extent to which the deed was carried out (mere threats or actual violence). There is every reason to think that if the basic propositions of this implicit axiomatics were spelled out more completely than is possible here (e.g. a crime is always more serious committed by night than committed by day), together with the laws by which they are combined (depending on the case, two propositions may either be added together or cancel each other out, which, within the logic of the rule, can only be described as an exception), it would be possible to *reproduce* all the provisions of all the customary laws which have been collected and even to produce the complete universe of all the acts of jurisprudence conforming to the "sense of justice" in its Kabyle form.

Thus the precepts of custom, very close in this respect to sayings and proverbs (such as those which govern the temporal distribution of activities), have nothing in common with the transcendent rules of a juridical code: everyone is able, not so much to cite and recite them from memory, as to reproduce them (fairly accurately). It is because each agent has the means of acting as a judge of others and of himself that custom has a hold on him: indeed, in social formations where, as in Kabylia, there exists no judicial apparatus endowed with a monopoly of physical or even symbolic violence and where clan assemblies function as simple arbitration tribunals, that is, as more or less expanded family councils, the rules of customary law have some practical efficacy only to the extent that, skilfully manipulated by the holders of authority within the clan (the "guarantors"), they "awaken", so to speak, the schemes of perception and appreciation deposited, in their incorporated state, in every member of the group, i.e. the dispositions of the habitus. They are therefore separated only by differences of degree from the partial and often fictitious explicit statements of the group's implicit axiomatics through which individual more-or-less "authorized" agents seek to counter the failures or hesitations of the habitus by stating the solutions appropriate to difficult cases. Talk of rules, a euphemized form of legalism, is never more fallacious than when applied to the most homogeneous societies (or the least codified areas of differentiated societies) where most practices, including those seemingly most ritualized, can be abandoned to the orchestrated improvisation of common dispositions: the rule is never, in this case, more than a second-best intended to make good the occasional misfirings of the collective enterprise of inculcation tending to produce habitus that are capable of generating practices regulated without express regulation or any institutionalized call to order.[18]

It goes without saying that the implicit philosophy of practice which pervades the anthropological tradition would not have survived all the denunciations of legalist formalism if it had not had an affinity with the presuppositions inscribed in the relationship between the observer and the object of his study, which impose themselves in the very construction of his object so long as they are not explicitly taken as an object. Native experience of the social world never apprehends the system of objective relations other than *in profiles*, i.e. in the form of relations which present themselves only one by one, and hence successively, in the emergency situations of everyday life. If agents are possessed by their habitus more than they possess it, this is because it acts within them as the organizing principle of their actions, and because this *modus operandi* informing all thought and action (including thought of action) reveals itself only in the *opus operatum*. Invited by the anthropologist's questioning to effect a reflexive and quasi-theoretical return on to his own practice, the best-informed informant produces a *discourse which compounds two opposing systems of lacunae*. Insofar as it is a *discourse of familiarity*, it leaves unsaid all that goes without saying: the informant's remarks – like the narratives or commentaries of those whom Hegel calls "original historians" (Herodotus, Thucydides, Xenophon, or Caesar) who, living "in the spirit of the event",[19] take for granted the presuppositions taken for granted by the historical agents – are inevitably subject to the censorship inherent in their habitus, a system of schemes of perception and thought which cannot give what it does give to be thought and perceived without *ipso facto* producing an unthinkable and an unnameable. Insofar as it is an *outsider-oriented discourse* it tends to exclude all direct reference to particular cases (that is, virtually all information directly attached to *proper names* evoking and summarizing a whole system of previous information). Because the native is that much less inclined to slip into the language of familiarity to the extent that his questioner strikes him as unfamiliar with the universe of reference implied by his discourse (a fact apparent in the form of the questions asked, particular or general, ignorant or informed), it is understandable that anthropologists should so often forget the distance between learned reconstruction of the native world and the native experience of that world, an experience which finds expression only in the silences, ellipses, and lacunae of the language of familiarity.

Finally, the informant's discourse owes its best-hidden properties to the fact that it is the product of a *semi-theoretical* disposition, inevitably induced by any learned questioning. The rationalizations produced from this standpoint, which is no longer that of action, without being that of science, meet and confirm the expectations of the juridical, ethical, or grammatical formalism to which his own situation inclines the observer. The relationship between informant and anthropologist is somewhat analogous to a pedagogical relationship, in which the master must bring to the state of explicitness, for the purposes of transmission, the unconscious schemes of his practice. Just as the teaching of tennis, the violin, chess, dancing, or boxing breaks down into individual positions, steps, or moves, practices which integrate all these artificially isolated elementary units of behaviour into the unity of an organized activity, so the informant's discourse, in which he strives to give himself the appearances of symbolic mastery of his practice, tends to draw attention to the most remarkable "moves", i.e. those most esteemed or reprehended, in the different social games (such as *elbahadla* in the honour game or marriage with the parallel cousin among the matrimonial strategies), rather than to the principle from which these moves and all equally possible moves can be generated and which, belonging to the universe of the undisputed, most often remain in their implicit state. But the subtlest pitfall doubtless lies in the fact that such descriptions freely draw on the highly ambiguous vocabulary of *rules*, the language of grammar, morality, and law, to express a social practice that in fact obeys quite different principles. The explanation agents may provide of their own practice, thanks to a quasi theoretical reflection on their practice, conceals, even from their own eyes, the true nature of their practical mastery, i.e. that it is *learned ignorance* (*docta ignorantia*), a mode of practical knowledge not comprising knowledge of its own principles. It follows that this learned ignorance can only give rise to the misleading discourse of a speaker himself misled, ignorant both of the objective truth about his practical mastery (which is that it is ignorant of its own truth) and of the true principle of the knowledge his practical mastery contains.

Native theories are dangerous not so much because they lead research towards illusory explanations as because they bring quite superfluous reinforcement to the intellectualist tendency inherent in the objectivist approach to practices. This academicism of the social "art" of living which, having extracted from the *opus operatum* the supposed principles of its production, sets them up as norms explicitly governing practices (with phrases like "good form requires...", "custom demands...", etc.), takes away understanding of the logic of practice in the very movement in which it tries to offer it. For example, the ideological use many societies make of the lineage model and, more generally, of genealogical representations, in order to justify and legitimate the established order (e.g. by choosing the more *orthodox* of two possible ways of classifying a marriage), would doubtless have become apparent to anthropologists at an earlier date if the theoretical use they themselves make of this theoretical construct had not prevented them from inquiring into the functions of genealogies and *genealogists*, and thereby from seeing the genealogy as the theoretical census of the universe of theoretical relationships within which individuals or groups define the real space of (in both senses) *practical* relationships in terms of their conjunctural interests.

The imposition and inculcation of the structures is never so perfect that all explicitness can be dispensed with. And inculcation is itself, together with institutionalizing, which is always accompanied by a certain amount of objectification in discourse (oral or written) or some other symbolic support (emblems, rites, etc.), one of the privileged moments for formulating the practical schemes and constituting them as principles. It is doubtless no accident that the question of the relations between the habitus and the "rule" should be brought to light with the historical emergence of an express and explicit action of inculcation:[20] the pedagogy of the Sophists, forced, in order to realize its aim, to produce systems of rules, such as grammars or rhetorics, came up against the problem of the rules defining the right way and right moment – *kairos* – to apply the rules, or, as the phrase so aptly goes, to *put into practice* a repertoire of devices or techniques, in short, the whole art of performance, in which the habitus inevitably reappears. And, no doubt because it still partakes of the ambiguous status of all grammars, which never make it clear whether they reconstitute the real mechanics of the schemes immanent in practice or the theoretical logic of the models constructed in order to account for practices, Chomskian generative grammar nowadays entails (objective) rediscovery that what creates the problem is not the possibility of producing coherent sentences in infinite number but the fact of coherently and appropriately using an infinite number of sentences in an infinite number of situations.

It is not easy to define rigorously the status of the semi-learned grammars of practice – sayings, proverbs, gnomic poems, spontaneous "theories" which always accompany even the most "automatic" practices, checking the functioning of the automatisms or, more or less successfully, making good their misfirings – and of all the *knowledges* produced by an "operation of the second power" which, as Merleau-Ponty observes, "presupposes the structures it analyses"[21] and more or less rigorously accounts for. Being the product of the same generative schemes as the practices they claim to account for, even the most false and superficial of these "secondary explanations" only reinforce the structures by providing them with a particular form of "rationalization". Even if they affect practice only within narrow limits,[22] the fact remains that whenever the adjustment between structures and dispositions is broken, the transformation of the generative schemes is doubtless reinforced and accelerated by the dialectic between the schemes immanent in practice and the norms produced by reflection on practices, which impose new meanings on them by reference to alien structures.

Reaction against legalist formalism in its overt or masked form must not lead us to make the habitus the exclusive principle of all practice. In reality, even in social formations where, as in Kabylia, the making explicit and objectifying of the generative schemes in a grammar of practices, a written code of conduct, is minimal, it is nonetheless possible to observe the first signs of a differentiation of the domains of practice according to the degree of codification of the principles governing them. Between the areas that are apparently "freest" because given over in reality to the regulated improvisations of the habitus (such as the distribution of activities and objects within the internal space of the house) and the areas most strictly regulated by customary norms and upheld by social sanctions (such as the great agrarian rites), there lies the whole field of practices subjected to traditional precepts, customary recommendations, ritual prescriptions, functioning as a regulatory device which orients practice without producing it. The absence of a genuine *law* – the product of the work of a body of specialists expressly mandated to produce a coherent corpus of juridical norms and ensure respect for its application, and furnished to this end with a coercive power – must not lead us to forget that any socially recognized formulation contains within it an intrinsic power to reinforce dispositions symbolically.

Our approach is thus radically opposed, on two essential points, to the interactionism which reduces the constructions of social science to "constructs of the second degree, that is, constructs of the constructs made by the actors on the social scene", as Schutz does,[23] or, like Garfinkel, to accounts of the accounts which agents produce and through which they produce the meaning of their world.[24] One is entitled to undertake to give an "account of accounts", so long as one does not put forward one's contribution to the science of pre-scientific representation of the social world as if it were a science of the social world. But this is still too generous, because the prerequisite for a science of commonsense representations which seeks to be more than a complicitous description is a science of the structures which govern both practices and the concomitant representations, the latter being the principal obstacle to the construction of such a science.[25] Only by constructing the objective structures (price curves, chances of access to higher education, laws of the matrimonial market, etc.) is one able to pose the question of the mechanisms through which the relationship is established between the structures and the practices or the representations which accompany them, instead of treating these "thought objects" as "reasons" or "motives" and making them the determining cause of the practices. Moreover, the constitutive power which is granted to ordinary language lies not in the language itself but in the group which authorizes it and invests it with authority. Official language, particularly the system of concepts by means of which the members of a given group provide themselves with a representation of their social relations (e.g. the lineage model or the vocabulary of honour), sanctions and imposes what it states, tacitly laying down the dividing line between the thinkable and the unthinkable, thereby contributing towards the maintenance of the symbolic order from which it draws its authority. Thus officialization is only one aspect of the objectifying process through which the group teaches itself and conceals from itself its own truth, inscribing in objectivity its representation of what it is and thus binding itself by this public declaration.[26]

The agent who "regularizes" his situation or puts himself in the right is simply beating the group at its own game; in abiding by the rules, falling into line with good form, he wins the group over to his side by ostentatiously honouring the values the group honours. In social formations in which the expression of material interests is heavily censored and political authority relatively uninstitutionalized, political strategies for mobilization can be effective only if the values they pursue or propose are presented in the misrecognizable guise of the values in which the group recognizes itself. It is therefore not sufficient to say that the rule determines practice when there is more to be gained by obeying it than by disobeying it. The rule's last trick is to cause it to be forgotten that agents have an interest in obeying the rule, or more precisely, in *being in a regular situation*. Brutally materialist reduction enables one to break with the naiveties of the spontaneous theory of practice; but it is liable to make one forget the advantage that lies in abiding by the rules, which is the principle of the second-order strategies through which the agent seeks to *put himself in the right*.[27] Thus, quite apart from the direct profit derived from doing what the rule prescribes, perfect conformity to the rule can bring secondary benefits such as the prestige and respect which almost invariably reward an action apparently motivated by nothing other than *pure*, *disinterested* respect for the rule. It follows that strategies directly oriented towards the primary profit of practice (e.g. the prestige accruing from a marriage) are almost always accompanied by second-order strategies whose purpose is to give apparent satisfaction to the demands of the official rule, and thus to compound the satisfactions of enlightened self-interest with the advantage of ethical impeccability.

The fallacies of the rule

The place which a notion as visibly ambiguous as that of the *rule* occupies in anthropological or linguistic theory cannot be fully understood unless it is seen that this notion provides a solution to the contradictions and difficulties to which the researcher is condemned by an inadequate or – which amounts to the same thing – an implicit theory of practice. Everything takes place as if, fulfilling the rôle of a refuge for ignorance, this hospitable notion, which can suggest at once the law constructed by science, the transcendent social norm and the immanent regularity of practices, enabled its user to escape from the dilemma of mechanism or finalism without falling into the most flagrant naiveties of the legalism which makes obedience to the rule the determining principle of all practices. One could go back to Durkheim and examine the place, at once central and empty, occupied in his system by the notion of social constraint. But it is sufficient to consider the quite exemplary theoretical operations whereby Saussure constitutes linguistics as a science by construct ing language as an autonomous object, distinct from its actualizations in speech, in order to bring to light the implicit presuppositions of any mode of knowledge which treats practices or works as symbolic facts, finished products, to be *deciphered* by reference to a code (which may be called culture).

Finding themselves in a position of theoretical dependence on linguistics, structural-ist anthropologists have often involved in their practice the *epistemological unconscious* engendered by unmindfulness of the acts through which linguistics constructed its own object. Heirs to an intellectual heritage which they did not make for themselves, they have too often been satisfied with literal translations of a terminology dissociated from the operations of which it is the product, sparing themselves the effort of an epistemological critique of the conditions and limits of validity of transposing the Saussurian construction. It is noteworthy, for example, that with the exception of Sapir, who was predisposed by his dual training as linguist and anthropologist to raise the problem of the relations between culture and language, no anthropologist has tried to bring out all the implications of the homology (which Leslie White is virtually alone in formulating explicitly) between the two oppositions, that between language and speech on the one hand, and on the other hand that between culture and conduct or works. When Saussure constitutes language as an autonomous object, irreducible to its concrete realizations, that is, to the utterances it makes possible, or when, by a procedure similar in every respect, Panofsky establishes that what he calls, following Aloïs Riegl, *Kunstwollen* – that is to say, roughly, the *objective sense* of the work – is no more reducible to the "will" of the artist than it is to the "will of the age" or to the experiences the work arouses in the spectator, they are performing an operation with regard to these particular cases which can be generalized to all practice. Just as Saussure shows that the true medium of communication between two subjects is not discourse, the immediate datum considered in its observable materiality, but the language, the structure of objective relations making possible both the production and the deciphering of discourse, so Panofsky shows that iconological interpretation treats the sensible properties of the work of art, together with the affective experiences it arouses, as mere "cultural symptoms", which yield their full meaning only to a reading armed with the cultural cipher the artist has engaged in his work.

Saussure first makes the point that speech appears as the precondition for language, as much from the individual as from the collective point of view, because language cannot be apprehended outside of speech, because language is learnt through speech, and because speech is the source of innovations in and transformations of language. This is so even though one might invoke the existence of dead languages or dumbness in old age as proving the possibility of losing speech while conserving language, and even though language mistakes reveal the language as the objective norm of speech (were it otherwise, every language mistake would modify the language and there would be no mistakes any more). But he then observes that the priority of speech over language is purely chronological and that the relationship is inverted as soon as one leaves the domain of individual or collective *history* in order to inquire into the *logical conditions* for deciphering. From this point of view, which is that of objectivism, language is the precondition for the *intelligibility* of speech, being the mediation which ensures the identity of the sound-concept associations made by the speakers and so guarantees mutual comprehension. Thus, in the *logical order of intelligibility*, speech is the product of language.[28] It follows that, because it is constructed from the strictly intellectualist standpoint of deciphering, Saussurian linguistics privileges the *structure* of signs, that is, the relations between them, at the expense of their *practical functions*, which are never reducible, as structuralism tacitly assumes, to functions of communication or knowledge.

The limits of Saussurian objectivism are never more clearly visible than in its inability to conceive of speech and more generally of practice other than as *execution*,[29] within a logic which, though it does not use the word, is that of the rule to be applied. Objectivism constructs a theory of practice (as execution) but only as a negative by-product or, one might say, waste product, immediately discarded, of the construction of the systems of objective relations. Thus, with the aim of delimiting, within the body of linguistic data, the "terrain of the language" and of extracting a "well-defined object", "an object that can be studied separately", "of homogeneous nature", Saussure sets aside "the physical part of communication", that is, speech as a preconstructed object, liable to stand in the way of constructing the language; he then isolates within the "speech circuit" what he calls the "executive side", that is, speech as a constructed object defined by the actualization of a certain sense in a particular combination of sounds, which he finally eliminates on the grounds that "execution is never the work of the mass", but "always individual". Thus the same concept, speech, is *divided* by theoretical construction into an immediately observable *preconstructed datum*, precisely that against which the operation of theoretical construction is carried out, and a *constructed object*, the negative product of the operation which constitutes the language as such, or rather, which produces both objects by producing the relation of opposition within which and by which they are defined. It would not be difficult to show that the construction of the concept of culture (in the cultural anthropology sense) or social structure (in Radcliffe-Brown's sense and that of social anthropology) similarly implies the construction of a notion of conduct as execution which coexists with the primary notion of conduct as simple behaviour taken at face value. The extreme confusion of debates on the relationship between "culture" (or "social structures") and conduct generally arises from the fact that the constructed meaning of conduct and the theory of practice it implies lead a sort of underground existence in the discourse of both the defenders and the opponents of cultural anthropology.[30] Objectivism is thus protected by the implicit state in which its theory of practice remains against the only decisive challenge, the one which would attack precisely that theory, the source of all the metaphysical aberrations on "the locus of culture", the mode of existence of the "structure", or the unconscious finality of the history of systems, not to mention the all-too-famous "collective consciousness".

It is indeed "on the executive side", as Saussure puts it, that one finds the essential weakness of the Saussurian model and of all the theories which, sometimes under new names, accept the fundamental presuppositions of its theoretical construction. Crediting the speaking subject with a potentially infinite generative capacity merely postpones the Saussurian difficulty: the power of innovation required in order to generate an infinite number of sentences in no way implies the power of adaptation that is required in order to make relevant use of those sentences in constantly changing situations. Hence the linguists' longstanding struggle to overcome the difficulties to which the Saussurian construction was condemned from the very beginning, inasmuch as the only way it could constitute the structural properties of the message was (simply by positing an indifferent sender and receiver) to neglect the functional properties the message derives from its *use* in a determinate situation and, more precisely, in a socially structured interaction.

As soon as one moves from the structure of language to the functions it fulfils, that is, to the uses agents actually make of it, one sees that mere knowledge of the *code* gives only very imperfect mastery of the linguistic interactions really taking place. As Luis Prieto observes, the meaning of a linguistic element depends at least as much on extra-linguistic as on linguistic factors, that is to say, on the *context* and *situation* in which it is used. Everything takes place as if, from among the class of "signifieds" abstractly corresponding to a speech sound, the receiver "selected" the one which seems to him to be compatible with the circumstances as he perceives them.[31] Thus reception depends to a large degree on the objective structure of the relations between the interacting agents' objective positions in the social structure (e.g. relations of competition or objective antagonism, or relations of power and authority, etc.), which governs the form and content of the interactions observed in a particular conjuncture. Bally shows how the very content of the communication, the nature of the language and all the forms of expression used (posture, gesture, mimickry, etc.) and above all, perhaps, their *style*, are affected by the structure of the social relation between the agents involved and, more precisely, by the structure of their relative positions in the hierarchies of age, power, prestige, and culture: "When I talk to someone, or talk about him, I cannot help visualizing the particular type of relationship (casual, formal, obligatory, official) between that person and myself; involuntarily I think not only of his possible action towards myself, but also of his age, sex, rank, and social background; all these considerations may affect my choice of expressions and lead me to avoid what might discourage, offend, or hurt. If need be, my language becomes reserved and prudent; it becomes indirect and euphemistic, it slides over the surface instead of insisting."[32] Hence communication is possible in practice only when accompanied by a practical spotting of cues which, in enabling speakers to situate others in the hierarchies of age, wealth, power, or culture, guides them unwittingly towards the type of exchange best suited in form and content to the objective situation between the interacting individuals. This is seen clearly in bilingual situations, in which the speakers adopt one or the other of the two available languages according to the circumstances, the subject of conversation, the social status of their interlocuter (and thus his degree of culture and bilingualism), etc. The whole content of the communication (and not just the language used) is unconsciously modified by the structure of the relationship between the speakers. The pressure of the socially qualified objective situation is such that, through the mediation of bodily mimesis, a whole way of speaking, a type of joke, a particular tone, sometimes even an accent, seem to be objectively called for by certain situations, and, conversely, quite excluded from others, whatever efforts are made to introduce them.

But the linguists and anthropologists who appeal to "context" or "situation" in order, as it were, to "correct" what strikes them as unreal and abstract in the structuralist model are in fact still trapped in the logic of the theoretical model which they are rightly trying to supersede. The method known as "situational analysis",[33] which consists of "observing people in a variety of social situations" in order to determine "the way in which individuals are able to exercise choices within the limits of a specified social structure",[34] remains locked within the framework of the rule and the exception, which Leach (often invoked by the exponents of "situational analysis") spells out clearly: "I postulate that structural systems in which all avenues of social action are narrowly institutionalized are impossible. In all viable systems, there must be an area where the individual is free to make choices so as to manipulate the system to his advantage."[35] In accepting as obligatory alternatives the model and the situation, the structure and the individual variations, one condemns oneself simply to take the diametrically opposite course to the structuralist abstraction which subsumes variations – regarded as simple variants – into the structure. The desire to "integrate variations, exceptions and accidents into descriptions of regularities" and to show "how individuals in a particular structure handle the choices with which they are faced – as individuals are in all societies"[36] – leads one to regress to the pre-structuralist stage of the individual and his choices, and to miss the very principle of the structuralist error.[37]

Not the least of Chomsky's merits is to have reopened discussion on the distinction between syntax and semantics (and secondarily, between syntax and pragmatics) and, more precisely, on the dependence or independence of these different levels of discourse relative to the situation, by affirming the independence of the structural properties of linguistic expressions relative to their uses and functions and the impossibility of making any inference from analysis of their formal structure – a position which has simply adopted explicitly the postulates implied in the Saussurian language/speech distinction.

In short, failing to construct practice other than negatively, objectivism is condemned either to ignore the whole question of the principle underlying the production of the regularities which it then contents itself with recording; or to reify abstractions, by the fallacy of treating the objects constructed by science, whether "culture", "structures", or "modes of production", as realities endowed with a social efficacy, capable of acting as agents responsible for historical actions or as a power capable of constraining practices; or to save appearances by means of concepts as ambiguous as the notions of the rule or the unconscious, which make it possible to avoid choosing between incompatible theories of practice. Thus Lévi-Strauss's use of the notion of the unconscious masks the contradictions generated by the implicit theory of practice which "structural anthropology" accepts at least by default, restoring the old entelechies of the metaphysics of nature in the apparently secularized form of a structure structured in the absence of any structuring principle.[38] When one is reluctant to follow Durkheim in positing that none of the rules constraining subjects "can be found entirely reproduced in the applications made of them by individuals, since they can exist even without being actually applied",[39] and unwilling to ascribe to these rules the transcendent, permanent existence he ascribes (as Saussure does to language) to all collective "realities", the only way to escape the crudest naivities of the legalism which sees practices as the product of obedience to the rules is to play on the polysemous nature of the word *rule*: most often used in the sense of a social *norm* expressly stated and explicitly recognized, like moral or juridical law, sometimes in the sense of a *theoretical model*, a construct devised by science in order to account for practices, the word is also, more rarely, used in the sense of a *scheme* (or principle) immanent in practice, which should be called implicit rather than unconscious, simply to indicate that it exists in a practical state in agents' practice and not in their consciousness, or rather, their discourse.[40]

Clearly a case in point is Chomsky, who holds, simultaneously, that the rules of grammar are inscribed in neuro-physiological mechanisms,[41] that they are systems of norms of which agents have a certain awareness, and lastly that they are instruments for description of language. But it is also instructive to reread a paragraph from Lévi-Strauss's preface to the second edition of *Les structures élementaires de la parenté* (*Elementary Structures of Kinship*), in which one may assume that particular care has been taken with the vocabulary of norms, models, or rules, since the passage deals with the distinction between "preferential systems" and "prescriptive systems": "Conversely, a system which *recommends* marriage with the mother's brother's daughter may be called prescriptive even if the *rule* is seldom observed, since what it says must be done. The question of how far and in what proportion the members of a given society respect the *norm* is very interesting, but a different question to that of where this society should properly be placed in a typology. It is sufficient

to acknowledge the likelihood that *awareness* of the *rule* inflects *choices* ever
so little in the *prescribed* direction, and that the percentage of *conventional*
marriages is higher than would be the case if marriages were made at random,
to be able to recognize what might be called a matrilateral '*operator*' at work
in this society and acting as a pilot: certain alliances at least follow the path
which it charts out for them, and this suffices to imprint a specific curve in
the genealogical space. No doubt there will be not just one curve but a great
number of local curves, merely incipient for the most part, however, and
forming closed cycles only in rare and exceptional cases. But the *structural*
outlines which emerge here and there will be enough for the system to be
used in making a probabilistic version of more rigid systems the *notion* of which
is completely *theoretical* and in which marriage would conform rigorously to
any rule the social group pleases to enunciate."[42]

The dominant tonality in this passage, as in the whole preface, is that of
the *norm*, whereas *Structural Anthropology* is written in the language of the
model or, if you like, the *structure*; not that such terms are entirely absent here,
since the mathematical-physical metaphors organizing the central passage
("operator", "curve" in "genealogical space", "structures") evoke the logic
of the theoretical model and of the equivalence, at once declared and repudiated, of the *model* and the *norm*: "A preferential system is prescriptive when
envisaged at the model level, a prescriptive system must be preferential when
envisaged on the level of reality."[43] But for the reader who remembers the
passages in *Structural Anthropology* on the relationship between language and
kinship (e.g. "'Kinship systems', like 'phonemic systems', are built up by
the mind on the level of unconscious thought")[44] and the imperious way in
which "cultural norms" and all the "rationalizations" or "secondary arguments" produced by the natives were rejected in favour of the "unconscious
structures", not to mention passages asserting the universality of the fundamental rule of exogamy, the concessions made here to "awareness of the rule"
and the dissociation from rigid systems "the notion of which is entirely
theoretical" may come as a surprise, as may this further passage from the same
preface: "It is nonetheless true that the empirical reality of so-called
prescriptive systems only takes on its full meaning when related to *a theoretical
model worked out by the natives themselves* prior to ethnologists",[45] or again:
"Those who practise them *know fully* that the spirit of such systems cannot
be reduced to the tautological proposition that each group obtains its women
from 'givers' and gives its daughters to 'takers'. They are also *aware* that
marriage with the matrilateral cross cousin (mother's brother's daughter)
provides the simplest illustration of the *rule*, the form most likely to *guarantee
its survival*. On the other hand, marriage with the patrilateral cross cousin
(father's sister's daughter) would violate it irrevocably."[46]

It is tempting to quote in reply a passage in which Wittgenstein effortlessly brings together all the questions evaded by structural anthropology and no doubt more generally by all intellectualism, which transfers the objective truth established by science into a practice which by its very essence rules out the theoretical stance which makes it possible to establish that truth:[47] "What do I call 'the rule by which he proceeds'? – The hypothesis that satisfactorily describes his use of words, which we observe: or the rule which he looks up when he uses signs; or the one which he gives us in reply when we ask what his rule is? – But what if observation does not enable us to see any clear rule, and the question brings none to light? – For he did indeed give me a definition when I asked him what he understood by 'N', but he was prepared to withdraw and alter it. So how am I to determine the rule according to which he is playing? He does not know it himself. – Or, to ask a better question: What meaning is the expression 'the rule by which he proceeds' supposed to have left to it here? "[48]

To consider regularity, that is, what recurs with a certain statistically measurable *frequency*, as the product of a consciously laid-down and consciously respected *ruling* (which implies explaining its genesis and efficacy), or as the product of an unconscious *regulating* by a mysterious cerebral and/or social mechanism, is to slip from the model of reality to the reality of the model.[49] "Consider the difference between saying 'The train is regularly two minutes late' and 'As a rule, the train is two minutes late'...there is the suggestion in the latter case that that the train be two minutes late is as it were in accordance with some policy or plan...Rules connect with plans or policies in a way that regularities do not...To argue that...there must be rules in the natural language is like arguing that roads must be red if they correspond to red lines on a map."[50] In one case – to take up Quine's distinction between *fitting* and *guiding* – one formulates a rule which fits the observed regularity in a purely descriptive way; in the other case one states a rule which guides the behaviour and which can do so only to the extent that it is known and recognized (and hence could be stated).[51] One is entitled to posit an "implicit guidance", as, according to Quine, Chomsky does, in order to account for a practice objectively governed by rules unknown to the agents; but only on condition that one does not mask the question of the mechanisms producing this conformity in the absence of the intention to conform, by resorting to the fallacy of the rule which implicitly places in the consciousness of the individual agents a knowledge built up against that experience, i.e. confers the value of an anthropological description on the theoretical model constructed in order to account for practices. The theory of action as mere *execution* of the model (in the twofold sense of norm and scientific construct) is just one example among others of the imaginary anthropology which objectivism engenders when, with the aid of words that obscure the distinction between "the things of logic and the logic of things", it presents the objective meaning of practices or works as the subjective purpose of the action of the producers of those practices or works, with its impossible *homo economicus* subjecting his decision-making to rational calculation, its actors performing rôles or acting in conformity with models, or its speakers "selecting" from among phonemes.

SECTION II: CASE STUDY: PARALLEL-COUSIN MARRIAGE

"Philosophy aims at the logical clarification of thoughts...Without philosophy thoughts are, as it were, cloudy and indistinct: its task is to make them clear and give them sharp boundaries."[52] In this sense, the foregoing analyses may be said to belong to philosophy. But unlike philosophical activity as Wittgenstein conceives it, they do not achieve their end in "the clarification of propositions". Arising in response to scientific difficulties and not to the reading of texts, they are intended to help surmount difficulties, by providing not only procedures for research but also procedures for validation, means of deciding between competing accounts of the same practices. The case of marriage – structuralist ground par excellence – and of parallel-cousin marriage – a sort of quasi-incest challenging both the unilineal-descent theories and the marriage-alliance theory – constitutes an ideal terrain for such a truth-test.[53]

Marriage with a patrilateral parallel cousin (*bent'amm*, father's brother's daughter)[54] appears as a sort of scandal, in Claude Lévi-Strauss's terms,[55] only to those who have internalized the categories of thought which it disturbs. In challenging the idea of *exogamy*, the precondition for the continuation of separate lineages and for the permanence and easy identification of consecutive units, it challenges the whole notion of unilineal descent as well as the theory of marriage as an exchange of one woman against another, which assumes an incest taboo, i.e. the absolute necessity of exchange. An exogamic system clearly divides alliance groups and descent groups, which by definition cannot coincide, genealogical lineages being by the same token clearly defined, since powers, privileges, and duties are transmitted either matrilineally or patrilineally. Endogamy, by contrast, results in a blurring of the distinction between lineages. Thus, in the extreme case of a system actually founded on parallel-cousin marriage, a particular individual could be related to his paternal grandfather equally through his father or his mother. But on the other hand, by choosing to keep the parallel cousin, a quasi-sister, within the lineage, the group would deprive itself of an opportunity to receive a woman from outside and of thus contracting new alliances. Is it sufficient to regard this type of marriage as the exception (or the "aberration") which proves the rule, or to rearrange the categories of thought which make it possible in order to find a place (i.e. a name) for it? Or should we radically question the categories of thought which have produced this "unthinkable" thing?

The contradiction posed by Arab and Berber traditions to currently available theories has at least the merit of reminding us that, as Louis Dumont says, the theory of unilineal descent groups and the alliance theory of marriage remain "regional theories" in the geographical and also the epistemological sense, even though they wear the cloak of universality.[56] Neither can the critical examination of certain of the bases of these theories, which is encouraged or even imposed by the particular characteristics of a cultural tradition, claim to be universal. But such a critical examination may contribute to progress towards a theory free from all geographical or epistemological regionalism by posing universal questions which are raised with particular insistence by the peculiarities of certain objects. For example, it is not sufficient to conclude that, while valid in the case of an exogamic tradition which strictly distinguishes between parallel and cross kin, the idea of a preferential marriage is not justified in the case of a society without exogamous groups. We must find in this exception a reason for questioning not only the very notion of prescription or preference, but also on the one hand, the notion of the genealogically defined group, an entity whose social identity is as invariable and uniform as the criteria for its delimitation and which confers on each of its members a social identity equally distinct and permanently fixed: and on the other hand, the notion of *rules* and *rule-governed behaviour* in the twofold sense of behaviour conforming objectively to rules and determined by obedience to rules.

The inadequacy of the language of prescription and rules is so clear in the case of patrilateral marriage that we cannot fail to be reminded of Rodney Needham's inquiries into the conditions of validity, perhaps never fulfilled, of such a language, which is in fact nothing other than legal language.[57] But this questioning of the epistemological status of concepts as commonly and as widely used as those of rule, prescription, and preference, inevitably challenges the *theory of practice* which they presuppose: can we, even implicitly, treat the "algebra of kinship", as Malinowski called it, as a theory of the practical uses of kinship and of "practical" kinship without tacitly postulating a deductive relationship between kinship terminology and "kinship attitudes"? And can we give an anthropological meaning to this relationship without postulating that regulated and regular relationships between kin are the results of obedience to a set of rules which, although a residual Durkheimian scruple makes Radcliffe-Brown call them "jural" rather than

legal are assumed to control behaviour in the same way as legal rules?[58]
Finally, can we make the genealogical definition of groups the only means
of differentiating between social units and of assigning agents to these groups
without implicitly postulating that the agents are defined in every respect
and for all time by their belonging to the group, and that, in short, *the* group
defines the agents and their interests more than the agents define *groups*
in terms of their interests?

The state of the question

The most recent theories of parallel-cousin marriage, those of Fredrik Barth[59] and of
Robert Murphy and Leonard Kasdan,[60] though diametrically opposed, do have in
common the fact that they appeal to those *functions* which structuralism either ignores
or brackets off, whether economic functions, such as the retention of the patrimony
within the lineage, or political functions, such as the reinforcement of lineage integration. It is difficult to see how they could do otherwise without making absurd
a marriage which obviously does not fulfil the function of exchange and alliance
commonly attributed to cross-cousin marriage.[61] Barth emphasizes that endogamous
marriage "plays a prominent role in solidifying the minimal lineage as a corporate group
in factional struggle". By contrast, Murphy and Kasdan criticize Barth for explaining
the institution "through reference to the consciously felt goals of the individual role
players", or more precisely by reference to the lineage head's interest in keeping a
close control over his nephews, who represent points of potential segmentation. Thus
Murphy and Kasdan relate this type of marriage to its "structural function", that is,
to the fact that it "contributes to the extreme fission of agnatic lines . . . and, through
in-marriage, encysts the patrilineal segments". Lévi-Strauss is perfectly justified
in stating that the two opposing positions amount to exactly the same thing: in fact
Barth's theory makes of this type of marriage a means of reinforcing lineage unity
and of limiting the tendency to fission; Murphy's theory sees in it the principle
of a quest for integration into larger units, founded on the appeal to a common
origin, and ultimately encompassing all Arabs. So both admit that parallel-cousin
marriage cannot be explained within the pure logic of the matrimonial exchange
system and that any explanation must refer to external economic or political
functions.[62]

Cuisenier simply draws out the consequences of this observation, in a construction
which attempts to account for the inconsistencies noted by all observers between the
"model" and actual practice, together with at least the economic external functions
of matrimonial exchanges. "It is native thinking itself which gives us a clue to an
explanatory model. This model represents in effect alliances knit together in one group
based on the fundamental opposition of two brothers, of whom one must marry
endogamously in order to maintain the coherence of the group, and the other must
marry exogamously in order to gain alliances for the group. This opposition between
the two brothers is found at all levels of the agnatic group; it expresses in the usual
genealogical terminology of Arab thought a choice between alternatives which may
be represented as a 'partial order' diagram in which the numerical values of a and
b are ⅓ and ⅔ respectively. If a represents the choice of endogamy and b the choice
of exogamy, and if one follows the branchings of the two-part family tree from the
roots upwards, the choice of a at the most superficial genealogical levels is the choice
of the parallel cousin (⅓ of the cases)."[63] One might be tempted to see it as a virtue

of this model that it seeks to account for the statistical data in contrast to traditional theories of preferential marriage which went no further than to state the divergence between the "norm" (or the "rule") and actual practice.[64] But one only has to adopt a more or less restrictive definition of the marriages assimilable to parallel-cousin marriage, to move away, to a greater or lesser extent, from the magical percentage (36 % = ⅓ ?) which, when combined with a native maxim, generates a "theoretical model"; and then there is no need to appeal to an epistemological critique to show that the model fits the facts so perfectly only because it has been *made to measure* to fit the facts, i.e. invented *ad hoc* to account for a statistical artefact, and not built up from a theory of the principles of the production of practices. There is an equation for the curve of each face, said Leibniz. And nowadays there will always be a mathematician to prove that two cousins parallel to a third are parallel to each other...

But the intention of submitting genealogies to statistical analysis has at least the virtue of revealing the most fundamental properties of the genealogy, an analytical tool which is never itself analysed. We can immediately see what is strange about the idea of calculating rates of endogamy when, as here, it is the very notion of the *endogamous group*, and therefore the basis of calculation, which is in question.[65] Are we to be satisfied with abstractly dissecting genealogies which have the same extent as the group memory, whose structure and extent depend on the *functions* actually given by the group to those whom it remembers or forgets? Recognizing in a lineage diagram an ideological representation resorted to by the Bedouin in order to achieve a "primary comprehension" of their present relationships, E. L. Peters[66] points out that the genealogy ignores the real power relations between genealogical segments, that it forgets about the women, and that it treats as "contingent accidents" the most basic ecological, demographic, and political factors.[67] Must we then resort to the units which the agents themselves recognize, using criteria which are not necessarily genealogical? We discover, however, that an individual's chances of making a marriage which can be treated as a marriage with the daughter of his 'amm are greater to the extent that his practical, effectively mobilizable lineage (as well as the number of potential partners) is larger, and the pressures on him to marry inside the lineage are stronger. Once the family property is divided and there is nothing to recall and maintain the genealogical relationship, the father's brother's daughter may be considered no closer in degree of kinship than any other patrilateral (or even matrilateral) cousin. On the other hand, a genealogically more distant cousin may be the practical equivalent of the *bent'amm* when the two cousins are part of a strongly united "house" living under one elder and owning all its property in common. And perhaps informants are simply victims of an illusion created by the decline of the great undivided families, when they repeat with insistence that people now marry less within the lineage than they did formerly.

The functions of kinship: official kin and practical kin

It is not sufficient to follow the example of the more circumspect fieldworkers, who prudently slip from the notion of preferential marriage with a parallel cousin to the notion of "lineage endogamy", trusting that this vague, high-sounding language will offer a way out of the problems raised by the notion of endogamy and concealed by the all-too-familiar concept of the *group*. It is first necessary to ask what is implied in defining a group by the genealogical relationship linking its members, and in thereby implicitly treating kinship as the necessary and sufficient condition of group unity. As soon as we ask explicitly about the *functions* of kin relationships, or more bluntly, about the usefulness of kinsmen, a question which kinship theorists prefer to treat as resolved, we cannot fail to notice that those uses of kinship which may be called genealogical are reserved for official situations in which they serve the function of ordering the social world and of legitimating that order.[68] In this respect they differ from the other kinds of practical use made of kin relationships, which are a particular case of the utilization of *connections*. The genealogical diagram of kin relationships which the anthropologist constructs merely reproduces the *official* representation of the social structures, a representation produced by application of the structuring principle that is *dominant in a certain respect*, i.e. in certain situations and with a view to certain functions.

Marriage provides a good opportunity for observing what in practice separates official kinship, single and immutable, defined once and for all by the norms of genealogical protocol, from practical kinship, whose boundaries and definitions are as many and as varied as its users and the occasions on which it is used. It is practical kin who make marriages; it is official kin who celebrate them. In ordinary marriages the contacts preceding the official proposal (*akhtab*) and the least avowable negotiations relating to areas which the official ideology tends to ignore, such as the economic conditions of the marriage, the status offered to the wife in her husband's home, relations with the husband's mother, and similar matters, are left to the persons least qualified to represent the group and to speak for it (who can therefore be disowned if need be), such as an old woman, usually a sort of professional in these secret meetings, a midwife, or some other woman used to moving from village to village. In the difficult negotiations between distant groups a well-known, prestigious man from a group sufficiently distant and distinct from the "wife-takers' to appear *neutral* and to be in a position to act in complicity with another man occupying approximately the same position in relation to the wife-givers (a friend or ally rather than a kinsman) will be entrusted with the delivery of the declaration of intent (*assiwaṭ wawal*). He will avoid coming straight to the point, but will try to find an opportunity to meet someone from "the girl's side" and to disclose to him the "intentions" of the interested family. The official marriage proposal (*akhtab*) is presented by the least responsible of those responsible, i.e. the elder brother and not the father, the paternal uncle and not the grandfather, etc., accompanied, especially if he is young, by a kinsman from another line. The men who present the request may be, for example, on the first occasion, an elder brother and a maternal uncle, then on the second occasion a paternal uncle and one of the notables of the group, then the third time the same people accompanied by several group and village notables such as the taleb, to be joined later by the village marabouts, and the fourth time the father together with notables from the neighbouring village and even the next tribe, etc. So progressively closer and more distinguished relatives of the bridegroom come to present their request (*ahallal*) to men in the bride's family who genealogically and spatially are increasingly distant. In the end it is the most important and most distant of the girl's kin who come to intercede with the girl's father and mother on behalf of the closest and most prestigious of the young man's kin, having been asked to do so by this latter group. Finally, acceptance (*aqbal*) is proclaimed before the largest possible number of men and conveyed to the most eminent kinsman of the young man by the most eminent of the girl's kinsmen, who has been asked to support the proposal. As negotiations proceed and begin to look successful, official kin may well take the place of practical kin, the hierarchy with respect to *utility* being almost the exact opposite of the hierarchy with respect to genealogical legitimacy. There are various reasons for this. First, it is not advisable to "commit" in the early stages kin who because of their genealogical and social position might compromise their principals too deeply – particularly in a situation of conjunctural inferiority, which is often associated with structural superiority (because the man is marrying beneath him). Secondly, not everyone can be asked to put himself in the position of a suppliant liable to receive a refusal, and *a fortiori* to take part in negotiations which will bring no glory, which are often painful, and sometimes bring dishonour on the two parties (like the practice of *thaj'alts*, which consists of paying money to secure the intervention of some of the prospective bride's kin). Finally, the search for maximum efficiency in the practical phase of negotiations directs the choice towards persons known to command great skill, to enjoy particular authority over the family in question, or to be on good terms with someone in a position to influence the decision. And it is natural that, in the official phase, those who have actually "made" the marriage should have to make do with the place assigned to them not by their usefulness but by their position in the genealogy; having played their parts as "utility men", they must make way for the "leading actors".

Thus, to schematize, official kinship is opposed to practical kinship in terms of the official as opposed to the non-official (which includes the unofficial and the scandalous); the collective as opposed to the individual; the public, explicitly codified in a magical or quasi-juridical formalism, as opposed to the private, kept in an implicit, even hidden state; collective ritual, subjectless practice, amenable to performance by agents interchangeable because collectively mandated, as opposed to strategy, directed towards the satisfaction of the practical interests of an individual or group of individuals. Abstract units produced by simple theoretical division, such as, here, the unilineal descent group (or elsewhere, age-groups) are available for all functions, that is, for no single one in particular, and have practical existence only for the most *official* uses of kinship; *representational kinship* is nothing other than the group's self-representation and the almost theatrical presentation it gives of itself when acting in accordance with that self-image. By contrast, practical groups exist only through and for the particular functions in pursuance of which they have been *effectively mobilized*; and they continue to exist only because they have been kept in working order by their very use and by maintenance work (including the matrimonial exchanges they make possible) and because they rest on a community of dispositions (habitus) and interests which is also the basis of undivided ownership of the material and symbolic patrimony.

To treat kin relationships as something people *make*, and with which they *do* something, is not merely to substitute a "functionalist" for a "structuralist" interpretation, as current taxonomies might lead one to believe; it is radically to question the implicit theory of practice which causes the anthropological tradition to see kin relationships "in the form of an object or an intuition", as Marx puts it, rather than in the form of the practices which produce, reproduce, and use them by reference to necessarily practical functions. The same is true, *a fortiori*, of affinal relationships: it is only when one records these relationships as a *fait accompli*, *post festum*, as the anthropologist does when he draws up a genealogy, that one can forget that they are the product of strategies (conscious or unconscious) oriented towards the satisfaction of material and symbolic interests and organized by reference to a determinate set of economic and social conditions. Once one forgets all that is implied in extracting from the product the principles of its production, from the *opus operatum* the *modus operandi*, one condemns oneself to proceed as if the regular product had been produced in accordance with the rules.[69]

The competition and conflicts provoked by the transmission of first names provide an opportunity to observe the practical and political functions of these genealogical markers: to appropriate these indices of genealogical position (so-and-so, son of so-and-so, son of so-and-so etc.) which are also *emblems*, symbolizing the whole symbolic capital accumulated by a lineage, is in a sense to take possession of a *title* giving special rights over the group's patrimony. The state of the relations of force and authority between contemporary kin determines what the collective history will be; but this symbolic projection of the power relations between competing individuals and groups also plays a part in reinforcing the initial state of affairs by giving those who are in a dominant position the right to profess the veneration of the past which is best suited to legitimate their present interests. To give a new-born child the name of a great forefather is not simply to perform an act of filial piety, but also in a sense to predestine the child thus named to bring the eponymous ancestor "back to life" (*isakrad djedi-s* "he has brought his grandfather 'back to life'"), i.e. to succeed him in his responsibilities and powers.[70]

Prestigious first names, like the noblest lands, are the object of regulated competition, and the "right" to appropriate the first name which is most coveted, because it continuously proclaims the genealogical connection with the ancestor whose name is preserved by the group and outside the group, is distributed in accordance with a hierarchy analogous to that governing the obligations of honour in the case of revenge, or of the rights to land belonging to the patrimony in the case of sale. Thus, since first names are transmitted in direct patrilineal line, the father cannot give a child the name of his own *'amm* or his own brother (the child's *'amm*) if either of the latter has left any sons who are already married and hence in a position to reuse their father's name for one of their sons or grandsons. Here as elsewhere, the convenient language of norms and obligations (must...cannot...etc.) must not be allowed to mislead us: thus, a younger brother has been known to take advantage of a favourable balance of power in order to give his children the first name of a prestigious brother who had died leaving only very young children; the children subsequently set their point of honour on retaking possession of the first name of which they considered themselves the legitimate bearers – even at risk of confusion. The competition is particularly evident when several brothers wish to give their children their father's first name: whereas the need to rescue it from neglect and fill up the gap that has appeared requires that the name should be given to the first boy born after the death of its bearer, the eldest may put off the attribution of the name in order to give it to one of his grandsons instead of leaving it for the son of one of his younger brothers, thus jumping a genealogical level. But it may also happen, on the other hand, that for lack of any male descendants, a name threatens to escheat, at which point the responsibility for "reviving" it falls first on the collaterals, and then on the group as a whole, which thereby demonstrates that its integration and its wealth of men enable it to reuse the names of all direct ancestors and, moreover, to make good any gaps that may appear elsewhere (one of the functions of marriage with the daughter of the *'amm* when the latter dies without male heirs, being to allow the daughter to see to it that her father's name does not disappear).

The ethnologist is in a particularly bad position to detect the distinction between official and practical kinship: as his dealings with kinship (at least, the kinship of others) are restricted to cognitive uses, he is disposed to take for gospel truth the official discourses which informants are inclined to present to him as long as they see themselves as spokesmen mandated to present the group's official account of itself. He has no reason to perceive that he is allowing the *official definition* of social reality to be imposed on him – a version which dominates or represses other definitions. Witness to this are the desperate efforts by generations of anthropologists to confirm or deny the existence of "preferential" cross-cousin marriage. As soon as one poses the problem of marriage in strictly genealogical terms, as informants always will, by referring to marriage with the *bent'amm*, all further discussion will take place within certain limits; all solutions are acceptable so long as they are expressed in genealogical language ... The ethnologist cannot break the complicity which binds him to the official ideology of his informants and reject the presuppositions implied in the mere fact of seeing exclusively genealogical relationships of filiation or alliance in relationships which can be read in other ways (e.g. in terms of siblingship) and are always *also* based on other principles (e.g. economic or political), unless he situates this special kind of use of kinship with respect to the various kinds of uses the agents may make of it. When the anthropologist treats native kinship terminology as a closed, coherent system of purely logical relationships, defined once and for all by the implicit axiomatics of a cultural tradition, he prohibits himself from apprehending the different practical functions of the kinship terms and relations which he unwittingly brackets; and by the same token he prohibits himself from grasping the epistemological status of a practice which, like his own, presupposes and consecrates neutralization of the practical functions of those terms and relationships.

The logical relationships constructed by the anthropologist are opposed to "practical" relationships – practical because continuously practised, kept up, and cultivated – in the same way as the geometrical space of a map, an imaginary representation of all theoretically possible roads and routes, is opposed to the network of beaten tracks, of paths made ever more practicable by constant use. The genealogical tree constructed by the anthropologist, a spatial diagram that can be taken in at a glance, *uno intuitu*, and scanned indifferently from any point in any direction, causes the complete network of kinship relations over several generations to exist as only theoretical objects exist, that is, *tota simul*, as a totality present in simultaneity.[71] Official relationships which do not receive continuous maintenance tend to become what they are for the genealogist: theoretical relationships, like abandoned roads on an old map. In short, the logical relations of kinship to which the structuralist tradition ascribes a more or less complete autonomy with respect to economic determinants, and correlatively a near-perfect internal coherence, exist in practice only through and for the official and unofficial uses made of them by agents whose attachment to keeping them in working order and to making them work intensively – hence, through constant use, ever more easily – rises with the degree to which they actually or potentially fulfil functions indispensable to them or, to put it less ambiguously, the extent to which they do or can satisfy vital material and symbolic *interests*.[72]

Officializing strategies

By the mere fact of talking of endogamy and of trying, out of a laudable desire for rigour, to measure its degrees, one assumes the existence of a purely genealogical definition of the lineage. In fact, every adult male, at whatever level on the genealogical tree, represents a point of potential segmentation which may become effective for a particular social purpose. The further back in time and genealogical space we place the point of origin – and nothing forbids a regression to infinity in this abstract space – the more we push back the *boundaries* of the lineage and the more the *assimilative* power of genealogical ideology grows, but only at the expense of its *distinctive* power, which increases as we draw nearer the point of common origin. Thus the kind of use which can be made of the expression *ath* ("the descendants of, the people of . . .") obeys a positional logic altogether similar to that which according to Evans-Pritchard characterizes the uses of the word *cieng*, the same person being able, depending on circumstance, situation, and interlocutor, to call himself a member of the Ath Abba (the house, *akham*), of the Ath Isa'd (*takharrubth*), of the Ath Ousseb'a (*adhrum*), or of the Ath Yahia (*'arch*). The absolute relativism which bestows upon the agents the power to manipulate without limit their own social identity (or that of the adversaries or partners whom they assimilate or exclude by manipulating the limits of the classes they each belong to), would at least have the merit of repudiating the naive realism of those who cannot characterize a group other than as a population defined by directly visible boundaries. However, the structure of a group (and hence the social identity of the individuals who make it up) depends on the function which is fundamental to its construction and organization. This is also forgotten by those who try to escape from genealogical abstraction by contrasting the descent line with the local line or the local descent group, that portion of a unilineal descent group which, by the mere fact of common residence, can act collectively as a group.[73] One again succumbs to realism if one forgets that the effects of spatial distance are dependent on the function which the social relationship aims to achieve. We may admit, for example, that the potential usefulness of a partner tends to decrease with distance (except in the case of prestige marriages, where the more distant the people between whom the relationship is established, the greater the symbolic profit). If unity of residence contributes to the integration of the group, the unity given to the group by its mobilization for a common function contributes towards minimizing the effect of distance. In short, although we could in theory maintain that there are as many possible groups as there are functions, the fact remains that, as we saw in the case of marriage, one cannot call on absolutely *anyone* for *any* occasion, any more than one can offer one's services to *anyone* for *any* end. Thus, to escape from relativism without falling into realism, we may posit that the constants of the field of potentially useful relationships (i.e. those that are actually usable, because spatially close, and useful, because socially influential) cause each group of agents to tend to keep up by continuous maintenance-work a privileged network of practical relationships which comprises not only the sum total of the genealogical relationships kept in working order (here called practical kinship) but also the sum total of the non-genealogical relationships which can be mobilized for the ordinary needs of existence (practical relationships).

The official set of those individuals amenable to definition by the same relationship to the same ancestor at the same level on the genealogical tree may constitute a practical group: this is the case when the genealogical divisions cover (in both senses) units founded on other principles, whether ecological (neighbourhood), economic (undivided patrimony), or political. The fact that the descriptive value of the genealogical criterion is greater when the common origin is nearer and the social unit is more limited does not mean that its *unificatory efficacy* rises in the same way. In fact, as we shall see, the closest genealogical relationship, that between brothers, is also the point of greatest tension, and only incessant work can maintain the community of interests. In short, the genealogical relationship is never strong enough on its own to provide a complete determination of the relationship between the individuals which it unites, and it has such predictive value only when it goes with the shared interests, produced by the common possession of a material and symbolic patrimony, which entails collective vulnerability as well as collective property. The extent of practical kinship depends on the capacity of the official group members to overcome the tensions engendered by the conflict of interests within the undivided production and consumption group, and to keep up the kind of practical relationships which conform to the official view held by every group which thinks of itself as a corporate unit. On that condition, they may enjoy both the advantages accruing from every practical relationship and the symbolic profits secured by the approval socially conferred on practices conforming to the official representation of practices.

Strategies aimed at producing "regular" practices are one category, among others, of *officializing strategies*, the object of which is to transmute "egoistic", private, particular interests (notions definable only within the relationship between a social unit and the encompassing social unit at a higher level) into disinterested, collective, publicly avowable, legitimate interests. In the absence of political institutions endowed with an effective monopoly of legitimate violence, political action proper can be exercised only by the effect of officialization and thus presupposes the *competence* (in the sense of a *capacity socially recognized in a public authority*) required in order to manipulate the collective definition of the situation in such a way as to bring it closer to the official definition of the situation and thereby to win the means of mobilizing the largest possible group, the opposite strategy tending to reduce the same situation to a merely private affair.[74] To possess the capital of authority necessary to impose a definition of the situation, especially in the moments of crisis when the collective judgment falters, is to be able to mobilize the group by solemnizing, officializing, and thus universalizing a private incident (e.g. by presenting an insult to a particular woman as an affront to the *ḥurma* of the whole group). It is also to be able to demobilize it, by disowning the person directly concerned, who, failing to identify his particular interest with the "general interest", is reduced to the status of a mere individual, condemned to appear unreasonable in seeking to impose his private reason – *idiotes* in Greek and *amahbul* in Kabyle.

In fact, groups demand infinitely less than legalist formalism would have us believe, but much more than those who "won't play the game" are willing to grant them. Between the *responsible* man, whom the excellence of a practice immediately in line with the official rule, because produced by a regulated habitus, predisposes to fulfil the functions of delegate and spokesman, and the *irresponsible* man who, not content with breaking the rules, does nothing to extenuate his infractions, groups make room for the *well-meaning rule-breaker* who by conceding the appearances or intent of conformity, that is, *recognition*, to rules he can neither respect nor deny, contributes to the – entirely official – survival of the rule. It is natural that politics should be the privileged arena for the dialectic of the official and the useful: in their efforts to draw the group's delegation upon themselves and withdraw it from their rivals, the agents in competition for political power are limited to ritual strategies and strategic rituals, products of the collectivizing of private interests and the symbolic appropriation of official interests.

But the struggle to monopolize the legitimate exercise of violence – that is to say, in the absence of economic accumulation, the struggle to accumulate symbolic capital in the form of collectively recognized *credit* – must not lead us to forget the necessarily hidden opposition between the official and the unofficial. Competition for official power can be set up only between men, while the women may enter into competition for a power which is by definition condemned to remain *unofficial* or even clandestine and occult. We find in fact in the political sphere the same division of labour which entrusts religion – public, official, solemn, and collective – to the men, and magic – secret, clandestine, and private – to the women. In this competition the men have the whole official institution on their side, starting with the mythico-ritual representations and the representations of kinship which, by reducing the opposition between the official and the private to the opposition between the outside and the inside, hence the male and the female, establish a systematic hierarchization condemning women's interventions to a shameful, secret, or, at best, unofficial existence. Even when women do wield the real power, as is often the case in matrimonial matters, they can exercise it fully only on condition that they leave the appearance of power, that is, its official manifestation, to the men; to have any power at all, women must make do with the unofficial power of the *éminence grise*, a *dominated power* which is opposed to official power in that it can operate only by proxy, under the cover of an official authority, as well as to the subversive refusal of the rule-breaker, in that it still serves the authority it uses.

The true status of kin relationships, principles of structuration of the social world which, as such, always fulfil a political function, is most clearly seen in the different uses which men and women can make of the same field of genealogical relationships, and in particular in their different "readings" and "uses" of genealogically ambiguous kinship ties (which are relatively frequent on account of the narrow area of matrimonial choice).

In all cases of genealogically ambiguous relationship, one can always bring closer the most distant relative, or move closer to him, by emphasizing what unites, while one can hold the closest relative at a distance by emphasizing what separates. What is at stake in these manipulations, which it would be naive to consider fictitious on the grounds that no one is taken in, is in all cases nothing other than the definition of the practical limits of the group, which can be redrawn by this means so as to go beyond or fall short of an individual one wants to annex or exclude. An idea of these subtleties may be got from considering the uses of the term *khal* (strictly, mother's

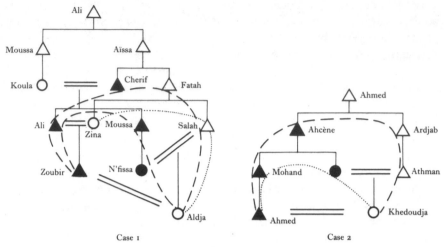

Fig. 1.

brother): used by a marabout to a common, lay peasant, it expresses the desire to distinguish oneself, within the limits of courtesy, by indicating the absence of any legitimate kin relationship; whereas between peasants, it manifests the intention of setting up a minimal relationship of familiarity by invoking a distant, hypothetical affinal relationship.

It is the official reading that the anthropologist is accepting when, with his informants' blessing, he assimilates to parallel-cousin marriage the relationship which unites, for example, second-degree patrilateral parallel cousins when one of them is himself the child of a parallel-cousin marriage, and *a fortiori* when both are children of such marriages (as in the case of an exchange of women between the sons of two brothers). The male, that is to say, the dominant reading, which imposes itself with particular insistence in all public, official situations – in short, in all honour relationships in which one man of honour is speaking to another – privileges the noblest aspect, the aspect most worthy of public proclamation, of a multi-faceted relationship, linking each of the individuals who are to be situated to his patrilineal forebears and, through the latter, to the patrilineal forebears they have in common. It represses the other possible pathway, albeit sometimes more direct and often more convenient practically, which would reckon through the women. Thus, genealogical propriety requires one to consider Zoubir as having married in Aldja his father's father's brother's son's daughter, or his father's brother's daughter's daughter, rather than his mother's brother's daughter, even if, as happens to be the case, this latter relationship lies at the origin of the marriage (see fig. 1, case 1); or again, to cite another case from the same genealogy, that Khedoudja should be seen as her husband

Ahmed's father's father's brother's son's daughter, instead of being treated as a cross cousin (father's sister's daughter), which she equally well is (case 2). The heretical reading, which privileges the relations through women that are included from the official account, is reserved for private situations, if not for magic, which, like insults, designates its victim as "his mother's son" and not "his father's son". Apart from the cases in which women are speaking to other women about a woman's kin relationships, when use of the language of kinship through women is taken for granted, this language may also be current in the most intimate sphere of family life, i.e. in a woman's conversations with her father and his brothers or her husband, her sons, or even perhaps her husband's brother, taking on then the value of an affirmation of the intimacy of the group of interlocutors as well as at least the symbolic participation in that intimacy of the person thus designated. The anthropologist is indeed the only person to undertake pure, disinterested research into all possible routes between two points in genealogical space: in practice, the choice of one route rather than another, the male or the female, which orients the marriage towards one or the other lineage, depends on the power relations within the domestic unit and tends to reinforce, by legitimating it, the balance of power which makes the choice possible.

Collective beliefs and white lies

The ambiguity of the strategies into which it enters is such as to lead us to ask whether parallel-cousin marriage should be seen as the ideal, hardly ever achieved in practice, of accomplished marriage; or as an ethical norm (a duty of honour) which bears on every marriageable person but which can conceivably be broken (when circumstances make it impossible); or simply as a "move" recommended in certain situations. It is because it is all these things at once that it is a favoured object of manipulation. In this case, the second-order strategies aimed at disguising the first-order strategies and the interests they pursue, under the appearances of obedience to the rule, arise from the ambiguity of a practice that is objectively amenable to a twofold reading, the genealogical reading, which everything encourages, and the economic and political reading, which would presuppose access to complete information on the exchanges between the groups in question. But the ideological trap works both ways: too much faith in native accounts can lead one to present a mere ideological screen as the norm of practice; too much distrust of them may cause one to neglect the social function of a lie socially devised and encouraged, one of the means agents have of correcting the symbolic effects of strategies imposed by other necessities.[75]

There is no doubt that the pre-eminent position enjoyed by parallel-cousin marriage in native accounts and, consequently, in ethnographic accounts, is due to the fact that it is the marriage most perfectly consistent with the mythico-ritual representation of the sexual division of labour, and more particularly of the functions assigned to the men and the women in inter-group relations. First, it constitutes the most absolute affirmation of the refusal to recognize the relationship of affinity for what it is, i.e. when it does not appear as a simple *duplication* of the relationship of filiation: there is praise for the result peculiar to a marriage between parallel cousins, the fact that the resulting children ("those whose extraction is unmixed, whose blood is pure") can be attached to the same lineage through their father or their mother ("he took his maternal uncles from the place where he has his roots" – *ichathel, ikhawel*, or in Arabic, "his maternal uncle is his paternal uncle" – *khalu 'ammu*). On the other hand we know that the husband is free (in theory) to repudiate his wife, and that a wife coming from outside is a virtual stranger until she has produced a male descendant and sometimes even beyond that time. We know too the ambivalence of the relationship between nephew and maternal uncle (*khal*): "he who has no enemies need only await his sister's son" (that is, the person who, in contempt of honour, can always claim his mother's inheritance portion).

But the refusal to recognize the affinity relationship ("the woman neither unites or separates", *thamaṭṭuth ur thazeddi ur theferreq*) finds reinforcement, if not a basis, in the mythical representation of woman as the source from which impurity and dishonour threaten to enter the lineage. Nothing entirely good can come fom a woman: she can bring nothing but evil or, at best, the lesser of two evils, her wickedness only being compensated for by her weakness ("God knew what he was creating in the donkey; he didn't give him any horns"). This lesser evil, this good in evil, always arises in women through the corrective and protective action of a man. "Shame is the maiden" – *al'ar thaqchichth* – the proverb says, and the son-in-law is sometimes called *seṭṭar la'yub* "the veil cast over shame".[76] It follows that a woman is never worth more than the worth of the men of her lineage. It follows too that the best, or least bad, of women is the one who is sprung from the men of the lineage, the patrilateral parallel cousin, the most masculine of women – the extreme instance of which, the impossible figment of a patriarchal imagination, is Athene, born of Zeus' *head*. "Marry the daughter of your *'amm*; even if she chews you, she won't swallow you." The patrilateral parallel cousin, a cultivated, straightened woman, is opposed to the matrilateral parallel cousin, a natural, twisted, maleficent, impure woman, as the *male–female* is opposed to the *female–female*, i.e. in accordance with the structure (of the type $a:b::b_1:b_2$) which also organizes the mythic space of the house and of the agrarian calendar.[77] Marriage to the father's brother's daughter is the most blessed of all marriages, and the one most likely to call down blessings on the group. It used to fulfil the rôle of the opening rite of the marriage season, intended, like the homologous rite in the case of ploughing, to exorcize the threat contained in the coming together of male and female, fire and water, sky and earth, ploughshare and furrow, in acts of inevitable sacrilege.[78]

The projection of the categories of mythic thought on to kin relationships produces oppositions which would remain relatively unreal if the divisions they engender did not correspond to a fundamental division in domestic politics: the interests of the mother, seeking to reinforce her position in her adoptive home by bringing into the family a woman sprung from her own lineage, are objectively opposed to the interests of the father, who, in arranging his son's marriage, as befits a man, by an agreement with his own kin, his own brother, or some other patrilineal kinsman, reinforces the agnatic unit and, thereby, his own position in the domestic unit.

The in-marrying woman (*thislith*), depending on whether she is linked to her husband's father (and in that case, whether she is so by her father, or more generally by a man, or by her mother) or to her husband's mother (and there again, whether it is by her father or her mother), carries very different weight in the power relationship with her husband's mother (*thamgharth*); this relationship clearly also varies depending on the *thamgharth's* genealogical relationship to the men of the lineage (i.e. to her husband's father). Thus the patrilateral parallel cousin finds herself from the outset in a position of strength when she has to deal with an "old woman" from outside the lineage, whereas the "old woman's" position may be strengthened in her relations with *thislith*, and also, indirectly, in her relations with her own husband, when *thislith* is her own sister's daughter, and, *a fortiori*, her brother's daughter. Since the mother and the father have (in a certain respect) structurally opposed interests, the son's marriage provokes a confrontation – albeit undeclared, because the women can have no official strategy – between the parents, the father tending to favour marriage within the lineage, i.e. the one which mythical representation, the ideological legitimation of male domination, presents as the best, while the mother directs her secret approaches towards her own lineage, and at the opportune moment will invite her husband to give his official sanction to the results. The women would not deploy in matrimonial exploration all the ingenuity and effort that is generally conceded to them by the sexual division of labour, at least up to the moment when official dialogue can be established between the men, if it were not the case that their son's marriage contains the potentiality of the subversion of their own power, and thus of a crisis in the domestic economy which would lead consumption (*lakhla ukham*, the emptiness of the house) to overtake the accumulation of stocks (*la'mara ukham*, the fullness of the house), resulting eventually in the break up of joint ownership. This means, incidentally, that the interests of "the old man" (*amghar*) and "the old woman" (*thamgharth*) are not necessarily antagonistic: conscious of the advantage to himself of the choice of a young wife (*thislith*) fully devoted to a *thamgharth* herself devoted to the lineage, *amghar* will authorize *thamgharth* to seek out a docile girl from her lineage: moreover, since the whole structure of practical relationships between kinsmen is present in each particular relationship, he may deliberately choose to take for his son his own sister's daughter (patrilateral cross cousin) or even, without being seen to do so, encourage his wife to marry him to her brother's daughter (matrilateral cross cousin) rather than strengthen the hold of a brother already dominant (by age or prestige), by agreeing to take his daughter (patrilateral parallel cousin).

Parallel-cousin marriage may in certain cases impose itself as a necessity which is, however, not that of a genealogical rule. In practice this ideal marriage is often a *forced* choice, which people sometimes try to pass off as a positive choice of the ideal, thus making a virtue of necessity. The native "theory", taken up with enthusiasm by legalist formalism, according to which everyone has a sort of "right of pre-emption" over his parallel cousin, is doubtless simply another expression of the ideology of masculinity which gives the man superiority, and therefore the initiative, in all relations between the sexes and especially in marriage.

It is impossible to find an informant or anthropologist who will not declare that in Arab and Berber countries every boy has a "right" to his parallel cousin: "If the boy wants his father's brother's daughter, he has a *right* to her. But if he doesn't, he isn't consulted. It's the same as with land." Although infinitely closer to the reality of practice than anthropological legalism, which does not even suspect the homology between a man's relation to the women of the lineage and his relation to the land, this remark by an informant, which adopts the official language of law, masks the real and infinitely more complex relation linking an individual with his parallel cousin. A man's supposed right to the *bent'amm*, the father's brother's daughter, may in fact be a *duty* which obeys the same principles as the obligation to avenge a kinsman or to buy up a piece of family land coveted by strangers, and is therefore totally binding only in very special and even somewhat exceptional circumstances.[79] The fact that, in the case of land, the right of pre-emption (*achfa'*) is formulated and codified by the learned legal tradition (furnished with an institutionalized authority and guaranteed by the courts) as well as by "custom" (*qanun*) in no way implies that the juridical or customary rule can be made the principle of the practices actually observed when land changes hands. Because the sale of a piece of land belonging to the patrimony is first and foremost an internal matter for the lineage, it is entirely exceptional for the group to have recourse to the authorities (the clan or village assembly) which transmute the obligation of honour into a right, and if they do invoke the right or custom of *chafa'* (or *achfa'*), they are almost always motivated by principles which have nothing to do with those of legal rights (e.g. the intention to *challenge* the purchaser of the lands by demanding the annulment of an allegedly illegal sale) and which govern most of the practices of buying or selling land. The obligation to marry a woman who is in a situation similar to that of fallow land, neglected by its masters (*athbur*, unmarried girl; *el bur*, fallow land) simply imposes itself with less urgency than the obligation to buy land put up for sale by a group member, or to buy back land fallen into the hands of outsiders, land ill defended and ill possessed; and it is infinitely less binding than the imperative of avenging the murder of a group member. In all these cases, the force of the duty depends on the agent's positions in the genealogy and also, of course, on their *dispositions*. Thus, in the case of revenge, the obligation of honour may become a right to honour in the eyes of some (the same murder is sometimes avenged twice), while others will back out or bring themselves to do it only under pressure. In the case of land, the material advantage of purchase is clear, and the hierarchy of rights to honour and obligations to buy is both more apparent and more often transgressed, with conflicts and complex transactions between those members of the family who feel obliged to purchase but cannot afford to, and those who have lesser duty-rights to purchase but could afford to.

In practice, parallel-cousin marriage does not take on the ideal significance and function which the official accounts attribute it, except in those families which are sufficiently strongly integrated to want this reinforcement of their integration. It only imposes itself, at least in an absolute way, in extreme circumstances, such as the case of the daughter of the *amengur*, the man who has "failed", who has not had a male heir. In this case interest and duty coincide to require the marriage of the parallel cousins, since the *amengur's* brother and his children will in any case inherit not only the land and the house of the "failed" man but also his obligations with regard to his daughters (particularly in the case of widowhood or repudiation), and since this marriage is, moreover, the only way of avoiding the threat which marriage to a stranger (*awrith*) would pose to the honour of the group and perhaps to its patrimony.

The obligation to marry the parallel cousin also imposes itself when a daughter has not found a husband, or at least not found one worthy of her family: "He who has a daughter and does not marry her off must bear her shame"; "The man whose daughter grows up without marrying would be better off dead than alive." The relationship between brothers is such that a man cannot withhold his daughter when his brother, especially an elder brother, asks for her for his son. In this limiting case, in which the taker is also the giver, inasmuch as he is the equivalent of and substitute for the father, shirking the obligation is scarcely thinkable, as when an uncle asks for his niece on behalf of someone to whom he has promised her; it would moreover, be a serious slight to a man's brothers to marry off his daughter without informing and consulting them, and a brother's disapproval, often given as a reason for refusing, is not always a ritual pretext. The demands of solidarity are even more binding, and refusal is unthinkable when, going against all propriety (it is always the man who "asks" for the woman in marriage), the girl's father offers her for his nephew, hinting at it as discreetly as possible, though to contravene custom in this way one has to be able to count on a relationship as strong as that between two closely united brothers. The fact remains that, since honour and dishonour are held in common, the two brothers have the same interest in "covering up the shame before it is unveiled", or, in the language of symbolic interest, before the family finds that its symbolic capital has been devalued by the lack of takers for its daughters on the matrimonial market.[80] So, even in these limiting situations where the choice of the parallel cousin imposes itself with extreme rigour, there is no need to appeal to ethical or juridical rules in order to account for practices which are the result of strategies consciously or unconsciously

directed towards the satisfaction of a determinate type of material and symbolic interests. The ethic of honour is the self-interest ethic of social formations, groups, or classes in whose patrimony symbolic capital figures
prominently. Only total unawareness of the terrible and permanent loss
which a slur on the honour of the women of the lineage can represent could
lead one to see obedience to an ethical or juridical rule as the principle
of the actions intended to prevent, conceal, or make good the outrage.

Marriages which are identical as regards genealogy alone may thus have
different, even opposite, meanings and functions, depending on the strategies
in which they are involved. These can only be grasped by means of a reconstruction of the entire system of relationships between the two associated
groups and of the state of these relationships at a given point in time. As soon
as one considers not simply the marriages already concluded, those counted
and classified by the genealogist, but also the conscious and unconscious
strategies and the objective conditions which made them possible and necessary, i.e. the individual and collective functions which they have fulfilled, one
cannot fail to notice that any two marriages between parallel cousins may have
nothing in common, depending on whether they were concluded during the
lifetime of the common paternal grandfather, and even perhaps by him (with
the agreement of the two fathers, or "over their heads"), or on the contrary
by direct agreement between the two brothers; whether in this latter case they
were arranged while the future spouses were still children, or once they were
of marriageable age (not to mention the case of the daughter who has already
passed that age); whether the two brothers live and work separately or have
kept undivided their farming activity (land, herds, and other goods) and their
domestic economy ("a single cooking pot"), not to mention the case in which
only the appearance of undivided property is maintained; whether it is the
elder brother (*dadda*) who gives his daughter to his junior, or on the contrary
who takes a daughter from him, a difference in age and especially in sibling
order sometimes being associated with differences in social rank and prestige;
whether the brother giving his daughter has a male heir or is an *amengur*;
whether the two brothers are alive at the moment when the marriage is
settled, or only one of them is, and more precisely whether the surviving
brother is the boy's father, the designated protector of the girl he is taking
for his son (especially if she has no adult brother), or on the contrary, the
girl's father, who may use his dominant position in order to secure the
allegiance of the son-in-law. And as if to add to the ambiguity of this type
of marriage, it is not unusual, as we have seen, that the duty to sacrifice
oneself, so as to be the "veil cast over shame", and to protect a suspect or
ill-favoured girl, should fall to a man from the poorest branch of the lineage,
whose act it is easy, useful and praiseworthy to praise as if it sprang from

his eagerness to fulfil a duty of honour towards the daughter of his *'amm* or even to exercise his right as a male member of the lineage.[81]

Informants constantly remind us by their very incoherences and contradictions that marriage can never be fully defined in genealogical terms, and that it may take on different, even opposite meanings and functions, according to its determining conditions. They also remind us that parallel-cousin marriage can be the worst or the best of marriages depending on whether it is seen as voluntary or forced, i.e. depending primarily on the relative positions of the families in the social structure. It may be the best kind of marriage ("to marry the daughter of your *'amm* is to have honey in your mouth"), not simply from the mythic point of view, but also in terms of practical satisfactions, since it is the least onerous economically and socially – the transactions and material and symbolic costs being reduced to a minimum – and at the same time the safest: the same terms are used to contrast a close marriage with a distant one as are used to contrast direct exchanges between peasants with market transactions.[82] It may also be the worst kind of union ("Marriage between 'paternal uncles' – *azwaj el la'mum* – is bitter in my heart; I pray you, oh my God, preserve me from that misfortune"),[83] and also the least prestigious ("Friends have come who overshadow you; you remain, you who are black") whenever it is forced on the group as a last resort. In short, the apparent incoherence of informants' accounts in fact draws our attention to the functional ambiguity of a *genealogically* (i.e. ideologically) *unequivocal marriage*, and thereby to the manipulations of the objective meaning of practice and its product which this combination of ambiguity and clarity allows and encourages.

Perhaps the only victim of these manipulations is the anthropologist: by putting into the same class all patrilateral parallel-cousin marriages (and assimilated cases) whatever their functions for the individuals and groups involved, he assimilates practices which may differ in all the respects left out of account by the genealogical model. One example will suffice to give an idea of the economic and symbolic inequalities which may be disguised beneath the mask of the genealogical relationship between classificatory parallel cousins and to bring to light the specifically *political* strategies cloaked under the legitimacy of this relationship. The spouses belong to the "house of Belaïd", a big family in terms both of its numbers (perhaps ten men of working age and about forty people in all) and of its economic capital. Because undivided property is never anything other than a refusal to divide, the inequalities which separate the potential "shares" and the respective contributions of different lines are strongly felt. Thus the line of the descendants of Ahmed, from which the bridegroom comes, is much richer in men than the line of Youcef, from which the bride comes, and which is correspondingly richer in land. Wealth in men, considered as reproductive strength and therefore as the promise of still greater wealth in men, is related, provided one knows how to make the capital work, to a great number of advantages the most important of which is authority in the conduct of the house's internal and external affairs: "The house of men is greater than the house of cattle" (*akham irgazen if akham izgaren*). The pre-eminent position of this line is shown by the fact that it has been able to take over the first names of the remote ancestors of the family and that it includes Ahcène, who represents the group in all major external encounters, whether conflict or ceremonies, and Ahmed, the "wise man" who by his mediation and counsel ensures the unity of the group. The girl's father (Youcef) is totally excluded from power, not so much on account of the difference in age separating him from his uncles (Ahcène and Ahmed), since Ahmed's sons, although much younger than he, are associated with the decisions, but above all because he has cut himself off from competition between men, from all exceptional contributions, and even to a certain extent from work on the land. (An only son, and, moreover, "son of the widow", coddled by a whole set of women (mother, aunts, etc.) as the only hope of the lineage, kept away from the games and work of the other children in order to go to school, he has kept in a marginal position all his life. After a period of army service and then agricultural labour abroad, he takes advantage, now that he is back in the village, of his favourable position as possessor of a large share of the patrimony with only a few mouths to feed, restricting himself to the work of overseeing, gardening, and tending (mills, gardens, and fig-driers) – those tasks which require the least initiative and entail the fewest responsibilities, in short, the least male of male jobs.) These are some of the elements which must be taken into account in order to understand the internal and external political function of the marriage between Belaïd – the last son of Amar, himself the son of Ahmed, the uncle of Youcef – and Youcef's daughter Yasmina, his classificatory parallel cousin (father's father's brother's son's daughter). This marriage, arranged by Ahmed and Ahcène, the holders of power – as usual without consulting Youcef, and leaving his wife to protest in vain against a union bringing little profit – reinforces the position of the dominant line, strengthening its links with the line rich in land, without in any way compromising its external prestige, since the structure of domestic power is never declared outwardly, and because even its most impoverished member nevertheless shares in the brilliance of the lineage. Thus the complete truth about this marriage resides in its twofold truth. The official image, that of a marriage between parallel cousins in a large family anxious to demonstrate its unity by a marriage able to reinforce it at the same time as displaying its adherence to the most sacred of the ancestral traditions, coexists without contradiction, even among strangers to the group, who are always sufficiently well informed never to be taken in by the representations they are given, with knowledge of the objective truth about a union which sanctions the forced *alliance* between two social units sufficiently attached to one another negatively, for better or for worse, i.e. genealogically, to be forced to unite their complementary riches. Endless examples could be given of this sort of collective bad faith.

It is understandable that, faced with such accomplished products of the art of masking constraints and interests under expressions capable of sidetracking spontaneous hermeneutics towards the less real but more presentable motives of morality and duty, the collective judgement should hesitate. But there is no case in which the objective meaning of a marriage is so strongly marked as to leave no room for symbolic transfiguration. Thus the marriage of the so-called *mechrut*, by which a man who has no male descendants gives his daughter in marriage to an "heir" (*awrith*) on condition that he comes to live in his father-in-law's house, is encountered only in tales or anthropology books in the form of the sort of purchase of a son-in-law, recruited for his powers of production and reproduction, that mechanical application of the official principles of the Kabyle world-view would lead us to see in it.[84] The informants who mention it, in whatever region, are right in saying that this form of marriage is unknown among them and only to be found in other areas. The most careful scrutiny of genealogies and family histories will not reveal a single case which perfectly matches the definition ("I give you my daughter, but you will come to my home"). But one is equally entitled to claim that there is no family which does not include at least one *awrith*, but an *awrith* disguised under the official image of the "associate" or the "adopted son". The word *awrith*, the "heir", is an official euphemism allowing people to name the unnameable, i.e. a man who could only be defined, in the house which welcomes him, as the husband of his wife. It is clear that the man of honour who plays the game fairly can count on the benevolent complicity of his own group when he attempts to disguise as an adoption a union which, viewed cynically, represents an inversion of all the honourable forms of marriage and which, as such, is no less dishonourable for the *awrith* ("he is the one who is playing the bride", they say) than for kinsmen sufficiently self-interested to give their daughter to this kind of unpaid domestic servant. And the group is quick to join in the circle of the calculated lies which tend to conceal its failure to find an honourable way of saving the *amengur* from resorting to such extremities in order to prevent the "bankruptcy" (*lakhla*) of his family.

But the genealogies also contain cases about which it is hard to understand how they can benefit from similar complicity. For example, in the history of one prestigious lineage one finds a series of acquisitions of sons-in-law who are neither seen as nor declared *mechrut*, although their annexation was imposed not by necessity, but as part of a quasi-systematic effort to increase the capital of men, a fact which one might expect to double the sense of scandal. In one such case, the fact that the "ill-gotten" son-in-law was a marabout no doubt lent credibility to the status of "adopted son" which he was supposed to have received, although he had put himself in the position of an *awrith* by coming to live with his wife's family (a sign that the latter were in a stronger position) after spending a few months with his own family (which he was made to do for the sake of appearances). Nevertheless, various subterfuges were resorted to in order to get over the problem of his presence in the house: he was given the job of miller, which made it possible to keep him at a distance; as is customary in such cases, his food was brought to him at the mill. Then the heads of the lineage discreetly suggested that he should take outside work, an ingenious solution which kept the profits of his labour while removing the embarrassing situation created by his presence in his wife's family. After the death of her husband, the woman remarried and had a son, whom she took back into her own lineage when her second husband died; this son was not regarded as an *awrith*, either, when his maternal uncles married him to an orphan under their protection, so as to bind him to her. The reason was that in bringing up their quasi-son as "their own son" (though he still calls them *khal* and not *dadda*, and is called Ahmed u Agouni, after his father's village) and marrying him to one of their quasi-daughters, they had given sufficient proof of their adherence to the official image of the *awrith* as "heir" and "adopted son" to impose a collective recognition of it. This is how the second-order strategies – which all tend to transform useful relationships into official ones and hence to ensure that practices which in fact obey altogether different principles appear to be *deduced* fom the genealogical definition – achieve in addition an unexpected result, in giving a representation of practice seemingly designed to confirm the representation the structuralist anthropologist has of practice.

The ordinary and the extra-ordinary

Thus, far from obeying a norm which would designate an obligatory spouse from among the whole set of official kin, the arrangement of marriages depends directly on the state of the practical kinship relations, relationships through the men usable by the men and relationships through the women usable by the women, and on the state of the power relations within the "house", that is, between the lineages united by marriage in the previous generation, which allow and favour the cultivation of one or the other field of relationships.

If one accepts that one of the principal functions of marriage is to reproduce the social relations of which it is the product, then it is immediately understandable why the different types of marriage which can be distinguished as much by the criterion of the objective characteristics of the groups brought together (their position in the social hierarchy, their remoteness in space, etc.) as by the characteristics of the ceremony itself, in particular its solemnity, should correspond very closely to the characteristics of the social relations which have made them possible and which they tend to reproduce. The official kin group, publicly named and socially recognized, is what makes possible and necessary the official marriages which provide its only opportunity to mobilize practically and thereby to reaffirm its unity, a unity at once as solemn and as artificial as the occasions on which it is celebrated. It is within practical kinship, that is, in the field of relationships *constantly* reused and thus reactivated for future use, that ordinary marriages are contracted, with a frequency which itself condemns them to the insignificance of the unmarked and the banality of the everyday. It is logical that the higher a group is placed in the social hierarchy and hence the richer it is in official relationships, the greater the proportion of its work of reproduction that is devoted to reproducing such relationships, whereas the poor relations, who have little to spend on solemnities, can make do with the ordinary marriages that practical kinship ensures for them.

The most insidious of the distortions inherent in informants' explanations is doubtless the fact that they give a disproportionate importance to extra-ordinary marriages, which distinguish themselves from ordinary marriages by a positive or a negative mark. As well as the various curios which the anthropologist often finds himself being offered by well-intentioned informants, such as marriage by exchange (*abdal*, two men "exchange" their sisters), marriage by "addition" (*thirni*, two brothers marry two sisters, the second sister being "added" to the first; the son marries the sister or even the daughter of the second wife of his father), or again, the levirate, a particular case of marriage as "reparation" (*thiririth*, from *err*, to give or take back), native discourse also defines the extreme cases: parallel-cousin marriage, the most perfect mythically, and marriage uniting the headmen of two tribes or two different clans, the most perfect politically.

Thus, the tale, a semi-ritualized didactic narrative, a simple paraphrase in parabolic form of the proverb or saying which serves as its moral, only ever relates marked, marking marriages. First, there are the different types of parallel-cousin marriage, whether intended to preserve a political heritage or to prevent the extinction of a lineage (in the case of an only daughter). Then there are the most flagrant misalliances, like the marriage of the tawny owl and the eagle's daughter – a pure model of upward marriage (upward socially, but also mythically, up being opposed to down as day, light, happiness, purity, honour are opposed to night, darkness, misfortune, impurity, and dishonour) between a man at the bottom of the social ladder, an *awrith* and a woman of a family of higher rank, in which the traditional relationship of assistance is inverted by the discrepancy between the partner's positions in the social and sexual hierarchies. It is the one who gives, in this case the higher, who must go to the aid of the one who has taken his son-in-law, the tawny owl, on his back, to spare him a humiliating defeat in competition with the young eagles – a scandalous situation denounced in the proverb "giving him your daughter and corn too".

Contrary to these official representations, observation and statistics establish that, in all the groups observed, the majority of the marriages belong to the class of ordinary marriages, generally arranged by the women, within the area of the practical kinship or practical relationships which make them possible and which they help to strengthen.[85] The marriages contracted within this area, between families united by frequent and ancient exchanges along age-old beaten paths continuously kept open for generation after generation, are those about which nothing is said, as with everything which can be taken for granted because it has always been as it is – those which have no other function, apart from biological reproduction, than the reproduction of those social relationships which make them possible.[86] These marriages, which are generally celebrated without ceremony, stand in the same relationship to extra-ordinary marriages, which are concluded by the men between different villages or tribes, or more simply, outside practical kinship, and for this reason always sealed by solemn ceremonies, as the exchanges of everyday life, the little presents (*thuntichin*) exchanged by women to "bind them in friendship", stand to the extra-ordinary exchanges on special occasions, the solemn gifts solemnly proclaimed (*lkhir*) which are expected between official kin.[87]

Extra-ordinary marriages exclude the women, as does parallel-cousin marriage, which differs in this respect – alone[88] – from ordinary marriages, which would be unthinkable without their intervention. But, in contrast to marriage arranged between brothers, or at any rate among the men of the lineage, with the blessing of the patriarch, a distant marriage is officially presented as political. Contracted outside the zone of everyday relationships, celebrated with ceremonies which mobilize extensive groups, its sole justification is political, as in the limiting case of the marriages intended to set the seal on peace or on an alliance between the "heads" of two tribes.[89] More often, it is marriage of the marketplace, a neutral ground from which women are excluded and where lineages, clans, and tribes warily meet. It is "published" in the market by the crier (*berrah*), unlike other marriages which, since they only bring together kinsmen, do not involve solemn invitations. It treats the woman as a political instrument, a sort of pledge or liquid asset, capable of earning symbolic profits. Being an opportunity to exhibit publicly and officially, and hence perfectly legitimately, the family's symbolic capital, to make a *show* of kinship ties, and thereby to increase this capital, at the cost of considerable economic expenditure, it is faithful at all times to the logic of the accumulation of symbolic capital. Thus marriage to a stranger who has been cut off from his group and has fled to one's village is shunned, while marriage to a stranger living at a distance is prestigious because it bears witness to the extent of the lineage's prestige. Similarly, political marriages, as opposed to ordinary marriages which follow well-worn tracks, are not and cannot be repeated, since the alliance would be devalued by becoming common. Furthermore, this type of marriage is fundamentally masculine and often causes conflict between the father of the bride and her mother, who is less appreciative of the symbolic profit which the marriage may bring and more concerned about the drawbacks it may entail for her daughter, condemned to a life of exile (*thaghribth*, the exile, she who has gone off to the west).[90] Insofar as it brings large groups into interrelationship through the families and lineages directly involved, it is totally official and every aspect of the celebration is strictly ritualized and magically stereotyped: this is doubtless because the stakes are so high and the chances of a rift so great that the agents dare not trust to the regulated improvisation of orchestrated habitus.

The marriages arranged in the sort of privileged sub-market (that of the *akham*) which the authority of the elder and agnate solidarity set up as a free zone from which all outbidding and all competition are absolutely excluded, unquestionably distinguish themselves from extra-ordinary marriages by their incomparably lower material and symbolic cost. The union is generally regarded as a self-evident necessity, and when this is not the case, the discreet mediation of the women of the family is sufficient to bring it about. The celebration of the marriage is reduced to a strict minimum. First, the expenses (*thaqufats*) incurred in the reception of the marriage procession by the girl's family are very modest; the *imensi* ceremony, at which the bridewealth is presented, brings together only the most important representatives of the two families being allied (perhaps twenty men); the bride's trousseau (*ladjaz*) is limited to three dresses, two scarves, and some other items (a pair of shoes, a *haïk*); the sum agreed upon as the bridewealth, negotiated in advance in relation to what the girl's parents have to buy in the market to deck their daughter (a mattress, a pillow, a trunk, as well as the blankets which are the family's own work and are handed down from mother to daughter), is presented without much ceremony, and without bluff or pretence; as for the wedding-feast expenses, they are minimized by arranging for the feast to coincide with the Aïd: the sheep traditionally sacrificed on that occasion is sufficient for the requirements of the wedding, and the guests are more likely to be kept at home at that time and present their excuses.

Compared with these ordinary marriages, which the old peasant morality eulogizes (in contrast to marriages which, like "widows' daughters' marriages", go beyond the socially recognized limits of each family), extra-ordinary marriages differ in every way. To conceive the ambition of seeking a wife at a distance, one has to be predisposed to do so by the habit of keeping up relationships that are out of the ordinary, which implies possession of the skills, especially the linguistic ones, indispensable in such circumstances; one also needs a large capital of very costly distant relationships, which are the only source of reliable information and of mediators necessary to the success of the project. In short, to be able to mobilize this capital at the right moment, it is necessary to have invested a lot and for a long time. For example, to take only one case, the heads of marabout families who have been asked to act as mediators are paid back in countless ways: the taleb of the village, or *a fortiori* the religious figure of higher rank who takes part in the procession of *iqafafen*, is given new clothes and shoes by the "master of the wedding", and the gifts he traditionally receives, in cash at the time of religious feasts and in provisions at harvest time, are in a sense proportionate to the services rendered; the Aïd sheep he is given that year is simply compensation for the "shame" (*ihachem udhmis*, he has covered his face with shame) he has incurred in going to solicit a layman (who, whatever his power, does not "hold in his heart" Koranic knowledge) and consecrating the marriage with his faith and knowledge. Once the agreement is reached (possibly involving the payment of *thaj'alts* to one or another of the girl's close relatives), the ceremony of "pledging" (*asarus*, the laying down of the pledge, *thimristh*), which functions as an appropriation rite (*a'ayam*, naming, or *a'allam*, marking, comparable to that of the first plot of land ploughed; or more exactly *amlak*, appropriation on the same terms as land) is in itself almost a wedding. Presents are brought not only for the bride (who receives her "pledge", a jewel of value, and money from all the men who see her on that day – *tizri*), but also for all the other women of the house; the visitors also bring provisions (semolina, honey, butter) and some cattle, to be slaughtered and eaten by the guests or added to the bride's capital. The men of the family demonstrate how numerous they are with the noise of their rifle volleys, as on the wedding day. All the feasts which take place between this feast and the wedding are opportunities to bring *thislith* her "share" (*el haq*): great families at a great distance from each other cannot be content with exchanging a few dishes of couscous; presents appropriate to the persons they unite are added. Though granted, that is to say "given", "appropriated", and "recalled to mind" by the many "shares" she has received, the girl is not yet acquired: a point of honour is set on allowing her family the time it wishes to wait and to keep one waiting.

The celebration of the marriage is obviously the high point of the symbolic confrontation of the two groups, and also the moment of the greatest expense. The girl's family is sent *thaqufats*, at least two hundred kilos of semolina, fifty kilos of flour, abundant meat (on the hoof) – which the senders know will not all be eaten – honey (twenty litres) and butter (twenty litres). The case was mentioned of a marriage in which the girl's family was taken a calf and five live and one slaughtered sheep. The delegation of *iqafafen* consisted, it is true, of forty rifle-bearing men, together with all the kinsmen and notables exempted by their age from shooting – fifty men in all. The bride's trousseau which may in such cases consist of up to thirty items, is matched by a similar number of items given to the various other women of the family. And if one often hears it said that between great families there are no *chrut* (conditions laid down by the father for his daughter before he grants her hand), it is because the status of the families is in itself a guarantee that the "conditions" explicitly stated elsewhere will here be surpassed. Although the value of the bridewealth is always subject to strict social supervision, exceptional marriages may ignore the limits tacitly set by the group. The proof may be seen in phrases nowadays used as challenges: "Who do you think you are? The woman of fourteen [*am arba'tach*]?" – an allusion to the fourteen *reals* paid for the most expensively bought wife who became the mistress of the house of the family which was richest and the most endowed with men. For women married around 1900–1910, the same expression speaks of a payment of forty *duros*, which, according to the popular notion of equivalence ("We got her for 'the equivalent of two pairs of oxen'", *elhaq nasnath natsazwijin*), must have corresponded to the price paid for two pairs of oxen; just before the Second World War, a typical bridewealth was worth around two thousand old francs (£20). A prestigious marriage celebrated with great ceremony in 1936, to which virtually all the men of the tribe were invited (together with a troupe of *tbal* who performed for three days and nights) cost the organizer in addition to all his liquid assets, the value of one of his best pieces of land (four days' ploughing for one man). To feed his guests he had to slaughter two oxen, a calf, and six sheep.

In fact the economic cost is probably insignificant in comparison with the symbolic cost of *imensi*. The ritual of the ceremony of presenting the bridewealth is the occasion for a total confrontation between the two groups, in which the economic stakes are no more than an index and pretext. To demand a large payment for one's daughter, or to pay a large sum to marry off one's son, is in either case to assert one's prestige, and thereby to acquire prestige: each side intends to prove its own "worth", either by showing what price men of honour, who know how to appreciate it, set on alliance with them, or by making a brilliant demonstration of their estimation of their own value through the price they are prepared to pay in order to have partners worthy of them. By a sort of inverted haggling, disguised under the appearance of ordinary bargaining, the two groups tacitly agree to step up the amount of the payment by successive bids, because they have a common interest in raising this indisputable index of the symbolic value of their products on the matrimonial exchange market. And no feat is more highly praised than the prowess of the bride's father who, after vigorous bargaining has been concluded, solemnly returns a large share of the sum received. The greater the proportion returned, the greater the honour accruing from it, as if, in crowning the transaction with an act of generosity, the intention was to make an exchange of honour out of bargaining which could be so overtly keen only because the pursuit of maximum material profit was masked under the contests of honour and the pursuit of maximum symbolic profit.[91]

The most distant marriages are perfectly unequivocal since, at least until recent times, it was impossible to marry at a distance for negative reasons, for lack of anyone to marry near at hand. Like all close marriages, parallel-cousin marriage, the only type of ordinary marriage to be positively and officially *marked*, often occurs in the poorest lineages or the poorest lines of the dominant lineages (the clients), who, in resorting to this, the most economical type of union, release the group in the most satisfactory way (if only by avoiding misalliances) from the obligation to marry off two of its particularly disadvantaged members. But at the same time, because it always has the objective effect of reinforcing the integration of the minimal unit and, consequently, its distinctiveness vis-à-vis other units, it is likely to be the tactic of groups characterized by a strong desire to assert their *distinction*. Thus its ambiguity predisposes it to play the rôle of the poor man's prestige marriage: it offers an elegant way out for all those who, like the ruined nobleman unable to indicate other than symbolically his refusal to derogate, seek in the affectation of rigour the means of affirming their distinction, such as a lineage cut off from its original group and anxious to maintain its originality, a family aiming to affirm the distinctive features of its lineage by going one better in purism (almost always the case with one family in a marabout community), a clan seeking to mark its distinction from the opposing clan by stricter observance of the traditions (like the Aït Madhi at Aït Hichem), and so on. Because it can appear as the most sacred and, under certain conditions, the most "distinguished" marriage, it is the cheapest form of extra-ordinary marriage, obviating expenditure on the ceremony, hazardous negotiations, and a costly bridewealth. And thus there is no more accomplished way of making a virtue of necessity and of putting oneself in line with the rule.

However, any particular marriage is meaningful only in relation to the totality of simultaneously possible marriages (or, more concretely, in relation to the range of potential partners); in other words, it is situated somewhere on a continuum running from parallel-cousin marriage to marriage between members of different tribes, the most risky but most prestigious type, and is therefore necessarily characterized from both standpoints, by the extent to which it reinforces integration and by the extent to which it expands alliances. These two types of marriage represent the points of maximum intensity of the two values which all marriages seek to maximize: on the one hand the integration of the minimal unit and its security, on the other hand alliance and prestige, that is, opening up to the outside world, towards strangers. The choice between fission and fusion, the inside and the outside, security and adventure, is posed anew with each marriage. If it ensures the maximum of integration for the minimal group, parallel-cousin marriage duplicates the relationship of filiation with a relationship of alliance, squandering by this redundancy the opportunity of creating new alliances which marriage represents. Distant marriage, on the other hand, secures prestigious alliances at the cost of lineage integration and the bond between brothers, the foundation of the agnatic unit. Native discourse repeats this obsessively.

The centripetal thrust – exaltation of the internal, of security, autarky, the excellence of the blood, agnate solidarity – always calls forth, if only to oppose it, the centrifugal thrust, exaltation of the prestigious alliance. The categorical imperative always masks calculation of the maximum and the minimum, the search for the maximum of alliance compatible with the maintenance or reinforcement of integration between brothers. This can be seen from the informants' syntax, which is always that of *preference*: "It is better to protect your point of honour [*nif*] than reveal it to others." "I don't sacrifice *adhrum* [the lineage] to *aghrum* [wheatcake]." "The inside is better than the outside." "First madness [daring, risky step]: to give the daughter of *'amm* to other men. Second madness to go penniless to market. Third madness: to vie with the lions on the mountain tops." This last saying is the most significant, because under the guise of absolute condemnation of distant marriage, it expressly recognizes the logic in which it belongs, that of the exploit, prowess, prestige. It takes great prestige and wild audacity to go to market without any money intending to buy things, just as it takes enormous courage to take on lions, the courageous strangers from whom the founders of the villages had to win back their wives, according to many legends of origin.

Matrimonial strategies and social reproduction

The characteristics of a marriage, and in particular the position it occupies at a determinate point on the continuum running from political marriage to parallel-cousin marriage, depend on the aims of the collective strategies of the groups involved. More precisely, given that the objectives themselves depend very closely on the means available, analysis of the operations which have led up to different types of marriage sends us back to analysis of the conditions which had to be fulfilled for them to be possible, i.e. conceivable and realizable. The matrimonial game is similar to a card game, in which the outcome depends partly on the deal, the cards held (their value itself being defined by the rules of the game, characteristic of the social formation in question), and partly on the players' skill: that is to say, firstly on the material and symbolic capital possessed by the families concerned, their wealth in instruments of production and in men, considered both as productive and reproductive power and also, in a previous state of play, as fighting strength and hence symbolic strength; and secondly on the competence which enables the strategists to make the best use of this capital, practical mastery of the (in the widest sense) economic axiomatics being the precondition for production of the practices regarded as "reasonable" within the group and positively sanctioned by the laws of the market in material and symbolic goods.

The collective strategy which leads up to a particular "move" (in the case of marriage or in any other area of practice) is but the product of a combination of the strategies of the interested parties which tends to give their respective interests the weight corresponding to their position, at the moment in question, within the structure of power relations within the domestic unit. It is a striking fact that matrimonial negotiations are really the business of the whole group, everyone playing his part at the appropriate moment, and thus being able to contribute to the success or failure of the project. First of all, the women with their unofficial and recoverable contacts make it possible to start semi-official negotiations without the risk of a humiliating rebuff. Then the most eminent men, those most representative of official kinship, acting as guarantors expressly *mandated* by the will of their group and as explicitly *authorized* spokesmen, mediate and intercede, presenting at the same time a striking testimony of the symbolic capital possessed by a family capable of mobilizing such prestigious men. Finally, each group in its entirety enters into the decision, passionately discussing the matrimonial projects, evaluating the reception given to the delegates' proposals, and directing the course which future negotiations should take. This means, incidentally – for the benefit of those ethnologists who count themselves satisfied when they have characterized a marriage in exclusively genealogical terms – that behind the quasi-theatrical image put forward by the official kin at the time of the marriage, the two groups carry out a systematic investigation to establish complete information on the variables characterizing not only the couple (age, and especially age difference, previous matrimonial history, sibling order, theoretical and practical kin relation to the family authority holder, etc.) but also their groups. Information is obtained on the economic and social history of the families about to be allied and of the larger groups to which they belong; the symbolic patrimony, especially the capital of honour and men of honour which they command; the quality of the network of alliances on which they count, and of the groups to which they are traditionally opposed; each family's position in its group – a particularly important factor because a display of prestigious kinsmen may disguise a dominated position within an eminent group – and the state of its relations with the other members of its group. i.e. the family's degree of integration (undivided ownership, etc.); the structure of the power and authority relations within the domestic unit (and, for a family marrying off a daughter, especially those among the women), etc.

In a social formation oriented towards simple reproduction, i.e. towards the biological reproduction of the group and the production of sufficient goods for its subsistence and biological reproduction, and, inseparably from this, towards reproducing the structure of social and ideological relations within which and through which the activity of production is carried on and legitimated, the strategies of the different categories of agents, whose interests within the domestic unit may be contradictory (among other occasions, at the time of a marriage), arise from the systems of interests objectively assigned to them by the system of principles which make up a particular *mode of reproduction*: these principles govern fertility, filiation, residence, inheritance, and marriage, and, in combining to fulfil the same function – the biological and social reproduction of the group – are objectively concerted.[92] In an economy characterized by the relatively equal distribution of the means of production (generally owned in common by the lineage) and by the weakness and stability of the productive forces, which rule out the production and accumulation of substantial surpluses and hence the development of clearly marked economic differentiation (although it is possible to see in the levying of labour in the "mutual-help/corvées" – *thiwizi* – a *disguised* form of the sale of labour-power), the family's efforts are directed towards the maintenance and reproduction of the family, not the production of assets.

If one insists on seeing *thiwizi* as a corvée (the better, for example, to force reality into the framework of a realist, reified definition of modes of production) one must at least take into account the fact that this corvée is disguised under the appearance of mutual aid. In fact *thiwizi* mainly profits the richer farmers and also the taleb (whose land is ploughed and sown collectively): the poor have no need of assistance with the harvest; but *thiwizi* may also benefit the poor man in the case of the building of a house (the transporting of stones and beams). Ostracism is a terrible sanction which is not only symbolic: owing to the limited technical resources, many activities would be impossible without the help of the group (e.g. the building of a house, with the transporting of stones, or the transporting of mill-wheels, which used to mobilize forty men in non-stop shifts for several days). Moreover, in this economy of insecurity, a capital of services rendered and gifts bestowed is the best and indeed the only safeguard against the "thousand contingencies" on which, as Marx observes, depends the maintenance or loss of working conditions, from the accident which causes the loss of an animal to the bad weather which destroys the crops.

In such conditions an abundance of men would no doubt be a liability if, taking a strictly economic view, one saw in it only "arms" and therefore "stomachs". In fact the political insecurity which perpetuates itself by generating the dispositions required in order to respond to war, brawling, robbery, or vengeance (*reqba*) was doubtless the basic reason why men were valued as "rifles", i.e. not only as a labour force but also as fighting power: the value of the land lies only in the men who cultivate and also defend it. The patrimony of the lineage, symbolized by its name, is defined not simply by the possession of the land and the house, goods which are precious and therefore vulnerable, but also by the possession of the means of protecting it, i.e. men; this is so because the land and the women are never reduced to the status of simple instruments of production or reproduction, and still less to the status of commodities or even "property". Attacks on the land, the house, or the women are attacks on their master, on his *nif*, his very being, as defined by the group – his "potency". Alienated land, unavenged rape or murder, are different forms of the same offence, which always elicits the same response from the group's point of honour. Just as a murder is "paid back", but at a higher rate, by striking if possible at the person closest to the murderer or the most prominent member in his group, so a piece of ancestral land, even a not very fertile one, is "bought back" *at any price* in order to wipe out the standing insult to the group's honour.[93] Just as, in the logic of challenge and riposte, the best land both technically and symbolically is that most closely tied to the patrimony, so the man through whom one can most cruelly strike at the group is its most representative member.

The ethos of honour is but the transfigured expression of these economic and political facts. A sharp distinction is drawn between *nif*, the point of honour, and *hurma*, the sum total of that which is *haram*, i.e. forbidden, all that goes to make up the vulnerability of the group, its most sacred possession (from which there follows a distinction between the challenge, which touches only the point of honour, and sacrilegious outrage).[94] Only the punctilious, active vigilance of the *point of honour* (*nif*) can guarantee the integrity of *honour* (*hurma*) – which, being sacred, is inherently exposed to sacrilegious outrage – and win the *consideration and respectability* accorded to the man who has sufficient point of honour to keep his honour safe from offence.[95] *Hurma* in the sense of the sacred (*haram*), *nif*, and *hurma* in the sense of respectability, are inseparable. The more vulnerable a family, the more *nif* it must possess to defend its sacred values, and the greater the merit and esteem opinion accords it; thus poverty, far from contradicting or prohibiting respectability, makes doubly meritorious the man who, though particularly exposed to outrage, nonetheless manages to win respect. Conversely, the point of honour has a meaning and a function only in a man for whom there exist things worthy of being defended. A being devoid of the sacred could dispense with the point of honour because he would in a sense be invulnerable. What is *haram* (i.e. literally, taboo) is essentially the sacred of the left hand, *hurma*, that is, the inside and more precisely the female universe, the world of the secret, the enclosed space of the house, as opposed to the outside, the open world of the public square (*thajma'th*), reserved for the men. The sacred of the right hand is essentially "the rifles", that is, the group of the agnates, the "sons of the paternal uncle", all those whose death must be avenged by blood and all those who are bound to carry out blood vengeance. The rifle is the symbolic embodiment of the *nif* of the agnatic group, *nif* defined as that which can be challenged and which enables one to take up the challenge. Thus to the passivity of *hurma*, female in nature, there is opposed the active susceptibility of *nif*, the male virtue par excellence. It is ultimately on *nif*, its (physical or symbolic) fighting capacity, that the defence of the group's material and symbolic patrimony – the source both of its potency and of its vulnerability – depends.

Men constitute a political and symbolic force on which depend the protection and expansion of the patrimony, the defence of the group and its goods against the encroachments of violence, and at the same time the imposition of its dominance and the satisfaction of its interests. Consequently, the only threat to the power of the group, apart from the sterility of its women, is the fragmentation of the material and symbolic patrimony which would result from quarrels between the men. Hence the fertility strategies which aim to produce as many men as possible as quickly as possible (through early marriage), and the educative strategies which, in inculcating an exalted adherence to the lineage and to the values of honour (the transfigured expression of the objective relation between the agents and an extremely vulnerable and perpetually threatened material and symbolic patrimony), collaborate to support the integration of the lineage and to divert aggressive tendencies outwards: "The land is copper (*nehas*), men's arms are silver." The very ambiguity of this saying – *nehas* also means jealousy – points to the principle of the contradiction which the successional custom engenders in *attaching* men to the land. The successional strategies, which objectively tend to attach as many men as possible to the patrimony by ensuring equality of inheritance and by guaranteeing the unity of the patrimony through the disinheriting of the women, introduce an unavoidable contradiction: not only do they threaten to fragment the ancestral lands by parcelling them out equally among very numerous heirs, but above all they set at the very heart of the system the principle of competition for power over the domestic economy and politics – competition and conflict between father and sons, whom this mode of power transmission condemns to subordination so long as the patriarch lives (many parallel-cousin marriages are arranged by the "old man" without the fathers being consulted); competition and conflict between brothers or cousins who, at least when they in their turn become fathers, are destined to find that their interests conflict.[96] The strategies of agnates are dominated by the antagonism between the symbolic profits of political and economic non-division and the material profits of a breakup which are continually recalled to mind by the spirit of economic calculation. The urge to calculate, repressed in men, finds more overt expression in women, who are structurally predisposed to be less concerned with the symbolic profits accruing from political unity, and to devote themselves more readily to strictly economic practices.

The ideology which makes woman a principle of division and discord thus finds an apparent basis in the effects of the division of labour between the sexes, which, as we have seen, predisposes the women to be less sensitive to symbolic profits and freer to pursue material profits.[97] Lending between women is regarded as the antithesis of the exchange of honour; and it is indeed closer to the economic truth of exchange than the men's dealings. Of the man who, unlike the man of honour anxious not to squander his capital of "credit", too readily seeks loans, especially of money, the man who has so often blanched with shame on asking for a loan that he has a "yellow face", it is said that "his borrowing (*arrtal*) is like that of women". The opposition between the two "economies" is so marked that the expression *err arrtal*, also used to express the taking of revenge, means the *returning of a gift*, an exchange, in the men's speech, whereas it means "giving back a loan" when used by the women. Loan conduct is certainly more frequent and more natural among the women, who will borrow and lend anything for any purpose; it follows that the economic truth, held back in swapping, is closer to the surface in female exchanges in which there may be specific dates for repayment ("when my daughter gives birth") and precise calculation of the quantities lent.

In short, the *symbolic and political* interests attached to the unity of land ownership, to the extent of alliances, to the material and symbolic power of the agnatic group, and to the values of honour and prestige which make a great house (*akham amoqrane*), militate in favour of the strengthening of corporate bonds. Conversely, as is shown by the fact that the breaking up of joint ownership has become more and more frequent with the generalizing of monetary exchanges and the spread of the (corresponding) calculative spirit, *economic* interests (in the narrow sense), those relating to consumption, are conducive to the breakup of undivided ownership.[98]

Even in cases in which a holder of domestic power has long prepared for his succession by the manipulation of individual aspirations, directing each of the brothers towards the "speciality" which suited him in the division of domestic labour, competition for internal power is almost inevitable, and can be sublimated into a competition of honour only at the cost of continuous control by the men over themselves and by the group over all of them. But the forces of cohesion represented by the non-division of the land and the integration of the family – institutions which reinforce each other – clash constantly with forces of fission such as the "jealousy" aroused by an unequal distribution of powers or responsibilities, or the imbalance between respective contributions to production and consumption ("The hard-working man's labour has been eaten up by the man who leans against the wall").[99] In general, authority over the delegation of work, the control of expenditure and the management of the patrimony, or over the family's external relations (alliances, etc.) resides in fact in a single person, who thus appropriates the symbolic profits which accrue from going to market, presence at clan assemblies or the more exceptional gatherings of tribal notables, etc. – not to mention the fact that these duties have the effect of exempting the person who assumes them from the exigencies of the daily work routine.

Objectively united, for the worse if not for the better, the brothers are subjectively divided, even in their solidarity. "My brother", said an informant, "is the man who would defend my honour if my point of honour failed, who would save me from dishonour but put me to shame." Another informant reported an acquaintance as saying: "My brother is he who, if I died, could marry my wife and would be praised for it." The homogeneity of the mode of production of habitus (i.e. of the material conditions of life, and of pedagogic action) produces a homogenization of dispositions and interests which, far from excluding competition, may in some cases engender it by inclining those who are the product of the same conditions of production to recognize and pursue the same goods, whose rarity may arise entirely from this competition. The domestic unit, a monopolistic grouping defined, as Weber said, by the exclusive appropriation of a determinate type of goods (land, names, etc.) is the locus of a competition for this capital, or rather, for control over this capital, which continuously threatens to destroy the capital by destroying the fundamental condition of its perpetuation.

The relationship between brothers, keystone of the family structure, is also its weakest point, which a whole series of mechanisms are designed to support and strengthen,[100] starting with parallel-cousin marriage, the ideological resolution, sometimes realized in practice, of the *specific contradiction of this mode of reproduction*. If parallel-cousin marriage is a matter for men,[101] consistent with the men's interests, that is, the higher interests of the lineage, often arranged without the women being informed, and *against their will* (when the two brothers' wives are on bad terms, one not wanting to admit the other's daughter to her house and the other not wishing to place her daughter under her sister-in-law's authority), the reason is that it is intended to counteract, practically, division between the men. This is taken so much for granted that the father's ritual advice to his son ("Don't listen to your wives, stay united amongst yourselves!") is naturally taken to mean "Marry your children to one another."

Everything takes places as if this social formation had had to grant itself officially a possibility rejected as incestuous by most societies, in order to resolve ideologically the tension which is at its very centre. Perhaps the exaltation of marriage with the *ben'amm* (parallel cousin) would have been better understood if it had been realized that *ben'amm* has come to designate the enemy, or at least, the intimate enemy, and that enmity is called *thaben'ammts* "that of the children of the paternal uncle". In fact, the forces of ideological cohesion are embodied in the elder, *djedd*, whose authority based on the power to disinherit, on the threat of malediction, and above all on adherence to the values symbolized by *thadjadith*, can secure equilibrium between the brothers only by maintaining the strictest equality between them (and their wives) both in work (the women, for example, taking turns to do the housework, prepare the meals, carry water, etc.) and in consumption. It is no accident that crisis so often coincides with the disappearance of this positive cohesive factor, arising when the father dies leaving adult sons none of whom wields a clear established authority (by virtue of the age gap or any other principle). But the extremely variable relative strength of the tendencies to fusion or fission depends fundamentally, at the level of the domestic unit as much as at the level of larger units like the clan or the tribe, on the relationship between the group and the external units: insecurity provides a negative principle of cohesion capable of making up for the deficiency of positive principles.[102] "I hate my brother, but I hate the man who hates him." The negative, forced solidarity created by a shared vulnerability, which is reinforced every time there is a threat to the jointly owned material and symbolic patrimony, rests on the same principle as the divisive tendency which it temporarily thwarts, that of the rivalry between agnates. So, from the undivided family up to the largest political units, the cohesion endlessly exalted by the mythological and genealogical ideology lasts no longer than the power relations capable of holding individual interests together.

Having restated the principles which define the systems of interests of the different categories of agents in the domestic power relations which result in the definition of a collective matrimonial strategy, if we now posit that the more the working of the system serves the agents' interests, the more they are inclined to serve the working of the system, we are able to understand the fundamental principles of the strategies which are confronted on the occasion of a marriage.[103] Though it is true that marriage is one of the principal opportunities to conserve, increase, or (by misalliance) diminish the capital of authority conferred by strong integration and the capital of prestige stemming from an extensive network of affines (*nesba*), the fact remains that the members of the domestic unit who take part in arranging the marriage do not all identify their own interests to the same degree with the collective interest of the lineage.

As the products of elaborate strategies, of which more is expected than simple biological reproduction, i.e. external or internal alliances intended to reproduce the domestic and political power relations, marriages are a sort of short-term and long-term investment in, among other things, the quality of the "maternal uncles" they procure. It is understandable that they cannot be lightly dissolved, the most long-standing and prestigious relationships naturally being best protected against an ill-considered break. If repudiation becomes inevitable, then all sorts of subterfuges are resorted to so as to prevent the total loss of the capital of alliances. The husband's relatives may go and "beg" the wife's relatives to give her back, attributing the divorce to the youth, recklessness, thoughtless choice of words, and irresponsibility of a husband too young to appreciate the value of alliances; it is pointed out that he did not pronounce the formula three times, but only once, impetuously, and without witnesses. The divorce becomes a case of *thutchḥa* (the wife who lost her temper and went home to her relatives); there may even be the offer of a new wedding (with *imensi* and a trousseau). If the repudiation proves to be final, there are several ways of "separating": the greater the importance and solemnity of the marriage, the more one has "invested" in it, the more one has therefore an interest in preserving relations with those from whom one is separating (either out of kinship or neighbourhood solidarity, or out of self-interested calculation), and the greater the discretion of the break; return of the bridewealth is not demanded immediately, nor is the return refused ("free" repudiation – *baṭṭal* – being a grave insult); it may not even be expected until the woman remarries; not too much attention is paid to the precise amount, and witnesses, especially outsiders, are kept away from the divorce settlement.

The inheritance tradition which excludes woman from the heritage, the mythic world-view which accords her only a limited existence and never grants her full participation in the symbolic capital of her adoptive lineage, the sexual division of labour which restricts her to domestic tasks leaving the representational functions to the man – everything combines to identify the interests of the men with the material and particularly the symbolic interests of the lineage; all the more so, the greater the men's authority in the agnatic group. And the typically masculine marriages – parallel-cousin and political marriages – testify unambiguously to the fact that mens' interests are more directly identified with the official interests of the lineage, and that their strategies are more directly designed to reinforce the domestic unit's integration or the family's network of alliances, contributing in both cases to the growth of the lineage's symbolic capital.

As for the women, it is no accident that the marriages for which they are responsible fall into the class of ordinary marriages, or more precisely, that they are left responsibility only for unremarkable, unceremonial marriages.[104] Being excluded from representational kinship, they are thrown back on to practical kinship and practical uses of kinship, investing more economic realism (in the narrow sense) than the men in the search for a partner for their sons or daughters.[105] Male and female interests are most likely to diverge when a daughter is to be married. Not only is the mother less sensitive to the "family interest" which tends to see the daughter as an *instrument* for strengthening the integration of the agnatic group, or as a sort of symbolic money allowing prestigious alliances to be set up with other groups; but also, in marrying her daughter into her own lineage and intensifying the exchanges between the groups, she tends to strengthen her own position in the domestic unit. The marriage of a son raises for the mistress of the house first and foremost the question of her dominance over the domestic economy. Her interest is only negatively adjusted to that of the lineage: in taking a daughter from the family she herself came from, she is following the path traced by the lineage, and a conflict among the women resulting from a bad choice would ultimately threaten the unity of the agnatic group.

The interest of the men, always dominant officially and tending always to be so in reality, imposes itself all the more fully the stronger the integration of the agnatic group and the more nearly equal (at least) the father's lineage is to the mother's in the social hierarchy. It is no exaggeration to claim that the group's whole matrimonial history is present in the internal transactions over each intended marriage. The lineage's interest, i.e. the male interest, requires that a man should not be placed in a subordinate position in the family by being married to a girl of markedly higher status (a man, they say, can raise a woman, but not the opposite; you give – a daughter – to a superior or an equal, you take – a daughter – from an inferior). It has more chance of asserting itself if the man who has the responsibility (at least the official responsibility) for the marriage has not himself been married above his status. In fact, a whole set of mechanisms, including the bridewealth and the wedding expenses, which rise in proportion to the prestige of the marriage, tend to exclude alliances between groups too unequally matched in terms of economic and symbolic capital (the frequent cases in which the family of one spouse is rich in one form of capital – e.g. in men – whereas the other possesses rather the other form of wealth – e.g. land – are no exceptions to this): "Men ally with their equals", the saying goes ("*tsnassaben (naseb) medden widh m'adhalen*").

In short, the structure of objective relations between the kin who make the matrimonial decision, as man or woman or as member of this or that lineage, helps to define the structure of relationships between the lineages united by the proposed marriage.[106] In fact it would be more accurate to say that the determinant relationship, between the lineage of the person to be married and the lineage offering a possible partner, is always mediated by the domestic power structure. Indeed, in order to describe completely the multi-dimensional and multi-functional relationship (irreducible to kinship ties) between the two groups, it is not sufficient to take into account only the spatial, economic, and social distance between them at the moment of marriage in terms of economic and symbolic capital (measured by the number of men and of men of honour, by the degree of integration of the family, etc.). We must also take into consideration the state, at that particular time, of the balance-sheet of their material and symbolic exchanges, i.e. the whole history of the official, extra-ordinary exchanges such as marriages brought about or at least consecrated by the men, and also the unofficial, ordinary exchanges continuously carried on by the women with the complicity of the men and sometimes without their knowledge, a mediation through which the objective relations predisposing two groups to come together are prepared for and realized.

Whereas economic capital is relatively stable, symbolic capital is relatively precarious: the death of a prestigious head of the family is sometimes enough to diminish it severely. Fluctuations in the group's symbolic fortunes are followed by corresponding changes in the whole image of itself which the group aims to present, and in the objectives – alliance or integration – which it sets for its marriages. Thus in the space of two generations, a great family, whose economic situation was in fact improving, declined from male marriages – marriages within the close kin or extra-ordinary marriages (arranged by men, outside the usual area, for purposes of alliance)

– to ordinary marriages, generally set up by the women, within their own network of relationships. This change in matrimonial policy coincided with the deaths of the two eldest brothers (Hocine and Laïd), the long absence of the oldest men (who had gone to France), and the weakening of the authority of *thamgarth*, who had become blind, with real power passing into the hands of Boudjemâa and, intermittently, Athman. Because it is not clear who is to succeed *thamgarth*, the woman who imposes order and silence (*ta'a n thamgarth, da susmi* "obedience to the old woman is silence"), the structure of relations between the wives reflects the structure of relations between the husbands, leaving vacant the position of mistress of the house; in such circumstances, marriages tend to go towards the women's respective lineages.[107]

The structural characteristics generically defining the value of a lineage's products on the matrimonial market are obviously specified by secondary characteristics such as the matrimonial status of the person to be married, his or her age, sex, etc. Thus the group's matrimonial strategies and the type of marriage which may result from them are quite different depending on whether the man to be married is a bachelor "of the marrying age" or has already "passed the age", or whether he is an already married man looking for a co-wife, or a widower or divorcee wanting to remarry (with the situation changing further depending on whether or not he has children from his first marriage). For a girl the principles of variation are the same, with the difference that the *depreciation* entailed by previous marriages is infinitely greater (because of the price put on virginity and in spite of the fact that a reputation as a "man who repudiates" is just as damaging as that of a "woman to be repudiated").

This is only one aspect of the dyssymmetry between the situation of the man and the woman before marriage: "The man", runs the saying, "is always a man, whatever his state [unlike the woman, who can disqualify herself, and cast herself into shame, *'ar*]; it is up to him to choose." Having the strategic initiative, he can afford to wait: he is sure to find a wife, even if he has to pay the price of his delay by marrying a woman who has already been married, or is of lower social status, or has some disability. The girl being the one traditionally "asked for" and "given" in marriage, it would be the height of absurdity for a father to solicit a husband for his daughter. Another difference is that "the man can wait for the woman [to be of age] but the woman cannot wait for the man": the father with daughters to marry can play with time so as to prolong the conjunctural advantage he derives from his position as the receiver of offers, but only up to a certain point, or he will see his products devalued because they are thought to be unsaleable, or simply because they are past their prime.

One of the most important constraints on matrimonial strategies is the urgency of marriage, which obviously weakens the agents' position. Among the reasons for hurrying the marriage, there may be the great age of the parents, who hope to see their son married and to have a daughter-in-law to look after them, or the fear of seeing a girl they had counted on getting being given to someone else (to avoid this happening, the parents "present a slipper", thus "marking" the girl at a very early age, and sometimes even have the *fatiha* recited). An only son is also married young, so that he can continue the lineage as quickly as possible. The symbolic profit accruing from remarrying after a divorce before the ex-spouse does so often leads both spouses to arrange hasty marriages (such marriages are unlikely to remain stable, which explains why some men seem "condemned" to marry many times). But there is great dyssymmetry on this point too: a man, divorced or widowed, is expected to remarry, whereas a divorced woman is devalued by the failure of her marriage, and a widow, even a very young one, is excluded from the matrimonial market by her status as a mother expected to bring up her husband's child, especially if it is a boy ("a woman cannot remain – a widow – for the sake of another woman" is the saying applied to a widow who, only having daughters, is encouraged to remarry, whereas a mother of sons is praised for her sacrifice, which is all the more meritorious if she is young and thus liable to have to live as an outsider among her husband's sisters and her husband's brothers' wives). But her situation varies further depending on whether she has "left" her children with her deceased husband's family or gone back to her own family with her children (in which case she is less free and hence harder to marry off). An interesting option arises: she may either be taken to wife by someone in her husband's family (the *official* practice, particularly recommended if she has sons) or be found a new husband by her father's family (which happens more often when she is childless) or by her husband's family. It is difficult to establish the universe of variables (doubtless including local traditions) determining the "choice" of one or the other of these strategies.

But it must also be borne in mind, contrary to the tradition which treats each marriage as an isolated unit, that the marrying of each of the children of the same family unit (i.e. the children of the same father, or in some cases the grandchildren of the same grandfather) depends on the marrying of all the others and thus varies as a function of each child's *position* (defined mainly by sibling order, sex, and relationship to the head of the family), within the particular *configuration* of the whole set of children to be married, itself characterized by their number and sex. Thus, for a man the situation is more favourable the closer his kin relationship to the statutory holder of authority over the marriage (which may range from son–father to younger brother–elder brother, or even the relationship between distant cousins). Moreover, although there is no official recognition of any privilege for the eldest (of the boys, of course), everything conspires to favour him to the detriment of his younger brothers, to marry him first and as well as possible, that is, outside rather than inside the lineage, the younger brothers being destined for *production* rather than the *exchanges* of the market or assembly, for work on the land rather than the house's external politics. His position is, however, very different depending on whether he is the eldest of several sons, or the bearer of all his family's hopes as an only son or one followed by several daughters.[108] The family with many daughters, especially if they are poorly "protected" (by sons) and hence little valued because vulnerable and promising few allies, is in an unfavourable position and finds itself forced to incur debts towards the families which receive its women. In contrast, a family rich in men has considerable room for manoeuvre: it can choose to invest each of its sons differently according to circumstances, to increase its alliances with one of them, to strengthen its integration with another, to put a cousin who only has daughters under an obligation by taking one of his girls for a third.[109] In this case, the strategist's skill can have free rein and can effortlessly reconcile the irreconcilable, both reinforcing integration and expanding alliances. The man who only has daughters, or has too many of them, is restricted to *negative* strategies, and his skill has to be limited to the manipulation of the relationship between the field of potential partners and the field of potential competitors, playing off the "near" against the "distant", the request of a close kinsman against that of a stranger (in order to refuse without offence or make him wait) in such a way as to reserve the power to opt for the most prestigious alternative.

It will doubtless have become clear how artificial it is to distinguish between the ends and the means of collective matrimonial strategies. Everything takes place as if, objectively oriented towards the reinforcing or increasing of integration within the limits of the maintenance of alliances (or the *reverse*) these strategies depended for their logic and their efficacy on the material and symbolic capital of the social unit in question, i.e. not only on the value of its material heritage but also on its symbolic heritage, which itself depends first on the size and integration of the agnatic group (marked by the joint production and consumption of material goods) and secondly on its capital of alliances, both these forms of symbolic capital obviously depending on the whole matrimonial history. It follows that every marriage *tends* to reproduce the conditions which have made it possible.[110] Matrimonial strategies, objectively directed towards the conservation or expansion of the material and symbolic capital jointly possessed by a more or less extended group, belong to the system of reproduction strategies, defined as the sum total of the strategies through which individuals or groups objectively tend to reproduce the relations of production associated with a determinate mode of production by striving to reproduce or improve their position in the social structure.[111]

This takes us a long way from the pure – because infinitely impoverished – realm of the "rules of marriage" and the "elementary structures of kinship". Having defined the system of principles from which the agents are able to produce regulated and regular matrimonial practices and to understand practically the matrimonial practices of other agents, we could use statistical analysis of the relevant information to establish the weight of the corresponding structural or individual variables. In fact, the important thing is that the agents' practice becomes intelligible as soon as one can construct the system of the principles and of the laws of combination of those principles (or, to put it another way, the system of variables and operators) which they put into practice when they identify immediately the individuals socio-logically matchable in a given state of the matrimonial market, or more precisely, when, in relation to a particular man, they designate, for example, the few women within practical kinship who are in some sense *promised* to him and those whom he would at a stretch be permitted to marry — and do so in such a clear and final way that any deviation from the most likely course, marriage into another tribe for example, is felt as a challenge to the family concerned, and also to the whole group.

2

Structures and the habitus

Methodological objectivism, a necessary moment in all research, by the break with primary experience and the construction of objective relations which it accomplishes, demands its own supersession. In order to escape the *realism of the structure*, which hypostatizes systems of objective relations by converting them into totalities already constituted outside of individual history and group history, it is necessary to pass from the *opus operatum* to the *modus operandi*, from statistical regularity or algebraic structure to the principle of the production of this observed order, and to construct the theory of practice, or, more precisely, the theory of the mode of generation of practices, which is the precondition for establishing an experimental science of the *dialectic of the internalization of externality and the externalization of internality*, or, more simply, of incorporation and objectification.

A false dilemma: mechanism and finalism

The structures constitutive of a particular type of environment (e.g. the material conditions of existence characteristic of a class condition) produce *habitus*, systems of durable, transposable *dispositions*,[1] structured structures predisposed to function as structuring structures, that is, as principles of the generation and structuring of practices and representations which can be objectively "regulated" and "regular" without in any way being the product of obedience to rules, objectively adapted to their goals without presupposing a conscious aiming at ends or an express mastery of the operations necessary to attain them and, being all this, collectively orchestrated without being the product of the orchestrating action of a conductor.

Even when they appear as the realization of the explicit, and explicitly stated, purposes of a project or plan, the practices produced by the habitus, as the strategy-generating principle enabling agents to cope with unforeseen and ever-changing situations, are only apparently determined by the future. If they seem determined by anticipation of their own consequences, thereby encouraging the finalist illusion, the fact is that, always tending to reproduce the objective structures of which they are the product, they are determined by the past conditions which have produced the principle of their production, that is, by the actual outcome of identical or interchangeable past practices, which coincides with their own outcome to the extent (*and only to the extent*) that the objective structures of which they are the product are prolonged in the structures within which they function. Thus, for example, in the interaction between two agents or groups of agents endowed with the same habitus (say A and B), everything takes place as if the actions of each of them (say, a_1 for A) were organized in relation to the reactions they call forth from any agent possessing the same habitus (say, b_1, B's reaction to a_1) so that they objectively imply anticipation of the reaction which these reactions in turn call forth (say a_2, the reaction to b_1). But the teleological description according to which each action has the purpose of making possible the reaction to the reaction it arouses (individual A performing action a_1, e.g. a gift or challenge, in order to make individual B produce action b_1, a counter-gift or riposte, so as to be able to perform action a_2, a stepped-up gift or challenge) is quite as naive as the mechanistic description which presents the action and the riposte as moments in a sequence of programmed actions produced by a mechanical apparatus. The habitus is the source of these series of moves which are objectively organized as strategies without being the product of a genuine strategic intention – which would presuppose at least that they are perceived as one strategy among other possible strategies.[2]

It is necessary to abandon all theories which explicitly or implicitly treat practice as a mechanical reaction, directly determined by the antecedent conditions and entirely reducible to the mechanical functioning of pre-established assemblies, "models" or "rôles" – which one would, moreover, have to postulate in infinite number, like the chance configurations of stimuli capable of triggering them from outside, thereby condemning oneself to the grandiose and desperate undertaking of the anthropologist, armed with fine positivist courage, who recorded 480 elementary units of behaviour in twenty minutes' observation of his wife in the kitchen.[3] But rejection of mechanistic theories in no way implies that, in accordance with another obligatory option, we should bestow on some creative free will the free and wilful power to constitute, on the instant, the meaning of the situation by projecting the ends aiming at its transformation, and that we should reduce the objective intentions and constituted significations of actions and works to the conscious and deliberate intentions of their authors.

Jean-Paul Sartre deserves credit for having given an ultra-consistent formulation of the philosophy of action accepted, usually implicitly, by all those who describe practices as strategies explicitly oriented by reference to purposes explicitly defined by a free project[4] or even, with some interactionists, by reference to the anticipated cues as to the reaction to practices. Thus, refusing to recognize anything resembling durable dispositions, Sartre makes each action a sort of unprecedented confrontation between the subject and the world. This is clearly seen in the passages in *Being and*

Nothingness where he confers on the awakening of revolutionary consciousness – a sort of "conversion" of consciousness produced by a sort of imaginary variation – the power to create the meaning of the present by creating the revolutionary future which negates it: "For it is necessary to reverse the common opinion and acknowledge that it is not the harshness of a situation or the sufferings it imposes that lead people to conceive of another state of affairs in which things would be better for everybody. It is on the day that we are able to conceive of another state of affairs, that a new light is cast on our trouble and our suffering and we *decide* that they are unbearable."[5] If the world of action is nothing other than this universe of interchangeable possibles, entirely dependent on the decrees of the consciousness which creates it and hence totally devoid of *objectivity*, if it is moving because the subject chooses to be moved, revolting because he chooses to be revolted, then emotions, passions, and actions are merely games of bad faith, sad farces in which one is both bad actor and good audience: "It is not by chance that materialism is serious; it is not by chance that it is found at all times and places as the favourite doctrine of the revolutionary. This is because revolutionaries are serious. They come to know themselves first in terms of the world which oppresses them...The serious man is 'of the world' and has no resource in himself. He does not even imagine any longer the possibility of *getting out* of the world...he is in *bad faith*."[6] The same incapacity to encounter "seriousness" other than in the disapproved form of the "spirit of seriousness" can be seen in an analysis of emotion which, significantly, is separated by *L'imaginaire* (*Psychology of the Imagination*) from the less radically subjectivist descriptions in *Sketch for a Theory of the Emotions*: "What will make me decide to choose the magical aspect or the technical aspect of the world? It cannot be the world itself, ,or this in order to be manifested waits to be discovered. Therefore it is necessary that the for-itself in its project must choose being the one by whom the world is revealed as magical or rational; that is, the for-itself must as a free project of itself give to itself rational or magical existence. It is responsible for either one, for the for-itself can *be* only if it has chosen itself. Therefore the for-itself appears as the free foundation of its emotions as of its volitions. My fear *is* free and manifests my freedom."[7] Such a theory of action was inevitably to lead to the desperate project of a transcendental genesis of society and history (the *Critique de la raison dialectique*) to which Durkheim seemed to be pointing when he wrote in *The Rules of Sociological Method*: "It is because the imaginary offers the mind no resistance that the mind, conscious of no restraint, gives itself up to boundless ambitions and believes it possible to construct, or rather reconstruct, the world by virtue of its own strength and at the whim of its desires."[8]

No doubt one could counterpose to this analysis of Sartrian anthropology the numerous texts (found especially in the earliest and the latest works) in which Sartre recognizes, for example, the "passive syntheses" of a universe of already constituted significations or expressly challenges the very principles of his philosophy, such as the passage in *Being and Nothingness* in which he seeks to distinguish his position from the *instantanéiste* philosophy of Descartes[9] or a sentence from the *Critique de la raison dialectique* in which he announces the study of "agentless actions, totalizer-less productions, counter-finalities, infernal circularities".[10] The fact remains that Sartre rejects with visceral repugnance "those gelatinous realities, more or less vaguely haunted by a supra-individual consciousness, which a shamefaced organicism still seeks to retrieve, against all likelihood, in the rough, complex but clear-cut field of passive activity in which there are individual organisms and inorganic material realities",[11] and that he leaves no room for everything that, as much on the side of the things of the world as on the side of the agents, might seem to blur the sharp line his rigorous dualism seeks to maintain between the pure transparency of the subject and the mineral opaci⸱⸱ ⸰f the thing. Within this logic, "objective" sociology can grasp only "the sociality of inertia", that is, for example, the class reduced to *inertia*, hence to impotence, class as a thing, an essence, "congealed" in its being, i.e. in its "having been": "Class seriality makes the individual (whoever he is and whatever the class) a being who defines himself as a commodified thing...The other form of class, that is, the group totalizing in a *praxis*, is born at the heart of the passive form and as its negation."[12] The social world, the site of these compromises between thing and meaning which define "objective meaning" as meaning-made-thing and dispositions as meaning-made-body, is a positive challenge to someone who can only live in the pure, transparent universe of consciousness or individual "praxis". The only limit this artificialism recognizes to the freedom of the ego is that which freedom sets itself by the free abdication of a pledge or the surrender of bad faith, the Sartrian name for alienation, or the submission imposed on it by the alienating freedom of the alter ego in the Hegelian struggles between master and slave. Seeing "in social arrangments only artificial and more or less arbitrary combinations", as Durkheim puts it,[13] without a second thought he subordinates the transcendence of the social – reduced to "the reciprocity of constraints and autonomies" – to the "transcendence of the ego", as the early Sartre used to put it: "In the course of this action, the individual discovers the dialectic as rational transparency, inasmuch as he produces it, and as absolute necessity inasmuch as it escapes him, in other words, *quite simply*, inasmuch as others produce it; finally, precisely insofar as he recognizes himself in overcoming his needs, he recognizes the law which others impose on him in overcoming their own (recognizes it: this does not mean that he submits to it), he recognizes his own autonomy (inasmuch as it can be used by another and daily is, bluffs, manoeuvres, etc.) as a foreign power and the autonomy of others as the inexorable law which allows him to coerce them."[14] The transcendence of the social can only be the effect of recurrence, that is to say, in the last analysis, of *number* (hence the importance accorded to the "series"), or of the "materialization of recurrence" in cultural objects;[15] alienation consists in the free abdication of freedom in favour of the demands of "worked upon matter": "the 19th century worker *makes himself what he is*, that is, he practically and rationally determines the order of his expenditure – hence he decides in his free praxis – and by his freedom he makes himself what he was, what he is, what he must be: a machine whose wages represent no more than its running costs... Class-being as practico-inert being comes to men by men through the passive syntheses of worked upon matter."[16] Elsewhere, affirmation of the "logical" primacy of "individual praxis", constituent Reason, over history, constituted Reason, leads Sartre to pose the problem of the genesis of society in the same terms as those employed by the theoreticians of the social contract: "History determines the content of human relationships in its totality and these relationships... relate back to everything. But it is not History which *causes* there to be human relationships in general. It is not the problems of organization and division of labour that have caused relations to be set up between those *initially separate* objects, men."[17] Just as for Descartes "creation is continuous", as Jean Wahl puts it, "because time is not" and because extended substance does not contain within itself the power to subsist – God being invested with the ever-renewed task of recreating the world *ex nihilo* by a free decree of his will – so the typically Cartesian refusal of the viscous opacity of "objective potentialities" and objective meaning leads Sartre to entrust to the absolute initiative of individual or collective "historical agents", such as the Party, the hypostasis of the Sartrian subject, the indefinite task of tearing the social whole, or the class, out of the inertia of the "practico-inert". At the end of his immense imaginary novel of the death and resurrection of freedom, with its twofold movement, the "externalization of internality", which leads from freedom to alienation, from consciousness to the materialization of consciousness, or, as the title puts it, "from praxis to the practico-inert", and the "internalization of externality" which, by the abrupt shortcuts of the awakening of consciousness and the "fusion of consciousnesses", leads "from the group to history", from the reified state of the alienated group to the authentic existence of the historical agent, consciousness and thing are as irremediably separate as they were at the outset, without anything resembling an institution or a socially constituted agent ever having been observed or constructed. The appearances of a dialectical discourse (or the dialectical appearances of the discourse) cannot mask the endless oscillation between the in-itself and the for-itself, or in the new language, between materiality and praxis, between the inertia of the group reduced to its "essence", i.e. to its outlived past and its necessity (abandoned to sociologists) and the continuous creation of the free collective project, seen as a series of acts of commitment indispensable for saving the group from annihilation in pure materiality.[18]

It is, of course, never ruled out that the responses of the habitus may be accompanied by a strategic calculation tending to carry on quasi-consciously the operation the habitus carries on in a quite different way, namely an estimation of chances which assumes the transformation of the past effect into the expected objective. But the fact remains that these responses are defined first in relation to a system of objective potentialities, immediately inscribed in the present, things to do or not to do, to say or not to say, in relation to a *forthcoming* reality which – in contrast to the future conceived as "absolute possibility" (*absolute Möglichkeit*), in Hegel's sense, projected by the pure project of a "negative freedom" – puts itself forward with an urgency and a claim to existence excluding all deliberation. To eliminate the need to resort to "rules", it would be necessary to establish in each case a complete description (which invocation of rules allows one to dispense with) of the relation between the habitus, as a socially constituted system of cognitive and motivating structures, and the socially structured situation in which the agents' *interests* are defined, and with them the objective functions and subjective motivations of their practices. It would then become clear that, as Weber indicated, the juridical or customary rule is never more than a *secondary principle* of the determination of practices, intervening when the primary principle, interest, fails.[19]

Symbolic – that is, *conventional* and *conditional* – stimulations, which act only on condition they encounter agents conditioned to perceive them, tend to impose themselves unconditionally and necessarily when inculcation of the arbitrary abolishes the arbitrariness of both the inculcation and the significations inculcated. The world of urgencies and of goals already achieved, of uses to be made and paths to be taken, of objects endowed with a "permanent teleological character", in Husserl's phrase, tools, instruments and institutions, the world of practicality, can grant only a conditional freedom – *liberet si liceret* – rather like that of the magnetic needle which Leibniz imagined actually enjoyed turning northwards. If one regularly observes a very close correlation between the scientifically constructed *objective probabilities* (e.g. the chances of access to a particular good) and *subjective aspirations* ("motivations" or "needs") or, in other terms, between the *a posteriori* or *ex post* probability known from past experience and the *a priori* or *ex ante* probability attributed to it, this is not because agents consciously adjust their aspirations to an exact evaluation of their chances of success, like a player regulating his bets as a function of perfect information as to his chances of winning, as one implicitly presupposes whenever, forgetting the "everything takes place as if", one *proceeds as if* game theory or the calculation of probabilities, each constructed *against* spontaneous dispositions, amounted to anthropological descriptions of practice.

Completely reversing the tendency of objectivism, we can, on the contrary, seek in the scientific theory of probabilities (or strategies) not an anthropological model of practice, but the elements of a *negative description* of the implicit logic of the *spontaneous interpretation of statistics* (e.g. the prospensity to privilege early experiences) which the scientific theory necessarily contains because it is explicitly constructed against that logic. Unlike the estimation of probabilities which science constructs methodically on the basis of controlled experiments from data established according to precise rules, practical evaluation of the likelihood of the success of a given action in a given situation brings into play a whole body of wisdom, sayings, commonplaces, ethical precepts ("that's not for the likes of us") and, at a deeper level, the unconscious principles of the *ethos* which, being the product of a learning process dominated by a determinate type of objective regularities, determines "reasonable" and "unreasonable" conduct for every agent subjected to those regularities.[20] "We are no sooner acquainted with the impossibility of satisfying any desire", says Hume in *A Treatise of Human Nature*, "than the desire itself vanishes." And Marx in the *Economic and Philosophical Manuscripts*: "If I have no money for travel, I have no *need*, i.e. no real and self-realizing need, to travel. If I have a vocation to study, but no money for it, I have *no* vocation to study, i.e. no *real, true* vocation."

Because the dispositions durably inculcated by objective conditions (which science apprehends through statistical regularities as the probabilities objectively attached to a group or class) engender aspirations and practices objectively compatible with those objective requirements, the most improbable practices are excluded, either totally without examination, as *unthinkable*, or at the cost of the *double negation* which inclines agents to make a virtue of necessity, that is, to refuse what is anyway refused and to love the inevitable. The very conditions of production of the ethos, *necessity made into a virtue*, are such that the expectations to which it gives rise tend to ignore the restriction to which the validity of any calculus of probabilities is sub-ordinated, namely that the conditions of the experiments should not have been modified. Unlike scientific estimations, which are corrected after each experiment in accordance with rigorous rules of calculation, practical esti-mates give disproportionate weight to early experiences: the structures charac-teristic of a determinate type of conditions of existence, through the economic and social necessity which they bring to bear on the relatively autonomous universe of family relationships, or more precisely, through the mediation of the specifically familial manifestations of this external necessity (sexual division of labour, domestic morality, cares, strife, tastes, etc.), produce the structures of the habitus which become in turn the basis of perception and appreciation of all subsequent experience. Thus, as a result of the *hysteresis effect* necessarily implied in the logic of the constitution of habitus, practices are always liable to incur negative sanctions when the environment with which they are actually confronted is too distant from that to which they are objectively fitted. This is why generation conflicts oppose not age-classes separated by natural properties, but habitus which have been produced by different *modes of generation*, that is, by conditions of existence which, in imposing different definitions of the impossible, the possible, and the probable, cause one group to experience as natural or reasonable practices or aspirations which another group finds unthinkable or scandalous, and vice versa.

Structures, habitus and practices

The habitus, the durably installed generative principle of regulated improvi-sations, produces practices which tend to reproduce the regularities immanent in the objective conditions of the production of their generative principle, while adjusting to the demands inscribed as objective potentialities in the situation, as defined by the cognitive and motivating structures making up the habitus. It follows that these practices cannot be directly deduced either from the objective conditions, defined as the instantaneous sum of the stimuli which may appear to have directly triggered them, or from the conditions which produced the durable principle of their production. These practices can be accounted for only by relating the objective *structure* defining the social conditions of the production of the habitus which engendered them to the conditions in which this habitus is operating, that is, to the *conjuncture* which, short of a radical transformation, represents a particular state of this structure. In practice, it is the habitus, history turned into nature, i.e. denied as such, which accomplishes practically the relating of these two systems of relations, in and through the production of practice. The "unconscious" is never anything other than the forgetting of history which history itself produces by incorporating the objective structures it produces in the second natures of habitus: "...in each of us, in varying proportions, there is part of yesterday's man; it is yesterday's man who inevitably predominates in us, since the present amounts to little compared with the long past in the course of which we were formed and from which we result. Yet we do not sense this man of the past, because he is inveterate in us; he makes up the unconscious part of ourselves. Consequently we are led to take no account of him, any more than we take account of his legitimate demands. Conversely, we are very much aware of the most recent attainments of civilization, because, being recent, they have not yet had time to settle into our unconscious."[21]

Genesis amnesia is also encouraged (if not entailed) by the objectivist apprehension which, grasping the product of history as an *opus operatum*, a *fait accompli*, can only invoke the mysteries of pre-established harmony or the prodigies of conscious orchestration to account for what, apprehended in pure synchrony, appears as objective meaning, whether it be the internal coherence of works or institutions such as myths, rites, or bodies of law, or the objective co-ordination which the concordant or conflicting practices of the members of the same group or class at once manifest and presuppose (inasmuch as they imply a community of dispositions).

Each agent, wittingly or unwittingly, willy nilly, is a producer and reproducer of objective meaning. Because his actions and works are the product of a *modus operandi* of which he is not the producer and has no conscious mastery, they contain an "objective intention", as the Scholastics put it, which always outruns his conscious intentions. The schemes of thought and expression he has acquired are the basis for the *intentionless invention* of regulated improvisation. Endlessly overtaken by his own words, with which he maintains a relation of "carry and be carried", as Nicolaï Hartmann put it, the virtuoso finds in the *opus operatum* new triggers and new supports for the *modus operandi* from which they arise, so that his discourse continuously feeds off itself like a train bringing along its own rails.[22] If witticisms surprise their author no less than their audience, and impress as much by their retrospective necessity as by their novelty, the reason is that the *trouvaille* appears as the simple unearthing, at once accidental and irresistible, of a buried possibility. It is because subjects do not, strictly speaking, know what they are doing that what they do has more meaning than they know. The habitus is the universalizing mediation which causes an individual agent's practices, without either explicit reason or signifying intent, to be none the less "sensible" and "reasonable". That part of practices which remains obscure in the eyes of their own producers is the aspect by which they are objectively adjusted to other practices and to the structures of which the principle of their production is itself the product.[23]

One of the fundamental effects of the orchestration of habitus is the production of a commonsense world endowed with the *objectivity* secured by consensus on the meaning (*sens*) of practices and the world, in other words the harmonization of agents' experiences and the continuous reinforcement that each of them receives from the expression, individual or collective (in festivals, for example), improvised or programmed (commonplaces, sayings), of similar or identical experiences. The homogeneity of habitus is what – within the limits of the group of agents possessing the schemes (of production and interpretation) implied in their production – causes practices and works to be immediately intelligible and foreseeable, and hence taken for granted. This practical comprehension obviates the "intention" and "intentional transfer into the Other" dear to the phenomenologists, by dispensing, for the ordinary occasions of life, with close analysis of the nuances of another's practice and tacit or explicit inquiry ("What do you *mean*?") into his intentions. Automatic and impersonal, significant without intending to signify, ordinary practices lend themselves to an understanding no less automatic and impersonal: the picking up of the objective intention they express in no way implies "reactivation" of the "lived" intention of the agent who performs them.[24] "Communication of consciousnesses" presupposes community of "unconsciouses" (i.e. of linguistic and cultural competences). The deciphering of the objective intention of practices and works has nothing to do with the "reproduction" (*Nachbildung*, as the early Dilthey puts it) of lived experiences and the reconstitution, unnecessary and uncertain, of the personal singularities of an "intention" which is not their true origin.

The objective homogenizing of group or class habitus which results from the homogeneity of the conditions of existence is what enables practices to be objectively harmonized without any intentional calculation or conscious reference to a norm and mutually adjusted *in the absence of any direct interaction* or, *a fortiori*, explicit co-ordination. "Imagine", Leibniz suggests, "two clocks or watches in perfect agreement as to the time. This may occur in one of three ways. The first consists in mutual influence; the second is to appoint a skilful workman to correct them and synchronize them at all times; the third is to construct these clocks with such art and precision that one can be assured of their subsequent agreement."[25] So long as, retaining only the first or at a pinch the second hypothesis, one ignores the true principle of the conductorless orchestration which gives regularity, unity, and systematicity to the practices of a group or class, and this even in the absence of any spontaneous or externally imposed organization of individual projects, one is condemned to the naive artificialism which recognizes no other principle unifying a group's or class's ordinary or extraordinary action than the conscious co-ordination of a conspiracy.[26] If the practices of the members of the same group or class are more and better harmonized than the agents know or wish, it is because, as Leibniz puts it, "following only [his] own laws", each "nonetheless agrees with the other".[27] The habitus is precisely this immanent law, *lex insita*, laid down in each agent by his earliest upbringing, which is the precondition not only for the co-ordination of practices but also for practices of co-ordination, since the corrections and adjustments the agents themselves consciously carry out presuppose their mastery of a common code and since undertakings of collective mobilization cannot succeed without a minimum of concordance between the habitus of the mobilizing agents (e.g. prophet, party leader, etc.) and the dispositions of those whose aspirations and world-view they express.

So it is because they are the product of dispositions which, being the internalization of the same objective structures, are objectively concerted that the practices of the members of the same group or, in a differentiated society, the same class are endowed with an objective meaning that is at once unitary and systematic, transcending subjective intentions and conscious projects whether individual or collective.[28] To describe the process of objectification and orchestration in the language of *interaction* and mutual adjustment is to forget that the interaction itself owes its form to the objective structures which have produced the dispositions of the interacting agents and which allot them their relative positions in the interaction and elsewhere. Every confrontation between agents in fact brings together, in an *interaction* defined by the *objective structure* of the relation between the groups they belong to (e.g. a boss giving orders to a subordinate, colleagues discussing their pupils, academics taking part in a symposium), systems of dispositions (carried by "natural persons") such as a linguistic competence and a cultural competence and, through these habitus, all the objective structures of which they are the product, structures which are active only when *embodied* in a competence acquired in the course of a particular history (with the different types of bilingualism or pronunciation, for example, stemming from different modes of acquisition).[29]

Thus, when we speak of class habitus, we are insisting, against all forms of the occasionalist illusion which consists in directly relating practices to properties inscribed in the situation, that "interpersonal" relations are never, except in appearance, *individual-to-individual* relationships and that the truth of the interaction is never entirely contained in the interaction. This is what social psychology and interactionism or ethnomethodology forget when, reducing the objective structure of the relationship between the assembled individuals to the conjunctural structure of their interaction in a particular situation and group, they seek to explain everything that occurs in an experimental or observed interaction in terms of the experimentally controlled characteristics of the situation, such as the relative spatial positions of the participants or the nature of the channels used. In fact it is their present and past positions in the social structure that biological individuals carry with them, at all times and in all places, in the form of dispositions which are so many marks of *social position* and hence of the social distance between objective positions, that is, between social persons conjuncturally brought together (in physical space, which is not the same thing as social space) and correlatively, so many reminders of this distance and of the conduct required in order to "keep one's distance" or to manipulate it strategically, whether symbolically or actually, to reduce it (easier for the dominant than for the dominated), increase it, or simply maintain if (by not "letting oneself go", not "becoming familiar", in short, "standing on one's dignity", or on the other hand, refusing to "take liberties" and "put oneself forward", in short "knowing one's place" and staying there).

Even those forms of interaction seemingly most amenable to description in terms of "intentional transfer into the Other", such as sympathy, friendship, or love, are dominated (as class homogamy attests), through the harmony of habitus, that is to say, more precisely, the harmony of ethos and tastes – doubtless sensed in the imperceptible cues of body *hexis* – by the objective structure of the relations between social conditions. The illusion of mutual election or predestination arises from ignorance of the social conditions for the harmony of aesthetic tastes or ethical leanings, which is thereby perceived as evidence of the ineffable affinities which spring from it.

In short, the habitus, the product of history, produces individual and collective practices, and hence history, in accordance with the schemes engendered by history. The system of dispositions – a past which survives in the present and tends to perpetuate itself into the future by making itself present in practices structured according to its principles, an internal law relaying the continuous exercise of the law of external necessities (irreducible to immediate conjunctural constraints) – is the principle of the continuity and regularity which objectivism discerns in the social world without being able to give them a rational basis. And it is at the same time the principle of the transformations and regulated revolutions which neither the extrinsic and instantaneous determinisms of a mechanistic sociologism nor the purely internal but equally punctual determination of voluntarist or spontaneist subjectivism are capable of accounting for.

It is just as true and just as untrue to say that collective actions produce the event or that they are its product. The conjuncture capable of transforming practices objectively co-ordinated because subordinated to partially or wholly identical objective necessities, into *collective action* (e.g. revolutionary action) is constituted in the dialectical relationship between, on the one hand, a *habitus*, understood as a system of lasting, transposable dispositions which, integrating past experiences, functions at every moment as a *matrix of perceptions, appreciations, and actions* and makes possible the achievement of infinitely diversified tasks, thanks to analogical transfers of schemes permitting the solution of similarly shaped problems, and thanks to the unceasing corrections of the results obtained, dialectically produced by those results, and on the other hand, an *objective event* which exerts its action of conditional stimulation calling for or demanding a determinate response, only on those who are disposed to constitute it as such because they are endowed with a determinate type of dispositions (which are amenable to reduplication and reinforcement by the "awakening of class consciousness", that is, by the direct or indirect possession of a discourse capable of securing symbolic mastery of the practically mastered principles of the class habitus). Without ever being totally co-ordinated, since they are the product of "causal series" characterized by different structural durations, the dispositions and the situations which combine synchronically to constitute a determinate conjuncture are never wholly independent, since they are engendered by the objective structures, that is, in the last analysis, by the economic bases of the social formation in question. The hysteresis of habitus, which is inherent in the social conditions of the reproduction of the structures in habitus, is doubtless one of the foundations of the structural lag between opportunities and the dispositions to grasp them which is the cause of missed opportunities and, in particular, of the frequently observed incapacity to think historical crises in categories of perception and thought other than those of the past, albeit a revolutionary past.

If one ignores the dialectical relationship between the objective structures and the cognitive and motivating structures which they produce and which tend to reproduce them, if one forgets that these objective structures are themselves products of historical practices and are constantly reproduced and transformed by historical practices whose productive principle is itself the product of the structures which it consequently tends to reproduce, then one is condemned to reduce the relationship between the different social agencies (*instances*), treated as "different translations of the same sentence" – in a Spinozist metaphor which contains the truth of the objectivist language of "articulation" – to the logical formula enabling any one of them to be derived from any other. The unifying principle of practices in different domains which objectivist analysis would assign to separate "sub-systems", such as matrimonial strategies, fertility strategies, or economic choices, is nothing other than the habitus, the locus of practical realization of the "articulation" of fields which objectivism (from Parsons to the structuralist readers of Marx) lays out side by side without securing the means of discovering the real principle of the structural homologies or relations of transformation objectively established between them (which is not to deny that the structures are objectivities irreducible to their manifestation in the habitus which they produce and which tend to reproduce them). So long as one accepts the canonic opposition which, endlessly reappearing in new forms throughout the history of social thought, nowadays pits "humanist" against "structuralist" readings of Marx, to declare diametrical opposition to subjectivism is not genuinely to *break* with it, but to fall into the fetishism of social laws to which objectivism consigns itself when in establishing between structure and practice the relation of the virtual to the actual, of the score to the performance, of essence to existence, it merely substitutes for the creative man of subjectivism a man subjugated to the dead laws of a natural history. And how could one underestimate the strength of the ideological couple subjectivism/objectivism when one sees that the critique of the *individual* considered as *ens realissimum* only leads to his being made an epiphenomenon of hypostatized structure, and that the well-founded assertion of the primacy of objective relations results in products of human action, the structures, being credited with the power to develop in accordance with their own laws and to determine and overdetermine other structures?

Just as the opposition of language to speech as mere execution or even as a preconstructed object masks the opposition between the objective relations of the language and the dispositions making up linguistic competence, so the opposition between the structure and the individual against whom the structure has to be won and endlessly rewon stands in the way of construction of the dialectical relationship between the structure and the dispositions making up the habitus.

If the debate on the relationship between "culture" and "personality" which dominated a whole era of American anthropology now seems so artificial and sterile, it is because, amidst a host of logical and epistemological fallacies, it was organized around the relation between two complementary products of the same realist, substantialist representation of the scientific object. In its most exaggerated forms, the theory of "basic personality" tends to define personality as a miniature replica (obtained by "moulding") of the "culture", to be found in all members of the same society, except deviants. Cora Du Bois's celebrated analyses on the Alor Island natives provide a very typical example of the confusions and contradictions resulting from the theory that "culture" and personality can each be deduced from the other: determined to reconcile the anthropologist's conclusions, based on the postulate that the same influences produce the same basic personality, with her own clinical observations of four subjects who seem to her to be "highly individual characters", each "moulded by the specific factors in his individual fate", the psychoanalyst who struggles to find individual incarnations of the basic personality is condemned to recantations and contradictions.[30] Thus, she can see Mangma as "the most typical" of the four ("his personality corresponds to the basic personality structure") after having written: "It is difficult to decide how typical Mangma is. I would venture to say that if he were typical, the society could not continue to exist." Ripalda, who is passive and has a strong super-ego, is "atypical", So is Fantan, who has "the strongest character formation, devoid of inhibitions toward women" (extreme heterosexual inhibition being the rule), and "differs from the other men as much as a city-slicker differs from a farmer". The fourth, Malekala, whose biography is typical at every point, is a well-known prophet who tried to start a revivalist movement, and his personality seems to resemble that of Ripalda, another sorcerer who, as we have seen, is described as atypical. All this is capped by the analyst's observation that "characters such as Mangma, Ripalda and Fantan can be found in any society". Anthony F. Wallace, from whom this critique is taken,[31] is no doubt right in pointing out that the notion of modal personality has the advantage of avoiding the illogicalities resulting from indifference to differences (and thus to statistics) usually implicit in recourse to the notion of basic personality. But what might pass for a mere refinement of the measuring and checking techniques used to test the validity of a theoretical construct amounts in fact to the substitution of one object for another: a system of hypotheses as to the *structure* of personality, conceived as a homeostatic system which changes by reinterpreting external pressures in accordance with its own logic, is replaced by a simple description of the central tendency in the distribution of the values of a variable, or rather a combination of variables. Wallace thus comes to the tautological conclusion that in a population of Tuscarora Indians, the modal personality type defined by reference to twenty-seven variables is to be found in only 37 per cent of the subjects studied. The construction of a class *ethos* may, for example, make use of a reading of statistical regularities treated as *indices*, without the principle which unifies and explains these regularities being reducible to the regularities in which it manifests itself. In short, failing to see in the notion of "basic personality" anything other than a way of pointing to a directly observable "datum", i.e. the "personality type" shared by the greatest number of members of a given society, the advocates of this notion cannot, in all logic, take issue with those who submit this theory to the test of statistical critique, in the name of the same realist representation of the scientific object.

The habitus is the product of the work of inculcation and appropriation necessary in order for those products of collective history, the objective structures (e.g. of language, economy, etc.) to succeed in reproducing themselves more or less completely, in the form of durable dispositions, in the organisms (which one can, if one wishes, call individuals) lastingly subjected to the same conditionings, and hence placed in the same material conditions of existence. Therefore sociology treats as identical all the biological individuals who, being the product of the same objective conditions, are the supports of the same habitus: social class, understood as a system of objective determinations, must be brought into relation not with the individual or with the "class" as a *population*, i.e. as an aggregate of enumerable, measurable biological individuals, but with the class habitus, the system of dispositions (partially) common to all products of the same structures. Though it is impossible for *all* members of the same class (or even two of them) to have had the same experiences, in the same order, it is certain that each member of the same class is more likely than any member of another class to have been confronted with the situations most frequent for the members of that class. The objective structures which science apprehends in the form of statistical regularities (e.g. employment rates, income curves, probabilities of access to secondary education, frequency of holidays, etc.) inculcate, through the direct or indirect but always convergent experiences which give a social environment its *physiognomy*, with its "closed doors", "dead ends", and limited "prospects", that "art of assessing likelihoods", as Leibniz put it, of anticipating the objective future, in short, the sense of reality or realities which is perhaps the best-concealed principle of their efficacy.

In order to define the relations between class, habitus and the organic individuality which can never entirely be removed from sociological discourse, inasmuch as, being given immediately to immediate perception (*intuitus personae*), it is also socially designated and recognized (name, legal identity, etc.) and is defined by a *social trajectory* strictly speaking irreducible to any other, the habitus could be considered as a subjective but not individual system of internalized structures, schemes of perception, conception, and action common to all members of the same group or class and constituting the precondition for all objectification and apperception: and the objective co-ordination of practices and the sharing of a world-view could be founded on the perfect impersonality and interchangeability of singular practices and views. But this would amount to regarding all the practices or representations produced in accordance with identical schemes as impersonal and substitutable, like singular intuitions of space which, according to Kant, reflect none of the peculiarities of the individual ego. In fact, it is in a relation of homology, of diversity within homogeneity reflecting the diversity within homogeneity characteristic of their social conditions of production, that the singular habitus of the different members of the same class are united; the homology of world-views implies the systematic differences which separate singular world-views, adopted from singular but concerted standpoints. Since the history of the individual is never anything other than a certain specification of the collective history of his group or class, *each individual system of dispositions* may be seen as a *structural variant* of all the other group or class habitus, expressing the difference between trajectories and positions inside or outside the class. "Personal" style, the particular stamp marking all the products of the same habitus, whether practices or works, is never more than a *deviation* in relation to the *style* of a period or class so that it relates back to the common style not only by its conformity – like Phidias, who, according to Hegel, had no "manner" – but also by the difference which makes the whole "manner".

The principle of these individual differences lies in the fact that, being the product of a chronologically ordered series of structuring determinations, the habitus, which at every moment structures in terms of the structuring experiences which produced it the structuring experiences which affect its structure, brings about a unique integration, dominated by the earliest experiences, of the experiences statistically common to the members of the same class. Thus, for example, the habitus acquired in the family underlies the structuring of school experiences (in particular the reception and assimilation of the specifically pedagogic message), and the habitus transformed by schooling, itself diversified, in turn underlies the structuring of all subsequent experiences (e.g. the reception and assimilation of the messages of the culture industry or work experiences), and so on, from restructuring to restructuring.

Springing from the encounter in an integrative organism of relatively independent causal series, such as biological and social determinisms, the habitus makes coherence and necessity out of accident and contingency: for example, the equivalences it establishes between positions in the division of labour and positions in the division between the sexes are doubtless not peculiar to societies in which the division of labour and the division between the sexes coincide almost perfectly. In a class society, all the products of a given agent, by an essential *overdetermination*, speak inseparably and simultaneously of his class – or, more, precisely, his position in the social structure and his rising or falling trajectory – and of his (or her) body – or, more precisely, all the properties, always socially qualified, of which he or she is the bearer – sexual properties of course, but also physical properties, praised, like strength or beauty, or stigmatized.

The dialectic of objectification and embodiment

So long as the work of education is not clearly institutionalized as a specific, autonomous practice, and it is a whole group and a whole symbolically structured environment, without specialized agents or specific moments, which exerts an anonymous, pervasive pedagogic action, the essential part of the *modus operandi* which defines practical mastery is transmitted in practice, in its practical state, without attaining the level of discourse. The child imitates not "models" but other people's actions. Body *hexis* speaks directly to the motor function, in the form of a pattern of postures that is both individual and systematic, because linked to a whole system of techniques involving the body and tools, and charged with a host of social meanings and values: in all societies, children are particularly attentive to the gestures and postures which, in their eyes, express everything that goes to make an accomplished adult – a way of walking, a tilt of the head, facial expressions, ways of sitting and of using implements, always associated with a tone of voice, a style of speech, and (how could it be otherwise?) a certain subjective experience. But the fact that schemes are able to pass from practice to practice without going through discourse or consciousness does not mean that acquisition of the habitus comes down to a question of mechanical learning by trial and error. Unlike an incoherent series of figures, which can be learnt only gradually, through repeated attempts and with continuous predictable progress, a numerical series is mastered more easily because it contains a structure which makes it unnecessary to memorize all the numbers one by one: in verbal products such as proverbs, sayings, maxims, songs, riddles, or games; in objects, such as tools, the house, or the village; or again, in practices such as contests of honour, gift exchanges, rites, etc., the material which the Kabyle child has to assimilate is the product of the systematic application of principles coherent in practice,[32] which means, that in all this endlessly redundant material, he has no difficulty in grasping the *rationale* of what are clearly series and in making it his own in the form of a principle generating conduct organized in accordance with the same rationale.

Experimental analyses of learning which establish that "neither the formation nor the application of a concept requires conscious recognition of the common elements or relationship involved in the specific instances"[33] enable us to understand the dialectic of objectification and incorporation whereby the systematic objectifications of systematic dispositions tend in their turn to give rise to systematic dispositions: when faced with series of symbols – Chinese characters (Hull) or pictures varying simultaneously the colour, nature, and number of the objects represented (Heidbreder) – distributed into classes with arbitrary but objectively based names, subjects who are unable to state the principle of classification nonetheless attain higher scores than they would *if they were guessing at random*, thereby demonstrating that they achieve a practical mastery of the classificatory schemes which in no way implies symbolic mastery – i.e. conscious recognition and verbal expression – of the processes practically applied. Albert B. Lord's analysis of the acquiring of structured material in a natural environment, based on his study of the training of the *guslar*, the Yugoslav bard, entirely confirms the experimental findings: the practical mastery of what Lord calls "the formula", that is, the capacity to improvise by combining "formulae", sequences of words "regularly employed under the same metrical conditions to express a given idea",[34] is acquired through sheer familiarization, "by hearing the poems",[35] without the learner's having any sense of learning and subsequently manipulating this or that formula or any set of formulae:[36] the constraints of rhythm are internalized at the same time as melody and meaning, without being attended to for their own sake.

Between apprenticeship through simple familiarization, in which the apprentice insensibly and unconsciously acquires the principles of the "art" and the art of living – including those which are not known to the producer of the practices or works imitated, and, at the other extreme, explicit and express transmission by precept and prescription, every society provides for *structural exercises* tending to transmit this or that form of practical mastery. Such are the riddles and ritual contests which test the "sense of ritual language" and all the games, often structured according to the logic of the wager, the challenge or the combat (duels, group battles, target-shooting, etc.), which require the boys to set to work, in the mode of "let's pretend", the schemes generating the strategies of honour.[37] Then there is daily participation in gift exchanges and all their subtleties, which the boys derive from their rôle as messengers and, more especially, as intermediaries between the female world and the male world. There is silent observation of the discussions in the men's assembly, with their effects of eloquence, their rituals, their strategies, their ritual strategies and strategic uses of ritual. There are the interactions with their relatives, which lead them to explore the structured space of objective kin relationships in all directions by means of *reversals* requiring the person who saw himself and behaved as a nephew of his father's brother to see himself and behave as a paternal uncle towards his brother's son, and thus to acquire mastery of the transformational schemes which permit the passage from the system of dispositions attached to one position to the system appropriate to the symmetrically opposite position. There are the lexical and grammatical commutations ("I" and "you" designating the same person according to the relation to the speaker) which instil the sense of the interchangeability of positions and of reciprocity as well as a sense of the limits of each. And, at a deeper level, there are the relationships with the mother and the father, which, by their dyssymmetry in antagonistic complementarity, constitute one of the opportunities to internalize, inseparably, the schemes of the *sexual division of labour* and of the *division of sexual labour*.

But it is in the dialectical relationship between the body and a space structured according to the mythico-ritual oppositions that one finds the form par excellence of the structural apprenticeship which leads to the em-bodying of the structures of the world, that is, the appropriating by the world of a body thus enabled to appropriate the world. In a social formation in which the absence of the symbolic-product-conserving techniques associated with literacy retards the objectification of symbolic and particularly cultural capital, inhabited space – and above all the house – is the principal locus for the objectification of the generative schemes; and, through the intermediary of the divisions and hierarchies it sets up between things, persons, and practices, this tangible classifying system continuously inculcates and reinforces the taxonomic principles underlying all the arbitrary provisions of this culture.[38] Thus, as we have seen, the opposition between the sacred of the right hand and the sacred of the left hand, between *nif* and *haram*, between man, invested with protective, fecundating virtues, and woman, at once sacred and charged with maleficent forces, and, correlatively, between religion (male) and magic (female), is reproduced in the spatial division between male space, with the place of assembly, the market, or the fields, and female space, the house and its garden, the retreats of *haram*. To discover how this spatial organization (matched by a temporal organization obeying the same logic) governs practices and representations – far beyond the frequently described rough divisions between the male world and the female world, the assembly and the fountain, public life and intimacy – and thereby contributes to the durable imposition of the schemes of perception, thought, and action, it is necessary to grasp the dialectic of objectification and embodiment in the privileged locus of the space of the house and the earliest learning processes.

This analysis of the relationship between the objectified schemes and the schemes incorporated or being incorporated presupposes a structural analysis of the social organization of the internal space of the house and the relation of this internal space to external space, an analysis which is not an end in itself but which, precisely on account of the (dangerous) affinity between objectivism and all that is already objectified, is the only means of fully grasping the structuring structures which, remaining obscure to themselves, are revealed only in the objects they structure. The house, an *opus operatum*, lends itself as such to a deciphering, but only to a deciphering which does not forget that the "book" from which the children learn their vision of the world is read with the body, in and through the movements and displacements which make the space within which they are enacted as much as they are made by it.

The interior of the Kabyle house, rectangular in shape, is divided into two parts by a low wall: the larger of these two parts, slightly higher than the other, is reserved for human use; the other side, occupied by the animals, has a loft above it. A door with two wings gives access to both rooms. In the upper part is the hearth and, facing the door, the weaving loom. The lower, dark, nocturnal part of the house, the place of damp, green, or raw objects – water jars set on the benches on either side of the entrance to the stable or against the "wall of darkness", wood, green fodder – the place too of natural beings – oxen and cows, donkeys and mules – and natural activities – sleep, sex, birth – and also of death, is opposed to the high, light-filled, noble place of humans and in particular of the guest, fire and fire-made objects, the lamp, kitchen utensils, the rifle – the attribute of the manly point of honour (*nif*) which protects female honour (*hurma*) – the loom, the symbol of all protection, the place also of the two specifically cultural activities performed within the house, cooking and weaving. The meaning objectified in things or places is fully revealed only in the practices structured according to the same schemes which are organized in relation to them (and vice versa). The guest to be honoured (*qabel*, a verb also meaning "to stand up to", and "to face the east") is invited to sit in front of the loom. The opposite wall is called the wall of darkness, or the wall of the invalid: a sick person's bed is placed next to it. The washing of the dead takes place at the entrance to the stable. The low dark part is opposed to the upper part as the female to the male: it is the most intimate place within the world of intimacy (sexuality, fertility). The opposition between the male and the female also reappears in the opposition between the "master" beam and the main pillar, a fork open skywards.

Thus, the house is organized according to a set of homologous oppositions – fire:water :: cooked:raw :: high:low :: light:shade :: day:night :: male:female :: *nif*:*hurma*::fertilizing:able to be fertilized. But in fact the same oppositions are established between the house as a whole and the rest of the universe, that is, the male world, the place of assembly, the fields, and the market. It follows that each of these two parts of the house (and, by the same token, each of the objects placed in it and each of the activities carried out in it) is in a sense qualified at two degrees, first as female (nocturnal, dark, etc.) insofar as it partakes of the universe of the house, and secondarily as male or female insofar as it belongs to one or the other of the divisions of that universe. Thus, for example, the proverb "Man is the lamp of the outside, woman the lamp of the inside" must be taken to mean that man is the true light, that of the day, and woman the light of darkness, dark brightness; and we also know that she is to the moon as man is to the sun. But one or the other of the two systems of oppositions which define the house, either in its internal organization or in its relationship with the external world, is brought to the foreground, depending on whether the house is considered from the male point of view or the female point of view: whereas for the man, the house is not so much a place he enters as a place he comes out of, movement inwards properly befits the woman.[39]

All the actions performed in a space constructed in this way are immediately qualified symbolically and function as so many structural exercises through which is built up practical mastery of the fundamental schemes, which organize magical practices and representations: going in and coming out, filling and emptying, opening and shutting, going leftwards and going rightwards, going westwards and going eastwards, etc. Through the magic of a world of objects which is the product of the application of the same schemes to the most diverse domains, a world in which each thing speaks metaphorically of all the others, each practice comes to be invested with an objective meaning, a meaning with which practices – and particularly rites – have to reckon at all times, whether to evoke or revoke it. The construction of the world of objects is clearly not the sovereign operation of consciousness which the neo-Kantian tradition conceives of; the mental structures which construct the world of objects are constructed in the practice of a world of objects constructed according to the same structures.[40] The mind born of the world of objects does not rise as a subjectivity confronting an objectivity: the objective universe is made up of objects which are the product of objectifying operations structured according to the very structures which the mind applies to it. The mind is a metaphor of the world of objects which is itself but an endless circle of mutually reflecting metaphors.

All the symbolic manipulations of body experience, starting with displacements within a mythically structured space, e.g. the movements of going in and coming out, tend to impose the *integration* of the body space with cosmic space by grasping in terms of the same concepts (and naturally at the price of great laxity in logic) the relationship between man and the natural world and the complementarity and opposed states and actions of the two sexes in the division of sexual work and sexual division of work, and hence in the work of biological and social reproduction. For example, the opposition between

4-2

movement outwards towards the fields or the market, towards the production and circulation of goods, and movement inwards, towards the accumulation and consumption of the products of work, corresponds symbolically to the opposition between the male body, self-enclosed and directed towards the outside world, and the female body, resembling the dark, damp house, full of food, utensils, and children, which is entered and left by the same inevitably soiled opening.[41]

The opposition between the *centrifugal*, male orientation and the *centripetal*, female orientation, which, as we have seen, is the true principle of the organization of domestic space, is doubtless also the basis of the relationship of each of the sexes to their "psyche", that is, to their bodies and more precisely to their sexuality. As in every society dominated by male values – and European societies, which assign men to politics, history, or war and women to the hearth, the novel, and psychology, are no exception – the specifically male relation to sexuality is that of *sublimation*, the symbolism of honour tending at once to refuse any direct expression of sexuality and to encourage its transfigured manifestation in the form of manly prowess: the men, who are neither conscious of nor concerned with the female orgasm but seek the affirmation of their potency in repetition rather than prolongation of the sexual act, are not unaware that, through the intermediary of the female gossip that they both fear and despise, the eyes of the group always threaten their intimacy. As for the women, it is true to say, with Erikson, that male domination tends to "restrict their verbal consciousness"[42] so long as this is taken to mean not that they are forbidden all talk of sex, but that their discourse is dominated by the male values of virility, so that all reference to specifically female sexual "interests" is excluded from this aggressive and shame-filled cult of male potency.

Psychoanalysis, the disenchanting product of the disenchantment of the world, which leads to a domain of signification that is mythically overdetermined to be constituted *as such*, forgets and causes it to be forgotten that one's own body and other people's bodies are only ever perceived through categories of perception which it would be naive to treat as sexual, even if, as is attested by the women's laughter during conversations, and the interpretations they give of graphic symbols – mural paintings, pottery or carpet designs, etc. – these categories always relate back, sometimes very concretely, to the opposition between the biologically defined properties of the two sexes. As naive as it would be to reduce to their strictly sexual dimension the countless acts of diffuse inculcation through which the body and the world tend to be set in order, by means of a symbolic manipulation of the relation to the body and to the world aiming to impose what has to be called, in Melanie Klein's term, a "body geography", a particular case of geography, or better, cosmology.[43] The child's initial relation to its father or mother, or in other terms, to the paternal body and maternal body, which offers the most dramatic opportunity to experience all the fundamental oppositions of mytho-poeic practice, cannot be found as the basis of the acquisition of the principles of the structuring of the ego and the world, and in particular of every homosexual and heterosexual relationship, except insofar as that initial relation is set up with objects whose sex is defined symbolically and not biologically. The child constructs its *sexual identity*, the major element in its social identity, at the same time as it constructs its image of the division of work between the sexes, out of the same socially defined set of inseparably biological and social indices. In other words, the awakening of consciousness of sexual identity and the incorporation of the dispositions associated with a determinate social definition of the social functions incumbent on men and women come hand in hand with the adoption of a socially defined vision of the sexual division of labour.

Psychologists' work on the perception of sexual differences makes it clear that children establish clear-cut distinctions very early (about age five) between male and female functions, assigning domestic tasks to women and mothers and economic activities to men and fathers. Everything suggests that the awareness of sexual differences and the distinction between paternal and maternal functions are constituted simultaneously. From the numerous analyses of the differential perception of mother and father it may be gathered that the father is generally seen as more competent and more severe than the mother, who is regarded as "kinder" and more affectionate than the father and is the object of a more emotional and more agreeable relationship. In fact, as Emmerich very rightly points out, underlying all these differences is the fact that children attribute more power to the father than to the mother.

It is not hard to imagine the weight that must be brought to bear on the construction of self-image and world-image by the opposition between masculinity and femininity when it constitutes the fundamental principle of division of the social and symbolic world. As is emphasized by the twofold meaning of the word *nif*, sexual potency inseparable from social potency, what is imposed through a certain social definition of maleness (and, by derivation, of femaleness), is a political mythology which governs all bodily experiences, not least sexual experiences themselves. Thus, the opposition between male sexuality, public and sublimated, and female sexuality, secret and, so to speak, "alienated" (with respect to Erikson's "utopia of universal genitality", i.e. the "utopia of full orgasmic reciprocity") is only a specification of the opposition between the extraversion of politics or public religion and the introversion of psychology or private magic, made up for the most part of rites aimed at domesticating the male partners.

Bodily *hexis* is political mythology realized, *em-bodied*, turned into a permanent disposition, a durable manner of standing, speaking, and thereby of *feeling* and *thinking*. The oppositions which mythico-ritual logic makes between the male and the female and which organize the whole system of values reappear, for example, in the gestures and movements of the body, in the form of the opposition between the straight and the bent, or between assurance and restraint. "The Kabyle is like the heather, he would rather break than bend." The man of honour's pace is steady and determined. His way of walking, that of a man who knows where he is going and knows he will arrive in time, whatever the obstacles, expresses strength and resolution, as opposed to the hesitant gait (*thikli thamahmahht*) announcing indecision, half-hearted promises (*awal amahmah*), the fear of commitments and the incapacity to fulfil them. At the same time it is a *measured* pace: it contrasts as much with the haste of the man who "throws his feet up as high as his head", "walks along with great strides", "dances" – running being weak and frivolous conduct – as it does with the sluggishness of the man who "trails along". The manly man stands up straight and honours the person he approaches or wishes to welcome by looking him right in the eyes; ever on the alert, because ever threatened, he lets nothing that happens around him escape him, whereas a gaze that is up in the clouds or fixed on the ground is the mark of an irresponsible man, who has nothing to fear because he has no responsibilities in his group. Conversely, a woman is expected to walk with a slight stoop, looking down, keeping her eyes on the spot where she will next put her foot, especially if she happens to have to walk past the *thajma'th*; her gait must avoid the excessive swing of the hips which comes from a heavy stride; she must always be girdled with the *thimehremth*, a rectangular piece of cloth with yellow, red, and black stripes worn over her dress, and take care that her headscarf does not come unknotted, revealing her hair. In short, the specifically feminine virtue, *laḥia*, modesty, restraint, reserve, orients the whole female body downwards, towards the ground, the inside, the house, whereas male excellence, *nif*, is asserted in movement upwards, outwards, towards other men.

If all societies and, significantly, all the "totalitarian institutions", in Goffman's phrase, that seek to produce a new man through a process of "deculturation" and "reculturation" set such store on the seemingly most insignificant details of *dress*, *bearing*, physical and verbal *manners*, the reason is that, treating the body as a memory, they entrust to it in abbreviated and practical, i.e. mnemonic, form the fundamental principles of the arbitrary content of the culture. The principles em-bodied in this way are placed beyond the grasp of consciousness, and hence cannot be touched by voluntary, deliberate transformation, cannot even be made explicit; nothing seems more ineffable, more incommunicable, more inimitable, and, therefore, more precious, than the values given body, *made* body by the transubstantiation achieved by the hidden persuasion of an implicit pedagogy, capable of instilling a whole cosmology, an ethic, a metaphysic, a political philosophy, through injunctions as insignificant as "stand up straight" or "don't hold your knife in your left hand".[44] The logic of scheme transfer which makes each technique of the body a sort of *pars totalis*, predisposed to function in accordance with the fallacy *pars pro toto*, and hence to evoke the whole system of which it is a part, gives a very general scope to the seemingly most circumscribed and circumstantial observances. The whole trick of pedagogic reason lies precisely in the way it extorts the essential while seeming to demand the insignificant: in obtaining the respect for form and forms of respect which constitute the most visible and at the same time the best-hidden (because most "natural") manifestation of submission to the established order, the incorporation of the arbitrary abolishes what Raymond Ruyer calls "lateral possibilities", that is, all the eccentricities and deviations which are the small change of madness. The concessions of *politeness* always contain *political* concessions. The term *obsequium* used by Spinoza to denote the "constant will" produced by the conditioning through which "the State fashions us for its own use and which enables it to survive"[45] could be reserved to designate the public testimonies of recognition which every group expects of its members (especially at moments of co-option), that is, the symbolic taxes due from individuals in the exchanges which are set up in every group between the individuals and the group. Because, as in gift exchange, the exchange is an end in itself, the tribute demanded by the group generally comes down to a matter of trifles, that is, to symbolic rituals (rites of passage, the ceremonials of etiquette, etc.), formalities and formalisms which "cost nothing" to perform and seem such "natural" things to demand ("It's the least one can do...": "It wouldn't cost him anything to...") that abstention amounts to a refusal or a challenge.[46]

Through the habitus, the structure which has produced it governs practice, not by the processes of a mechanical determinism, but through the mediation of the orientations and limits it assigns to the habitus's operations of invention.[47] As an acquired system of generative schemes objectively adjusted to the particular conditions in which it is constituted, the habitus engenders all the thoughts, all the perceptions, and all the actions consistent with those conditions, and no others. This paradoxical product is difficult to conceive, even inconceivable, only so long as one remains locked in the dilemma of determinism and freedom, conditioning and creativity (like Chomsky, for example, who thought the only escape from Bloomfieldian behaviourism lay in seeking "freedom" and "creativity" in the "structure" – i.e. the "nature" – of the human mind). Because the habitus is an endless capacity to engender products – thoughts, perceptions, expressions, actions – whose limits are set by the historically and socially situated conditions of its production, the conditioned and conditional freedom it secures is as remote from a creation of unpredictable novelty as it is from a simple mechanical reproduction of the initial conditionings.[48]

3
Generative schemes and practical logic: invention within limits

The opposite gesture, that of inverting a spoon, should automatically, as it were, provoke a contrary action. This is what the wife of a *fqih* does, among the Mtougga, to ward off imminent rainfall.

E. Laoust, *Mots et choses berbères*

"I think I've made a new theological discovery..."
"What is it?"
"If you hold your hands upside down, you get the opposite of what you pray for!"

Charles M. Schulz, *There's No One Like You, Snoopy*

Man differs from other animals in that he is the one most given to mimicry (*mimetikotaton*) and learns his first lessons through mimesis (*dia mimeseos*).

Aristotle, *Poetics*, 1448b

Objectivism constitutes the social world as a spectacle presented to an observer who takes up a "point of view" on the action, who stands back so as to observe it and, transferring into the object the principles of his relation to the object, conceives of it as a totality intended for cognition alone, in which all interactions are reduced to symbolic exchanges. This point of view is the one afforded by high positions in the social structure, from which the social world appears as a representation (in the sense of idealist philosophy but also as used in painting or the theatre) and practices are no more than "executions", stage parts, performances of scores, or the implementing of plans. With the Marx of the *Theses on Feuerbach*, the theory of practice as practice insists, against positivist materialism, that the objects of knowledge are *constructed*, and against idealist intellectualism, that the principle of this construction is practical activity oriented towards practical functions. It is possible to abandon the sovereign point of view from which objectivist idealism orders the world, without being forced to relinquish the "active aspect" of apprehension of the world by reducing cognition to a mere recording: it suffices to situate oneself *within* "real activity as such", i.e. in the practical relation to the world, the quasi-bodily "aiming" which entails no representation of either the body or the world, still less of their relationship, that active presence in the world through which the world imposes its presence, with its urgencies, its things to be done or said, things "made" to be said and said "to be done", which

[96]

directly command words and deeds without ever deploying themselves as a spectacle.

The arguments that have developed as much among anthropologists (ethno-science) as among sociologists (ethnomethodology) around classifications and classificatory systems have one thing in common: they forget that these instruments of cognition fulfil as such functions other than those of pure cognition. Practice always implies a cognitive operation, a practical operation of construction which sets to work, by reference to practical functions, systems of classification (taxonomies) which organize perception and structure practice. Produced by the practice of successive generations, in conditions of existence of a determinate type, these schemes of perception, appreciation, and action, which are acquired through practice and applied in their practical state without acceding to explicit representation, function as practical opera-tors through which the objective structures of which they are the product tend to reproduce themselves in practices. Practical taxonomies, instruments of cognition and communication which are the precondition for the establish-ment of meaning and the consensus on meaning, exert their *structuring* efficacy only to the extent that they are themselves *structured*. This does not mean that they can be adequately treated by "structural", "componential", or any other form of strictly *internal* analysis which, in artificially wrenching them from their conditions of production and use, inevitably fails to understand their social functions.[1]

The coherence to be observed in all products of the application of the same habitus has no other basis than the coherence which the generative principles constituting that habitus owe to the social structures (structures of relations between groups – the sexes or age-classes – or between social classes) of which they are the product and which, as Durkheim and Mauss saw, they tend to reproduce.[2] The practical operators which constitute the habitus and which function in their practical state in gesture or utterance reproduce in a *trans-formed form*, inserting them into the structure of a system of symbolic relations, the oppositions and hierarchies which actually organize social groups, and which they help to legitimate by presenting them in a misrecog-nizable form.

The calendar and the synoptic illusion

Analysis of the agrarian calendar will enable us to demonstrate, by a sort of proof *per absurdum*, the error which results from the intellectualist theory of social systems of classification. Owing to the extremely important social function which it fulfils in orchestrating the group's activity, the calendar is indeed one of the most codified aspects of social existence.[3] The organization of practices is not entrusted in this case exclusively to the practical schemes of the habitus: it is the object of explicit injunctions and express recommendations, sayings, proverbs, and taboos, serving a function analogous to that performed in a different order by customary rules or genealogies. Although they are never more than *rationalizations* devised for semi-scholarly purposes, these more or less codified objectifications are, of all the products of habitus structured in accordance with the prevailing system of classification, those which are socially recognized as the most representative and successful, those worthiest of being preserved by the collective memory; and so they are themselves organized in accordance with the structures constituting that system of classification. They thereby come to be endowed with a common "physiognomy" rendering them immediately "intelligible" for any agent equipped with the "sense" of linguistic and/or mythic roots, and are thus predisposed to make up for the lapses or uncertainties of the habitus by setting out codified references and strict guidelines.[4]

What one derives from questioning informants, thereby inviting them to adopt a quasi-scientific attitude, is a mixture, in variable proportions, of knowledges drawn from one or the other of the available traditions which, except when mechanically reproduced, is selected and often *reinterpreted* in terms of the schemes of the habitus and of representations produced *ad hoc* from the same schemes. As soon as one undertakes to draw up a synoptic calendar which combines the features most frequently attested and indicates the most important variants (instead of presenting a single calendar chosen for the sake of its particular "quality", or a set of particular calendars) one comes up against a primary difficulty: identical periods are given different names, and still more often, identical names cover periods varying considerably in length and situated at different times in the year, depending on the region, the tribe, the village, and even the informant. Moreover, at two different points in the same conversation, an informant may offer two different names (e.g. one Berber, one drawn from the Islamic tradition) for the same moment of the year.

There is a great temptation to amass and collate these different productions in order to construct a lacuna-free, contradiction-free whole, a sort of *unwritten score* of which all the calendars derived from informants are then regarded as imperfect, impoverished *performances*.[5] The problem is that the calendar cannot be understood unless it is set down on paper, and that it is impossible to understand how it works unless one fully realizes that it exists only on paper (see fig. 2).[6] Moreover, when it is a matter of transmitting all the useful information as quickly as possible, there is no more efficient and convenient way than a linear narrative, which permits the rapid unfolding of the succession of "periods" and "moments" (treating rival accounts as "variants").

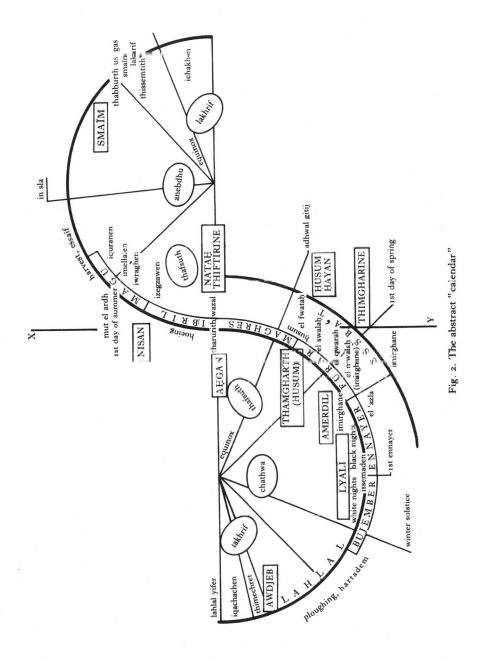

Fig. 2. The abstract "calendar"

Most informants spontaneously make the year start with autumn (*lakhrif*). For some of them, the season starts around the 1st of September in the Julian calendar; for others, it starts on about the 15th of August, on the day called "the door of the year" (*thabburth usugas*), which marks the entry into the wet period, after the dogdays of *smaïm* and at the beginning of *lakhrif*: on that day, each family sacrifices a cock, and associations and contracts are renewed. But for other informants, the "door of the year" is the first day of ploughing (*lahlal natsharats* or *lahlal n thagersa*), the most decisive turning-point of the transitional period.

The tillage period (usually called *lahlal*, but sometimes *hartadem*) begins with the first day's ploughing (*awdjeb*), after an ox bought collectively has been sacrificed (*thimechret*) and the meat shared out amongst all the members of the community (*adhrum* or village). Ploughing and sowing, which begin immediately after the inaugural ceremony (which is also a rain-making rite), as soon as the land is sufficiently moist, may go on until mid-December or even longer, depending on the region and the year.

It is doubtless incorrect to speak of *lahlal* as a "period": this term, and the corresponding temporal unit, are defined practically, within the universe of the wet season, in opposition to *lakhrif* (ploughing and sowing being opposed to the picking and drying of the figs, gardening work in *thabhirth*, the summer garden, and with *la'laf*, the special attention given to the oxen weakened by treading out, so as to prepare them for ploughing); but within the same universe it may also be defined in opposition to *lyali*, the slack moment in winter. Within a quite different logic it can also be contrasted with all the other periods held to be licit for a particular type of work which would be *haram* (the illicit) if done outside those periods: for example, *lahlal lafth*, the licit period for sowing turnips (from the seventeenth day of autumn, the 3rd of September in the Julian calendar), *lahlal yifer*, the licit period for stripping the fig-trees (the end of September), etc.

For some informants, winter begins on the 15th of November, for others on the 1st of December, without any special rite (which tends to show that the opposition between autumn and winter is not strongly marked).[7] The heart of winter is called *lyali*, the nights, "a period of forty days", within which a distinction is almost always drawn between two equal parts, *lyali thimella-line*, the white nights, and *lyali thiberkanine*, the black nights (a distinction which, as is suggested by its range of applications, is the product of an entirely abstract, formal principle of division, although informants find justifications for it in climatic changes). Once the autumn work is over, the peasants keep themselves busy, repairing their tools when they cannot leave the house, gathering grass and leaves for the cattle, and clearing the paths after heavy snowfalls. This is the slack season of the year, contrasted, as such, with *smaïm*, the slack period of the dry season, or, as we have seen, with *lahlal*, a time of intense activity; but it is contrasted in another respect with the transition from winter to spring (*essba't* or *essubu'*, the "sevens"); and from yet another point of view, these are the "great nights" (*lyali kbira*) as opposed to the "lesser nights" (*lyali esghira*) of February and March, to the "shepherd's nights" and to the "nights of Hayan". The first day of *ennayer* (January), in the depth of winter, is marked by a whole set of renewal rites and taboos (in particular on sweeping and weaving), which some informants extend to the whole period of *issemaden* (the cold days) running from late December to early January.

The end of *lyali* is marked by the ritual celebration of *el'azla gennayer*, separation from *ennayer*: life has emerged on the face of the earth, the first shoots are appearing on the trees, it is "the opening" (*el ftuh*). The farmer goes out into the fields and sets up oleander branches, which have the power to drive away *maras*, the cockchafer grub; as he does so, he says, "Come out, *maras*! The *khammes* is going to kill you!" On the same day, it is said, the peasants go to their stables before sunrise and shout in the ears of the oxen: "Good news! *Ennayer* is over!" Some informants say *'azri*, the bachelor, for *'azla* ("because from that day on, spring is coming, and marriages start to be celebrated"), with a sort of play on words which is no doubt also a play on mythic roots. This is beginning of a long transitional period, a time of waiting, covered by a terminology as rich as it is confused: whereas autumn is "a whole", as one informant put it, the passage from winter to spring is a patchwork of moments which are ill defined, almost all malign, and variously named.

Thus, the term *thimgharine*, the old women, or *thamgharth*, the old woman,[8] also known as *amerdil* (the loan) in Great Kabylia, denotes either the moment of transition from one month to another (from December to January, or January to February, or February to March, and even, at Aïn Aghbel, from March to April), or the moment of transition from winter to spring. *Husum*, a learned term of Arabic origin, referring to a sura of the Koran, coexists with *hayan* (or *ahgan*) to denote the passage from *furar* to *maghres*.[9] But the logic of magic insists that it is never possible to know exactly which is the most unpropitious moment in a period which is uncertain as a whole,[10] so that the terms *thimgharine* or *husum*, relating to highly unpropitious periods, are sometimes used to denote the whole transitional period from late January to mid-March: in this case, they are made to include the four "weeks" which divide up the month of February, known collectively as *essba't* ("the sevens"), i.e. *el mwalah* (sometimes called *imirghane*), the salt days; *el quarah*, the pungent days; *el swalah*, the benign days; *el fwatah*, the open days.[11] As the names of this series themselves testify, we find here, as in the case of the nights of January, one of the semi-explicit dichotomies which always involve an attempt at rationalization: the first two periods are malign and come at the end of winter; the last two are benign and come at the beginning of spring. In the same way, informants who identify *husum* with the fortnight straddling the end of January and the beginning of February, concentrating within it all the features characteristic of the period as a whole, distinguish a first, dangerous week and a second, more favourable week. And similarly, numerous informants (especially in the Djurdjura region) distinguish two *ahgans* (or *hayans*) – *ahgan bu akli*, the *hayan* of the Negro, seven intensely cold days during which work is suspended, and *ahgan u hari*, the *hayan* of the freeman, seven days in which "everything on earth comes back to life".

During "*hayan* week" (the first week of March), life completes its work. Man must not disturb it by going into the fields or orchards.[12] The animals too seem to have completed their growth: weaning (*el hiyaz*) is carried out at the end of *hayan* week, on the day of the spring equinox (*adhwal gitij*, the lengthening of the sun). A tin can is struck to make a noise which will prevent the oxen – who can understand human speech on that day – from hearing what is said about "the lengthening of the days", for if they heard it, they would take fright at having to work harder. By virtue of its position, *husum* (or *hayan*) is endowed with an inaugural – and augural – character very similar to that conferred on the morning, in the cycle of the day (for example, if it does not rain, the wells will not be full all year; if it rains, that is a sign of plenty; if there is snow at the beginning, there will be many partridge eggs); it is therefore an occasion for acts of propitiation (almsgiving) and divination.

Once the days of the old woman and *husum* are over, the flock is reckoned to be saved: it is now *el fwatah*, the time for coming out, the time of births, both on the cultivated land and among the flock, and the younglings are no longer threatened by the rigours of winter. The first day of spring (*thafsuth*), the feast of greenness and infancy,[13] has already been celebrated. All the ritual of this inaugural day of an augural period is placed under the sign of *joy* and of objects that bring good fortune and prosperity. The children go out into the fields to meet spring. In the open air they will eat a semolina of grilled cereals and butter. The couscous served on that day is cooked in the steam of a broth containing *adhris* (*seksu wadhris*), thapsia, a plant which causes swelling. The women abandon the taboos of the ploughing period and dye their hands with henna. They go off in groups of fifteen or twenty and bring back heath shrubs to make brooms, the euphemistic name for which is *thafarahth*, from *farah*, joy, and which, made in joy, will bring joy.

The days grow longer. There is not much work to be done (apart from tillage in the fig orchards); man has to wait for life to do its work. "In March", they say in Great Kabylia, "go and look at your crops, and take a good look"; and elsewhere: "the sun of the flowering [of the long-awaited peas and beans] empties the *douar*." The food stocks are exhausted, and the lengthening of the days is accentuated by the ban on going out into the fields (*natah* is not over) and on eating beans or other green vegetables. Hence the proverbs: "March (*maghres*) climbs like a hillside"; and "The days of March are seven-snack days."

With *natah* or *thiftirine*, the transitional period comes to an end. These terms, which denote the same period to within a few days, are both of Arabic origin and are rarely known to the peasants of the Djurdjura region (where *hayan*, or rather *ahgan*, as it is known locally, has shifted to this time of the year). During *natah* "the trees are shaken and knock together"; excessive rain is likely, and the weather is so cold that "the boar shivers in its lair". As in *husum*, there is a ban on entering the cultivated fields and the orchards (for fear of causing the death of a person or an animal). For *natah* is also the season of nature's awakening, of the blossoming of crops, life, and marriages. It is the moment for weddings and village feasts.[14] And so, by a familiar device, some informants divide *thiftirine* or *natah* into an unfavourable period, in March ("the difficult days") and a favourable period ("the easy days") in April.

The passage from the wet season to the dry season is effected ritually and collectively, during *natah*, on the day of *tharurith wazal* (the return of *azal*),[15] on a date which varies from region to region because of climatic differences, coming either in March, after weaning, *el hiyaz*, or in April, at shearing time or just after, or, at the very latest, at the beginning of May: from that day on, the flock, which up to then went out late in the morning and came back relatively early, leaves early in the morning, comes back and goes out again in the early afternoon, and returns at sunset.

The bad weather is over for good; the *green* fields and the gardens are now ready to receive the rays of the sun. This is the start of the cycle of dryness and ripening; with *ibril*, a particularly beneficent month ("April is a downward slope"), a trouble-free period of relative plenty begins. Work of all sorts starts up again: in the fields, where the critical period of growth is over, the men can start the hoeing, the only important activity (which used to be inaugurated by the abduction of Mata, the "bride" of the field, a rite intended to call down the rain needed for the ears of the corn to develop); in the gardens, the first beans are picked. During the period of *nisan*, whose beneficent rain, bringing fertility and prosperity to every living thing, is invoked with all sorts of rites, the sheep are shorn and the new lambs are branded. The fact that *nisan*, like all transitional periods (*natah*, for example), is an ambiguous period, ill defined in relation to the opposition between the dry and the wet, is here expressed not in a division into two periods, one auspicious and the other inauspicious, but by the existence of inauspicious moments (*eddbagh*, the 1st of May, at a mysterious hour known to none), marked by various taboos (pruning or grafting, celebrating weddings, whitewashing houses, setting up the loom, setting eggs to be hatched, etc.).

As the period known as *izegzawen* "the green days" comes to an end, the last traces of greenery fade from the landscape; the cereals, which had been as "tender" (*thaleqaqth*) as a new-born baby, now begin to turn yellow. The changing appearance of the cornfields is indicated by the names of the ten- or seven-day periods into which the month of *magu* (or *mayu*) is divided. After *izegzawen* come *iwraghen*, the yellow days, *imellalen*, the white days, and *iquranen*, the dry days. Summer (*anebdhu*) has begun. The characteristic tasks of the wet season, tillage (in the fig orchards) and sowing, which is still permitted in the "green days", are absolutely banned from the period known as the "yellow days". The only concern is to protect the ripening crops against the dangers which threaten them (hail, birds, locusts, etc.). The means used against predators – showers of stones, shouts (*aḥaḥi*), scarecrows – like the collective expulsion rites (*aṣifedh*) that are intended to transfer the malignant forces from the territory to be protected into a cave, bush, or heap of stones, after "fixing" them on objects (dolls) or animals (e.g. a pair of birds) which are then sacrificed, are simply applications of the scheme of "transference of evil" which is set to work in the treatment of a large number of diseases – fever, madness (possession by a *djin*), sterility – and also in rites performed on fixed dates in certain villages.

According to most informants, summer begins on the seventeenth day of the month of *magu*, also called *mut el ardh* "the death of the land".[16] By the last day of *iquraranen*, known as "a fiery ember has fallen into the water" (*thagli thirgith egwaman*), an expression which alludes to the tempering of iron, the action proper to the smith, everyone should have started harvesting (*essaïf*), which is completed around *in sla*, the day of the summer solstice (24 June), when purificatory fires are lit everywhere.[17] When treading-out and winnowing are completed, the forty dogdays of *smaïm* begin and work is suspended (just as it is in *lyali*, a period to which *smaïm* is always opposed).[18]

In opposition to the harvesting and treading-out, *lakhrif* is seen as a slack period in the agrarian year, or rather in the grain cycle. It is also a period devoted to rest and to the celebrations of a plentiful harvest;[19] as well as the newly harvested grain there are figs, grapes, and various fresh vegetables, tomatoes, sweet peppers, gourds, melons, etc. *Lakhrif* is sometimes said to begin in mid-August, at *thissemtith* (from *semti*, to start ripening), the moment when the first ripe figs appear, and *el haq* "the law" is imposed – a ban on fig-picking, even from one's own trees, with fines for disobedience. When *ichakhen* comes round (*ichakh lakhrif*, it is *lakhrif* everywhere), the fig-harvest is at its peak, and the men, the women, and the children are all kept busy; the 1st of October is *lahal yifer* (of the leaves), and now the leaves may be stripped from the fig-trees (*achraw*, from *chrew*, to strip) to feed the oxen. This date is the signal for the "withdrawal of life", the work of *iqachachen* ("the last days"), which are devoted to a thorough cleaning of the kitchen gardens, orchards, and fields, with *thaqachachth lakhrif* (the last fruit is shaken from the trees and the remaining leaves are stripped off) and "the rooting up of the garden". When all traces of life persisting in the fields after the harvest have thus been removed, the land is ready for ploughing.

This linear diagram of the agrarian year (like all discourse) at once masks and reveals the difficulties that are encountered as soon as one ceases to take practical relations of analogy or homology singly (or in pairs) and successively, and endeavours instead to fix them simultaneously so as to cumulate them systematically. These difficulties would, no doubt, not merit our attention (in spite of the trouble and time they have cost) were it not that, as with, in another order, the statistical analysis of genealogies, they have the effect of forcing us to call into question the very operation which gave rise to them. Rigour demands not that one should occlude these contradictions by means of some rhetorical or mathematical device, so as to fall into line with the rules of the profession, but rather that one should make them the object of a reflection capable of discovering in them both the logic of the practical use of temporal oppositions (from which the contradictions arise) and, inseparably from this, the principle of the transmutation to which scholarly objectification subjects this logic.

Just as genealogy substitutes a space of unequivocal, homogeneous relationships, established once and for all, for a spatially and temporally discontinuous set of islands of kinship, ranked and organized to suit the needs of the moment and brought into practical existence gradually and intermittently, and just as a map replaces the discontinuous, patchy space of practical paths by the homogeneous, continuous space of geometry, so a calendar substitutes a linear, homogeneous, continuous time for practical time, which is made up of incommensurable islands of duration, each with its own rhythm, the time that flies by or drags, depending on what one is *doing*, i.e. on the *functions* conferred on it by the activity in progress. By distributing *guide-marks* (ceremonies and tasks) along a continuous line, one turns them into *dividing marks* united in a relation of simple succession, thereby creating *ex nihilo* the question of the intervals and correspondences between points which are no longer topologically but metrically equivalent.

Proof that *lyali*, which every informant mentions, is not "a period of forty days" (all that is said is "We are entering *lyali*") but a simple scansion of passing time, is found in the fact that different informants ascribe to it different durations and different dates: one of them even situates the first day of *ennayer* both in the middle of winter and in the middle of *lyali*, although he does not set *lyali* in the (geometric) middle of winter, thereby demonstrating that the practical grasp of the structure which leads him to think of *lyali* as the winter of winter overrides calculative reason. A number of ill-defined guide-marks (e.g. the "old women") shift according to the region and the informant, but never beyond the bounds of winter. The same logic is found in the belief that it is impossible to know exactly when a certain action should be avoided, the "period" being nothing other than the field of uncertainty between two guide-marks. A question as innocuous in appearance as "And what comes next?", inviting an informant to situate two "periods" in relation to one another in a continuous time (which does no more than state what the genealogical or chronological diagram does implicitly), has the effect of imposing an attitude to temporality which is the exact opposite of the attitude involved practically in the ordinary use of temporal terms. Quite apart from the form which the questioning must take so as to elicit an ordered sequence of answers, everything about the inquiry relationship itself betrays the interrogator's "theoretical" (i.e. "non-practical") disposition and invites the interrogatee to adopt a quasi-theoretical attitude: the situation in which the interrogation is carried on rules out any reference to the use and conditions of use of the temporal guide-marks; the interrogation itself tacitly substitutes for discontinuous marks, intended to be used for practical ends, the calendar as an *object of thought*, predisposed to become an object of discourse and to be unfolded as a totality existing beyond its "applications" and independently of the needs and interests of its users. This explains why informants who are invited to give the calendar often start by setting out the scholarly series of successive units, such as *mwalah*, *swalah*, and *fwatah*, or *izegzawen*, *iwraghen*, *imellalen*, and *iquranen*. And also why, when they do not send the anthropologist (whom they always see as a scholar) to other scholars with his scholar's questions, they endeavour to produce the forms of learning which seem to them worthiest of being offered in reply to scholarly interrogation, substituting for the guides which really organize their practice as much as they can mobilize of the series of the constructed calendar, the months of the Moslem calendar or the "houses".[20] In short, by tacitly excluding all reference to the practical interest which a socially characterized agent – a man or a woman, an adult or a shepherd, a farmer or a smith, etc. – may have in dividing up the year in such-and-such a way, and in using such-and-such a temporal guide, one unwittingly constructs an *object* which exists only by virtue of this unconscious construction of both it and its operations.

The cancelling out of the practical functions of temporal guide-marks that results from the context of interrogation and from scientific recording is the hidden condition of cumulating and seriating the aggregate of the oppositions which can be produced in relation to different universes of discourse, that is, with different functions. By cumulating information which is not and cannot always be mastered by any single informant – at any rate, never on the instant – the analyst wins the *privilege of totalization* (thanks to the power to *perpetuate* that writing and all the various techniques for recording give him, and also to the abundant time he has for analysis). He thus secures the means of apprehending the logic of the system which a partial or discrete view would miss; but by the same token, there is every likelihood that he will overlook the change in status to which he is subjecting practice and its products, and consequently that he will insist on trying to answer questions which are not and cannot be questions for practice, instead of asking himself whether the essential characteristic of practice is not precisely the fact that it excludes such questions.

The totalization which the *diagram* effects by juxtaposing in the simultaneity of a single space the complete series of the temporal oppositions applied successively by different agents at different times, which can never all be mobilized together in practice (because the necessities of existence never require this sort of synoptic apprehension, tending rather to discourage it by their urgency) gives full rein to the *theoretical neutralization* which the inquiry relationship itself produces. The establishment of a single series thus creates *ex nihilo* a whole host of relations (of simultaneity, succession, or symmetry, for example) between terms and guide-marks of different levels, which, being produced and used in different situations, are never brought face to face in practice and are thus compatible practically even when logically contradictory. The synoptic diagram takes all the temporal oppositions which can be collected and assembled and distributes them in accordance with the laws of succession (i.e. (1) "y follows x" excludes "x follows y"; (2) if y follows x and z follows y, then z follows x; (3) either y follows x or x follows y). This makes it possible to apprehend at a glance, *uno intuitu et tota simul*, as Descartes said, *monothetically*, as Husserl put it,[21] meanings which are produced and used polythetically, that is to say, not only one after another, but one by one, step by step.[22]

Depending on the precision with which the event considered has to be localized, on the nature of the event, and on the social status of the agent concerned, different systems of oppositions are seen to emerge: for example, the period known as *lyali*, far from being defined – as in a perfectly ordinate series – in relation to the period which preceded it and the period which follows it, and only in relation to them, can be opposed to *smaïm* as well as to *el husum* or *thimgharine*; as we have seen, it can also be opposed, as "*lyali* of December", to "*lyali* of January", or, by a different logic, be opposed as the "great nights" to the "lesser nights of *furar*" and the "lesser nights of *maghres*" (the same combinative logic which leads to the oppositions between "*essba't* of winter" and "*essba't* of spring"; between "*es-ba't* of late spring", with the "green days" and the "yellow days", and "*essba't* of summer", with the "white days" and the "dry days"; and between *smaïm* of summer and *smaïm* of autumn). The same informant may at one moment, thinking in terms of ritual practices, oppose *lakhrif* taken as a whole ("autumn is without divisions") to *lahlal*, the licit period for ploughing; and the very next moment, thinking in terms of the cycle of the fig harvest, oppose *lahlal* to *achraw*, which is the end of *lakhrif* and one of the activities of *thaqachachth*, through which it is implicitly opposed to *thissemtith* (the first figs), or *achakh* (the ripeness of the figs).

When one knows that many other oppositions could be produced, one sees the artificiality and indeed unreality of a calendar which assimilates and aligns units of different levels and of very unequal importance. Given that all the divisions and sub-divisions which the observer may record and cumulate are produced and used in different situations and on different occasions, the question of how each of them relates to the unit at a higher level, or, *a fortiori*, to the divisions or sub-divisions of the "periods" to which they are opposed, never arises in practice. If another seemingly ethnocentric analogy be permitted, one might suggest that the relation between the constructed series obeying the laws of succession, and the temporal oppositions put into practice successively so that they cannot be telescoped into the same spot, is homologous with the relation between the continuous, homogeneous, political space of graduated scales of opinion, and practical political positions, which are always taken up in response to a particular situation and particular interlocutors or opponents and make distinctions and divisions of greater or lesser refinement depending on the political distance between the interlocutors (left:right::left of the left:right of the left::left of the left of the left:right of the left of the left::etc.) so that the same agent may find himself successively on his own right and on his own left in the "absolute" space of geometry, contradicting the third law of succession.

The same analysis applies to the terminologies serving to designate social units: ignorance of the uncertainties and ambiguities which these products of a practical logic owe to their functions and to the conditions in which they are used leads to the production of *artefacts* as impeccable as they are unreal. Perhaps no anthropologist has been more sensitive than Edmund Leach to "the essential difference between the ritual description of structural relations and the anthropologist's scientific description", or, in particular, to the opposition between the "completely unambiguous" terminology of the anthropologist, with his arbitrarily devised concepts, and the concepts which agents use in ritual actions to express structural relations. Indeed, nothing is more suspect than the ostentatious rigour of the diagrams of the social organization of Berber societies offered by anthropologists. Jeanne Favret provides an example in a recent article in which she follows Hanoteau on to a "field" on which her general ideas are most redolent of generals' ideas, as Virginia Woolf would have put it. If her taste for provocative paradox had not led her to rehabilitate the worthy brigadier-general's "wild [*sauvage*] ethnography" against professional ethnology (which happens to be somewhat under-professionalized in this area), Ms Favret would not have gone to the "innocent and meticulous ethnography of Hanoteau and Letourneux" for the basis of the pure, perfect taxonomy of political organization which she opposes to the anthropological tradition, accusing the latter both of being "merely more sophisticated and more ignorant of its limits" than the general's military anthropology and of failing to observe the distinctions which his work makes it possible to draw.[23] A more penetrating reading of the texts in question, produced in the main by administrators and soldiers (or law professors), would show that the vagueness of the social terminologies they offer could only result from a certain familiarity with Kabyle reality combined with ignorance of the theoretical traditions and of the corresponding pretensions to theoretical systematicity. Without entering into detailed discussion of Ms Favret's schematic presentation of the terminology collected by Hanoteau, one can only restate certain basic points of the description of the structure of the village of Aït Hichem[24] which perhaps erred only by excessive "rationalization" of native categories. Though the vocabulary of social divisions varies from place to place, the fact remains that the hierarchy of the basic social units, those designated by the words *thakharubth* and *adhrum*, is almost always the *opposite* of what Ms Favret, following Hanoteau, says it is. A few cases can be found in which, as Hanoteau maintains, *thakharubth* includes *adhrum*, probably because terminologies collected at particular times and places designate the results of different *histories*, marked by the splitting up, the (no doubt frequent) disappearance, and the annexation of lineages. It also often happens that the words are used indifferently to refer to social divisions at the same level; this is the case in the Sidi Aïch region, in which the terms used, starting with the most restricted and hence most real unit, are (a) *el hara*, the undivided family (called *akham*, the house, *akham n'Aït Ali*, at Aït Hichem), (b) *akham*, the extended family, covering all the people bearing the name of the same ancestor (as far as the third or fourth generation) – *Ali ou X*, sometimes also designated by a term probably suggested by the topography, since the path bends as one passes from one *akham* to another: *thaghamurth*, the elbow, (c) *adhrum*, *akharub* (or *thakharubth*), or *aharum*, bringing together the people whose common origin goes back beyond the fourth generation, (d) the *ṣuff*, or simply "those above" or "those below", (e) the village, a purely local unit, in this case including the two leagues. The synonyms, to which must be added *tha'rifth* (from *'arf*, to know one another), a group of acquaintances, equivalent to *akham* or *adhrum* (elsewhere, *thakharubth*) may not have been used haphazardly, since they emphasize either integration and internal cohesion (*akham* or *adhrum*) or the contrast with other groups (*taghamurth, aharum*). *Ṣuff*, used to suggest an "arbitrary" unit, a conventional alliance as opposed to the other terms which denote individuals bearing a common name (Aït...), is often distinguished from *adhrum*, with which it coincides at Aït Hichem. Everything takes place as if one passed by insensible gradations from the patriarchal family to the clan (*adhrum* or *thakharubth*), the fundamental social unit, with the intermediate units corresponding to more-or-less arbitrary points of segmentation (which would explain the informants' uncertainty with vocabulary they often inadequately master). These points become especially apparent when conflict arises (by virtue of the fact that the units are separated only by differences of degree, as can be seen, for example, in the different shades of obligation in the case of mourning, with the closest relatives offering the meal, and the others making their own small contribution, by helping with the cooking, bringing jars of water or some vegetables, and the most distant relatives – or friends from another clan – giving a meal for the family of the deceased after the mourning is over); and they are subject to constant change: the virtual limits may become real ones when the group extends itself (thus at Aït Hichem, the Aït Mendil, who were originally united, constitute two *thakharubth*) and the real limits may disappear (the Aït Isaad group together several reduced *thakharubth* in a single *thakharubth*). In short, the systematic picture of interlocking units, presented by "wild" or civilized anthropologists from Hanoteau through Durkheim to Jeanne Favret, ignores the unceasing dynamism of units which are constantly forming and reforming, and the *fuzziness* which is an integral part of native notions inasmuch as it is at once the precondition and the product of their functioning. What is true of genealogical and political taxonomies is equally true of the temporal taxonomies of the agrarian calendar: the level at which the oppositions actually mobilized are situated depends fundamentally on the situation – that is to say, on the relationship between the groups or individuals who are to be *demarcated* by means of taxonomies.

Economy of logic

Symbolic systems owe their *practical coherence*, that is, their regularities, and also their irregularities and even incoherences (both equally *necessary* because inscribed in the logic of their genesis and functioning) to the fact that they are the product of practices which cannot perform their practical functions except insofar as they bring into play, in their practical state, principles which are not only coherent – i.e. capable of engendering intrinsically coherent practices compatible with the objective conditions – but also practical, in the sense of convenient, i.e. immediately mastered and manageable because obeying a "poor" and economical logic.

One thus has to acknowledge that practice has a logic which is not that of logic, if one is to avoid asking of it more logic than it can give, thereby condemning oneself either to wring incoherences out of it or to thrust upon it a forced coherence.[25] Analysis of the various but closely interrelated aspects of the theorization effect (forced synchronization of the successive, fictitious totalization, neutralization of functions, substitution of the system of products for the system of principles of production, etc.) brings out, in negative form, certain properties of the logic of practice which by definition escape theoretical apprehension, since they are constitutive of that apprehension. Practical logic – practical in both senses of the word – is able to organize the totality of an agent's thoughts, perceptions, and actions by means of a few generative principles, themselves reducible in the last analysis to a fundamental dichotomy, only because its whole economy, which is based on the principle of the economy of logic, presupposes a loss of rigour for the sake of greater simplicity and generality and because it finds in "polythesis" the conditions required for the correct use of polysemy.

Thanks to "polythesis", the "confusion of spheres", as the logicians call it, resulting from the highly economical, but necessarily approximate, application of the same schemes to different logical universes, can pass unnoticed because it entails no practical consequences. No one takes the trouble to systematically record and compare the successive products of the application of the generative schemes: these discrete, self-sufficient units owe their immediate transparency not only to the schemes which are realized in them, but also to the *situation* apprehended through these schemes and to the agent's practical relation to that situation. The principle of the economy of logic, whereby no more logic is mobilized than is required by the needs of practice, means that the universe of discourse in relation to which this or that class (and therefore the complementary class) is constituted, can remain implicit, because it is implicitly defined in each case in and by the practical relation to the situation. Given that it is unlikely that two contradictory applications of the same schemes will be brought face to face in what we must call a *universe of practice* (rather than a universe of discourse), the same thing may, in different universes of practice, have different things as its complement and may, therefore, receive different, even opposed, properties, according to the universe.[26] The house, for example, is globally defined as female, damp, etc., when considered from outside, from the male point of view, i.e. in opposition to the external world, but it can be divided into a male-female part and a female-female part when it ceases to be seen by reference to a universe of practice coextensive with *the* universe, and is treated instead as a universe (of practice and discourse) in its own right, which for the women it indeed is, especially in winter.[27]

The fact that symbolic objects and practices can enter without contradiction into successive relationships set up from different points of view means that they are subject to *overdetermination through indetermination*: the application to the same objects or practices of different schemes (such as opening/closing, going in/coming out, going up/going down, etc.) which, at the degree of precision (i.e. of imprecision) with which they are defined, are all *practically* equivalent, is the source of the polysemy characterizing the fundamental relationships in the symbolic system, which are always determined in several respects at once. Thus a relationship such as that between the house and the *thajmu'th* (for which one could substitute the market, or the fields) condenses a good number of the system's fundamental oppositions – the full and the empty, the female and the male, night and day, etc. – which are also found, with only slight differences, in relationships as accessary in appearance as those between the cooking-pot and the wheatcake griddle or the stable and the *kanun*.

The most specific properties of a ritual corpus, those which define it as a system coherent in practice, cannot be perceived or adequately understood unless the corpus is seen as the product (*opus operatum*) of a practical mastery (*modus operandi*) owing its practical efficacy to the fact that it makes connections based on what Jean Nicod calls *overall resemblance*.[28] This mode of apprehension never explicitly or systematically limits itself to any one aspect of the terms it links, but takes each one, each time, as a whole, exploiting to the full the fact that two "data" are never entirely alike in *all* respects but are always alike in some respect, at least indirectly (i.e. through the mediation of some common term). This explains, first, why among the different aspects of the at once undetermined and overdetermined symbols it manipulates, ritual practice never clearly opposes aspects symbolizing something to aspects symbolizing nothing and hence disregarded (such as, in the case of the letters of the alphabet, the colour or size of the strokes, or, in a page of writing, the vertical word-order). For example, although one of the different aspects through which a "datum" like gall can be connected with other (equally equivocal) data – viz. bitterness (it is equivalent to oleander, wormwood, or tar, and opposed to honey), greenness (it is associated with lizards and the colour green), and hostility (inherent in the previous two qualities) – necessarily comes to the forefront, the other aspects do not thereby cease to be perceived simultaneously; the symbolic chord may be sounded either in its fundamental form, when the fundamental quality is emphasized, or in its inverted form. Without wishing to push the musical metaphor too far, one might nonetheless suggest that a number of ritual sequences can be seen as *modulations*: occurring with particular frequency because the specific principle of ritual action, the desire to stack all the odds on one's own side, is conducive to the logic of *development*, with variations against a background of redundancy, these modulations play on the harmonic properties of ritual symbols, whether duplicating one of the themes with a strict equivalent in all respects (gall evoking wormwood, which, like gall, unites bitterness and greenness) or modulating into remoter tonalities by playing on the associations of the secondary harmonics (lizard → toad).[29]

Ritual practice effects a *fluid*, *"fuzzy" abstraction*, bringing the same symbol into different relations through different aspects or bringing different aspects of the same referent into the same relation of opposition; in other words, it excludes the Socratic question of the *respect in which* the referent is apprehended (shape, colour, function, etc.), thereby obviating the need to define in each case the principle governing the choice of the aspect selected, and, *a fortiori*, the need to stick to that principle at all times. But in relating objects and selecting aspects, this practical taxonomy applies, successively or simultaneously, principles which are all indirectly reducible to one another, and this enables it to classify the same "data" from several different standpoints without classifying them in different ways (whereas a more rigorous system would make as many classifications as it found properties). The universe thus undergoes a division which can be said to be logical, though it seems to break all the rules of logical division (for example, by making divisions which are neither exclusive nor exhaustive), for all its dichotomies are indefinitely redundant, being in the last analysis the product of a single *principium divisionis*. Because the principle opposing the terms which have been related (e.g. the sun and the moon) is not defined and usually comes down to a simple contrariety (whereas contradiction implies a preliminary analysis) *analogy* (which, when it does not function purely in its practical state, is always expressed elliptically – "woman is the moon") establishes a homology between oppositions (man:woman::sun:moon) set up in accordance with two indeterminate, overdetermined principles (hot:cold::male: female::day:night::etc.) which differ from the principles generating other homologies into which either of the two terms in question might enter (man:woman::east:west or sun:moon::dry:wet). In other words, fluid abstraction is also false abstraction. Because the properties distinguishing one "datum" from another remain attached to non-pertinent properties, the assimilation is comprehensive and complete even when fundamentally motivated in only one respect. The aspect of each of the terms which is (implicitly) selected from a single standpoint in any particular connection made between them remains attached to the other aspects through which it can subsequently be opposed to other aspects of another referent in other connections. The same term could thus enter into an infinite number of connections if the number of ways of relating to what is not itself were not limited to a few fundamental oppositions. Ritual practice proceeds no differently from the child who drove André Gide to despair by insisting that the opposite of "blanc" was "blanche" and the feminine of "grand", "petit". In short, the "analogical sense" inculcated in the earliest years of life is, as Wallon says of thinking in couples, a sort of "sense of the contrary", which gives rise to the countless applications of a few basic contrasts capable of providing a minimum of determination (a man is not a woman → a toad is not a frog) and cannot give any information about the relations it relates, because it is precisely their indeterminacy and fuzziness that permit it to operate. The uncertainties and misunderstandings inherent in this logic of suggestion and ambiguity are thus the price that has to be paid for the *economy* which results from reducing the universe of the relations between opposites and of the relations between these relations to a few basic relations from which all the others can be generated.

Sympatheia ton holon, as the Stoics called it, the affinity between all the objects of a universe in which meaning is everywhere, and everywhere superabundant, is achieved at the cost of the fuzziness and vagueness of each of the elements and each of the relationships between them: logic can be everywhere only because it is really nowhere. If ritual practices and representations are objectively endowed with partial, approximate systematicity, this is because they are the product of a small number of generative schemes that are *practically interchangeable*, i.e. capable of producing equivalent results from the point of view of the "logical" demands of practice. If they never have *more* than partial and approximate systematicity, this is because the schemes of which they are the product can be quasi-universally applied only because they function *in their practical state*, i.e. on the hither side of explicit statement and consequently outside of all logical control, and by reference to practical ends which are such as to impose on them a *necessity* which is not that of logic.

It is by "practical sense" that an agent knows, for example, that a given act or object requires a particular place inside the house; that a given task or rite corresponds to a particular period of the year or is excluded from another. He only needs to possess, in their practical state, a set of schemes functioning in their implicit state and in the absence of any precise delimitation of the universe of discourse, to be able to produce or understand a symbolic series such as the following: when a cat enters the house with a feather or a wisp of white wool in its fur, if it heads for the hearth, this presages the arrival of guests, who will be given a meal with meat; if it goes towards the stable, this means that a cow will be bought if the season is spring, an ox if it is autumn. The question-begging and the approximations in this series are obvious: the cat, an intruder which enters by chance and is driven out again, is only there as a bearer of symbols, which realizes practically the movement of entering; the feather is implicitly treated as the equivalent of the wool, no doubt because both substances are called upon to function as the mere supports of a beneficent quality, "the white"; the opposition between the hearth and the stable, the centre of the rite, is engendered by the scheme which structures the internal space of the house, opposing the top and the bottom, the dry and the wet, the male and the female, the noble part where guests are received and where meat is roasted (the dish served to guests par excellence), and the lower part, the place reserved for the animals. This scheme only has to be combined with the scheme generating the opposition between two seasons – autumn, the time of the collective sacrifice of an ox followed by the ploughing, and spring, the season of milk – to give the ox and the cow.[30]

Another example occurs in a well-known tale, the story of Ḥeb-Ḥeb-er-Remman. A girl who has seven brothers falls foul of the jealousy of her sisters-in-law. They make her eat seven snake's eggs, concealed in dumplings: her belly swells and people think she is pregnant; she is driven from the house. A wise man discovers the cause of her ailment: to cure her, a sheep must be slaughtered and its meat roasted, with a lot of salt. The girl must eat it and then be suspended by her feet with her mouth open over a pan of water. When this is done, the snakes come out and they are killed. The girl marries; she has a child whom she calls Ḥeb-Ḥeb-er-Remman "pomegranate seeds". She goes back to her brothers, who recognize her when she tells them her story, showing them the seven snakes which she has dried and salted. It can immediately be seen that to produce this narrative, or to decode (at least in an approximate form) its significance, it is sufficient to possess the set of schemes which are at work in the production of any fertility rite. To fecundate is to penetrate, to introduce something which swells and/or causes swelling: the ingestion of food, and of food which swells (*ufthyen*) is homologous with sexual intercourse and ploughing.[31] But here there is a false fecundation: the snakes, a symbol of the male life-principle, of semen, of the ancestor who must die in order to be reborn, and thus of the dry, are ingested in the form of eggs, i.e. in their female state, and return to maleness inopportunely, in the girl's stomach (in a fertility rite reported by Westermarck, it is the heart – a male part of the snake – that is eaten). The swelling which results from this inverted procreation is sterile and pernicious. The cure is logically self-evident. The dry must be made to move in the opposite direction, from the high to the low – the girl simply has to be turned upside down – and from the inside to the outside – which cannot be done by a simple mechanical operation: the dry must be further dried, parched, by adding to it what is pre-eminently dry, salt, and reinforcing its propensity towards the moist, which in normal fecundation – procreation or sowing – carries it towards the inside, towards the damp womb of woman or of the earth opened by the ploughshare. At the end of the story, the woman's fecundity is proved by the birth of Heb-Heb-er-Remman "pomegranate seeds" (the symbol par excellence of female fecundity, identified with the womb), i.e. the many sons born (or to be born) from the fertile womb of a woman herself sprung from a womb prolific of men (her seven brothers). And the seven snakes end up dried and salted, i.e. in the state to which they are structurally assigned as symbols of male seed, capable of growing and multiplying through the cycle of immersion in the wet followed by emergence towards the dry.

The body as geometer: cosmogonic practice

Understanding ritual practice is not a question of decoding the internal logic of a symbolism but of restoring its practical necessity by relating it to the real conditions of its genesis, that is, to the conditions in which its functions, and the means it uses to attain them, are defined. It means, for example, reconstituting – by an operation of logical reconstruction which has nothing to do with an act of empathic projection – the significance and functions that agents in a determinate social formation can (and must) confer on a determinate practice or experience, given the practical taxonomies which organize their perception. When confronted with myth and ritual, social theory has always hesitated between the lofty distance which the most comprehensive science seeks to keep between itself and the elementary forms of reason and the mystical participation of the great initiates of the gnostic tradition. The objectivist reduction which brings to light the so-called objective functions of myths and rites (for Durkheim, functions of moral integration; for Lévi-Strauss, functions of logical integration) makes it impossible to understand how these functions are fulfilled, because it brackets the agents' own representation of the world and of their practice. "Participant" anthropology, on the other hand – when it is not merely inspired by nostalgia for the agrarian paradises, the principle of all conservative ideologies – regards the human invariants and the universality of the most basic experiences as sufficient justification for seeking eternal answers to the eternal questions of the cosmogonies and cosmologies in the practical answers which the peasants of Kabylia or elsewhere have given to the practical, historically situated problems which were forced on them in a determinate state of their instruments of material and symbolic appropriation of the world. Even when they are asymptotic with scientific truth, the inspired interpretations fostered by such a disposition are never more than the inversion of the false objectification performed by colonial anthropology. By cutting practices off from their real conditions of existence, in order to credit them with alien intentions, by a false generosity conducive to stylistic effects, the exaltation of lost wisdom dispossesses them, as surely as its opposite, of everything that constitutes their reason and their *raison d'être*, and locks them in the eternal essence of a "mentality". The Kabyle woman setting up her loom is not performing an act of cosmogony; she is simply setting up her loom to weave cloth intended to serve a technical function. It so happens that, given the symbolic equipment available to her for thinking her own activity – and in particular her language, which constantly refers her back to the logic of ploughing – she can only think what she is doing in the enchanted, that is to say, mystified, form which spiritualism, thirsty for eternal mysteries, finds so enchanting.

Rites take place because and only because they find their *raison d'être* in the conditions of existence and the dispositions of agents who cannot afford the luxury of logical speculation, mystical effusions, or metaphysical anxiety. It is not sufficient to ridicule the more naive forms of functionalism in order to have done with the question of the practical functions of practice. It is clear that a universal definition of the functions of marriage as an operation intended to ensure the biological reproduction of the group, in accordance with forms approved by the group, in no way explains Kabyle marriage ritual. But, contrary to appearances, scarcely more understanding is derived from a structural analysis which ignores the specific functions of ritual practices and fails to inquire into the economic and social conditions of the production of the dispositions generating both these practices and also the collective definition of the practical functions in whose service they function. The

Kabyle peasant does not react to "objective conditions" but to the practical interpretation which he produces of those conditions, and the principle of which is the socially constituted schemes of his habitus. It is this interpretation which has to be constructed in each case, if we want to give an account of ritual practices which will do justice both to their reason and to their *raison d'être*, that is, to their inseparably logical and practical necessity.

Thus, technical or ritual practices are determined by the material conditions of existence (that is, in this particular case, by a certain relationship between the climatic and ecological conditions and the available techniques) as treated in practice by agents endowed with schemes of perception of a determinate sort, which are themselves determined, negatively at least, by the material conditions of existence (the relative autonomy of ritual being attested by the invariant features found throughout the Maghreb, despite the variations in the climatic and economic conditions). It is in a particular relationship between a mode of production and a mode of perception that the *specific contradiction* of agrarian activity is defined as the hazardous or even sacrilegious confrontation of antagonistic principles, together with the ritual apparatus whose function it is to resolve that contradiction. It is through the mediation of the function thereby assigned to technical or ritual practice that the relationship observed between the economic system and the mythico-ritual system is established practically.[32]

Rites, more than any other type of practice, serve to underline the mistake of enclosing in concepts a logic made to dispense with concepts; of treating movements of the body and practical manipulations as purely logical operations; of speaking of analogies and homologies (as one sometimes has to, in order to understand and to convey that understanding) when all that is involved is the practical transference of incorporated, quasi-postural schemes.[33] Rite is indeed in some cases no more than a practical *mimesis* of the natural process which needs to be facilitated: unlike metaphor and explicit analogy, *mimetic representation* (*apomimema*) establishes a relationship between the swelling of grain in the cooking-pot, the swelling of a pregnant woman's belly, and the germination of wheat in the ground, which entails no explicit statement of the properties of the terms related or the principles of their relationship; the most characteristic operations of its "logic" – inverting, transferring, uniting, separating, etc. – take the form of movements of the body, turning to the right or left, putting things upside down, going in, coming out, tying, cutting, etc.

To speak, as we have here, of overall resemblance and uncertain abstraction, is still to use the intellectualist language of representation – the language which an analyst's relation to a corpus spread out before him in the form of documents quite naturally forces on him – to express a logic which is acted out directly in the form of bodily gymnastics without passing through the express apprehension of the "aspects" selected or rejected, of the similar or dissimilar "profiles". The logicism inherent in the objectivist standpoint leads those who adopt it to forget that scientific construction cannot grasp the principles of practical logic without changing the nature of those principles: when made explicit for objective study, a practical succession becomes a represented succession; an action oriented in relation to a space objectively constituted as a structure of demands (things "to be done" and "not to be done") becomes a reversible operation carried out in continuous, homogeneous space. For example, as long as mythico-ritual space is seen as an *opus operatum*, that is, as a timeless order of things coexisting, it is never more than a theoretical space, in which the only landmarks are provided by the terms of relations of opposition (up/down, east/west), and where only theoretical operations can be effected, i.e. logical displacements and transformations which differ *toto coelo* from movements and actions actually performed, such as falling or rising. Having established that the internal space of the Kabyle house receives a symmetrically opposite signification when re-placed in the total space outside, we are justified in saying, as we did earlier, that each of these two spaces, inside and outside, can be derived from the other by means of a semi-rotation, only on condition that the mathematical language expressing such operations is reunited with its basis in practice, so that terms like displacement and rotation are given their practical senses as *movements of the body*, such as going forwards or backwards, or turning round. Just as, in the time of Lévy-Bruhl, there would have been less amazement at the oddities of the "primitive mentality" if it had been possible to conceive that the logic of magic and "participation" might have some connection with the experience of emotion, so nowadays there would be less astonishment at the "logical" feats of the Australian aborigines if the "savage mind" had not been unconsciously credited, by a sort of inverted ethnocentrism, with the relation to the world that intellectualism attributes to every "consciousness" and if anthropologists had not remained silent about the transformation leading from operations mastered in their practical state to the formal operations isomorphic with them, failing by the same token to inquire into the social conditions of production of that transformation.

The science of myth is at liberty to describe the syntax of myth in the language of group theory, so long as it is not forgotten that this language destroys the truth it makes available to apprehension, because it has been won and built up *against* the experience it enables one to name: it is scarcely necessary to insist that we can no more identify the scientific study of oxidation with the experience of fire than we can offer the continuous, homogeneous space of geometry as the practical space of practice, with its dyssymmetries, its discontinuities, and its directions conceived as substantial properties, left and right, east and west. We may say that gymnastics or dancing are geometry so long as we do not mean to say that the gymnast and the dancer are geometers. Perhaps there would be less temptation to treat the agent implicitly or explicitly as a logical operator if (without entering into the question of chronological priority) one went back from the mythic logos to the ritual praxis which enacts in the form of real actions, i.e. body movements, the operations which objective analysis discovers in mythic discourse, an *opus operatum* concealing the constituting moment of "mythopoeic" practice under its reified significations. Like the acts of jurisprudence, ritual practice owes its *practical coherence* (which may be reconstituted in the form of an objectified diagram of operations) to the fact that it is the product of a single system of *conceptual schemes immanent in practice*, organizing not only the perception of objects (and in this particular case, the classification of the possible instruments, circumstances – place and time – and agents of ritual action) but also the production of practices (in this case, the gestures and movements constituting ritual action). Performing a rite presupposes something quite different from the conscious mastery of the sort of catalogue of oppositions that is drawn up by academic commentators striving for symbolic mastery of a dead or dying tradition (e.g. the Chinese mandarins' tables of equivalences) and also by anthropologists in the first stage of their work. Practical mastery of principles neither more complex nor more numerous than the principles of solid statics applied when using a wheelbarrow, a lever, or a nutcracker[34] makes it possible to produce ritual actions that are *compatible* with the ends in view (e.g. obtaining rain or fertility for the livestock) and intrinsically (at least relatively) *coherent*, that is, combinations of a particular type of circumstances (times and places), instruments, and agents and, above all, of displacements and movements ritually qualified as propitious or unpropitious. These include going (or throwing something) upwards or eastwards, downwards or westwards, together with all the equivalent actions – putting something on the roof of the house or throwing it towards the *kanun*; burying it on the threshold or throwing it towards the stable; going or throwing to the left or with the left hand, and going or throwing to the right or with the right hand; turning something from left to right, or right to left; closing (or tying) and opening (or untying), etc. In fact, an analysis of the universe of mythically or ritually defined objects, starting with the circumstances, instruments, and agents of ritual action, makes it clear that the countless oppositions observed in every area of existence can all be brought down to a small number of couples which appear as fundamental, since, being linked to one another only by weak analogies, they cannot be reduced to one another except in a forced and artificial way. And almost all prove to be based on movements or postures of the human body, such as going up and coming down (or going forwards and going backwards), going to the left and going to the right going in and coming out (or filling and emptying), sitting and standing (etc.). The reason why this practical geometry, or geometrical practice ("geometry in the tangible world", as Jean Nicod puts it),[35] makes so much use of inversion is perhaps that, like a mirror bringing to light the paradoxes of bilateral symmetry, the human body functions as a practical operator which reaches to the left to find the right hand it has to shake, puts its right arm in the sleeve of the garment which had been lying on the left, or reverses right and left, east and west, by the mere fact of turning about to "face" someone or "turn its back" on him, or again, turns "upside down" things which were "the right way up" – so many movements which the mythic world-view charges with social significations and which rite makes intensive use of.

> I catch myself defining the threshold
> As the geometric locus
> Of arrivals and departures
> In the House of the Father.[36]

The poet goes straight to the heart of the relationship between the space inside the house and the outside world: the reversal of directions (*sens*) and meanings (*sens*) in going in and coming out. As a belated, small-scale producer of private mythologies, it is easier for him to sweep aside dead metaphors and go straight to the principle of mythopoeic practice, that is, to the movements and gestures which, as in a sentence of Albert the Great's picked up by René Char, can reveal the duality underlying the seeming unity of the object: "In Germany there was a pair of twins, one of whom opened doors with his right arm, the other of whom shut them with his left arm."[37]

If we simply follow the opposition defined by Wilhelm von Humboldt, and move from *ergon* to *energeia*, i.e. from objects or acts to the principles of their production, or, more precisely, from the *fait accompli* and dead letter of the already effected analogy ($a:b::c:d$), which objectivist hermeneutics considers, to analogical practice as *scheme transfer* carried out by the habitus on the basis of acquired equivalences facilitating the interchangeability of reactions[38] and enabling the agent to master by a sort of practical generalization all similar problems likely to arise in new situations, then at once we break the spell of the *panlogism* encouraged by the exoteric version of structuralism, in which the revelation of a non-intentional coherence, often described by linguists (Sapir and Trubetzkoy, for example) and even anthropologists as an "unconscious finality", serves as the basis for a metaphysics of nature dressed up in the language of natural science. We are then in a position to question the perfect coherence which tends to be conferred on historical systems by those who convert the methodological postulate of intelligibility into an ontological thesis. The fallacy, which Ziff points out, of converting regularity into a rule, thus presupposing a plan, is only apparently corrected in the hypothesis of the *unconscious*, held to be the only alternative to final causes as a means of explaining cultural phenomena presenting themselves as totalities endowed with structure and meaning.[39] In fact this plannerless plan is no less mysterious than the plan of a supreme planner, and it is understandable that the structuralist vulgate should have become for some people an intellectually acceptable form of Teilhardism – that is to say, one acceptable in intellectual circles.

The language of the body, whether articulated in gestures or, *a fortiori*, in what psychosomatic medicine calls "the language of the organs", is incomparably more ambiguous and more overdetermined than the most overdetermined uses of ordinary language. This is why ritual "roots" are always broader and vaguer than linguistic roots, and why the gymnastics of ritual, like dreams, always seems richer than the verbal translations, at once unilateral and arbitrary, that may be given of it. Words, however charged with connotation, limit the range of choices and render difficult or impossible, and in any case explicit and therefore "falsifiable", the relations which the language of the body suggests. It follows that simply by bringing to the level of discourse – as one must, if one wants to study it scientifically – a practice which owes a number of its properties to the fact that it falls short of discourse (which does not mean it is short on logic) one subjects it to nothing less than a change in ontological status the more serious in its theoretical consequences because it has every chance of passing unnoticed.[40]

Ritual practice, which always aims to facilitate *passages* and/or to authorize encounters between opposed orders, never defines beings or things otherwise than in and through the relationship it establishes practically between them, and makes the fullest possible use of the polysemy of the fundamental actions, mythic "roots" whose polysemy is partially reproduced by linguistic roots: for example, the root FTH may mean – figuratively as well as literally – to open (transitive) a door or a path (in ritual, extra-ordinary contexts), the heart (cf. opening one's heart), a speech (e.g. with a ritual formula), the sitting of an assembly, an action, the day, etc.; or to be open – applied to the "door" in the sense of the beginning of a series, the heart (i.e. the appetite), the sky, a knot; or to open (intransitive) – applied to a bud, a face, a shoot, an egg; and more generally, to inaugurate, bless, make easy, place under good auspices ("May God open the doors"), a cluster of senses covering virtually all the meanings attached to spring. But, being broader and vaguer than the linguistic root, the mythical root lends itself to richer and more varied interplay, and the scheme: to open (trans.) – to open (intrans.) – to be open makes it possible to set up associations among a whole set of verbs and nouns that go far beyond simple morphological affinity: it can evoke the roots FSU, to unbind, untie, resolve, dissolve, open, appear (used of young shoots; hence the name *thafsuth* given to spring); FRKh, to blossom, give birth (hence *asafrurakh*, blossoming, and *lafrakh*, the sprouts which appear on the trees in spring, and more generally, offspring, the outcome of any business), to proliferate, multiply; FRY, to form (trans.), to form (intrans.) (applied to figs), to begin to grow (applied to wheat or a baby), to multiply (a nestful of birds: *ifruri el'ach*, the nest is full of fledglings ready to take wing), to shell, or be shelled (peas and beans), and thus, to enter the period when fresh beans can be picked (*lahlal usafruri*), to sift and be sifted (wheat being prepared for grinding), separate or be separated (opponents), and thus, to reconcile, appease, pacify, dawn (daylight which "fights" with the night and "separates" from it, *ifruri was*), to become brighter (the weather, *ifruri elhal*); finally, by opposition, it can evoke the root FLQ, to break, burst, smash, to be broken, burst, smashed, to split and be split like the egg or pomegranate broken at the time of marriage and ploughing.[41]

One would only have to let oneself be carried along by the logic of associations in order the reconstruct the whole system of synonyms and antonyms, synonyms of synonyms and antonyms of antonyms, and so on. On one side, one could approach the roots 'MR, fill – be filled, or FTH, increase (intrans.), multiply (intrans.), or UFF, inflate, and through them pass to the root ZDY, unite (trans.) – unite (intrans.) – be in unity (the house "full" of men and goods is a numerous, united house); on the other side, through the antonyms, one would find empty – be emptied or ruin – be ruined (KHL), separate (trans.) – separate (intrans.) – be separated (FRQ), cut – be sharp (QD'), extinguish – be extinguished (TF), etc.[42] Similarly, starting from the mythical root "go up" one would find go eastward or be turned eastward, go toward the light, go toward the open country, go rightward, go forward, go into the future, be born, sprout, grow up (a bridge to the previous set of roots), stand up, be awake, be above, etc. or, through the antonyms, go down, go toward the darkness, go leftward, decline, fall, lie down, sleep, be below, etc.

The nearest equivalent to this series of generative schemes bound together by relations of practical equivalence is the system of adjectives (*lourd/léger*, *chaud/froid*, *terne/brillant*, etc.)[43] which are available in French to express the ultimate values of taste and which can be applied equally well to a dish or a school exercise, a play or a painting, a joke or a walk, an accent or a garment, and so on. This practical taxonomy owes its efficacy to the fact that, as is evidenced by the numerous senses recorded in the dictionaries, the meaning of each adjective, and of its relationship with its antonym, is specified in each case in terms of the logic of each of the fields in which it is applied: *froid* may be synonymous with *calme* or *indifférent*, but also with *frigide* or *grave*, or again with *austère* and *distant*, *dur* (hard) and *sec* (dry), *plat* (flat) and *terne* (dull), depending on whether it is applied to a man or a woman, a head or a heart, a melody or a tone of voice, a tint or a work of art, a calculation or a fit of anger, etc.; and it will have as many antonyms as it has different senses: *chaud* (hot) or course, but also *ardent* or *emporté* (irascible), *sensuel* or *chaleureux* (cordial), *brillant* or *expressif*, *éclatant* (dazzling) or *piquant* (pungent), etc. It follows that, considered in each of their uses, the pairs of qualifiers which as a system constitute the equipment of the judgment of taste are extremely "poor", quasi-indeterminate, and extremely rich, their indefiniteness predisposing them to inspire or express the sense of the indefinable: on the one hand, each use of one of these pairs is only meaningful in relation to a universe of practice which is different each time, usually implicit, and always self-sufficient, ruling out the possibility of comparison with other universes. On the other hand, the meaning which these pairs are given in a particular field has for harmonics all the meanings which they themselves, or any of the couples that are interchangeable with them to within a matter of nuances, may be given in other fields, i.e. in slightly different contexts.

This is true, for example, of the way in which the opposition between "in front" and "behind" functions in ritual practice: behind is where things one wants to get rid of are sent[44] (e.g. in one of the rites associated with the loom, these words are uttered: "May the angels be before me and the devil behind me"; in another rite, a child is rubbed behind the ear so that he will send evil "behind his ear"); behind is where ill fortune comes from (a woman on her way to market to sell the products of her industry, a blanket, yarn, etc., or the produce of her husbandry, hens, eggs, etc., must not look behind her or the sale will go badly; the whirlwind – *thimsiwray* – attacks from behind the man who faces the *qibla* to pray); "behind" is naturally associated with "inside", with the female (the eastern, front door is male, the western, back door is female), with all that is private, hidden, and secret; but it also is associated with that which follows, trailing behind on the earth, the source of fertility, *abruʿ*, the train of a garment, an amulet, happiness: the bride entering her new house strews fruit, eggs, and wheat behind her, symbolizing prosperity. These meanings interweave with all those associated with "in front", going forward, confronting (*qabel*), going into the future, going eastward, toward the light, and it would not be difficult to reconstruct the quasi-totality of Kabyle ritual practices from this one scheme.

This plurality of meanings at once different and more or less closely interrelated is a product of scientific collection. Each of the significations collected exists in its practical state only in the relationship between a scheme (or the product of a scheme, a word for example) and a specific situation. This is why it is not legitimate to speak of the different meanings of a symbol unless it is borne in mind that the assembling of these meanings in simultaneity (or on the same page of a dictionary, in the case of words) is a scientific artefact and that they never exist simultaneously in practice. On the one hand, as Vendryès pointed out, a word cannot always appear with all its meanings at once, without turning discourse into an endless play on words; on the other hand, if all the meanings a word is capable of taking were perfectly independent of the basic meaning, no play on words would ever be possible. This is equally true of the symbols of ritual. Among the forms which a basic opposition may take, there are always some which function as "switchers", concretely establishing the relationship between the universes of practice: here, for example, the relationship between "behind" and "inside", which provides the passage from "behind" to female prosperity, i.e. fertility – male prosperity being linked to "in front" through the intermediary of the bond between "in front", the future, and light. The objectified path of these passages is sometimes marked out by sayings which state the analogies ("the maiden is the wall of darkness", or "woman is the west", or "woman is the moon") between the different series.

The universes of meaning corresponding to different universes of practice are at once self-contained – hence protected from logical control through systematization – and *objectively* consistent with all the others, insofar as they are the loosely systematic products of a system of more or less completely integrated generative principles functioning in a structurally invariant way in the most diverse fields of practice. Within the "*fuzzy" logic of approximation* which immediately accepts as equivalents "flat", "dull", and "insipid", favourite value-judgment terms of the French aesthete or teacher, or, in the Kabyle tradition, "full", "closed", "inside", "underneath", which on closer inspection are perfectly incommensurable, the generative schemes are interchangeable practically; this is why they can only generate products that are indeed systematic but are so by virtue of a fuzzy systematicity and an approximate logic which cannot withstand the test of rational systematization and logical criticism.[45] Lacking symbolic mastery of the schemes and their products – schemes which they *are*, products which they *do* – the only way in which agents can adequately master the productive apparatus which enables them to generate correctly formed ritual practices is by making it operate.[46] This is what the observer is likely to forget, because he cannot recapture the logic immanent in the recorded products of the apparatus except by constructing a model which is precisely the substitute required when one does not have (or no longer has) immediate mastery of the apparatus.

Every successfully socialized agent thus possesses, in their incorporated state, the instruments of an ordering of the world, a system of classifying schemes which organizes all practices, and of which the linguistic schemes (to which the neo-Kantian tradition – and the ethnomethodological school nowadays – attribute unjustified autonomy and importance) are only one aspect. To grasp through the constituted reality of myth the constituting moment of the mythopoeic act is not, as idealism supposes, to seek in the conscious mind the universal structures of a "mythopoeic subjectivity" and the unity of a spiritual principle governing all empirically realized configurations regardless of social conditions. It is, on the contrary, to reconstruct the principle generating and unifying all practices, the system of inseparably cognitive and evaluative structures which organizes the vision of the world in accordance with the objective structures of a determinate state of the social world: this principle is nothing other than the *socially informed body*, with its tastes and distastes, its compulsions and repulsions, with, in a word, all its *senses*, that is to say, not only the traditional five senses – which never escape the structuring action of social determinisms – but also the sense of necessity and the sense of duty, the sense of direction and the sense of reality, the sense of balance and the sense of beauty, common sense and the sense of the sacred, tactical sense and the sense of responsibility, business sense and the sense of propriety, the sense of humour and the sense of absurdity, moral sense and the sense of practicality, and so on.

Union and separation

To the foregoing list should be added what might be called the *sense of limits and of the legitimate transgression of limits*, which is the basis at once of the ordering of the world (known, since Parmenides, as *diakosmesis*) and of the ritual actions intended to authorize or facilitate the necessary or unavoidable breaches of that order. "The world is based on the limit [*thalasth*]", said an old Kabyle. "Heaven and earth are separated by the limit. The eyes have an enclosure [*zerb*]. The mouth has a limit. Everything has a limit." To bring order is to bring distinction, to divide the universe into opposing entities, which the primitive speculation of the Pythagoreans set out as two "columns of contraries" (*sustoichiai*).[47] But the necessities of practice demand the reunion of things which practical logic has sundered – in marriage or ploughing, for example – and one function of ritual is precisely to euphemize, and thus to make licit, these unavoidable transgressions of the boundary. Not surprisingly, it proved difficult to find a place in the "columns of contraries" for an opposition as productive as that of the *odd* and the *even*, and more generally, for all the symbolic objects and actions which can be generated from the scheme *unite* (trans.) – *unite* (intrans.) – *be in unity* (the root ZDY) and its opposite *separate* (trans.) – *separate* (intrans.) – *be separated* (the root FRQ, or QD', cut – be sharp, and all the roots associated with them from the point of view of ritual meaning, close – be closed, extinguish – be extinguished, kill, slaughter, harvest, etc.). The principle of division cannot easily be classified among the things that it makes it possible to classify. This difficulty was encountered by Empedocles, who set aside *philia* and *neikos*, love and strife, as two ultimate principles irreducible to the oppositions which thanks to them can be dialectically combined.[48] When Empedocles gives as synonyms of *diakrisis* and *synkrisis* – an opposition which seems to belong to the order of logic, in which union and division do indeed figure, but in a very sublimated form – words as loaded as *phthora*, corruption, or *genesis*, generation, and for the second, *mixis*, which can also be translated as union, but this time in the sense of marriage, he points to the principle of the practical logic of rite, whose operations are inseparably logical and biological, as are the natural processes which it reproduces, when thought in accordance with the schemes of magical thought.[49]

It is thus possible to describe the whole system of ritual symbols and actions by means of a small number of *antagonistic symbols* (the paradigm of which is the opposition between the sexes, and which are produced from a small number of schemes) and a small number of (logical and biological) *practical operators* which are nothing other than natural processes culturally constituted in and through ritual practice, such as marriage and ploughing seen as *the union of contraries* and murder or harvesting seen as *the separation of contraries* (processes which the logic of ritual *mimesis*, as such, reproduces). Because the union of contraries does not destroy the opposition (which it presupposes), the reunited contraries are just as much opposed, but now in a quite different way, thereby manifesting the duality of the relationship between them, at once antagonism and complementarity, *neikos* and *philia*, which might appear as their own twofold "nature" if they were conceived outside that relationship. Thus the house, which has all the negative characteristics of the dark, nocturnal, female world, and is in this respect the equivalent of the tomb or the maiden, changes its definition when it becomes what it equally is, the place par excellence of cohabitation and of the marriage of contraries, which, like the wife, "the lamp of the inside", encloses its own light. When the roof has been put on a new house, it is the marriage lamp that is called upon to bring the first light. Each thing thus receives different properties according as it is apprehended in the state of union or the state of separation, but it is not possible to consider either of these states as its objective truth, with the other being regarded as an imperfect, mutilated form of that truth. Thus cultivated nature, the sacred of the left hand, the male-female, or male-dominated female, for example married woman or

ploughed land, is opposed not only to the male in general – united or separated – but also and especially to natural nature, which is still wild and
untamed – fallow land and the maiden – or has returned to the twisted,
maleficent naturalness into which it falls outside marriage – the harvested field
or the old witch, with the cunning and treachery which relate her to the
jackal.[50]

This opposition between a female-female and a male-female is attested in countless
ways. The female woman par excellence is the woman who does not depend on
any man, who has escaped from the authority of her parents, her husband, and her
husband's family, and has no children. Such a woman is without *hurma*: "she is bad
wood"; "she is twisted wood". She is akin to fallow land, the wilderness; she has
affinities with the dark forces of uncontrolled nature. Magic is her business (*thamgarth
thazemnith*, the old witch; *settuth*, the witch in the tales). A sterile woman must not
plant in the garden or carry seeds. Every woman partakes of the diabolic nature of
the female woman, especially during menstruation, when she must not prepare meals,
work in the garden, plant, pray, or fast (*elkhaleth*, the collective noun for
"womanhood" is also emptiness, the void, the desert, ruin). And conversely, the
unbridled, sterile old woman who no longer has any "restraint" brings the virtualities
inherent in every woman to their full realization. Like the young shoot which, left
to itself, tends to the left and has to be brought back to the right (or the upright)
at the cost of a "knot", "woman is a knot in the wood" (*thamṭṭuth diriz*). The "old
woman" is in league with all that is twisted (*a'waj*, to twist) and all that is warped
or warping: she is credited with *thi'iwji*, the maleficent, suspect craftiness which also
defines the *smith*; she specializes in the magic which uses the left hand, the cruel hand
(a "left-hander's blow" is a deadly blow), and turns *from right to left* (as opposed to
man, who uses the right hand, the hand used in swearing an oath, and turns from
left to right); she is adept in the art of slyly "twisting her gaze" (*abran walan*) away
from the person to whom she wishes to express her disapproval or annoyance (*abran*,
to turn from right to left, to make a slip of the tongue, to turn back to front, in short,
to turn in the wrong direction, is opposed to *geleb*, to turn one's back, to overturn,
as a discreet, furtive, passive movement, a female sidestepping, a "twisted" move,
a magical device, is to open, honest, straightforward, male aggression).[51]

The fundamental operators, uniting and separating, are the practical equivalents of filling and emptying (*plerosis* and *kenosis*): to marry is *'ammar*, to
be full. Through this, they can even be reduced to the fundamental
oppositions: to moisten and to dry, to feminize and to masculinize. This is
seen clearly in the significance assigned to everything symbolizing the union
of contraries. Thus the crossroads, which is opposed to the fork as the place
"where the paths meet" (*anidha itsamyagaran ibardhan*) to the place "where
the paths divide" (*anidha itsamfaraqen ibardhan*), is the point of convergence
of the four cardinal directions and of those who come and go in those
directions. As such, it is the symbol of fullness (*i'mar ubridh*, the path is
peopled, full), and, more precisely, of male fullness, which is opposed on the
one hand to the emptiness of the field and forest (*lakhla*) and on the other
hand to female fullness (*la'mara*), the village or the house.[52] A sterile woman,

or a girl who cannot find a husband, goes to a *crossroads*, a full place peopled by men, to bathe naked in the water from the tempering vat just before sunrise, that is, at the moment when the day is struggling with the night; and the water in which she has bathed is poured away at a crossroads regularly used by the flocks (a promise of fecundity).[53] The fearfulness of any operation reuniting contraries is particularly emphasized in the case of tempering (*asqi*, also meaning broth, sauce, and poisoning), which stands in the same relation to copulation as the crossroads – fullness in emptiness, male fullness – to the house: *sequi* is to unite the wet and the dry, in the action of sprinkling couscous with sauce: to unite the hot and the cold, fire and water, the dry and the wet, in tempering; to pour out burning (or burnt) water, poison. Tempering is a terrible act of violence allied with cunning, performed by a terrible being, the smith, whose ancestor, Sidi-Daoud, could hold red-hot iron in his bare hands and would punish tardy payers by offering them one of his products with an innocent air after first heating it white-hot.

Uniting and separating each entail the same sacrilegious violence, which breaks the natural order of things to impose on them the counter-natural order which defines culture. Witness the fact that the acts consisting of mixing or cutting, uniting or dividing, in fact fall to the same persons, all equally feared and despised – the smith, the butcher, and the corn-measurer.[54] It is almost always the smith who is appointed to perform all the sacrilegious, sacred acts of cutting, whether it be the slaughter of the sacrificial ox or circumcision (although he does not sit in the assembly, his opinion is always taken into account in matters of war or violence), and, if certain testimonies are to be believed, in some villages he is even entrusted with the inaugural ploughing. Conversely, in at least one village, the person charged with starting the ploughing, the last descendant of the man who found a piece of iron in the earth at the spot where lightning had struck, and made his ploughshare out of it, is responsible for all the acts of violence by fire and iron (circumcision, scarification, tatooing, etc.).[55] The reason for this is that in all such cases man's intervention, his very presence at the crossroads of the opposing forces which he must bring into contact in order to ensure the survival of the group, is a supremely dangerous operation. Just as a man cannot confront woman until assured of the magical protection given by circumcision, so the ploughman puts on a white woollen skull-cap and *arkasen*, leather sandals which must not enter the house, in order to avoid making himself the meeting-point of sky and earth and their antagonistic forces (whereas, to glean and clear the fields, the women, who partake of the terrestrial powers, go barefoot into the fields).[56]

The temporal distribution of tasks and rites, that is, the chronological structure of the agrarian year or of the cycle of life, is the product at once of the *diacritical intent* (separation) which orders by opposing, and the *synthetic intent* (union) which creates *passages* between the contraries by means of *rites* (of passage) which attain their full intensity when the union or separation of the antagonistic principles is effected by human agency. On the one hand, there is the fundamental opposition, always mentioned by informants, between the two "upbeats" structuring the year, *lyali*, "the nights", and *smaïm*, the dogdays, in which the properties of the wet season and the dry season are brought to their highest degree of intensity; on the other hand, there are the insensible, ever-threatened transitions between opposing principles, and the rites of passage of a particular kind which are intended to ensure that men and the elements respect "the order of time" (*chronou taxis*), that is, the order of the world: feminization of the male in autumn, with ploughing and sowing and the rain-making rites which accompany them, and masculinization of the female in spring, with the progressive separation of the grain and the earth which is completed with the harvest.

The primary reason why *lyali*, "the nights", is referred to by all informants, and always in relation to *smaïm*, is that the winter of winter and the summer of summer in a sense concentrate within themselves all the oppositions structuring the world and the agrarian year. The period of forty days which is believed to represent the time the seed sown in autumn takes to emerge is the prime example of the slack periods, during which nothing happens and all work is suspended, and which are marked by no major rite (expect a few prognostication rites).[57] The fecundated field, duly protected, like a woman, with a thorn fence (*zerb*), is the site of a mysterious, unpredictable toil which no outward sign betrays, and which resembles the cooking of wheat or beans in the pot or the work accomplished in woman's womb. This period is indeed the winter of winter, the night of night, when the boar mates, the moment when the natural world is given over to the female forces of fecundity – natural, wild forces which can never be said to be perfectly, finally domesticated.[58] The continuing assaults of winter, cold, and night serve to remind men of the hidden violence of the female nature. In the "quarrel between winter and man",[59] winter is presented as a woman (the name of the season, *chathwa*, being treated as a personified woman's name), and doubtless an *old woman*, the incarnation of the maleficent forces of death and destruction, disorder and division, who is forced to renounce her lust for violence and show more moderation and clemency when defeated in her struggle with man. This is a sort of origin myth emphasizing the fact that winter, like woman, is dual-natured: winter contains both the purely female woman, unadulterated, untamed, incarnated in the old woman, empty, dry, sterile woman, i.e. the female principle which old age reduces to its objective, purely negative truth;[60] but there is also the tamed, domesticated woman, woman fulfilled, i.e. fertility, the work of gestation and germination accomplished by nature when fecundated by man. It is within this logic that the famous "days of the old woman", and the other moments of transition and rupture, must be understood. The whole of nature – the earth with its buried seed, but also the womb – is the scene of a struggle similar to that between the cold and darkness of winter, an evil, sterile old woman, and the springtime forces of light with which man is in league. In all the legends of the borrowed days (*amerdil*, the loan), which are perhaps more than just a way of accounting for the unexpected return of bad weather, a being partaking of the nature of winter, usually an old woman (like Winter herself), a goat, or a Negro (the slave Ḥayan), sometimes even a jackal, the embodiment of natural disorder,[61] is sacrificed by winter, or, no doubt, sacrificed *to* winter, as a scapegoat. This is perhaps the price that has to be paid for the old witch Winter to agree to respect the *limits* assigned to her, as she does when she asks the following period to lend her a few days.

Smaïm, the dogdays, is to the dry season exactly what *lyali* is to the wet season: this slack period, which is opposed to *essaïf*, the harvest, just as within the wet season *lyali*, another slack period, is opposed to *lahlal*, ploughing, presents all the properties of the dry season. The dry, sterile kingdom of summer is entered in May, a month regarded as unpropitious for any act of procreation (hence for marriages).[62] The rites which mark the "first day of summer", also known as "the death of the land", and even more, the rites of the summer solstice, *in sla*, which occurs at the beginning of *smaïm*, make use of iron and fire, and instruments forged with fire – the ploughshare, the sickle, the carding-comb, and also the dagger (which cuts the throats of sacrificial animals and men's throats too) – instruments used to cut, chop, pierce, burn, or bleed (tattooing; preventive or curative scarification with a stick of oleander, a plant not used in the *azal* bouquet; piercing the little girls' ears; bleeding performed on the men and the animals, etc.).[63] The night of *in sla*, in the course of which sterile, purifying fires are lit in the house, in the midst of the flock, in the orchards, in the fields, by the hives, on the threshing-floor, etc., is given over to sterility; it is said that women cannot conceive then, and that children born on that day are themselves condemned to sterility (as are marriages celebrated then). The time of the dry is also the time for salt, for roast, spiced food, virile and virilizing, like the dried herbs used to make it, the time for wheatcake and oil, which is to summer food as butter is to winter food.[64] According to Destaing, the Beni Snous used to set an *upturned* cooking pot (a symbol of the blackness and wetness of winter) with its bottom coated with lime (blackness whitened) in the kitchen gardens (the place for female cultivation) at the time of *in sla*. *Smaïm* presents all the features of summer in their pure state, i.e. without admixture or attenuation: it is to the year what *azal* (the hottest time of the day) or, more exactly, the middle of *azal* (*thalmasth uzal*), is to the cycle of the day. Like *azal*, *smaïm*, the desert (*lakhla*) of the harvested fields, the time of iron and fire, violence and death (the time of the sword-edge, *semm*) is the male time par excellence.

Thresholds and rites of passage

The transitional periods have all the properties of the *threshold*, a sort of sacred boundary between two spaces, where the antagonistic principles confront one another and the world is reversed. The rites of these moments also obey the principle, already encountered, of the maximization of magical profit. They aim to ensure the concordance of the mythical calendar, which requires rain to come *at the right moment*, ploughing time, and the climatic calendar, with its whims and vagaries, by facilitating the passages, accompanying or if need be accelerating the passage from the dry to the wet in autumn or from the wet to the dry in spring, endeavouring at the same time to conserve for as long as possible the advantages of the declining season. This is obviously the case with all the autumn rites intended to aid the coming of rain: not only the ritual games, which are played in every season when rain is needed, such as *kura* (a ball game in which two teams, east and west, equipped with wooden sticks, try to push a ball, the *kura*, into the opposing camp), but also *thimechret*, the sacrifice of an ox (chosen for the rain-cloud colour (*azegzaw*) of its coat and evoking thunder by its lowing) and the inauguration of the ploughing (*awdjeb*), which insofar as it ritually mimes the fearful union of contraries, is in itself an invocation of rain. It is also true of the composition and preparation of the food consumed on ordinary and extraordinary occasions, which, practically treated as a ritual of *participation*, manifests the significance conferred on the transition from one season to another. The diet of autumn, generated in accordance with the scheme of soaking the dry, is made up of dry foods (cereals, dry vegetables, dried meat) which are *boiled in water*, *without spices*, in the cooking-pot, or (which amounts to the same thing) steamed, or raised with yeast. But autumn is also the point where the course of the world turns round and everything is turned over to enter its opposite, the male into the female, the seed into the womb of the earth, men and beasts into the house, light (with the lamp) into darkness, until the return of spring, which will set back on its feet a world turned upside down, momentarily abandoned to the supremacy of the female principle, the womb, woman, the house, and the darkness of night.[65]

Indeed, more so than autumn, which is dominated by the sharp break that ploughing marks, and by the logic of fecundation, interwoven with the ritual work of moistening the dry, spring is an interminable transition, constantly suspended and threatened, between the wet and the dry, beginning immediately after *lyali*; or, better, a struggle between two principles with unceasing reversals and changes in fortune. The rôle of mankind in this struggle, which resembles the battle fought out every morning between darkness and light, can only be that of anxious onlookers: hence perhaps, among other signs, the multitude of calendar terms almost all describing the state of the weather or the crops. In this time of waiting, when the fate of the seedlings depends on a female, ambiguous nature, and man cannot intervene without danger, the virtual cessation of activity reflects his limited control over the processes of germination and gestation; it falls to woman to play the part of a midwife and to offer nature a sort of ritual and technical assistance (hoeing, for example) in its labour.[66]

This time of rupture and separation has the same rôle in the cycle of the grain as that played in the cycle of life by the rites intended to ensure the progressive virilization of the growing boy (initially a female being), beginning at birth and always involving fire or instruments made with fire.[67] All the characteristic features of this difficult transition are in a sense concentrated in the series of *critical moments*, like *ḥusum* and *natah*, times of crisis when all the evil powers of winter seem to revive and to endanger growth and life one last time, or *nisan*, which though regarded as benignant is not exempt from threats – ambiguous periods which, even at their worst, contain the hope of the best and, even at their best, the threat of the worst. Everything takes place as if each of them bore within it the conflict which overshadows the whole season – and also the uncertainty about the future which causes these inaugural periods (especially *ḥusum* or the first day of spring) to be, like morning, times for the rites of prognostication and inaugural practices.

The ambiguity is in spring itself: springtime means growth and childhood, to be celebrated with *joy*, like the inaugural day of the season, but it also means the vulnerability and fragility of all beginnings. Spring is to summer as green and raw (*azegzaw*) and tender (*thalaqaqth*) things – the unripe corn or the baby, and green produce, the eating of which is seen as untimely destruction (*a'dham*) – are to full-grown, yellow (*iwraghen*), ripe, dry, hardened produce.[68] The women are logically charged with all the tasks involving the protection of things that grow and shoot, that are green and tender; it is the women's duty to watch over the growth of the young humans and animals, the morning of life. As well as hoeing, the women's work includes gathering herbs and vegetables in the garden, looking after the cow, milking it, and making butter, a female product which is opposed to oil as the inside and the wet to the outside and the dry.

The precise locus of the threshold, where the order of things turns upside down (*aqlab*), "like a wheatcake in the pan", is explicitly marked by the "return of *azall*" (*tharurith wazal*), the point of division between the wet season and the dry season, where the year tips over: the rhythm of the working day – defined by the moment when the flock goes out – changes, and with it the group's whole existence. The *fire is brought out* and the *kanun* is set up in the courtyard. The flock with its shepherd, the housewife busy with the tasks of milking and treating the milk, bring into the rites new elements partaking more of the dry than of the wet. The flock ceases to be fed on tender green plants from the cultivated fields and goes and grazes instead on wild, dry plants. The herbs, flowers, and branches that the shepherd brings back with him on his first return at the hour of *azal*, which go to make up the bouquet, called *azal*, that is ritually placed above the threshold (fern, cytisis, bramble, thyme, lentisk, male fig-tree branches, asparagus, elm, thapsia, myrtle, tamarind, heather, broom – in short, "everything the wind shakes in the countryside") are the wild products of fallow land (and not the product, even parasitically, of cultivated land, like the plants gathered by the women while hoeing). The change in food is even clearer: the special dishes of *tharurith wazal* give a prominent place to milk, as in the previous period, but it is now eaten in cooked or boiled form.

Reunion of contraries and denial

The times of separation, when the opposing principles may be said to exist in their pure state, as in summer, or to threaten, in the case of winter, to return to it, and the times of reunion, when the dry returns to the wet, as in autumn, or the wet returns to the dry, as in spring, are moments opposed to one another; but they are also opposed in a different way, as moments in which reunion and separation are accomplished without any more than symbolic participation on the part of man, to the times when reunion and separation take on a critical form because it falls to man himself to bring them about. It is precisely here that the structure of ritual practice is articulated with the structure of farming activity: the opposition between the propitiatory rites of the transitional periods and the sanctioning rites which are obligatory for the whole group and above all for the men, during the periods of human intervention in nature, harvesting and ploughing, appears in fact as the retranslation into the specific logic of ritual of the opposition – structuring the agrarian year – between the time of work and the much longer time of production, during which the grain – like the pottery set out to dry – undergoes a purely natural process of transformation. The high moments in the agrarian year, those which Marx designates *working periods*, are marked by rites contrasting in their gravity, solemnity, and imperative character with the rites of the *production periods*, whose sole function is to lend magical assistance to *nature in its labour* (see fig. 3).[69]

The rites which accompany ploughing or marriage have the function of disguising and thereby sanctioning the inevitable collision of two contrary principles that the peasant brings about in forcing nature, doing it violence and violation, as he must, with ploughshare and knife, sickle and loom – instruments fearful in themselves, being the work of the smith, the master of fire. The aim is to transform into intentionally performed, and hence judiciously euphemized, ritual acts the objectively sacrilegious acts of separating, cutting, and dividing things which nature (i.e. the taxonomy) has united (when reaping, cutting the yarn after weaving, or cutting the throat of the sacrificial ox);[70] or to reunite – in tempering, marriage, or ploughing – things which nature (i.e. the taxonomy) has put asunder. When objectively sacrilegious acts cannot be delegated to an inferior being, a sacrificer and scapegoat whose rôle is to "take away ill fortune"[71] (like the slaughter of the ox in the collective sacrifices, which is entrusted to the smith or a Negro, and tempering, the task of the smith, a man both feared and respected) but must be shouldered by those who undertake and benefit from them (like the defloration of the bride, turning the first furrow, cutting the last thread in weaving, harvesting the last sheaf), they are transfigured by a collective *mise en scène* intended to impose on them a collectively proclaimed symbolic value which is the exact opposite of their socially recognized, and hence no less objective, truth. The whole truth of magic and collective belief is contained in this game of twofold objective truth, a double game played with truth, through which the group, the source of all objectivity, in a sense lies to itself, producing a truth whose sole meaning and function are to deny a truth known and recognized by all, a lie which would deceive no one, were not everyone determined to deceive *himself*.

In the case of the harvest, the social truth to be collectively denied is an unambiguous one: the harvest (*thamegra*) is a murder (*thamgert*, the throat, violent death, revenge; *amgar*, sickle), in which the earth, fecundated by ploughing, is stripped of the produce it has brought to maturity.

The ritual of the last sheaf, of which we have countless descriptions – no doubt because attention was drawn to it by Frazer's analyses[72] – and hence almost as many variants, always consists essentially in symbolically denying the inevitable murder of the field, or of the source of its fecundity, the "spirit of the corn" of "spirit of the field", by transforming it into a sacrifice conducive to resurrection. From the names given to the last sheaf, it seems that the "spirit of the field" whose perpetuation is to be affirmed is practically identified, depending on the variant, either with an *animal* (informants speak of "the mane of the field" and "the tail of the field") or with a bride, *thislith*, destined to die after having borne her fruit (informants speak of "the curl of the field" and "the plait of the field"). To these different representations

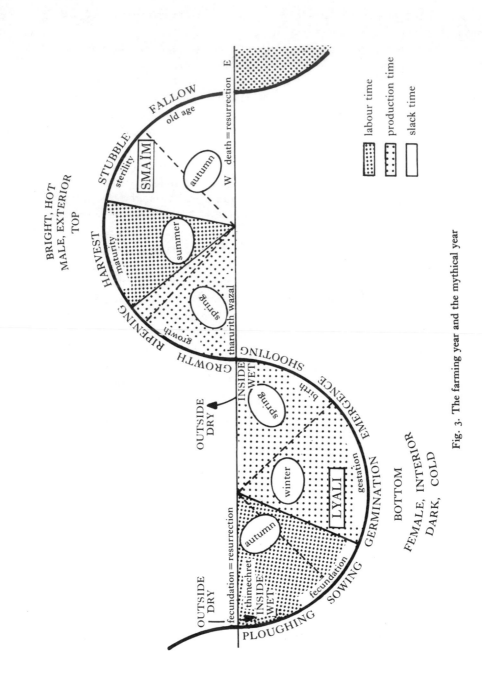

Fig. 3. The farming year and the mythical year

BRIGHT, HOT
MALE, EXTERIOR
TOP

FALLOW
old age
STUBBLE
SMAÏM
sterility
autumn
HARVEST
maturity
summer
RIPENING
growth
spring
GROWTH
tharurith wazal
SHOOTING

W death = resurrection E

OUTSIDE
DRY

INSIDE
WET
spring
EMERGENCE
birth
GERMINATION
gestation
LYALI
winter
SOWING
fecundation
PLOUGHING
autumn
thimechret
INSIDE
WET
fecundation = resurrection
OUTSIDE
DRY

BOTTOM
FEMALE, INTERIOR
DARK, COLD

labour time
production time
slack time

correspond different rituals: in some villages it is held to be a sin to reap the last sheaf, which is left standing in the middle of the field for the poor, the oxen, or the birds; in other villages, it is mown (or uprooted by hand to avoid contact with the sickle), but always in accordance with a special ritual. The ritual murder of the field may be enacted in the sacrifice of an animal which is both its embodiment and its substitute.[73] It may also be performed on the last sheaf itself, treated like a sacrificial animal: in one tradition (observed in central Kabylia by Jean Servier), the master of the field turns to face the east, lays the last sheaf on the ground with its "head" towards the east, as if it were an ox, and simulates cutting its throat, letting a handful of soil trickle from his left hand in the middle of the wound to represent bleeding. Finally, in the Soummam region, the last sheaf may be treated as if it were a dead man and be buried in an eastward-facing grave to the accompaniment of prayers (*chahada*) and chants announcing its resurrection (e.g. "Die, die, O field, our master can bring you back to life!"). Even when what seems to be the original form of the ritual has disappeared (as it has in Great Kabylia), it is still the master of the field who reaps the last sheaf and brings it back to the house, where it is hung from the main beam. Resurrection can come only through repetition of the primal marriage of sky and earth: and for this reason the harvest rites reapply the logic of the rain-making rites at a time when rain is not required for its specifically technical function (which is never autonomized) and can only serve the purpose of revivifying the sacred strength of the corn or the field. Thus the whole apparatus of the rain-making rites reappears, with the characters (Anzar and his wife Ghonja, he representing rain and the sky, and she the young virgin soil, the bride, etc.) and the objects (dolls, banners) which figure in it. Sometimes one even finds the marriage by abduction of the hoeing games.

The ploughing ceremony, another ritual intended to sanction the union of contraries, cannot be fully understood unless one knows that the period following the harvest, with its rites to ensure the perpetuation of the fecundating principle, is a *time of separation*, devoted to the manly virtues, the point of honour and combats.[74] *Lakhrif*, an *extra-ordinary* period of plenty and rest, which cannot be defined either as a labour period, like ploughing and harvesting, or as a production period, like winter and spring, is the male time par excellence, when the group opens up to the outside world and must confront *outsiders*, in feasts and in war, so as to knit alliances which, like extra-ordinary marriages, are far from excluding challenge. Like the grain set aside as seed corn, which will be kept in a state of separation, the young boy is symbolically torn from the female world by circumcision, a ceremony from which women are rigorously excluded, the function of which is to co-opt the boy into the world of men by means of an operation regarded as a second birth, a purely male event this time, one which, as the saying goes, "makes men". In one variant of the ritual, the newly circumcised boys are surrounded by two or three concentric circles of men seated on ploughshares with their rifles in their hands.[75] The land itself is divested of every trace of life as the trees are stripped, the last fruit picked, and any remaining vegetation uprooted from the fields and gardens. The state of separation ends, for the natural world, with *awdjeb*, the solemn inauguration of the ploughing, which celebrates the marriage of the sky and the earth, the ploughshare and the furrow, by the collective enactment of a whole range of mimetic practices, including human marriage.

The return to the ordinary order is also marked by the reassertion of the primacy of the strengthening of kin-group unity over the pursuit of distant alliances, with *thimechret*, the sacrifice of an ox at the door of the year; its throat is cut, its blood is sprinkled on the ground, calling down rain, and the consecrated meat is shared out among all members of the community. This sacrifice, intended to sanction the imposition of the human order on fecund but wild nature (symbolized by the jackal, "who has no house" and feeds on raw flesh – *azegzaw* – and blood), is a meal of alliance. In solemnly reaffirming the bonds of real or official blood kinship which unite all living members of the *adhrum* (*thaymats*) in and through the original community (*thadjadith*), that is, the relation to common ancestors, the source of all fecundity, this act of sacred commensality proclaims the specifically human (i.e. male) order of the oath of loyalty, against nostalgia for the struggle of all against all, again embodied in the jackal (or woman, the source of division) and his sacrilegious cunning (*thahraymith*). Like the natural world, within whose domesticated fertility lie the only half-tamed forces of a wild nature (those embodied and exploited by the old witch), the social order sprung from the oath which tears the assembly of men from the disorder of individual interests remains haunted by consciously repressed nostalgia for the state of nature.

This philosophy of history, implicit in the whole ritual calendar, is expressed in a tale: "The animals once met together in an *assembly* and *swore* not to prey on one another any longer, and to live on earth in peace. They chose the lion to be their king...devised laws, and defined sanctions...The animals lived in peace...Life would have been fine if Jackal, the lion's counsellor, had not ruined everything. He was an old hand at every sort of *treachery*...and he regretted the former state of affairs; the smell of *fresh meat and warm blood*, which were now forbidden, used to send him into a frenzy...He decided to resort to *guile* (*thahraymith*) and secretly to incite the courtiers to disobey, one after another – the work of a demon."[76] In the same tale, the jackal eats the animals he is supposed to bury. He has the task of fetching water. Another feature he shares with woman is that he is *twisted*: "they put a jackal's tail down a rifle barrel for forty days, and when they took it out again, it was just as before." Moreover, like woman, he *divides*, and does so by his cunning.

Rite must resolve by means of an operation socially approved and collectively assumed – that is, in accordance with the logic of the taxonomy that gives rise to it – the specific contradiction which the primal dichotomy makes inevitable in constituting as separate and antagonistic principles that must be reunited in order to ensure the reproduction of the group. By a practical denial, not an individual, asocial one like that described by Freud, but a collective, public denial (as in all belief), rite neutralizes the dangerous forces contained in the wild, untamed, natural nature of woman or the earth, as well as those that may be unleashed by violation of its *haram*, transgression of the sacred limit.[77] Enacted in this way, collectively and publicly, through the inter-mediary of an authorized delegate, in accordance with the arbitrarily pre-scribed rules of a ritual, sacrilege is symbolically denied in the very act in which it is performed. Acting as a delegated representative of the group, and also as a scapegoat designated to confront the curse of the earth, the man to whom it falls to open the ploughing, "the man of the wedding"[78] as he is sometimes known, solemnly reproduces, with his ploughshare born of a thunderbolt, the marriage of sky and earth, the archetypal fecundation which is the condition of the success of all human acts of fecundation.[79] Male and female, wet and dry, are in a sense separated only so as to be reunited, since only their union – in ploughing or marriage – can free them from the negative properties (negative only in the respect in question, that of fecundity) that are associated with them so long as they remain in the *odd-numbered, imperfect* state of separateness.[80] The ploughshare, an instrument which is forged in another reunion of contraries, the *tempering* of iron, and has the same name as the thunderbolt, *thagursa*, is in itself dry and sterile, like the seed it introduces into the earth: it is a source of fertility only through the violence it inflicts. As for the earth, left to itself it returns to sterility or the wild fecundity of fallow land, which, twisted and malignant like the maiden, cannot produce all its benefits unless it is forced and violated, and also raised and straightened.

The rites of ploughing owe their complexity to the fact that they must not only sanction the union of opposites but also facilitate that state of the union of contraries in which *supremacy* temporarily passes to the female principle: the seed temporarily condemned to dryness and sterility returns to life only through immersion in female wetness;[81] but the future of the grain (for the earth, like the ewe, may fail to bring forth – *thamazgults*, from *zgel*, to misfire) depends on female powers which the act of fecundation has had to force. The "door of the year" is not the moment when the year begins (it has no beginning, being an everlasting beginning anew); it is the moment when, like the house, which must remain open to the fecundating light of the sun, the year opens up to the male principle which fecundates and fills it. Ploughing and sowing mark the culmination of the movement of the outside into the inside, the empty into the full, the dry into the wet, sunlight into earthly shadows, the fecundating male into the fertile female.

Marriage rites and ploughing rites owe their numerous similarities to the fact that their *objective intention* is to sanction the union of contraries which is the condition of the resurrection of the grain and the reproduction of the group. This dialectic of death and resurrection is expressed in the saying (often used nowadays in another sense when speaking of generation conflicts): "From life they draw death, from death they draw life" (a scheme which reappears in the riddle: "Something dead out of something living" – an egg. "Something living out of something dead" – a chick). The sacrifice and collective eating of the ox is a mimetic representation of the cycle of the grain, which must die so as to feed the whole community, and whose resurrection is symbolized by the solemn meal bringing together the whole community in a recalling of the dead. As is shown by the status of the outsider, the man who cannot "cite" any ascendant and will not be "cited" by any descendant (*asker*, to cite and also to resurrect) the group membership that is affirmed by gathering together in commensality implies the power to recall ascendants and the certainty of being recalled by descendants. The return of the dead, that is, resurrection, is called for by every aspect of symbolism, particularly that of cooking: thus the broad bean, the male, dry seed par excellence, akin to the bones, the refuge of the soul waiting for resurrection, is served in the couscous offered to the dead at the start the ploughing (and also on the eve of feast days, especially the eve of *Achura*); it is one of the articles thrown into the first furrow; it is used in the boiled dishes always served on such occasions: an almost transparent symbol of the dead ("I put a bean in the ground", runs a riddle, "and it didn't come up" – a dead man), whose food it is ("I saw the dead nibbling beans" – I almost died), it is predisposed to carry the symbolism of death and resurrection as a desiccated seed which, after ritual burial in the damp womb of nature, swells and comes up again, more numerous, in spring (when it is the first sign of plant life to appear).[82]

As acts of procreation, that is, of re-creation, marriage and ploughing are both conceived of as male acts of opening and sowing destined to produce a female action of swelling, and it is logical that ritual enactment should mobilize on the one hand everything that opens (keys, nails), everything that is open (untied hair and girdles, trailing garments), everything that is sweet, soft, and white (sugar, honey, dates, milk), and on the other hand everything that swells and rises (pancakes, fritters, seeds which swell while cooking – *ufthyen*), everything that is multiple and tightly packed (grains of *seksu*, couscous, or *berkukes*, coarse couscous, pomegranate seeds, fig seeds), everything that is full (eggs, nuts, almonds, pomegranates, figs), the most effective objects and actions being those which compound the various properties.[83] Such are the egg, the symbol par excellence of that which is full and pregnant with life, or the pomegranate, which is at once full, swollen, and multiple, and of which one riddle says, "Granary upon granary, the corn inside is red", and another: "No bigger than a pounding-stone, and its children are more than a hundred." And a whole aspect of the multi-functional action performed in ploughing and marriage is summed up in the ploughman's gesture of breaking (*felleq*, to burst, split, deflower) a pomegranate or an egg on his ploughshare.

The first time the yoke of oxen, the plough, and the seed corn set out for the fields and the moment of the bride's arrival in her new house are marked by the same rites. The girl is welcomed on the threshold by the "old woman" who holds the "sieve of the traditions", containing fritters, eggs, wheat, beans, dates, nuts, dried figs, pomegranates, etc. The bride breaks the eggs on the head of the mule that bears her, wipes her hands on its mane, and throws the sieve behind her, and the children who have followed her scramble (number = abundance) to pick up the titbits it contained. Similarly, the "ploughing sieve" which, depending on the local traditions, may be carried by various persons (the ploughman, his wife) at various times (in the morning, when the ploughman leaves the house, or on his arrival in the fields, when he yokes the oxen, or at the time of the midday meal), always contains pancakes, dried beans, wheat, and a pomegranate, which the ploughman throws into the furrows over the oxen and the plough, and which the children scramble for (with countless variants, such as these: the ploughman breaks two pomegramates, a few wheatcakes, and some fritters on the ploughshare, and distributes the rest among those present; the offerings are buried in the first furrow). Endless examples could be given of features common to the two rituals: the bride (and her procession) are sprinkled with milk and she herself often sprinkles water and milk as she enters her new house, just as the mistress of the house sprinkles the plough with water or milk as it leaves for the fields. The bride is presented with a key with which she strikes the lintel of the door (elsewhere a key is put under her clothes as she is being dressed); a key is put in the bag of seed corn and sometimes thrown into the furrow. The bridal procession is preceded by a woman bearing a lamp (*mesbaḥ*) which represents sexual union, with the clay, the oil and the flame of which it is composed symbolizing the constituent parts of the human being – the body, the damp, female, vegetative soul, *nefs* (a word sometimes used as a euphemism for the genitals, the seat of the "bad instincts" – *thinefsith*) and the dry, male, subtle soul, *ruḥ* (a euphemism for the penis);[84] and on the first day of ploughing, a lamp is taken to the fields and kept alight until the first delimited plot of land (*thamtirth*) has been sown. The bride must not wear a girdle for seven days, and on the seventh day her girdle must be tied by the mother of many sons; the woman who carries the seed corn must avoid tying her girdle too tight and she must also wear a long dress which trails behind in a lucky *train* (*abru'*). The bride's hair must remain untied for the first seven days; the woman who carries the seed corn always lets her hair hang loose. Also common to both rituals are: rifle shots (in even numbers), stone-throwing, and target-shooting, all of which frequently figure in the rain-making rites as symbols of male sprinkling which have the power of *untying* that which is tied.[85] The bride's life continues in this way under the sign of fertility: on the seventh day, when she comes out of the house to go to the fountain for the first time, before drawing water she throws into the spring the grains of corn and the beans which had been placed under her bed; the first work she does is to sift the wheat, the noble task par excellence.

Making use of indeterminacy

The propitiatory *mise-en-scène* through which ritual action aims at creating
the conditions favourable to the success of the miracle of the resurrection of
the grain by reproducing it symbolically presents a certain number of
ambiguities which appear, for example, when one considers the ritual of the
last sheaf. In some places the last sheaf is "treated practically"[86] as a female
personification of the field ("the strength of the earth", "the bride"), on whom
male rain, sometimes personified as Anzar,[87] is called down; in others it is
a male (phallic) symbol of "the spirit of the corn", destined to return for a
while to dryness and sterility before inaugurating a new cycle of life by
pouring down in rain onto the parched earth. The same ambiguities reappear
in the ploughing ritual, although at first sight the acts tending to favour the
world's return to wetness (and in particular the rites specifically intended to
provoke rain, which are performed in identical form in spring) can be
combined quite logically with the actions intended to favour the act of
fecundation, ploughing or marriage, as the immersion of the dry in the wet,
celestial seed in the fertile earth. In the presence of rain, dry water, which
through its heavenly origin partakes of solar maleness, while on the other hand
it partakes of wet, terrestrial femininity, the system of classification hesitates.
The same is true of tears, urine, and blood, much used in the homoeopathic
strategies of the rain-making rites, and also semen, which gives new life to
woman as rain does to the earth, and of which it may be said indifferently
either that it swells or that it makes swell, like beans or wheat in the cooking
pot.[88] Hence the hesitations of magical practice, which, far from being
troubled by these ambiguities, takes advantage of them.[89] After systematically
cataloguing the multiple variants of the rain-making rites, Laoust (the only
anthropologist to have seen the contradiction clearly) infers the female nature
of *thislith*, the betrothed (or *thlonja*, the ladle), a doll made out of a ladle
dressed like a bride, which is taken round in a procession while rain is called
down. The meticulousness and rigour of his inventory provide us with the
means of grasping the properties which make of the "doll" of the rain-making
rites, hoeing rites (it is "Mata" whose abduction is simulated), and harvest
rites a being which is unclassifiable from the point of view of the very system
of classification of which its properties are the product. First, there is a name,
thislith, which may well be no more than a euphemism to denote a phallic
symbol, and which, by encouraging the "female" reading, orients the ritual
actions, since being male it sprinkles and being female it is sprinkled. Then
there is a shape, an ambiguous one for the taxonomy itself, since the ladle
can be treated as a hollow, liquid-filled object which sprinkles, or as a hollow,

empty object asking to be sprinkled. Finally, there is a function, that of the ladle itself, an implement made to sprinkle or to serve from the (female) cooking-pot.

Here is a series of scattered, contradictory observations, which were collected in the hope of removing the ambiguity of the ladle but only serve to confirm it. (1) On her wedding day the bride plunges the ladle into the pot: she will bear as many sons as she brings up pieces of meat. (2) A proverb: "Whatever there is in the cooking-pot, the ladle will bring it up." (3) The ladle is hung on a piece of string so that it balances evenly, in front of a piece of wheatcake; if it dips towards the wheatcake, the hoped-for event will occur. (4) Of a man who cannot do anything with his hands: "He's like the ladle." (5) You must never hit anyone with a ladle: either the implement would break (there is only one in the house) or the person struck would break. (6) A man must never eat out of the ladle (to taste the soup, as the women do): the consequence would be storms and rain when he marries. (7) If a man scrapes the bottom of the pot with the ladle, it is bound to rain on his wedding day. (8) To someone using a tool clumsily: "Would you have eaten with the ladle?" – if one eats with the ladle one is liable to be cheated. This sort of taxonomic hesitation is not uncommon: it can be found in relation to moonlight (*tiziri*), the unlooked-for light, or embers (*times*, a word which is taboo in the presence of men and is replaced by euphemisms), a female fire which consumes and is consumed, like passion (*thinefsith*, a diminutive of *nefs* which we have already encountered), under the ashes, a crafty, treacherous fire which suggests female sexuality (as opposed to the flame, *ahajuju*, which purifies and sets alight); or even in relation to clearly attributed objects like the egg, the symbol par excellence of female fertility, which also partakes of the male through its colour (white) and its name (*thamellalts*, plural *thimellalin*, egg; *imellalen*, the white (masculine plural), the testicles of the adult; *thimellalin*, the white (feminine plural), eggs, the child's testicles). But, because the fundamental schemes are roughly congruent, the divergences never run, as they do here, into contradiction.

The uncertainty of usage duplicates the uncertainty of significance: because the ritual use that can be made of an object depends on the meanings it is given by the taxonomy, it is not surprising that when agents are dealing, as they are here, with objects whose properties are a challenge to the system of classification, they should put them to uses quite incompatible with some of the meanings that they could have outside that relationship (especially in situations like drought, when the urgency of practical necessity requires agents to relax the demands of logic even further and to make use of anything that will serve). And because the meaning of a symbol is only ever fully determined in and through the actions it effects or undergoes (the raven, for example, being less ominous when it flies from west to east), the uncertainties of the interpretation simply reflect the uncertainties of the use that the agents themselves may make of a symbol so overdetermined as to be indeterminate even from the point of view of the schemes which determine it (the error in this case lying in wanting to impose decision on the undecidable, in decreeing male or female a symbol which different practices treat indifferently as dry or wet, fecundating or fecundable). The cultural artefact, *thislith* thought and fashioned for the specifically cultural needs of rite, is thus endowed with the *plurality of aspects* (different or even contradictory ones) which the objects of the world possess until the cultural system of classifications frees them from it through the arbitrary selection which it effects.

With this example we draw near the principle of practical logic, which functions practically only by taking all sorts of liberties with the most elementary principles of logical logic: thus the same symbol can relate to realities that are opposed even from the standpoint of the axiomatics of the system – or rather, we must include in that axiomatics the fact that the system does not exclude contradiction. If being able to write out the algebra of practical logics is not *a priori* unthinkable, it can be seen that the precondition of doing so would be the knowledge that logical logic, which only ever speaks of them *negatively* in the very operations through which it constitutes itself by denying them, is not prepared to describe them without destroying them. It would simply be a question of constructing the model of this *partially integrated* system of generative schemes which, *partially mobilized* to deal with each particular situation, in each case produces, without acceding to discourse and the logical verifiablity which it makes possible, a practical "definition" of the situation and of the functions of the action – almost always multiple and overlapping – and, in accordance with a combinative logic at once complex and inexhaustible, generates the appropriate actions to fulfil these functions given the means available. More precisely, one only has to compare the diagrams corresponding to the different domains of practice – the agrarian year, cooking, the women's work, the day – to see that these different series spring from different schemes: the oppositions between the wet and the dry, the cold and the hot, and the full and the empty, in the case of the agrarian year; between the wet and the dry (in the form of the boiled and the roast, two forms of the cooked), the bland and the spiced, in the case of cooking; between the dark and the light, the cold and the hot, the inside (or the closed) and the outside in the case of the day; between the female and the male, the tender (green) and the hard (dry), in the case of the cycle of life. Then one would only have to add other structured universes, such as the space inside the house or the parts of body, to see other principles at work: above and below, east and west, etc. These different schemes are at once partially independent and more or less closely interconnected: thus the opposition dry/wet (or drying/soaking) can be used to generate practices or symbols that cannot be produced directly from the opposition inside/outside or darkness/light, and vice versa; on the other hand, there is a direct passage from hot/cold to dry/wet, whereas hot/cold is connected with inside/outside only through the intermediary of light/darkness, and the path to oppositions like standing up/lying down, empty/full, or above/below is even longer. In other words, each of the oppositions constituting the system can be linked with all the others, but along paths of varying length (which may or may not be reversible), i.e. at the end of a series of equivalences which progressively empty the relationship of its content (e.g. waking/sleeping ∼ outside/inside ∼ standing up/lying down ∼ east/west ∼ light/darkness ∼ hot/cold ∼ spiced/bland); moreover, each opposition can be linked with several others in different respects by relations of differing intensity and meaning (e.g. spiced/bland can be directly related to male/female and less directly to strong/weak or empty/full, through the intermediary, in the latter case, of male/female and dry/wet, themselves interconnected). It follows that all the oppositions do not have the same rôle in the system; it is possible to distinguish secondary oppositions which specify the principal oppositions in a particular respect and have a low yield on account of this (yellow/green, a simple specification of dry/wet), and central oppositions (such as male/female or dry/wet) strongly interconnected with all the others by logically very diverse relations which constitute arbitrary cultural necessity (e.g. the relations between female/male and inside/outside or left/right, twisted/straight, below/above). Given that, in practice, no more than one particular sector of the system of schemes is mobilized at any one time (without all the connections with the other oppositions ever being entirely severed) and that the different schemes mobilized in different situations are partially autonomous and partially linked with all the others, it is natural that all the products of the application of these schemes, both individual rites and series of ritual actions such as the rites of passage, should be partially congruent and should appear as roughly, that is practically, equivalent to anyone possessing practical mastery of the system of schemes.[90]

The habitus and homologies

The presence of symbolically identical objects or acts in the rituals associated with such different events in the existence of man and the land as funerals, ploughing, harvesting, circumcision, or marriage cannot and need not be explained in any other way. The partial coincidence of the significations which the practical taxonomies confer on these events is matched by the partial coincidence of the ritual acts and symbols, whose polysemy is perfectly appropriate to the requirements of essentially "multi-functional" practices. An agent does not need symbolic mastery of the concepts of *swelling* (or *durable swelling*) and *resurrection* to associate the dish called *ufthyen*, a mixture of wheat and beans which swells when boiled, with the ceremonies of marriage, ploughing, or burial, through the intermediary of what is there subordinate to the "resurrection" function; or to rule out eating this dish ("because the gum would stay swollen") when teeth are being cut (in favour of *thibu'jajin*, a sort of pancake which as it cooks forms bubbles which burst at once) and on the occasion of circumcision, which as a rite of purification and virilization, that is to say, of breaking with the female world, is seen syncretically as associated with the dry, fire, and violence, gives a prominent place to target-shooting, and is accompanied by roast meat. But this does not prevent the dish being associated with target-shooting in at least one variant of the ritual of a multi-functional ceremony like marriage, in which "intentions" of virilization (opening) and fertilization (swelling) are combined.

Application of the same schemes in fields as different as the "calendars" of cooking or of the women's tasks, the series of moments in the day or the cycle of life, is the principle underlying the homologies which analysis discovers in practices and works. Thus, to explain the essential features of the series of ordinary and extraordinary dishes which, on account of the participation-rite function conferred on eating,[91] are associated with the different periods of the agrarian year (see fig. 4) one only has to go to the opposition between two classes of food and two classes of operations: on one side there are the dry foods (cereals (wheat and barley), dried vegetables (beans, peas, chick peas, lentils, etc.), dried meat) which are *boiled in water*, *unspiced*, in the *cooking-pot*, indoors, or (which amounts to the same thing)

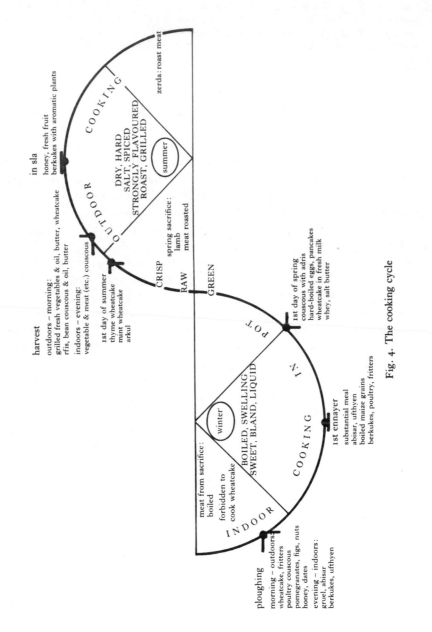

harvest

outdoors – morning:
grilled fresh vegetables & oil, butter, wheatcake
rfis, bean couscous & oil, butter
indoors – evening:
vegetable & meat (etc.) couscous

in sla
honey, fresh fruit
berkukes with aromatic plants

1st day of summer
thyme wheatcake
mint wheatcake
arkul

COOKING

OUTDOOR

DRY, HARD
SALT, SPICED
STRONGLY FLAVOURED
ROAST, GRILLED

summer

zerda: roast meat

CRISP

RAW

GREEN

spring sacrifice:
lamb
meat roasted

1st day of spring
couscous with adris
hard-boiled eggs, pancakes
wheatcake in fresh milk
whey, salt butter

POT

BOILED, SWELLING
SWEET, BLAND, LIQUID

winter

COOKING IN

1st ennayer
substantial meal
abisar, ufthyen
boiled maize grains
berkukes, poultry, fritters

meat from sacrifice:
boiled
forbidden to
cook wheatcake

INDOOR

ploughing

morning – outdoors:
wheatcake, fritters
poultry couscous
pomegranates, figs, nuts
honey, dates
evening – indoors:
gruel, abisar
berkukes, ufthyen

Fig. 4. The cooking cycle

steamed, or raised with leaven (fritters), operations which all make the food *swell*; and on the other side there are the raw, green, or fresh foods (three meanings of the word *azegzaw*, associated with spring and unripe corn) which are eaten *raw* (as tends to be the case in spring) and/or *boiled* or *grilled* (on the griddle, *bufraḥ*) and heavily spiced (as in summer).[92] And the variations observed are fully accounted for when one has noted that the first combination is characteristic of late autumn and winter, the period when the dry is moistened and the fertilized earth and woman are expected to swell, whereas the second is associated with spring, a transitional season, and summer, the period of desiccation of the wet and separation from the female, when everything that has developed inwardly, like grains of wheat and beans (*ufthyen*) must open out and ripen in the light of day.[93]

Without entering into a description – strictly speaking, an interminable one, owing to the innumerable variants – of the feast-day dishes which in a sense concentrate the characteristic properties of the cooking associated with the various periods, it is nonetheless possible briefly to indicate their pertinent features, bearing in mind that the dishes differ not so much in their ingredients as in the processes applied to them, which strictly define cooking (so that certain "polysemous" items reappear at different times of the year and in very different rites: for example wheat, of course, but also broad beans, which figure in the meals of ploughing time, the first day of January, harvest time, funerals, etc.). On ploughing days, the meal eaten outside in the fields is, as always, more male, i.e. "drier", than the food of autumn and winter as a whole, which is *boiled* or steamed, like the food eaten at the time of weddings or burials; but the meal taken in the evening after the first day's ploughing always consists of boiled cereals, with numerous variants, or a coarse-grained, unspiced couscous, a dish explicitly excluded from the meal of the first day of spring ("because the ants would multiply like the grains of semolina") or *ufthyen*, made from grains of wheat and beans cooked in water or steam, or *abisar*, a sort of thick bean purée, the food of the dead and of resurrection (these dishes are always associated with many-seeded fruit, pomegranates, figs, grapes, nuts, or sweet foods, honey, dates, etc., symbols of "easiness"). Wheatcake, the dry, male food par excellence, must not be cooked during the first three days of ploughing; it is even said that if roast meat were eaten (the meat of the *thimechret* ox is eaten boiled), the oxen would before long be injured in the neck. The couscous (*berkukes*) eaten on the first day of *ennayer* contains poultry, typically female (among other reasons because the fowl are the women's personal property). But it is no doubt on the eve of this day (sometimes called the "old women" of *ennayer*) that the scheme generating winter food, that of moistening the dry, shows through most clearly: on that day, people must eat nothing but boiled, dry grains (sometimes with fritters), and must eat their fill; they must not eat meat ("so as not to break the bones") or dates ("so as not to expose the stones"). The meal eaten on the first day of *ennayer* (*Achura*) is very similar to that of the first day of ploughing: it is always substantial (being an inaugural rite) and consists of *abisar* or *berkukes* and fritters, or boiled cereal. From the first day of spring, as well as the traditional elements of fertility-giving food (couscous cooked in the steam of *adhris*, thapsia, which causes swelling, hard-boiled eggs, which must be eaten to satiety), the diet includes grilled cereals (which the children eat *outdoors*), raw, green produce (beans and other vegetables) and milk (warmed or cooked). With the return of *azal*, dry pancakes dipped in hot milk, and semolina with butter, announce the dry, male food of summer. The combination characterizing the feast-day meals of the dry season is wheatcake and grilled meat with or without couscous (depending mainly on whether it is eaten in the fields or in the house); more ordinary meals consist of wheatcake dipped in *oil* (a dry, male food contrasting with wet, female butter) and dried figs and also, for indoor meals, grilled fresh vegetables.

The same structure reappears in the "calendar" of the women's work, which complements the farming "calendar" to which it is directly subordinated (see fig. 5). The action homologous with marriage and ploughing, the assembly of the loom, whose two uprights and two beams – called the "sky beam" and the "earth beam", or the east beam and west beam – delimit the weaving just as the furrow delimits the field, takes place in autumn ("the figs and blackberries are ripe, and we have no blankets"): passers-by are offered figs, dates, and almonds, and a meal of moist, swelling food (*tighrifin*, fritters) is eaten.[94] Like ploughing, weaving is a marriage of sky and earth, and the cloth is the product of a birth: *thanslith*, the triangular motif with which weaving starts, is a symbol of fecundity (from the root NSL, to begin, to engender); unmarried girls must not sit astride the thread, married women may; the crossing of the thread is called *ruh*, the soul.[95] Weaving is the winter activity, which ends with the wet season, in May. Just as the last sheaf is often cut by hand, by the master of the field, so it falls to the mistress of the house to unfasten the woven cloth, without the use of iron and after sprinkling it with water, as is done to the dead. Care is taken not to perform this dangerous operation in the presence of a man: every birth being a rebirth, the law of the equivalence of lives, a "soul" for a "soul", is capable of exacting the death of a human being as the price of the birth of the cloth.[96] When the cloth has been removed, the loom is dismantled and put away for the duration of "the death of the field".

Wool and pottery, natural products, have much the same cycle. Pottery, being derived from the earth, partakes of the life of the field; the clay is collected in autumn, but it is never worked in that season, nor in winter, when the earth is pregnant, but in spring. The unfired (*azegzaw*) pottery dries slowly in the sun (wet-dry) while the ears of corn are ripening (the wet-dry period). So long as the earth bears the ears, it cannot be baked; it is only after the harvest, when the earth is bare and no longer producing, and fire is no longer liable to dry up the ears (the dry-dry period) that baking can be carried out, in the open air (dry-dry).

The wool, which is sheared at the end of the cold period, is washed with soap and water, at the moment when everything is opening and swelling (*thafsuth*) and boiled in a pot into which some wheat and beans (*ufthyen*) have been thrown, so that the flocks of wool will swell like the ears of corn in the

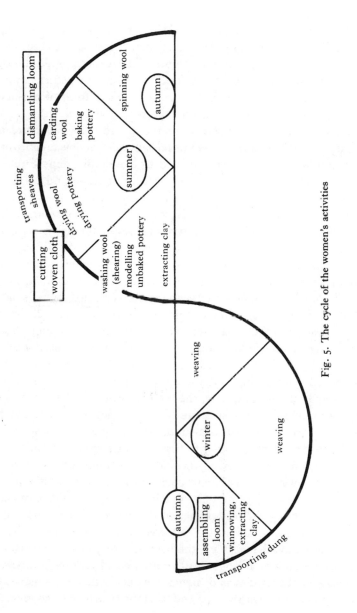

Fig. 5. The cycle of the women's activities

fields. It dries at the same time as the pottery, in the wet-dry period. It is carded with instruments as typically "sharp" and male as the carding-comb, the symbol of separation and male roughness, a product of the work of the smith which is used in the virilization rites and in the prophylactic rites intended to ward off the diseases associated with evening and the wet.[97]

The structure of the day (which integrates the five Moslem prayers very naturally) constitutes another, particularly legible, product of the application of the same structuring principles. The wet-season day is nocturnal even in its diurnal part: because the flock goes out and returns only once in the course of this day, it appears as an incomplete form of the dry-season day (see fig. 6).[98] On the day called "the return of *azal*", the threshold of the dry season, when the mistress of the house brings the fire out into the courtyard and lights the *kanun* in *thimetbakth*, there is an abrupt changeover to a more complex rhythm, defined by the double departure and return of the flocks:[99] they go out for the first time at dawn and come back as soon as the heat becomes burdensome, that is, around *eddoha*; the second departure coincides with the midday prayer, *eddohor*, and they return at nightfall.

Just as the year runs from autumn towards summer, moving from west to east, so the day (*as*) runs from the evening towards midday: although the whole system is organized in accordance with the perfect cycle of an eternal recurrence – evening and autumn, old age and death, being also the locus of procreation and sowing – time is nonetheless oriented towards the culminating point represented by midday, summer, or mature age (see fig. 7). Night, in its darkest part, the "shadows" of "the middle of the night", which brings men, women, and children together in the most secret part of the house, close to the animals, in the closed, damp, cold place of sexual relations, a place associated with death and the grave, is opposed to the day, and more precisely to its summit, *azal*, the moment when the light and heat of the sun at its zenith are at their strongest. The link between night and death, which is underscored by nocturnal sounds like the howling of dogs and the grating of the sleepers' teeth, similar to that of the dying, is marked in all the taboos of the evening: the practices forbidden – bathing, or even wandering round stretches of water, especially stagnant, black, muddy, stinking water, looking in mirrors, anointing the hair, touching ashes – would have the effect of in a sense doubling the malignancy of the nocturnal darkness through contact with substances which are all endowed with the same properties (and are in some cases interchangeable – the hair, mirrors, black waters).

The morning is a moment of *transition* and *rupture*, a *threshold*. Dawn is a struggle between day and night: it is during the hours before daybreak, as the reign of night comes to an end, that the rites of expulsion and purification

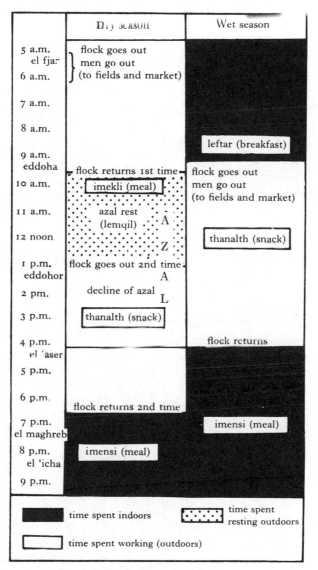

Fig. 6. Daily rhythms in summer and winter

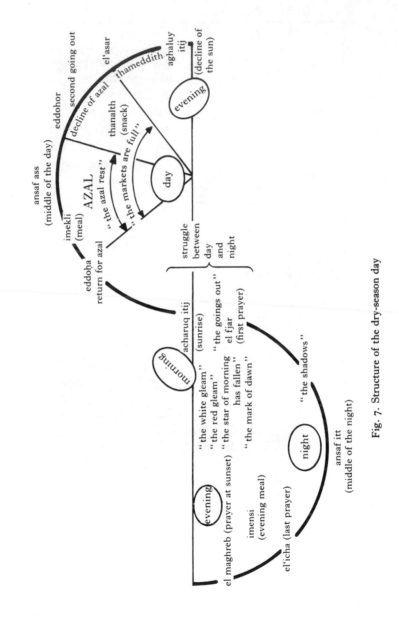

Fig. 7. Structure of the dry-season day

are performed, and the break is made with darkness, evil, and death, so that one may "be in the morning", i.e. open to the light, the good, and the luck that are associated with it (this is, for example, the moment when the semolina left overnight near the head of a jealous baby, or one afflicted by transferred evil – *aqlab* – is poured over him). Every morning is a *birth*. Morning is the time for going out, the *opening* of the day and an opening up to light (*fatah*, to open, blossom, is synonymous with *sebah*, to be in the morning). It is an opening first in the sense that this is the moment when the day is born (*thallalith wass*, the birth of the day), when "the eye of the light" (*thit antafath*) opens and the house and the village, which had closed in upon themselves for the night, pour out their men and their flocks into the fields. An opening too in the sense of "beginning": morning is an inaugural moment which men worthy of the name feel it right to be present at and take part in (*esbah*, to be present, to be alive in the morning). "Morning", it is said, "means facility." To get up early is to place oneself under favourable auspices (*leftah*, opening, good augury). The early riser is safe from the encounters which bring misfortune; whereas the man who is last to set out on the road can have no other companion than the one-eyed man (associated, like the blind, with night) who waits for broad daylight before setting out, or the lame man who lags behind. To rise at cockcrow is to put one's days in the protection of the angels of the morning and to do them honour; it is, so to speak, to put oneself in a state of grace, to act in such a way that "the angels decide in one's stead". In fact the morning, an inaugural time blessed by the return of light and life, is the best moment for making decisions and undertaking action: the inauguration rites which mark the days of transition are performed at daybreak, whether it be the waking of the cattle at the winter solstice, the renewal rites on the first day of the year (*ennayer*), the shepherds' departure to gather plants on the first day of spring, the flock's going out on the return of *azal*, etc.

The morning, like the homologous period in the agrarian year or human life, spring or childhood, would be entirely favourable – since it marks the victory of light, life, and the future over night, death, and the past – did not its position confer on it the fearful power to determine the future to which it belongs and which it governs as the inaugural term of the series:[100] though intrinsically beneficent, it is fraught with the danger of misfortune, inasmuch as it can decide, for good or for ill, the fate of the day. We must take a closer look at this logic, that of magic, which has perhaps never been fully understood, because it is all too easily half understood on the basis of the quasi-magical experience of the world which, under the effect of emotion, for example, imposes itself even on those whose material conditions of existence, and an institutional environment tending to discourage it, best protect them against this "regression". When the world is seen as "a fatal system"[101] whose starting-point is its cause, what happens in the world and what people do govern what will happen and what will be done. The future is already inscribed in the present in the form of omens.[102] Men must decipher these warnings, not in order to submit to them as a destiny (like the emotion which accepts the future announced in the present) but in order to be able, if necessary, to change them: this is only an apparent contradiction, since it is in the name of the hypothesis of the fatal system that a man will try to *remake* the future announced in the present by making a new present. Magic is fought with magic: the magical potency of the omen-present is fought with conduct aiming to change the starting-point, in the name of the belief, which was the whole strength of the omen, that the system's starting-point is its cause.

Morning is the time when everything becomes a sign announcing good or ill to come. A man who meets someone carrying milk sees a good omen in the encounter; a man who hears the shouts of a quarrel while he is still in bed draws a bad omen from them. Men anxiously watch for the signs (*esbuḥ*, the first encounter of the morning, portending good or ill) through which evil forces may announce their imminence, and an effort is made to exorcize their effect: a man who meets at dawn a blacksmith, a lame man, a one-eyed man, a woman with an empty goatskin bottle, or a black cat must "remake his morning", return to the night by crossing the threshold in the opposite direction, sleep again, and remake his "going out". The whole day (and sometimes the whole year or a man's whole life, when it is the morning of an inaugural day) hangs on his knowing how to defeat the malignant tricks of chance. The magical potency of words and things works with particular intensity here, and it is more than ever necessary to use the euphemisms which replace baleful words: of all the words tabooed, the most dreadful are those expressing terminal acts or operations – shutting, extinguishing, leaving, spreading – which might invoke an interruption, an untimely destruction, emptiness (e.g. "There are no dried figs left in the store", or the mere word "nothing") or sterility.[103]

Azal, and in particular *thalmaṣth uzal*, the middle of *azal*, the moment when the sun is at its zenith, noon, the moment when "azal is at its hottest" (*iḥma uzal*), broad daylight, is opposed both to night and to morning, first light, the nocturnal part of the day.[104] Homologous with the hottest, driest, brightest time of the year, it is the day of the daytime, the dry of the dry, in a sense bringing the characteristic properties of the dry season to their fullest expression. It is the male time par excellence, the moment when the markets, paths, and/or fields are full (of men), when the men are outdoors at their men's tasks.[105] Even the sleep of *azal* (*lamqil*) is the ideal limit of male rest, just as the fields are the limit of the habitual places for sleep, such as the threshing floor, the driest and most masculine spot in the space close to the house, where the men often sleep; one can see why *azal*, which in itself partakes of the dry and the sterile, should be strongly associated with the desert (*lakhla*) of the harvested field.

Eddohor, the second prayer, roughly coincides with the end of the *azal* rest: this is the start of "the decline of *azal*", the and of the fiercest heat (*azghal*), when for the second time the flocks set out for the fields and the men go off to work. With the third prayer, *el'asar*, *azal* ends and *thameddith* (or *thadugwath*) begins: now "the markets have emptied" and now too the taboos of the evening take effect. The decline of the sun (*aghaluy itij*), which "slopes to the west", is in a sense the paradigm of all forms of decline, in particular old age and all kinds of political decadence (*yeghli itij-is*, his sun has fallen) or physical decay (*yeghli lwerq-is*): to go westward, towards the setting sun (*ghereb*, as opposed to *cherraq*, to go towards the rising sun), is to go towards darkness, night, death, like a house whose westward-facing door can only receive shadows.

Pursuing the analysis of the different fields of application of the system of generative schemes, we could build up a sort of synoptic diagram of the cycle of life as structured by the rites of passage: birth (with the practices associated with the cutting of the umbilical cord by the *qabla* and the rites intended to protect the child against evil spells); name-giving on the third or seventh day; the first time the mother and child come out of the house, on the fortieth day (with, in the meantime, all the rites of "the breaking of the link with the month", *thuksa an-tsucherka wayur*, on the third, seventh, fourteenth, thirtieth, and fortieth days, to "break the association with the month" – to drive out evil and also to separate the child progressively from the female world); the "first ventures" (into the courtyard, away from the family); the first haircut, a purificatory ritual often associated with the first visit to the market; circumcision, marriage, and burial. The cycle of the rites of passage is in fact subordinated to the agrarian calendar which, as we have seen, is itself nothing other than a succession of rites of passage.

This is primarily because in a number of cases the rites of passage are more or less explicitly associated with particular moments in the year, by virtue of the homology between them and the moment in question; thus, for example, a birth is auspicious if it comes at *lahlal* (or in the morning), ill omened if it comes at *husum* or *in sla* (or in the afternoon between *el'asar* and *el maghreb*); early afternoon is the best time for circumcision, but not winter, and *el'azla gennayer* is the propitious moment for the first haircut; autumn and spring (after *el'azla*) are the right times for marriage, which is ruled out on the last day of the year, at *husum* and *nisan*, and in May and June. The springtime rites (and in particular those of the first day of spring and the return of *azal*) set to work a symbolism which applies as much to the unripe corn, still "bound, fettered, knotted" (*igan*), as to the limbs of the baby which cannot yet walk (*aqnan ifadnis*) and remains in a sense attached to the earth.[106] Those rites of passage that are not linked to a particular period of the year always owe some of their properties to the ritual characteristics of the period in which they are performed, a fact which explains the essential features of the variants observed. For example, the beneficent water of *nisan*, a necessary component in the rites specific to that period (like the first milk in spring, the ears of the last sheaf in summer, etc.), also appears as a supplementary element in the rites of passage which happen to take place at that time.

But, at a deeper level, it is the whole of human existence that, being the product of the same system of schemes, is organized in a manner homologous to that of the agrarian year and the other great temporal "series". Thus procreation (*akhlaq*, creation) is very clearly associated with evening, autumn, and the damp, nocturnal part of the house. Similarly, gestation corresponds to the underground life of the grain, i.e. the "nights" (*lyali*): the taboos of pregnancy (of fecundity) are the taboos of evening and death (looking in a mirror at nightfall, etc.); the pregnant woman, like the earth swollen in spring, partakes of the world of the dead (*juf*, which denotes the belly of the pregnant woman, also means north, the homologue of night and winter). Gestation, like germination, is identified with cooking in the pot: after childbirth the woman is served the boiled food of winter, of the dead, and of ploughing, in particular *abisar* (the food of the dead and of funerals) which, except on this occasion, is never eaten by women, coarse-grained couscous boiled in water (*abazin*), pancakes, fritters, and eggs. Childbirth is associated with the "opening" of the end of winter, and all the taboos on closing that are observed at that time reappear here (crossing the legs, folding the arms, clasping the hands together, wearing bracelets or rings). The homology between spring, childhood, and morning, inaugural periods of uncertainty and expectation, manifests itself in, among other things, the abundance of prognostication rites which are practised then. Although described as an untimely destruction (*an'adam*), the harvest is not a death without issue (*ma'dum*, the bachelor, who dies childless), and magic, which allows the profits of contradictory actions to be compounded without contradiction, is expected to bring about resurrection in and through a new act of fecundation. Similarly, old age, which faces the west, the setting sun, night and death, the dark direction par excellence, is at the same time turned towards the east of resurrection in a new birth. The cycle ends in death, that is, the west, only for the outsider (*aghrib*), the man of the west (*el gharb*) and of exile (*el ghorba*), hence without issue (*anger*). His grave is often used – as an exemplary realization of utter oblivion and annihilation – in the rites for the expulsion of evil: in a universe in which a man's social existence requires that he be linked to his ancestors through his ascendants and be "cited" and "resurrected" (*asker*) by his descendants, the death of the outsider is the only absolute form of death.[107]

The different generations occupy different positions in this cycle, diametrically opposed for successive generations, those of father and son (since one conceives when the other is conceived, and enters old age when the other is in childhood), and identical for alternate generations, those of grandfather and grandson (see fig. 8). Such is the logic which, making of birth a rebirth, leads the father whenever possible to give his first-born son the name of his own father (*asker*: to name and to resurrect). And the fields go through a perfectly analogous cycle, that of *two-year rotation*: just as the *cycle of generation* is closed by A's death and resurrection, i.e. when B conceives C, so the cycle of the field is closed when field A, which has lain fallow, awaiting its resurrection, for the duration of the life of the fecundated field B, is "raised from the dead" by ploughing and sowing, i.e. when field B is laid fallow.

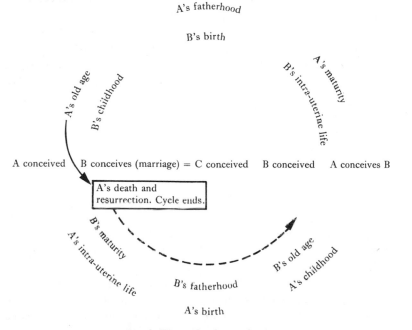

Fig. 8. The cycle of reproduction

It is no accident that the difficulties of the Greek and Chinese exegetes begin when they try to construct and superimpose *series* (in the sense of asymmetrical, transitive, "connected" relationships which Russell gives the word in his *Introduction to Mathematical Philosophy*):[108] when one tries to push the superimposition of the various series beyond a certain degree of refinement, behind the fundamental homologies (brought together in fig. 9), difficulties begin to multiply systematically, demonstrating that true rigour does not lie in an analysis which tries to push the system beyond its limits, by abusing the powers of the discourse which gives voice to the silences of practice and by exploiting the magic of the writing which tears practice and discourse out of the flow of time.[109] It is only when practical metaphor, scheme-transfer effected on the hither side of discourse, becomes *metaphor* or *analogy* that it is possible, for example, to wonder like Plato whether "it was the earth that imitated woman in becoming pregnant and bringing a being into the world, or woman that imitated the earth" (*Menexenus*, 238a).

Ignorance of the objective truth of practice as learned ignorance is the source of innumerable theoretical errors, not least the error from which Western philosophy originated (and which anthropological science endlessly reproduces).[110] Rites and myths which were "acted out" in the mode of belief and fulfilled a practical function as collective instruments of symbolic action on the natural world and above all on the group, receive from learned reflection a function which is not their own but that which they have for scholars. The slow evolution "from religion to philosophy", as Cornford and the Cambridge school put it, i.e. from analogy as a practical scheme of ritual action to analogy as an object of reflection and a rational method of thought, is correlative with a transformation of the function which the groups concerned confer on myth and rite in their practice.[111] Myth tends to cease to have any function other than the one it receives in the relations of competition between the literate scholars who question and interpret its letter by reference to the questions and readings of past and contemporary interpreters: only then does it become explicitly what it always was, but only implicitly or practically so, i.e. a system of solutions to cosmological or anthropological problems which scholarly reflection thinks it finds in them but which it in fact creates *ex nihilo* by a *mistaken reading* that is implied in any *reading* ignorant of its objective truth as a literary reading.[112]

The problems which nascent philosophy thinks it raises in fact arise of their own accord from its unanalysed relationship to an object which never raised them as such. And this is no less true of its most specific modes of thought: the pre-Socratic thinkers would not hold such fascination for certain philosophers (who practically never possess the means of really understanding them) were it not that they supply its most accomplished models to the tradition (most "eminently" represented by Heidegger) of the play on words of common origin which establishes a *doubly determined* relationship between the linguistic root and the mythic root, or the (Hegelian) tradition of etymology seen as a means of reappropriating the treasures accumulated by the historical work of reason.[113] It is indeed the essence of learned reflection that it situates the principle of relations confusedly sensed in the order of meaning (*sens*), in relations which manifest themselves at the level of the *letter* (homophony, homography, paronymy, etymological kinship, etc.). The inanity of meta-

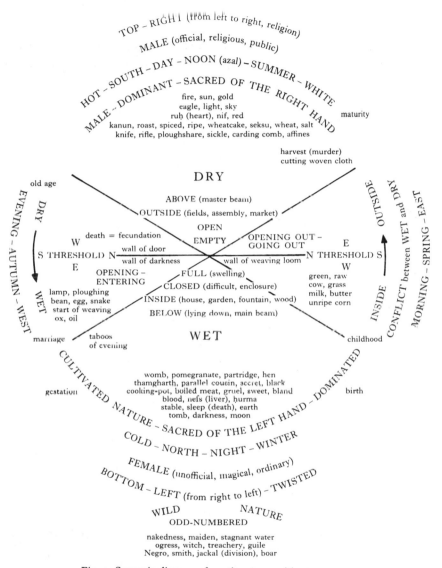

Fig. 9. Synoptic diagram of pertinent oppositions

physics would escape no one if, as Carnap thinks, its "pseudo-propositions" were only "an inadequate means of expressing the feeling of life".[114] Plato's remark must be taken literally: "The philosopher is a mythologist." Logical criticism inevitably misses its target: because it can only challenge the relationships consciously established between words, it cannot bring out the incoherent coherence of a discourse which, springing from underlying mythic or ideological schemes, has the capacity to survive every *reductio ad absurdum*.

4
Structures, habitus, power: basis for a theory of symbolic power

Doxa, orthodoxy, heterodoxy

There is, perhaps, no better way of *making felt* the real function of classificatory systems than to evoke as concretely as possible the abrupt and total transformation of daily life which occurs on "the return of *azal*". Everything, without exception, in the activities of the men, the women, and the children, is abruptly altered by the adoption of a new rhythm: the movements of the flock, of course, but also the men's work and the domestic activities of the women, the place where the cooking is done, the rest periods, the food eaten, the times and the itinerary of the women's movements and outdoor work, the rhythm of the men's assembly meetings, of the ceremonies, prayers, markets, and meetings outside the village.

In the wet season, in the morning, before *eddoha*, all the men are in the village; with the exception of the meeting sometimes held on a Friday after collective prayer, this is the time of day for meetings of the clan assembly and all the conciliation committees (before a divorce, or to prevent a divorce, before division of an estate or to avoid division); this is also the time when announcements concerning all the men are made from the top of the minaret (summoning them to participate in collective work, repairing roads, digging drains, transporting flagstones, etc.). About the time of *eddoha* the shepherd sets out with his flock and the men go off to the fields and gardens, either to work on the major seasonal tasks such as ploughing or digging or to spend their time on the minor activities which occupy the slack periods of the agrarian year or day (collecting grass or diss, digging or clearing ditches, gathering wood, digging up tree-stumps, etc.). When rain, snow, or cold rule out work in the fields and the earth is too wet to be trodden on without jeopardizing the future crop or the ploughing to come, and when the state of the roads and the fear of being weather-bound far from the house suspend traditional relations with the outside world, the men's imperative duty to be outside brings them all to the communal house (even across clan and/or league divisions). Indeed, at that time of the year, not a man is missing from the village (to which the inhabitants of the *azib* – hamlet – return at *thaqachachth* – end of October).

The evening meal (*imensi*) is served very early, as soon as the men have taken off their moccasins and work-clothes and have had a short rest. By

nightfall, everyone is at home, except those who want to offer evening prayer
in the mosque, where the last prayer (*el'icha*) is generally brought forward
so as to be said at the same time as *maghreb*. Because the men eat all their
meals indoors (except the afternoon snack), the women, ousted from their
own space, strive to reconstitute a separate universe, making the preparations
for the meal over by the wall of darkness, during the afternoon, while the
men are away, taking care not to attract attention, even when busy, or be
found doing nothing: the loom, which is up throughout the wet season, affords
them a sort of veil, behind which they can withdraw, and also the alibi of
a permanently available activity. The same strategies appear in the use made
of the village space: if the men are present, the wife cannot go to the fountain
all morning, especially since the risk of a fall requires special precautions;
so the "old woman" is the one who goes and gets the water in the morning
and, if there is no little girl available, keeps chickens and animals away from
the matting on which the olives or grain are spread out before being taken
to the press or the mill.

The group's withdrawal into itself, and also into its own past, its traditions
– with the tales and legends in the long evenings in the room reserved for the
men – is followed by the opening on to the outside world in the dry season.[1]
Whereas during the wet season the village awoke every morning without much
ado, once *azal* returns it awakes with a great deal of noise and bustle: the
tread of mules as men make their way to market is followed by the
uninterrupted tread of the outgoing flocks, and then by the clattering hooves
of the asses ridden or led by the men going off to the fields or the forest. About
the time of *eddhoḥa*, the shepherd brings back his flock and some of the men
return to the village for their midday rest. The muezzin's call to *eddohor* is
the signal for the second going out of the day. In less than half an hour, the
village is this time almost completely emptied: in the morning, the women
were kept in the house by their domestic tasks and above all by the impropriety
there would be in taking their midday rest outside, under a tree, like the men,
or in hurrying to get home, which is a woman's proper place at a moment
reserved for intimacy; by contrast, in the afternoon, all but a few of the women
accompany the men, at least on certain occasions: there are first, of course,
the "old women" who, after "giving their orders" to the daughters-in-law
whose turn it is to prepare dinner, taking the measure of flour from the *akufi*,
getting the bunch of onions and the other vegetables required for *imensi* out
of *tha'richth* and putting the keys to all the stores back on their girdles, go
and make their contribution to the work and assert their authority in their
own way, by inspecting the gardens, making good the men's negligence –
the stray piece of wood, the handful of fodder dropped on the way, the branch
left behind under a tree – and in the evening bringing back, on top of the

jar of water from the spring in the garden, a bunch of herbs, vine-leaves, or maize, for the domestic animals. There are also the young wives who, especially at the time of the fig-harvest, follow their husbands around the orchard, picking up the fruit the men have beaten down, sorting it and setting it out on trays, and go home in the evening, each a few paces behind her husband, alone or accompanied by the "old woman".

Thus the double going out delimits *azal*, a sort of "dead" time which everyone feels he must respect: all is silent, still, and austere; the streets are "desertlike". Most of the men are scattered far from the village, some living in the *azib*, others away from home for long periods looking after the garden and the pair of oxen that are being fatted, others watching over the fig-drying shed (in this season every family's fear is that in an emergency it would not be able to assemble its men). No one can say whether the public space of the village belongs to man or to woman. So each of them takes care not to occupy it: there is something suspicious about anyone who ventures into the streets at that hour. The few men who have not stayed in the fields to sleep under a tree take their siesta in any spot that is to hand, in the shade of a porch or a hedge, in front of the mosque, on the flagstones or indoors, in the courtyards of their houses, or in side rooms if they have one. Furtive shadows slip across the street from one house to another: the women, equally unoccupied, are taking advantage of the limited presence of the men to meet together or visit one another. Only the shepherds[2] who have returned to the village with their flocks bring life to the outer crossroads and the minor meeting-places with their games – *thigar*, a kicking contest, *thighuladlh*, stone-throwing at targets, *thimrith*, a sort of draughts, etc.

Doing one's duty as a man means conforming to the social order, and this is fundamentally a question of respecting rhythms, keeping pace, not falling out of line. "Don't we all eat the same wheatcake (or the same barley)?" "Don't we all get up at the same time?" These various ways of reasserting solidarity contain an implicit definition of the fundamental virtue of conformity, the opposite of which is the desire to stand apart from others. Working while the others are resting, staying in the house while the others are working in the fields, travelling on deserted roads, wandering round the streets of the village while the others are asleep or at the market – these are all suspicious forms of behaviour. The eccentric who does everything differently from other people is called *amkhalef* (from *khalef*, to stand out, to transgress) and there is often a play on words to the effect that *amkhalef* is also the man who arrives late (from *khellef*, to leave behind). Thus, as we have seen, a worthy man, conscious of his responsibilities, must get up early.[3] "The man who does not settle his business early in the morning will never settle it"; "It's the morning that gives the hunters their game; bad luck for late sleepers!" and again "The *suq* is the morning"; "The man who sleeps until the middle of *azal* will find the market empty" (*sebah*, to be present in the morning, also means to be fitting, becoming).[4] But getting up early is not a virtue in itself: if they are ill-used, wasted, the first hours are no more than "time taken from the night", an offence against the principle that "there is a time for everthing", and that "everything should be done in its time" (*kul waqth salwaqth-is* "everything in its time"). What is the use of a man's getting up at the muezzin's call if he is not going to say the morning prayer? There is only mockery for the man who, despite getting up "under the stars" or when "dawn has not taken shape" (*'alam*) has achieved little. Respect for collective rhythms implies respects for *the* rhythm that is appropriate to each action – neither excessive haste nor sluggishness. It is simply a question of being in the proper place at the proper time. A man must walk with a "measured pace" (*ikthal uqudmis*) neither lagging behind nor running like a "dancer", a shallow, frivolous way to behave, unworthy of a man of honour. So there is mockery too for the man who hurries without thinking, who runs to catch up with someone else, who works so hastily that he is likely to "maltreat the earth", forgetting the teachings of wisdom:

> "It is useless to pursue the world,
> No one will ever overtake it."

> "You who rush along,
> Stay and be rebuked;
> Daily bread comes from God,
> It is not for you to concern yourself."

The over-eager peasant moves ahead of the collective rhythms which assign each act its particular moment in the space of the day, the year, or human life; his race with time threatens to drag the whole group into the escalation of diabolic ambition, *thahraymith*, and thus to turn circular time into linear time, simple reproduction into indefinite accumulation.[5]

The tasks of farming, *horia erga*, seasonable works, as the Greeks called them, are defined as much in their rhythm, which determines their duration, as in their moment. The sacred tasks, such as ploughing and sowing, fall to those who are capable of treating the land with the respect it deserves, of approaching it (*qabel*) with the measured pace of a man meeting a partner whom he wants to welcome and honour. This is underlined by the myth of the origin of wheat and barley. Adam was sowing wheat; Eve brought him some wheatcake. She saw him sowing grain by grain, "covering each seed with earth", and invoking God each time. She accused him of *wasting his time*. While her husband was busy eating, she started to broadcast the grain, without invoking the name of God. When the crop came up, Adam found his field full of strange ears, delicate and brittle, like woman. He called this plant (barley) *ech'ir* "weak". One of the effects of the ritualization of practices is precisely that of assigning them a time – i.e. a moment, a tempo, and a duration which is relatively independent of external necessities, those of climate, technique, or economy, thereby conferring on them the sort of arbitrary necessity which specifically defines cultural arbitrariness.

. The reason why submission to the collective rhythms is so rigorously demanded is that the temporal forms or the spatial structures structure not only the group's representation of the world but the group itself, which orders itself in accordance with this representation: this may be clearly seen, for example, in the fact that the organization of the existence of the men and the women in accordance with different times and different places constitutes two interchangeable ways of securing separation and hierarchization of the male and female worlds, the women going to the fountain at an hour when the men are not in the streets, or by a special path, or both at once.[6] The social calendar tends to secure integration by compounding the *synchronization* of identical practices with the *orchestration* of different but structurally homologous practices (such as ploughing and weaving).[7] All the divisions of the group are projected at every moment into the spatio-temporal organization which assigns each category its place and time: it is here that the fuzzy logic of practice works wonders in enabling the group to achieve as much *social and logical* integration as is compatible with the diversity imposed by the division of labour between the sexes, the ages, and the "occupations" (smith, butcher).[8] Synchronization, in the case of rites or tasks, is that much more associated with spatial grouping the more there is collectively at stake: rites thus range in importance from the great solemn rites (e.g. *awdjeb*) enacted by everyone at the same time, through the rites performed at the same time but by each family separately (the sacrifice of a sheep at the Aïd), through those which may be practised at any time (e.g. the rite to cure sties), and finally to those which must only take place in secret and at unusual hours (the rites of love magic).

Practical taxonomies, which are a transformed, misrecognizable form of the real divisions of the social order, contribute to the reproduction of that order by producing objectively orchestrated practices adjusted to those divisions. Social time as *form*, in the musical sense, as succession organized by the application to passing time of the principle which organizes all dimensions of practice, tends to fulfil, even more effectively than the division of space, a function of integration in and through division, that is, through hierarchization. But more profoundly, the organization of time and the group in accordance with mythical structures leads collective practice to appear as "realized myth", in the sense in which for Hegel tradition is "realized morality"

(*Sittlichkeit*), the reconciliation of subjective demand and objective (i.e. collective) necessity which grounds the *belief* of a whole group in what the group believes, i.e. in the group: a reflexive return to the principles of the operations of objectification, practices or discourses, is prevented by the very reinforcement which these productions continuously draw from a world of objectifications produced in accordance with the same subjective principles.

Every established order tends to produce (to very different degrees and with very different means) the naturalization of its own arbitrariness. Of all the mechanisms tending to produce this effect, the most important and the best concealed is undoubtedly the dialectic of the objective chances and the agents' aspirations, out of which arises the *sense of limits*, commonly called the *sense of reality*, i.e. the correspondence between the objective classes and the internalized classes, social structures and mental structures, which is the basis of the most ineradicable adherence to the established order. Systems of classification which reproduce, in their own specific logic, the objective classes, i.e. the divisions by sex, age, or position in the relations of production, make their specific contribution to the reproduction of the power relations of which they are the product, by securing the misrecognition, and hence the recognition, of the arbitrariness on which they are based: in the extreme case, that is to say, when there is a quasi-perfect correspondence between the objective order and the subjective principles of organization (as in ancient societies) the natural and social world appears as self-evident. This experience we shall call *doxa*, so as to distinguish it from an orthodox or heterodox belief implying awareness and recognition of the possibility of different or antagonistic beliefs. Schemes of thought and perception can produce the objectivity that they do produce only by producing misrecognition of the limits of the cognition that they make possible, thereby founding immediate adherence, in the doxic mode, to the world of tradition experienced as a "natural world" and taken for granted. The instruments of knowledge of the social world are in this case (objectively) political instruments which contribute to the reproduction of the social world by producing immediate adherence to the world, seen as self-evident and undisputed, of which they are the product and of which they reproduce the structures in a transformed form. The political function of classifications is never more likely to pass unnoticed than in the case of relatively undifferentiated social formations, in which the prevailing classificatory system encounters no rival or antagonistic principle. As we have seen in the case of the domestic conflicts to which marriages often give rise, social categories disadvantaged by the symbolic order, such as women and the young, cannot but recognize the legitimacy of the dominant classification in the very fact that their only chance of neutralizing those of its effects most contrary to their own interests lies in submitting to them in order to make use of them (in accordance with the logic of the *éminence grise*).

The taxonomies of the mythico-ritual system at once divide and unify, legitimating unity in division, that is to say, hierarchy.[9] There is no need to insist on the function of legitimation of the division of labour and power between the sexes that is fulfilled by a mythico-ritual system entirely dominated by male values. It is perhaps less obvious that the social structuring of temporality which organizes representations and practices, most solemnly reaffirmed in the rites of passage, fulfils a political function by symbolically manipulating *age limits*, i.e. the boundaries which define age-groups, but also the limitations imposed at different ages. The mythico-ritual categories cut up the age continuum into discontinuous segments, constituted not biologically (like the physical signs of ageing) but socially, and marked by the symbolism of cosmetics and clothing, decorations, ornaments, and emblems, the tokens which express and underline the representations of the uses of the body that are legitimately associated with each socially defined age, and also those which are ruled out because they would have the effect of disrupting the system of oppositions between the generations (such as rejuvenation rites, which are the exact inversion of the rites of passage). Social representations of the different ages of life, and of the properties attached by definition to them, express, in their own logic, the power relations between the age-classes, helping to reproduce at once the union and the division of those classes by means of temporal divisions tending to produce both continuity and rupture. They thereby rank among the institutionalized instruments for maintenance of the symbolic order, and hence among the mechanisms of the reproduction of the social order whose very functioning serves the interests of those occupying a dominant position in the social structure, the men of mature age.[10]

We see yet again how erroneous it would be to consider only the cognitive or, as Durkheim put it, "speculative", functions of mythico-ritual representations: these mental structures, a transfigured reproduction of the structures constituting a mode of production and a mode of biological and social reproduction, contribute at least as efficaciously as the provisions of custom towards defining and maintaining the delimitation of powers between the sexes and generations, through the ethical dispositions they produce, such as the sense of honour or respect for elders and ancestors. The theory of knowledge is a dimension of political theory because the specifically symbolic power to impose the principles of the construction of reality – in particular, social reality – is a major dimension of political power.

In a determinate social formation, the stabler the objective structures and the more fully they reproduce themselves in the agents' dispositions, the

greater the extent of the field of doxa, of that which is taken for granted.
When, owing to the quasi-perfect fit between the objective structures and the
internalized structures which results from the logic of simple reproduction,
the established cosmological and political order is perceived not as arbitrary,
i.e. as one possible order among others, but as a self-evident and natural order
which goes without saying and therefore goes unquestioned, the agents'
aspirations have the same limits as the objective conditions of which they are
the product.

It is not easy to evoke the subjective experience associated with this world of the
realized ought-to-be, in which things that could scarcely be otherwise nonetheless are
what they are only because they are what they ought to be, in which an agent can
have at one and the same time the feeling that there is nothing to do except what he
is doing and also that he is only doing what he ought.[11] And so it is in all seriousness
that I juxtapose two particularly striking evocations of this experience, one by an old
Kabyle woman, underlining the fact that to be ill and dying was a social status, with
its attendant rights and duties, and the other by Marcel Proust, describing the
subjective effects of the ritualization of practices:
"In the old days, folk didn't know what illness was. They went to bed and they
died. It's only nowadays that we're learning words like liver, lung [*albumun*; Fr. *le
poumon*], intestines, stomach [*listuma*; Fr. *l'estomac*], and I don't know what! People
only used to know [pain in] the belly [*th'abuṭ*]; that's what everyone who died died
of, unless it was fever [*thawla*]...In the old days sick people used to call for death,
but it wouldn't come. When someone was ill, the news soon spread everywhere, not
just in the village, but all over the 'arch. Besides, a sick man's house is never empty:
in the daytime all his relatives, men and women, come for news...At nightfall, all
the women relatives, even the youngest, would be taken to his bedside. And once a
week there was 'the sick man's market' [*suq umuṭin*]: they would send someone to
buy him meat or fruit. All that's forgotten nowadays; it's true, there aren't any sick
people now, not as there used to be. Now everyone's sick, everyone's complaining
of something. Those who were dying used to suffer a lot; death came slowly, it could
take a night and a day or two nights and a day. Death 'always struck them through
their speech': first they became dumb. Everyone had time to see them one last time;
the relatives were given time to assemble and to prepare the burial. They would give
alms to make the dying easier: they would give the community a tree, generally a fig-tree
planted beside the road. Its fruit would not be picked, but left for passing travellers
and the poor [*chajra usufagh*, the tree of the outgoing; *chajra n'esadhaqa*, the alms
tree]...Who's ill nowadays? Who's well? Everyone complains but no one stays in bed;
they all run to the doctor. Everyone knows what's wrong with him now."[12]
"From the position of the bed, my side recalled the place where the crucifix used
to be, the breath of the recess in the bedroom in my grandparents' house, in the days
when there were still bedrooms and parents, a time for each thing, when you loved
your parents not because you found them intelligent but because they were your
parents, when you went to bed not because you wanted to but because it was time,
and when you marked the desire, the acceptance and the whole ceremony of sleeping
by going up two steps to the big bed, where you closed the blue rep curtains with
their raised-velvet bands, and where, when you were ill, the old remedies kept you
for several days on end, with a nightlight on the Siena marble mantelpiece, without
any of the immoral medicines that allow you to get up and imagine you can lead the

life of a healthy man when you are ill, sweating under the blankets thanks to perfectly harmless infusions, which for two thousand years have contained the flowers of the meadows and the wisdom of old women."[13]

Moreover, when the conditions of existence of which the members of a group are the product are very little differentiated, the dispositions which each of them exercises in his practice are confirmed and hence reinforced both by the practice of the other members of the group (one function of symbolic exchanges such as feasts and ceremonies being to favour the circular reinforcement which is the foundation of *collective belief*) and also by institutions which constitute collective thought as much as they express it, such as language, myth, and art. The self-evidence of the world is reduplicated by the instituted discourses about the world in which the whole group's adherence to that self-evidence is affirmed. The specific potency of the explicit statement that brings subjective experiences into the reassuring unanimity of a socially approved and collectively attested sense imposes itself with the *authority* and *necessity* of a collective position adopted on data intrinsically amenable to many other structurations.

"Nature" as science understands it – a cultural fact which is the historical product of a long labour of "disenchantment" (*Entzauberung*) – is never encountered in such a universe. Between the child and the world the whole group intervenes, not just with the warnings that inculcate a fear of supernatural dangers,[14] but with a whole universe of ritual practices and also of discourses, sayings, proverbs, all structured in concordance with the principles of the corresponding habitus. Furthermore, through the acts and symbols that are intended to contribute to the reproduction of nature and of the group by the analogical reproduction of natural processes, mimetic representation helps to produce in the agents temporary reactions (such as, for example, the collective excitement associated with *lakhrif*) or even *lasting dispositions* (such as the generative schemes incorporated in the body schema) attuned to the objective processes expected from the ritual action – helps, in other words, to make the world conform to the myth.

Because the subjective necessity and self-evidence of the commonsense world are validated by the objective consensus on the sense of the world, what is essential *goes without saying because it comes without saying*: the tradition is silent, not least about itself as a tradition; customary law is content to enumerate specific applications of principles which remain implicit and unformulated, because unquestioned; the play of the mythico-ritual homologies constitutes a perfectly closed world, each aspect of which is, as it were, a reflection of all the others, a world which has no place for *opinion* as liberal ideology understands it, i.e. as one of the different and equally legitimate answers which can be given to an explicit question about the established political order; and nothing is further from the correlative notion of the *majority* than the *unanimity* of doxa, the aggregate of the "choices" whose subject is everyone and no one because the questions they answer cannot be explicitly asked. The adherence expressed in the doxic relation to the social world is the absolute form of recognition of legitimacy through misrecognition of arbitrariness, since it is unaware of the very question of legitimacy, which arises from competition for legitimacy, and hence from conflict between groups claiming to possess it.

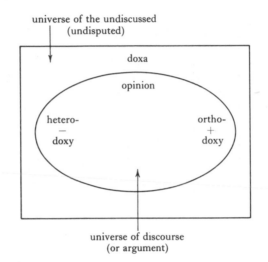

The truth of doxa is only ever fully revealed when negatively constituted by the constitution of a *field of opinion*, the locus of the confrontation of competing discourses – whose political truth may be overtly declared or may remain hidden, even from the eyes of those engaged in it, under the guise of religious or philosophical oppositions. It is by reference to the universe of opinion that the complementary class is defined, the class of that which is taken for granted, doxa, the sum total of the theses tacitly posited on the hither side of all inquiry, which appear as such only retrospectively, when they come to be suspended practically. The practical questioning of the theses implied in a particular way of living that is brought about by "culture contact" or by the political and economic crises correlative with class division is not the purely intellectual operation which phenomenology designates by the term *epoche*, the deliberate, methodical suspension of naive adherence to the world.[15] The critique which brings the undiscussed into discussion, the unformulated into formulation, has as the condition of its possibility objective crisis, which, in breaking the immediate fit between the subjective structures and the objective structures, destroys self-evidence practically. It is when the social world loses its character as a natural phenomenon that the question of the natural or conventional character (*phusei* or *nomo*) of social facts can be raised.[16] It follows that the would-be most radical critique always has the limits that are assigned to it by the objective conditions. Crisis is a necessary condition for a questioning of doxa but is not in itself a sufficient condition for the production of a critical discourse. In class societies, in which the definition of the social world is at stake in overt or latent class struggle, the drawing of the line between the field of opinion, of that which is explicitly questioned, and the field of *doxa*, of that which is beyond question and which each agent tacitly accords by the mere fact of acting in accord with social convention, is itself a fundamental objective at stake in that form of class struggle which is the struggle for the imposition of the dominant systems of classification. The dominated classes have an interest in pushing back the limits of *doxa* and exposing the arbitrariness of the taken for granted; the dominant classes have an interest in defending the integrity of doxa or, short of this, of establishing in its place the necessarily imperfect substitute, *orthodoxy*.

It is only when the dominated have the material and symbolic means of rejecting the definition of the real that is imposed on them through logical structures reproducing the social structures (i.e. the state of the power relations) and to lift the (institutionalized or internalized) censorships which it implies, i.e. when social classifications become the object and instrument of class struggle, that the arbitrary principles of the prevailing classification can appear as such and it therefore becomes necessary to undertake the work of conscious systematization and express rationalization which marks the passage from doxa to orthodoxy.

Orthodoxy, straight, or rather *straightened*, opinion, which aims, without ever entirely succeeding, at restoring the primal state of innocence of doxa, exists only in the objective relationship which opposes it to heterodoxy, that is, by reference to the choice – *hairesis*, heresy – made possible by the existence of *competing possibles* and to the explicit critique of the sum total of the alternatives not chosen that the established order implies. It is defined as a system of euphemisms, of acceptable ways of thinking and speaking the natural and social world, which rejects heretical remarks as blasphemies.[17] But the manifest censorship imposed by orthodox discourse, the official way of speaking and thinking the world, conceals another, more radical censorship: the overt opposition between "right" opinion and "left" or "wrong" opinion, which delimits *the universe of possible discourse*, be it legitimate or illegitimate, euphemistic or blasphemous, masks in its turn the fundamental opposition between the universe of things that can be stated, and hence thought, and the universe of that which is taken for granted. The universe of discourse, in the classic definition given by A. de Morgan in his *Formal Logic*, "a range of ideas which is either expressed or understood as containing the whole matter under discussion",[18] is practically defined in relation to the necessarily unnoticed complementary class that is constituted by the universe of that which is undiscussed, unnamed, admitted without argument or scrutiny. Thus in class societies, everything takes place as if the struggle for the power to impose the legitimate mode of thought and expression that is unceasingly waged in the field of the production of symbolic goods tended to conceal, not least from the eyes of those involved in it, the contribution it makes to the delimitation of the universe of discourse, that is to say, the universe of the thinkable, and hence to the delimitation of the universe of the unthinkable; as if euphemism and blasphemy, through which the expressly censored unnameable nonetheless finds its way into the universe of discourse, conspired in their very antagonism to occult the "aphasia" of those who are denied access to the instruments of the struggle for the definition of reality. If one accepts the equation made by Marx in *The German Ideology*, that "language is real, practical consciousness", it can be seen that the boundary between the universe of (orthodox or heterodox) discourse and the universe of doxa, in the twofold sense of what goes without saying and what cannot be said for lack of an available discourse, represents the dividing-line between the most radical form of misrecognition and the awakening of political consciousness.

The relationship between language and experience never appears more clearly than in crisis situations in which the everyday order (*Alltäglichkeit*) is challenged, and with it the language of order, situations which call for an extraordinary discourse (the *Ausseralltäglichkeit* which Weber presents as the decisive characteristic of charisma) capable of giving systematic expression to the gamut of extra-ordinary experiences that this, so to speak, objective *epoche* has provoked or made possible. "Private" experiences undergo nothing less than a *change of state* when they recognize themselves in the *public objectivity* of an already constituted discourse, the objective sign of recognition of their right to be spoken and to be spoken publicly: "Words wreck havoc", says Sartre, "when they find a name for what had up to then been lived namelessly."[19] Because any language that can command attention is an "authorized language", invested with the authority of a group, the things it designates are not simply expressed but also authorized and legitimated. This is true not only of establishment language but also of the heretical discourses which draw their legitimacy and authority from the very groups over which they exert their power and which they literally produce by expressing them: they derive their power from their capacity to *objectify* unformulated experiences, to make them public – a step on the road to officialization and legitimation – and, when the occasion arises, to manifest and reinforce their concordance. Heretical power, the strength of the sorcerer who wields a liberating potency – that of all logotherapies – in offering the means of expressing experiences usually repressed, the strength of the prophet or political leader who mobilizes the group by announcing to them what they want to hear, rests on the dialectical relationship between authorized, authorizing language and the group which authorizes it and acts on its authority.

Symbolic capital

The theoretical construction which retrospectively projects the counter-gift into the project of the gift has the effect of transforming into mechanical sequences of obligatory acts the at once risky and necessary improvisation of the everyday strategies which owe their infinite complexity to the fact that the giver's undeclared calculation must reckon with the receiver's undeclared calculation, and hence satisfy his expectations without appearing to know what they are. In the same operation, it removes the conditions making possible the *institutionally organized and guaranteed misrecognition*[20] which is the basis of gift exchange and, perhaps, of all the symbolic labour intended to transmute, by the sincere fiction of a disinterested exchange, the inevitable, and inevitably interested relations imposed by kinship, neighbourhood, or work, into elective relations of reciprocity: in the work of reproducing established relations – through feasts, ceremonies, exchanges of gifts, visits or courtesies, and, above all, marriages – which is no less vital to the existence of the group than the reproduction of the economic bases of its existence, the labour required to conceal the function of the exchanges is as important an element as the labour needed to carry out the function.[21] If it is true that the lapse of time interposed is what enables the gift or counter-gift to be seen and experienced as an inaugural act of generosity, without any past or future, i.e. without *calculation*, then it is clear that in reducing the polythetic to the monothetic, objectivism destroys the specificity of all practices which, like gift exchange, tend or pretend to put the law of self-interest into abeyance. A rational contract would telescope into an instant a transaction which gift exchange disguises by stretching it out in time; and because of this, gift exchange is, if not the only mode of commodity circulation practised, at least the only mode to be fully recognized, in societies which, because they deny "the true soil of their life", as Lukács puts it, have an economy in itself and not for itself. Everything takes place as if the essence of the "archaic" economy lay in the fact that economic activity cannot explicitly acknowledge the economic ends in relation to which it is objectively oriented: the "idolatry of nature" which makes it impossible to think of nature as a raw material, or, consequently, to see human activity as *labour*, i.e. as man's struggle against nature, tends, together with the systematic emphasis on the symbolic aspect of the activities and relations of production, to prevent the economy from being grasped *as* an economy, i.e. as a system governed by the laws of interested calculation, competition, or exploitation.

In reducing the economy to its objective reality, economism annihilates the specificity located precisely in the socially maintained discrepancy between the misrecognized or, one might say, socially repressed, objective truth of economic activity, and the social representation of production and exchange. It is no accident that the vocabulary of the archaic economy should be entirely composed of double-sided notions that are condemned to disintegrate in the course of the history of the economy, since, owing to their duality, the social relations they designate represent unstable structures which are condemned to split in two as soon as there is any weakening of the social mechanisms aimed at maintaining them. Thus, to take an extreme example, *rahnia*, a contract by which the borrower grants the lender the usufruct of some of his land for the duration of the loan, and which is regarded as the worst form of usury when it leads to dispossession, differs only in the nature of the social relation between the two parties, and thus in the detailed terms of the agreement, from the aid granted to a relative in difficulties so as to save him from having to sell a piece of land, which, even when it continues to be used by its owner, constitutes a sort of security on the loan.[22] "It was precisely the Romans and Greeks", writes Mauss, "who, possibly following the Northern and Western Semites, drew the distinction between personal rights and real rights, separated purchases from gifts and exchanges, dissociated moral obligations from contracts, and, above all, conceived of the difference between ritual, rights and interests. By a genuine, great and venerable revolution they passed beyond the excessively hazardous, costly and elaborate gift economy, which was encumbered with personal considerations, incompatible with the development of the market, trade and production, and, in a word, uneconomic."[23] The historical situations in which the unstable, artificially maintained structures of the good-faith economy break up and make way for the *clear, economic* (i.e. *economical*) concepts of the undisguised self-interest economy reveal the cost of operating an economy which, by its refusal to acknowledge and confess itself as such, is forced to devote as much time to concealing the reality of economic acts as it expends in carrying them out: the generalization of monetary exchange, which exposes the objective workings of the economy, also brings to light the institutional mechanisms, proper to the archaic economy, which have the function of limiting and disguising the play of economic interest and calculation (economic in the narrow sense of the word). For example, a well-known mason, who had learnt his trade in France, caused a scandal, around 1955, by going home when his work was finished without eating the meal traditionally given in the mason's honour when a house is built, and then demanding, in addition to the price of his day's work (one thousand old francs), an allowance of two hundred francs in lieu of the meal: his demand for the cash equivalent of the meal was a sacrilegious reversal of the formula used by symbolic alchemy to transmute the price of labour into an unsolicited gift, and it thus exposed the device most commonly employed to keep up appearances by means of a collectively concerted make-believe. As an act of exchange setting the seal on alliances ("I set the wheatcake and the salt between us"), the final meal at the time of the *thiwizi* of harvest or house-building naturally became a *closing rite* intended to transmute an interested transaction retrospectively into a generous exchange (like the gifts which mark the successful conclusion of a deal).[24] Whereas the greatest indulgence was accorded to the subterfuges used by some to minimize the cost of the meals at the end of the *thiwizi* (e.g. inviting only the "notables" of each group, or one man from each family) – a departure from principles which at least paid lip-service to their legitimacy – the reaction could only be scandal and shock when a man took it upon himself to declare that the meal had a cash equivalent, thus betraying the best-kept and worst-kept secret (one that everyone must keep), and breaking the law of silence which guarantees the complicity of collective bad faith in the good-faith economy.

The *good-faith economy* calls forth the strange incarnation of *homo economicus* known as the *bu niya* (or *bab niya*), the man of good faith (*niya* or *thi'ugganth*, from *a'ggun*, the child still unable to speak, contrasted with *thahraymith*, calculating, technical intelligence). The man of good faith would not think of selling certain fresh food products – milk, butter, cheese, vegetables, fruit – to another peasant, but always distributes them among friends or neighbours. He practises no exchanges involving money and all his relations are based on total confidence; unlike the shady dealer, he has recourse to none of the guarantees (witnesses, written documents, etc.) with which commercial transactions are surrounded. The general law of exchanges means that the closer the individuals or groups are in the genealogy, the easier it is to make agreements, the more frequent they are, and the more completely they are entrusted to good faith. Conversely, as the relationship becomes more impersonal, i.e. as one moves out from the relationship between brothers to that between virtual strangers (people from two different villages) or even complete strangers, so a transaction is less likely to occur at all, but it can become and increasingly does become purely "economic" in character, i.e. closer to its economic reality, and the interested calculation which is never absent even from the most generous exchange (in which both parties account – i.e. count – themselves satisfied) can be more and more openly revealed. This explains why recourse to formal guarantees becomes more and more exceptional as the social distance between the parties decreases, and also as the solemnity of the guarantees increases, because the authorities responsible for authenticating and enforcing them are more remote and/or more venerated. (First there is the word of witnesses, which is enhanced if they are distant and influential; then there is a simple paper drawn up by someone not specialized in the production of legal documents; then the contract signed before a taleb, providing a religious but not a legal guarantee, which is less solemn when drawn up by the village taleb than by a well-known taleb; then the Cadi's written document; and finally the contract signed in front of a lawyer.) It would be insulting to presume to authenticate a transaction based on trust between trustworthy people, and still more so between relatives, before a lawyer, a cadi, or even witnesses. Similarly, the share of the loss which partners agree to accept when there is an accident to an animal may be entirely different depending on the assessment of their responsibilities which they come to in accordance with the relationship between them: a man who has lent an animal to a close relative feels he must minimize his partner's responsibility. By contrast, a regular contract, signed before the Cadi or before witnesses, governed the arrangement by which the Kabyles handed over their oxen to the southern Nomads to be looked after for one, two, or three working years (from autumn to autumn) in exchange for twenty-two double decalitres of barley per ox per year, with costs to be shared in the case of loss and profits shared in the case of sale. Private arrangements between kin and affines are to market transactions what ritual war is to total war. The "goods or beasts of the fellah" are traditionally contrasted with the "goods or beasts of the market": old informants will talk endlessly of the tricks and frauds which are common practice in the "big markets", that is to say, in exchanges between strangers. There are countless tales of mules which run off as soon as the purchaser has got them home, oxen made to look fatter by rubbing them with a plant which makes them swell (*adhris*), and purchasers who band together to force prices down. The incarnation of economic war is the shady dealer, the man who fears neither God nor man. Men avoid buying animals from him, just as they avoid buying from any complete stranger: as one informant said, for straightforward goods such as land, it is the choice of the thing to be purchased which determines the buyer's decision; for problematic goods, such as beasts of burden, especially mules, it is the choice of seller which decides, and at least an effort is made to substitute a personalized relationship ("on behalf of . . .") for a completely impersonal, anonymous one. Every intermediate stage can be found, from transactions based on complete distrust, such as that between the peasant and the shady dealer, who cannot demand or obtain guarantees because he cannot guarantee the quality of his product or find guarantors, to the exchange of honour which can dispense with conditions and depend entirely on the good faith of the "contracting parties". But in most transactions the notions of buyer and seller tend to be dissolved in the network of middlemen and guarantors designed to transform the purely economic relationship between supply and demand into a genealogically based and genealogically guaranteed relationship. Marriage itself is no exception: quite apart from parallel-cousin marriage, it almost always occurs between families already linked by a whole network of previous exchanges, underwriting the specific new agreement. It is significant that in the first phase of the highly complex negotiations leading up to the marriage agreement, the families bring in prestigious kinsmen or affines as "guarantors", the symbolic capital thus displayed serving both to strengthen their hand in the negotiations and to guarantee the deal once it has been concluded.

Similarly, the indignant comments provoked by the heretical behaviour of peasants who have departed from traditional ways draw attention to the mechanisms which formerly inclined the peasant to maintain a magical relationship with the land and made it impossible for him to see his toil as labour: "It's sacrilege, they have profaned the land; they have done away with fear [*elhiba*]. Nothing intimidates them or stops them; they turn everything upside down, I'm sure they'll end up ploughing in *lakhrif* if they are in a hurry and if they mean to spend *lahlal* [the licit period for ploughing] doing something else, or in *rbi'* [spring] if they've been too lazy in *lahlal*. It's all the same to them." Everything in the peasant's practice actualizes, in a different mode, the objective intention revealed by ritual. The land is never treated as a raw material to be exploited, but always as the object of respect mixed with fear (*elhiba*): it will "settle its scores", they say, and take revenge for the bad treatment it receives from a clumsy or over-hasty farmer. The accomplished peasant "presents himself" to his land with the stance appropriate when one man meets another (i.e. face to face), and with the attitude of trusting familiarity he would show a respected kinsman. During the ploughing, he would not think of delegating the task of leading the team, and the only task he leaves for his "clients" (*ichikran*) is that of breaking up the soil behind the plough. "The old men used to say that to plough properly, you had to be the master of the land. The young men were left out of it: it would have been an insult to the land to 'present' it [*qabel*] with men one would not dare to present to other men." "It is the man who confronts [receives] other men", says a proverb, "who must confront the land." To take up Hesiod's opposition between *ponos* and *ergon*, the peasant does not *work*, he takes *pains*. "Give to the earth and the earth will give to you", says a proverb. This can be taken to mean that in obedience to the logic of gift exchange, nature bestows its bounty only on those who bring it their care as a tribute. And the heretical behaviour of those who leave to the young the task of "opening the earth and ploughing into it the wealth of the new year" provokes the older peasants to express the principle of the relationship between men and the land, which could remain unformulated as long as it was taken for granted: "The earth no longer gives because we give it nothing. We openly mock the earth and it is only right that it should pay us back with lies." The self-respecting man should always be busy doing something; if he cannot find anything to do, "at least he can carve his spoon". Activity is as much a duty of communal life as an economic necessity. What is valued is activity for its own sake, regardless of its strictly economic function, inasmuch as it is regarded as appropriate to the function of the person doing it.[25] Only the application of categories alien to peasant experience (those imposed by economic domination and the generalization of monetary exchanges) brings up the distinction between the technical aspect and the ritual or symbolic aspect of agricultural activity. The distinction between productive and unproductive work or between profitable and unprofitable work is unknown: the ancient economy knows only the opposition between the idler who fails in his social duty and the worker who performs his socially defined proper function, whatever the product of his effort.

Everything conspires to conceal the relationship between work and its product. Thus the distinction which Marx makes between the *working period* proper – the time devoted to ploughing and harvest – and the *production period* – the nine months or so between sowing and harvesting, during which time there is hardly any productive work to be done – is disguised in practice by the apparent continuity conferred on agricultural activity by the countless minor tasks intended to assist nature in its labour. No one would have thought of assessing the technical efficiency or economic usefulness of these indissolubly technical *and* ritual acts, the peasant's version, as it were, of art for art's sake, such as fencing the fields, pruning the trees, protecting the new shoots from the animals, or "visiting" (*asafqadh*) and looking after the fields, not to mention practices generally regarded as rites, such as actions intended to expel or transfer evil (*asifedh*) or celebrate the coming of spring. Similarly, no one would dream of trying to evaluate the profitability of all the activities which the application of alien categories would lead one to regard as unproductive, such as the functions carried out by the head of the family as leader and representative of the group – co-ordinating the work, speaking in the men's assembly, bargaining in the market, and reading in the mosque. "If the peasant counted", runs a proverb, "he would not sow." Perhaps we should say that the relationship between work and its product is in reality not unknown, but *socially repressed*; that the productivity of labour is so low that the peasant must refrain from counting his time, in order to preserve the meaningfulness of his work; or – and this is only an apparent contradiction – that in a world in which time is so plentiful and goods are so scarce, his best and indeed only course is to spend his time without counting it, to squander the one thing which exists in abundance.[26]

In short, the reality of production is no less repressed than the reality of circulation, and the peasant's "pains" are to *labour* what the gift is to commerce (an activity for which, as Emile Benveniste points out, the Indo-European languages had no name). The discovery of labour presupposes the constitution of the common ground of production, i.e. the disenchantment of a natural world henceforward reduced to its economic dimension alone; ceasing to be the tribute paid to a necessary order, activity can be directed towards an exclusively economic end, the end which money, henceforward the measure of all things, starkly designates. This means the end of the primal undifferentiatedness which made possible the play of individual and collective misrecognition: measured by the yardstick of monetary profit, the most sacred activities find themselves constituted negatively, as *symbolic*, i.e., in a sense the word sometimes receives, as lacking concrete or material effect, in short, *gratuitous*, i.e. disinterested but also useless.

Those who apply the categories and methods of economics to archaic economies without taking into account the ontological transmutation they impose on their object are certainly not alone nowadays in treating this type of economy "as the Fathers of the Church treated the religions which preceded Christianity": Marx's phrase could also be applied to those Marxists who tend to limit research on the formations they call "pre-capitalist" to scholastic discussion about the typology of modes of production. The common root of this ethnocentrism is the unconscious acceptance of a *restricted definition of economic interest*, which, in its explicit form, is the historical product of capitalism: the constitution of relatively autonomous areas of practice is accompanied by a process through which symbolic interests (often described as "spiritual" or "cultural") come to be set up in opposition to strictly economic interests as defined in the field of economic transactions by the fundamental tautology "business is business"; strictly "cultural" or "aesthetic" interest, disinterested interest, is the paradoxical product of the ideological labour in which writers and artists, those most directly interested, have played an important part and in the course of which symbolic interests become autonomous by being opposed to material interests, i.e. by being symbolically nullified as interests. Economism knows no other interest than that which capitalism has produced, through a sort of concrete application of abstraction, by establishing a universe of relations between man and man based, as Marx says, on "callous cash payment". Thus it can find no place in its analyses, still less in its calculations, for the strictly symbolic interest which is occasionally recognized (when too obviously entering into conflict with "interest" in the narrow sense, as in certain forms of nationalism or regionalism) only to be reduced to the irrationality of feeling or passion. In fact, in a universe characterized by the more or less perfect interconvertibility of economic capital (in the narrow sense) and symbolic capital, the *economic calculation* directing the agents' strategies takes indissociably into account profits and losses which the narrow definition of economy unconsciously rejects as *unthinkable* and *unnameable*, i.e. as economically irrational. In short, contrary to naively idyllic representations of "pre-capitalist" societies (or of the "cultural" sphere of capitalist societies), practice never ceases to conform to economic calculation even when it gives every appearance of disinterestedness by departing from the logic of interested calculation (in the narrow sense) and playing for stakes that are non-material and not easily quantified.

Thus the theory of strictly economic practice is simply a particular case of a general theory of the economics of practice. The only way to escape from the ethnocentric naiveties of economism, without falling into populist exaltation of the generous naivety of earlier forms of society, is to carry out in full what economism does only partially, and to extend economic calculation to *all* the goods, material and symbolic, without distinction, that present themselves as *rare* and worthy of being sought after in a particular social formation – which may be "fair words" or smiles, handshakes or shrugs, compliments or attention, challenges or insults, honour or honours, powers or pleasures, gossip or scientific information, distinction or distinctions, etc. Economic calculation has hitherto managed to appropriate the territory objectively surrendered to the remorseless logic of what Marx calls "naked self-interest" only by setting aside a "sacred" island miraculously spared by the "icy water of egoistical calculation" and left as a sanctuary for the priceless or worthless things it cannot assess. But an accountancy of symbolic exchanges would itself lead to a distorted representation of the archaic economy if it were forgotten that, as the product of a principle of differentiation alien to the universe to which it is applied – the distinction between economic and symbolic capital – the only way in which such accountancy can apprehend the undifferentiatedness of economic and symbolic capital is in the form of their perfect interconvertibility. If the constitution of art *qua* art, accompanying the development of a relatively autonomous artistic field, leads one to conceive of certain primitive or popular practices as aesthetic, one inevitably falls into the ethnocentric errors unavoidable when one forgets that those practices cannot be conceived as such from within; similarly, any partial or total objectification of the ancient economy that does not include a theory of the *theorization effect* and of the social conditions of objective apprehension, together with a theory of that economy's relation to its objective reality (a relation of misrecognition), succumbs to the subtlest and most irreproachable form of ethnocentrism.

In its full definition, the patrimony of a family or lineage includes not only their land and instruments of production but also their kin and their clientele, *nesba*, the network of alliances, or, more broadly, of relationships, to be kept up and regularly maintained, representing a heritage of commitments and debts of honour, a capital of rights and duties built up in the course of successive generations and providing an additional source of strength which can be called upon when extra-ordinary situations break in upon the daily routine. For all its power to regulate the routine of the ordinary course of events through ritual stereotyping, and to overcome crises by producing them symbolically or ritualizing them as soon as they appear, the archaic economy is nonetheless familiar with the opposition between ordinary and extraordinary occasions, between the regular needs which the household can satisfy and the exceptional needs for material and symbolic goods and services (in unusual circumstances of economic crisis, political conflict, or simply urgent farm work) requiring the unpaid assistance of a more extended group. If this is so, it is because, contrary to what Max Weber suggests when he draws a crude contrast between the traditionalist type and the charismatic type, the ancient economy has its discontinuities, not only in the political sphere, with conflicts which may start with a chance incident and escalate into tribal war through the interplay of the "leagues", but also in the economic sphere, with the opposition between the *labour period*, which in traditional cereal cultivation is particularly short, and the *production period* – an opposition giving rise to one of the basic contradictions of that social formation and also, in consequence, to the strategies designed to overcome it.[27] The strategy of accumulating a capital of honour and prestige, which produces the clients as much as they produce it, provides the optimal solution to the problem the group would face if it had to *maintain continuously* (throughout the production period as well) the whole (human and animal) workforce it needs during the labour period: it allows the great families to make use of the maximum workforce during the labour period, and to reproduce consumption to a minimum during the unavoidably long production period. Both human and animal consumption are cut, the former by the reduction of the group to the minimal unit, the family; and the latter through hire contracts, such as the *charka* of an ox, by which the owner lends his animal in exchange for nothing more than compensation in cash or in kind for "depreciation of the capital". These services, provided at precise moments and limited of periods of intense activity, such as harvest time, are repaid either in the form of labour, at other times of the year, or with other services such as protection, the loan of animals, etc.

Thus we see that symbolic capital, which in the form of the prestige and renown attached to a family and a name is readily convertible back into economic capital, is perhaps *the most valuable form of accumulation* in a society in which the severity of the climate (the major work – ploughing and harvesting – having to be done in a very short space of time) and the limited technical resources (harvesting is done with the sickle) demand collective labour. Should one see in it a disguised form of purchase of labour power, or a covert exaction of corvées? By all means, as long as the analysis holds together what holds together in practice, the *double reality* of instrinsically *equivocal, ambiguous* conduct. This is the pitfall awaiting all those whom a naively dualistic representation of the relationship between practice and ideology, between the "native" economy and the "native" representation of that economy, leads into self-mystifying demystifications:[28] the complete reality of this appropriation of services lies in the fact that it *can only* take place in the disguise of the *thiwizi*, the voluntary assistance which is also a corvée and is thus a voluntary corvée and forced assistance, and that, to use a geometrical metaphor, it implies a double half-rotation returning to the starting-point, i.e. a conversion of material capital into symbolic capital itself reconvertible into material capital.

The acquisition of a clientele, even an inherited one, implies considerable *labour* devoted to making and maintaining relations, and also substantial material and symbolic *investments*, in the form of political aid against attack, theft, offence, and insult, or economic aid, which can be very costly, especially in times of scarcity. As well as material wealth, *time* must be invested, for the value of symbolic labour cannot be defined without reference to the time devoted to it, *giving* or *squandering time* being one of the most precious of gifts.[29] It is clear that in such conditions symbolic capital can only be accumulated at the expense of the accumulation of economic capital. Combining with the objective obstacles stemming from the inefficiency of the means of production, the action of the social mechanisms inclining agents to repress or disguise economic interest and tending to make the accumulation of symbolic capital the only recognized, legitimate form of accumulation, was sufficient to restrain and even prohibit the accumulation of material capital; and it was no doubt rare for the assembly to have to step in and order someone "not to get any richer".[30] It is a fact that collective pressure – with which the wealthy members of the group have to reckon, because they draw from it not only their authority but also, at times, political power, the strength of which ultimately reflects their capacity to mobilize the group for or against individuals or groups – requires the rich not only to pay the largest share of the cost of ceremonial exchanges (*tawsa*) but also to make the biggest contributions to the maintenance of the poor, the lodging of strangers, and the organization of festivals. Above all, wealth implies duties. "The generous man", it is said, "is the friend of God." Belief in immanent justice, which inspires a number of practices (such as collective oath-swearing), no doubt helps to make of generosity a sacrifice designed to win in return the blessing of prosperity: "Eat, you who are used to feeding others"; "Lord, give unto me that I may give." But the two forms of capital are so inextricably linked that the mere exhibition of the material and symbolic strength represented by prestigious affines is likely to be in itself a source of material profit in a good-faith economy in which good repute is the best, if not the only, economic guarantee: it is easy to see why the great families never miss a chance (and this is one reason for their predilection for distant marriages and vast processions) to organize exhibitions of symbolic capital (in which conspicuous consumption is only the most visible aspect), with processions of relatives and friends to solemnize the pilgrim's departure or return; the bride's escort, assessed in terms of the number of "rifles" and the intensity of the salutes fired in the couple's honour; prestigious gifts, including sheep, given on the occasion of the marriage; witnesses and guarantors who can be mobilized at any time and place, to attest the good faith of a market transaction or to strengthen the position of the lineage in matrimonial negotiation and to solemnize the contract. Once one realizes that symbolic capital is always *credit*, in the widest sense of the word, i.e. a sort of advance which the group alone can grant those who give it the best material and symbolic *guarantees*, it can be seen that the exhibition of symbolic capital (which is always very expensive in economic terms) is one of the mechanisms which (no doubt universally) make capital go to capital.

It is thus by drawing up a *comprehensive balance-sheet* of symbolic profits, without forgetting the undifferentiatedness of the symbolic and material aspects of the patrimony, that it becomes possible to grasp the economic rationality of conduct which economism dismisses as absurd: the decision to buy a second pair of oxen after the harvest, on the grounds that they are needed for treading out the grain – which is a way of making it known the crop has been plentiful – only to have to sell them again for lack of fodder, before the autumn ploughing, when they would be technically necessary, seems economically aberrant only if one forgets all the material and symbolic profit accruing from this (albeit fictitious) addition to the family's symbolic capital in the late-summer period in which marriages are negotiated. The perfect rationality of this strategy of bluff lies in the fact that marriage is the occasion for an (in the widest sense) economic circulation which cannot be seen purely in terms of material goods; the profit a group can expect to draw from the transaction rises with its material and especially its symbolic patrimony, in other words, its standing in the eyes of other groups. This standing, which depends on the capacity of the group's point of honour to guarantee the invulnerability of its honour, and constitutes an undivided whole indissolubly uniting the quantity and quality of its goods and the quantity and quality of the men capable of turning them to good account, is what enables the group, mainly through marriage, to acquire powerful affines (i.e. wealth in the form of "rifles", measured not only by the number of men but also by their quality, i.e. their point of honour), and defines the group's capacity to preserve its land and honour, and in particular the honour of its women (i.e. the capital of material and symbolic strength which can actually be mobilized for market transactions, contests of honour, or work on the land). Thus the interest at stake in the conduct of honour is one for which economism has no name, and which has to be called symbolic, although it is such as to inspire actions which are very directly material; just as there are professions, like law and medicine, in which those who practise them must be "above suspicion", so a family has a vital interest in keeping its capital of honour, i.e. its capital of honourability, safe from suspicion. And the hypersensitivity to the slightest slur or innuendo (*thasalqubth*), and the multiplicity of strategies designed to belie or avert them, can be explained by the fact that symbolic capital is less easily measured and counted than land or livestock and that the group, ultimately the only source of credit for it, will readily withdraw that credit and direct its suspicions at the strongest members, as if in matters of honour, as in land, one man's greater wealth made the others that much poorer.

We must analyse in terms of the same logic the mechanisms which some- times endow a piece of land with a value not always corresponding to its strictly technical and (in the narrow sense) economic qualities. Doubtless the nearest fields, those best maintained and best farmed, and hence the most "productive", those most accessible to the women (by private paths, *thik- huradjiyin*), are predisposed to be more highly valued by *any* purchaser; however, a piece of land will sometimes take on a symbolic value dispro- portionate to its economic value, as a function of the socially accepted definition of the symbolic patrimony. Thus the first plots to be relinquished will be the land least integrated into the estate, least associated with the name of its present owners, the land which was bought (especially by a recent purchase) rather than inherited, the land bought from strangers rather than that bought from kinsmen. When a field endowed with all the properties which define a strong integration into the patrimonial estate is owned by strangers, buying it back becomes a question of honour, analogous to avenging an insult, and it may rise to exorbitant prices. They are purely theoretical prices most of the time, since, within this logic, the symbolic profits of making the challenge are greater than the material profits that would accrue from cynical (hence reprehensible) exploiting of the situation. So, the point of honour the possessors set on keeping the land, especially if their appropriation is sufficiently recent to retain its value as a challenge to the alien group, is equal to the other side's determination to buy it back and to avenge the injury done to the *ḥurma* of their land. It may happen that a third group will step in with a higher bid, thereby challenging not the seller, who only profits from the competition, but the "legitimate" owners.[31]

Only an inconsistent – because reduced and reductive – materialism can fail to see that strategies whose object is to conserve or increase the honour of the group, in the forefront of which stand blood vengeance and marriage, are dictated by interests no less vital than are inheritance or fertility strategies.[32] The interest leading an agent to defend his symbolic capital is inseparable from the tacit adherence, inculcated in the earliest years of life and reinforced by all subsequent experience, to the axiomatics objectively inscribed in the regularities of the (in the broad sense) economic order which constitutes a determinate type of symbolic capital as worthy of being pursued and pre- served. The objective harmony between the agents' dispositions (here, their propensity and capacity to play the game of honour) and the objective regularities of which their dispositions are the product, means that membership in this economic cosmos implies unconditional recognition of the stakes which, by its very existence, it presents as taken for granted, that is, misrecognition of the arbitrariness of the value it confers on them. This value is such as to induce investments and over-investments (in both the economic and the psychoanalytic senses) which tend, through the ensuing competition and rarity, to reinforce the well-grounded illusion that the value of symbolic goods is inscribed in the nature of things, just as interest in these goods is inscribed in the nature of men.

Thus, the homologies established between the circulation of land sold and bought, the circulation of "throats" "lent" and "returned" (murder and vengeance), and the circulation of women given and received, that is, between the different forms of capital and the corresponding modes of circulation, oblige us to abandon the dichotomy of the economic and the non-economic which stands in the way of seeing the science of economic practices as a particular case of a *general science of the economy of practices*, capable of treating all practices, including those purporting to be disinterested or gratuitous, and hence non-economic, as economic practices directed towards the maximizing of material or symbolic profit. The capital accumulated by groups, the energy of social dynamics – in this case their capital of physical strength (related to their mobilizing capacity, and hence to the number of men and their readiness to fight), their economic capital (land and livestock) and their symbolic capital, always additionally associated with possession of the other kinds of capital, but susceptible of increase or decrease depending on how they are used – can exist in *different forms* which, although subject to strict laws of equivalence and hence mutually convertible, produce specific effects.[33] Symbolic capital, a transformed and thereby *disguised* form of physical "economic" capital, produces its proper effect inasmuch, and only inasmuch, as it conceals the fact that it originates in "material" forms of capital which are also, in the last analysis, the source of its effects.

Modes of domination

In societies which have no "self-regulating market" (in Karl Polyani's sense), no educational system, no juridical apparatus, and no State, relations of domination can be set up and maintained only at the cost of strategies which must be endlessly renewed, because the conditions required for a *mediated, lasting appropriation* of other agents' labour, services, or homage have not been brought together. By contrast, domination no longer needs to be exerted in a direct, personal way when it is entailed in possession of the means (economic or cultural capital) of appropriating the mechanisms of the field of production and the field of cultural production, which tend to assure their own reproduction by their very functioning, independently of any deliberate intervention by the agents. So, it is in the degree of objectification of the accumulated social capital that one finds the basis of all the pertinent differences between the modes of domination: that is, very schematically, between, on the one hand, social universes in which relations of domination are made, unmade, and remade in and by the interactions between persons, and on the other hand, social formations in which, mediated by objective, institutionalized mechanisms, such as those producing and guaranteeing the distribution of "titles" (titles of nobility, deeds of possession, academic degrees, etc.), relations of domination have the opacity and permanence of things and escape the grasp of individual consciousness and power. Objectification guarantees the permanence and cumulativity of material and symbolic acquisitions which can then subsist without the agents having to recreate them continuously and in their entirety by deliberate action; but, because the profits of these institutions are the object of differential appropriation, objectification also and inseparably ensures the reproduction of the structure of the distribution of the capital which, in its various forms, is the precondition for such appropriation, and in so doing, reproduces the structure of the relations of domination and dependence.

Paradoxically, it is precisely because there exist relatively autonomous fields, functioning in accordance with rigorous mechanisms capable of imposing their necessity on the agents, that those who are in a position to command these mechanisms and to appropriate the material and/or symbolic profits accruing from their functioning are able to *dispense with* strategies aimed *expressly* (which does not mean manifestly) and directly (i.e. without being mediated by the mechanisms) at the domination of individuals, a domination which in this case is the condition of the appropriation of the material and symbolic profits of their labour. The saving is a real one, because strategies designed to establish or maintain lasting relations of dependence are generally very expensive in terms of material goods (as in the potlatch or in charitable acts), services, or simply *time*; which is why, by a paradox constitutive of this mode of domination, the means eat up the end, and the actions necessary to ensure the continuation of power themselves help to weaken it.[34]

Economic power lies not in wealth but in the relationship between wealth and a field of economic relations, the constitution of which is inseparable from the development of a *body of specialized agents*, with specific interests; it is in this relationship that wealth is constituted, in the form of capital, that is, as the instrument for appropriating the institutional equipment and the mechanisms indispensable to the functioning of the field, and thereby also appropriating the profits from it. Thus Moses Finley convincingly shows that the ancient economy lacked not resources but the means "to overcome the limits of individual resources". "There were no proper credit instruments – no negotiable paper, no book clearance, no credit payments...There was moneylending in plenty but it was concentrated on small usurious loans to peasants or consumers, and in large borrowings to enable men to meet the political or other conventional expenditures of the upper classes...Similarly in the field of business organization: there were no long-term partnerships or corporations, no brokers or agents, no guilds – again with the occasional and unimportant exception. In short, both the organizational and the operational devices were lacking for the mobilization of private capital resources."[35] This analysis is even more relevant to ancient Kabylia, which lacked even the most elementary instruments of an economic institution. Land was in fact more or less totally excluded from circulation (though, occasionally serving as security, it was liable to pass from one group to another). Village and tribal markets remained isolated and there was no way in which they could be linked up in a single mechanism. The opposition made by traditional morality, incarnated by the *bu niya*, between the "sacrilegious cunning" customary in market transactions and the good faith appropriate to exchanges among kinsmen and friends[36] – which was marked by the spatial distinction between the place of residence, the village, and the place of transactions, the market – must not be allowed to mask the opposition between the small local market, still "embedded in social relationships", as Polyani puts it, and the market when it has become the "dominant transactional mode".[37]

The strategies of honour are not banished from the market: though a man may enhance his prestige by tricking a stranger, he may also take pride in having bought something at an exorbitant price, to satisfy his point of honour, just "to show he could do it"; or he may boast of having managed to strike a bargain without laying out a penny in cash, either by mobilizing a number of guarantors, or, better still, by drawing on the *credit* and the *capital of trust* which come as much from a reputation for honour as from a reputation for wealth. It is said of such a man that "he could come back with the whole market even if he left home with nothing in his pockets". Men whose reputation is known to all are predisposed to play the part of guarantors – either for the seller, who vouches for the quality of his animal in their presence, or for the buyer, who, if he is not paying in cash, promises that he will repay his debt promptly.[38] The trust in which they are held, and the connections which they can mobilize, enable them to "go to the market with only their faces, their names, and their honour for money" – in other words, the only things which can take the place of money in this economy – and even "to wager [to make an offer], *whether they have money on them or not*". *Strictly personal qualities*, "which cannot be borrowed or lent", count at least as much as wealth or solvency. In reality, even in the market the degree of mutual information is such as to leave little scope for overpricing, cheating, and bluff. If, exceptionally, a man "who has not been brought up for the market" tries to "make a bid", he is soon put in his place. "The market will judge", they say, meaning by "market" not the laws of the market, which in a very different universe sanction reckless undertakings, but rather the collective judgment shaped and manifested in the market. Either a man *is* a "market man" (*argaz naṣuq*) or he isn't; a total judgment is passed on *the whole man*, and like all such judgments in every society, it involves the ultimate values laid down in the mythical taxonomies. A "house man" (*argaz ukhamis*) who takes it upon himself to overstep his "natural" limits is put in his place with the words "Since you're only a fireside man, remain a fireside man" (*thakwath*, the alcove in the wall of the house which is used to hide the small, typically female objects which must not be seen in broad daylight – spoons, rags, weaving tools, etc.).

The village/market dichotomy is no doubt a means of preventing the impersonal exchanges of the market from obtruding the dispositions of calculation into the world of reciprocity relationships. In fact, whether a small tribal market or a big regional market, the *ṣuq* represents a transactional mode intermediate between two extremes, neither of which is ever fully actualized: on the one hand there are the exchanges of the familiar world of acquaintance, based on the *trust* and *good faith* that are possible when the purchaser is well informed about the products exchanged and the seller's strategies, and when the relationship between the parties concerned exists before and after the exchange; and on the other hand there are the rational strategies of the self-regulating market, which are made possible by the standardization of its products and the quasi-mechanical necessity of its processes. The *ṣuq* does not provide all the traditional information, but neither does it create the conditions for rational information. This is why all the strategies applied by the peasants aim to minimize the risk implied in the unpredictability of the outcome, by transforming the impersonal relationships of commercial transactions, which have neither past nor future, into lasting relationships of reciprocity: by calling upon guarantors, witnesses, and mediators they are able to establish, or re-establish, the functional equivalent of a traditional network of relationships between the contracting parties.

Just as economic wealth cannot function as capital until it is linked to an economic apparatus, so cultural competence in its various forms cannot be constituted as cultural capital until it is inserted into the objective relations between the system of economic production and the system producing the producers (which is itself constituted by the relation between the school system and the family). When a society lacks both the literacy which would enable it to preserve and accumulate in objectified form the cultural resources it has inherited from the past, and also the educational system which would give its agents the aptitudes and dispositions required for the symbolic reappropriation of those resources, it can only preserve them *in their incorporated state*.[39] Consequently, to ensure the perpetuation of cultural resources which would otherwise disappear along with the agents who bear them, it has to resort to systematic inculcation, a process which, as is shown by the case of the bards, may last as long as the period during which the resources are actually used. The transformations made possible by an instrument of cultural communication such as writing have been abundantly described:[40] by detaching cultural resources from persons, literacy enables a society to move beyond immediate human limits – in particular those of individual memory – and frees it from the constraints implied by mnemonic devices such as poetry, the preservation technique par excellence in non-literate societies;[41] it enables a society to accumulate culture hitherto preserved in embodied form, and correlatively enables particular groups to practise *primitive accumulation of cultural capital*, the partial or total monopolizing of the society's symbolic resources in religion, philosophy, art, and science, by monopolizing the instruments for appropriation of those resources (writing, reading, and other decoding techniques) henceforward preserved not in memories but in texts.

But the objectification effects of literacy are nothing in comparison with those produced by the educational system. Without entering into detailed analysis, it must suffice to point out that academic qualifications are to cultural capital what money is to economic capital.[42] By giving the same value to all holders of the same certificate, so that any one of them can take the place of any other, the educational system minimizes the obstacles to the free circulation of cultural capital which result from its being incorporated in individual persons (without, however, sacrificing the advantages of the charismatic ideology of the irreplaceable individual); it makes it possible to relate all qualification-holders (and also, negatively, all unqualified individuals) to a single standard, thereby setting up a *single market* for all cultural capacities and guaranteeing the convertibility of cultural capital into money, at a determinate cost in labour and time. Academic qualifications, like money, have a conventional, fixed value which, being guaranteed by law, is freed from local limitations (in contrast to scholastically uncertified cultural capital) and temporal fluctuations: the cultural capital which they in a sense guarantee once and for all does not constantly need to be proved. The objectification accomplished by academic degrees and diplomas and, in a more general way, by all forms of credentials, is inseparable from the objectification which the law guarantees by defining *permanent positions* which are distinct from the biological individuals holding them, and may be occupied by agents who are biologically different but interchangeable in terms of the qualifications required. Once this state of affairs is established, relations of power and domination no longer exist directly between individuals; they are set up in pure objectivity between institutions, i.e. between socially guaranteed qualifications and socially defined positions, and through them, between the social mechanisms which produce and guarantee both the social value of the qualifications and the positions and also the distribution of these social attributes, among biological individuals.[43]

Law does no more than symbolically consecrate – by *recording* it in a form which renders it both eternal and universal – the structure of the power relation between groups and classes which is produced and guaranteed practically by the functioning of these mechanisms. For example, it records and legitimates the distinction between the position and the person, the power and its holder, together with the relationship obtaining at a particular moment between qualifications and jobs (reflecting the relative bargaining power of the buyers and sellers of qualified, i.e. scholastically guaranteed, labour power) which appears concretely in a particular distribution of the material and symbolic profits assigned to the holders (or non-holders) of qualifications. The law thus contributes its own (specifically symbolic) force to the action of the various mechanisms which render it superfluous constantly to reassert power relations by overtly resorting to force.

Thus the task of legitimating the established order does not fall exclusively to the mechanisms traditionally regarded as belonging to the order of ideology, such as law. The system of symbolic goods production and the system producing the producers fulfil in addition, i.e. by the very logic of their normal functioning, ideological functions, by virtue of the fact that the mechanisms through which they contribute to the reproduction of the established order and to the perpetuation of domination remain hidden. The educational system helps to provide the dominant class with what Max Weber terms "a theodicy of its own privilege", not so much through the ideologies it produces or inculcates (as those who speak of "ideological apparatuses" would have it); but rather through the practical justification of the established order which it achieves by using the overt connection between qualifications and jobs as a smokescreen for the connection – which it *records surreptitiously*, under cover of formal equality – between the qualifications people obtain and the cultural capital they have inherited – in other words, through the legitimacy it confers on the transmission of this form of heritage. The most successful ideological effects are those which have no need of words, and ask no more than complicitous silence. It follows, incidentally that any analysis of ideologies, in the narrow sense of "legitimating discourses", which fails to include an analysis of the corresponding institutional mechanisms is liable to be no more than a contribution to the efficacy of those ideologies: this is true of all internal (semiological) analyses of political, educational, religious, or aesthetic ideologies which forget that the political function of these ideologies may in some cases be reduced to the effect of displacement and diversion, camouflage and legitimation, which they produce by reproducing – through their oversights and omissions, and in their deliberately or involuntarily complicitous silences – the effects of the objective mechanisms.[44]

It has been necessary at least to sketch an analysis of the objective mechanisms which play a part both in setting up and in concealing lasting relations of domination, in order to understand fully the radical difference between the different modes of domination and the different political strategies for conservation characteristic of social formations whose accumulated social energy is unequally objectified in mechanisms. On the one side there are social relations which, not containing within themselves the principle of their own reproduction, must be kept up through nothing less than a process of continuous creation; on the other side, a social world which, containing within itself the principle of its own continuation, frees agents from the endless work of creating or restoring social relations. This opposition finds expression in the history or prehistory of sociological thought. In order to "ground social being in nature", as Durkheim puts it,[45] it has been necessary to break with the propensity to see it as founded on the arbitrariness of individual wills, or, with Hobbes, on the arbitrariness of a sovereign will: "For Hobbes", writes Durkheim, "it is an act of will which gives birth to the social order and it is a perpetually renewed act of will which upholds it."[46] And there is every reason to believe that the break with this artificialist vision, which is the precondition for scientific apprehension, could not be made before the constitution, in reality, of objective mechanisms like the self-regulating market, which, as Polyani points out, was intrinsically conducive to belief in determinism. But social reality had another trap in store for science: the existence of mechanisms capable of reproducing the political order, independently of any deliberate intervention, makes it possible to recognize as political, amongst the different types of conduct directed towards gaining or keeping power, only such practices as tacitly exclude control over the reproduction mechanisms from the area of legitimate competition. In this way, social science, taking for its object the sphere of legitimate politics (as so-called "political science" does nowadays) adopted the preconstructed object which reality foisted upon it.

The greater the extent to which the task of reproducing the relations of domination is taken over by objective mechanisms, which serve the interests of the dominant group without any conscious effort on the latter's part, the more indirect and, in a sense, impersonal, become the strategies objectively oriented towards reproduction: it is not by lavishing generosity, kindness, or politeness on his charwoman (or on any other "socially inferior" agent), but by choosing the best investment for his money, or the best school for his son, that the possessor of economic or cultural capital perpetuates the relationship of domination which objectively links him with his charwoman and even her descendants. Once a system of mechanisms has been constituted capable of objectively ensuring the reproduction of the established order by its own motion (*apo tou automatou*, as the Greeks put it), the dominant class have only to *let the system they dominate take its own course* in order to exercise their domination; but until such a system exists, they have to work directly, daily, personally, to produce and reproduce conditions of domination which are even then never entirely trustworthy. Because they cannot be satisfied with appropriating the profits of a social machine which has not yet developed the power of self-perpetuation, they are obliged to resort to *the elementary forms of domination*, in other words, the direct domination of one person by another, the limiting case of which is appropriation of persons, i.e. slavery. They cannot appropriate the labour, services, goods, homage, and respect of others without "winning" them personally, "tying" them – in short, creating a bond between persons.

This is why a social relationship such as that between the master and his *khammes* (a sort of *métayer* who gets only a very small share of the crop, usually a fifth, with local variations), which might at first sight seem very close to a simple capital–labour relation, cannot in fact be kept up without the direct application of material or symbolic violence to the person who is to be tied. The master may bind his *khammes* by a debt which forces him to keep renewing his contract until he finds a new master willing to pay off the debt to the former employer – in other words, indefinitely. He may also resort to brutal measures such as seizing the entire crop in order to recover his loan. But each particular relationship is the product of complex strategies whose efficacy depends not only on the material and symbolic strength of either party but also on their skill in arousing sympathy or indignation so as to mobilize the group. The value of the relationship for the dominator does not lie exclusively in the resultant material profits, and many masters who are not much richer than their *khammes* and would gain by cultivating their lands themselves refrain from doing so because they prefer the prestige of possessing a "clientele". But a man who wants to be treated as a "master" must show he has the virtues corresponding to his status, and the first of these is generosity and dignity in his relations with his "clients". The compact uniting the master and his *khammes* is an arrangement between one man and another guaranteed by nothing beyond the "loyalty" which honour demands. It involves no abstract discipline, no rigorous contracts, and no specific sanctions. But the "great" are expected to show that they are worthy of their rank by affording material and symbolic "protection" to those dependent upon them.

Here again, it is all a question of strategy, and the reason why the "enchanted" relations of the pact of honour are so frequent is that, in this economy, the strategies of symbolic violence are often ultimately more economical than pure "economic" violence. Given that there is no real labour market, and that money is rare (and therefore dear), the best way in which the master can serve his own interests is to work away, day in, day out, with constant care and attention, weaving the ethical and affective, as well as economic, bonds which durably tie his *khammes* to him. To reinforce the bonds of obligation, the master may arrange the marriage of his *khammes* (or his son) and instal him, with his family, in the master's own house; the children, brought up together, with the goods (the flock, fields, etc.) being owned in common, often take a long time to discover what their position is. It is not uncommon for one of the sons of a *khammes* to go and work for wages in the town, together with one of the master's sons, and like him, bring back his savings to the master. In short, if the master wants to persuade the *khammes* to devote himself over a long period to the pursuit of the master's interests, he has to *associate* him completely with those interests, masking the dyssymmetry of the relationship by symbolically denying it in his behaviour. The *khammes* is the man to whom one entrusts one's goods, one's house, and one's honour (as is shown by the formula used by a master leaving to go and work in a town or in France: "Associate, I'm counting on you; I'm going off to be an associate myself"). The *khammes* "treats the land as if he owned it", because there is nothing in his master's conduct to belie his claim to have rights over the land on which he works; and it is not unusual to hear a *khammes* saying, long after leaving his "master", that the sweat of his brow entitles him to pick fruit or enter the estate. And just as he never feels entirely freed from his obligations towards his former master, so, after what he calls a "change of heart" he may accuse his master of "treachery" in abandoning someone he had "adopted".

Thus this system contains only two ways (and they prove in the end to be just one way) of getting and keeping a lasting hold over someone: gifts or debts, the overtly economic obligations of debt, or the "moral", "affective" obligations created and maintained by exchange, in short, overt (physical or economic) violence, or symbolic violence – censored, euphemized, i.e. unrecognizable, socially recognized violence. There is an intelligible relation – not a contradiction – between these two forms of violence, which coexist in the same social formation and sometimes in the same relationship:[47] when domination can only be exercised in its *elementary form*, i.e. directly, between one person and another, it cannot take place overtly and must be disguised under the veil of enchanted relationships, the official model of which is presented by relations between kinsmen; in order to be socially recognized it must get itself misrecognized.[48] The reason for the pre-capitalist economy's great need for symbolic violence is that the only way in which relations of domination can be set up, maintained, or restored, is through strategies which, being expressly oriented towards the establishment of relations of personal dependence, must be disguised and transfigured lest they destroy themselves by revealing their true nature; in a word, they must be *euphemized*. Hence the *censorship* to which the overt manifestation of violence, especially in its naked economic form, is subjected by the logic characteristic of an economy in which interests can only be satisfied on condition that they be disguised in and by the strategies aiming to satisfy them.[49] It would be a mistake to see a contradiction in the fact that violence is here both more present and more hidden.[50] Because the pre-capitalist economy cannot count on the implacable, hidden violence of objective mechanisms, it resorts *simultaneously* to forms of domination which may strike the modern observer as more brutal, more primitive, more barbarous, or at the same time, as gentler, more humane, more respectful of persons.[51] This coexistence of overt physical and economic violence and of the most refined symbolic violence is found in all the institutions characteristic of this economy, and at the heart of every social relationship: it is present both in the debt and in the gift, which, in spite of their apparent opposition, have in common the power of founding either dependence (and even slavery) or solidarity, depending on the strategies within which they are deployed. The fundamental ambiguity of all the institutions which modern taxonomies tend to present as economic is evidence that contrary strategies, which, as we have also seen in the case of the master–*khammes* relationship, may coexist under the same name, are *interchangeable* ways of performing the same function, with the "choice" between overt violence and gentle, hidden violence depending on the relative strengths of the two parties at a particular time, and on the degree of integration and ethical integrity of the arbitrating group. In a society in which overt violence, the violence of the usurer or the merciless master, meets with collective reprobation[52] and is liable either to provoke a violent riposte from the victim or to force him to flee (that is to say, in either case, in *the absence of any other recourse*, to provoke the annihilation of the very relationship which was intended to be exploited), symbolic violence, the gentle, invisible form of violence, which is never recognized as such, and is not so much undergone as chosen, the violence of credit, confidence, obligation, personal loyalty, hospitality, gifts, gratitude, piety – in short, all the virtues honoured by the code of honour – cannot fail to be seen as the most economical mode of domination, i.e. the mode which best corresponds to the economy of the system.

Gentle, hidden exploitation is the form taken by man's exploitation of man whenever overt, brutal exploitation is impossible. It is as false to identify this essentially *dual* economy with its official reality (generosity, mutual aid, etc.), i.e. the form which exploitation has to adopt in order to take place, as it is to reduce it to its objective reality, seeing mutual aid as a corvée, the *khammes* as a sort of slave, and so on. The gift, generosity, conspicuous distribution – the extreme case of which is the potlatch – are operations of social alchemy which may be observed whenever the direct application of overt physical or economic violence is negatively sanctioned, and which tend to bring about the transmutation of economic capital into symbolic capital. Wastage of money, energy, time, and ingenuity is the very essence of the social alchemy through which an interested relationship is transmuted into a disinterested, gratuitous relationship, overt domination into misrecognized, "socially recognized" domination, in other words, *legitimate authority*. The active principle is the labour, time, care, attention, and savoir-faire which must be squandered to produce a personal gift irreducible to its equivalent in money, a present in which what counts is not so much what you give as the way you give it, the seemingly "gratuitous" surrender not only of goods or women but of things that are even more personal and therefore more precious, because, as the Kabyles say, they can "neither be borrowed nor lent", such as *time* – the time that has been taken to do the things that "won't be forgotten", because they are done the right way at the right time – marks of appreciation, "gestures", "kindnesses", and "considerations".[53] The exercise of gentle violence demands a "*personal*" price from its users. Authority, charisma, grace, or, for the Kabyles, *sar*, are always seen as a property of the person. *Fides*, as Benveniste points out, is not "trust" but the fact that "the inherent quality of a person inspires confidence in him and is exercised in the form of a protective authority over those who entrust themselves to him".[54] The illusion implied by personal fidelity – that the object is the source of the feelings responsible for the particular representation of the object – is not entirely an illusion; the "grace" which gratitude recognizes is indeed, as Hobbes observes, the recognition of an "*antecedent grace*".

Gentle exploitation is much more costly – and not only in economic terms – for those who practise it. "Responsibilities" such as those of the *tamen*, the "spokesman" or "guarantor" who represented his group (*thakharrubth* or *adhrum*) at the meetings of the men's assembly and on all solemn occasions, gave rise to little competition or envy, and it was not uncommon for the most influential and most important members of a group to refuse the job or soon ask to be replaced: the tasks of representation and mediation which fell to the *tamen* did indeed demand a great deal of time and effort. Those on whom the group bestows the title "wise men" or "great men", and who, in the absence of any official mandate, find themselves invested with a sort of tacit delegation of the group's authority, feel *obliged* (by a sense of duty towards themselves resulting from considerable self-esteem) constantly to recall the group to the values it officially recognizes, both by their exemplary conduct and by their express utterances; if they see two women of their group quarrelling they feel it incumbent upon them to separate them and even to beat them (if they are widows or if the men responsible for them are without authority) or fine them; in cases of serious conflict between members of their own clan, they feel required to recall both parties to wisdom, never an easy task and sometimes a dangerous one; in any situation liable to lead to inter-clan conflict (in cases of crime, for example) they meet together in an assembly with the marabout so as to reconcile the antagonists; they feel it their duty to protect the interests of the clients and the poor, to give them presents when the traditional collections are made (for the *thimechret*, for example), to send them food at feast times, to assist the widows, to arrange marriages for the orphans, etc.

In short, because the delegation which is the basis of personal authority remains diffuse and is neither officially declared nor institutionally guaranteed, it can only be lastingly maintained through actions whose conformity to the values recognized by the group is a practical reaffirmation of that authority.[55] It follows that in such a system, the "great" are those who can least afford to take liberties with the official norms, and that the price to be paid for their outstanding value is outstanding conformity to the values of the group, the source of all symbolic value. The constitution of institutionalized mechanisms makes it possible for a single agent (a party leader or union delegate, a member of a board of directors, a member of an academy, etc.) to be entrusted with the totality of the capital which is the basis of the group, and to exert over this capital, collectively owned by all the "shareholders", a delegated authority not strictly related to his personal contribution; but in pre-capitalist societies, each agent shares directly in the collective capital, symbolized by the name of the family or lineage, to an extent directly proportionate to his own contribution, i.e. exactly to the extent that his words, deeds, and person are a credit to the group.[55] The system is such that the dominant agents have a vested interest in virtue; they can accumulate political power only by paying a *personal* price, and not simply by redistributing their goods and money; they must have the "virtues" of their power because the only basis of their power is "virtue".

Generous conduct, of which the potlatch (a curio for anthropologists) is simply the extreme case, might seem to suspend the universal law of interest and "fair exchange", whereby nothing is ever given for nothing, and to set up instead relationships which are their own end – conversation for conversation's sake (and not in order to say something), giving for giving's sake, and so on. But in reality such denials of interest are never more than *practical disclaimers*: like Freud's *Verneinung*, the discourse which says what it says only in a form that tends to show that it is not saying it, they satisfy interest in a (disinterested) manner designed to show that they are not satisfying interest. (A parenthesis of the benefit of the moralists: an absolute, i.e. ethical, justification of the enchantment felt by the observer of enchanted social relations may be found in the fact that, as with desire, so with material interest: society cannot ask or expect of its members anything more or better than denial, a "lifting of repression" which, as Freud says, does not amount to "an acceptance of what is repressed".)[57] Everyone knows that "it's not what you give but the way you give it" that counts, that what distinguishes the gift from mere "fair exchange" is the labour devoted to *form*: the *presentation*, the manner of giving, must be such that the outward forms of the act present a practical denial of the content of the act, symbolically transmuting an interested exchange or a simple power relation into a relationship set up in due form for form's sake, i.e. inspired by pure respect for the customs and conventions recognized by the group. (A parenthesis for the benefit of the aesthetes: archaic societies devote more time and effort to the forms, because in them the censorship of direct expression of personal interest is stronger; they thus offer connoisseurs of beautiful forms the enchanting spectacle of an art of living raised to the level of an art for art's sake founded on the refusal to acknowledge self-evident realities such as the "business is business" or "time is money" on which the unaesthetic life-style of the *harried leisure classes*[58] in so-called advanced societies is based.)

Goods are for giving. The rich man is "rich so as to be able to give to the poor" say the Kabyles.[59] This is an exemplary disclaimer: because giving is also a way of possessing (a gift which is not matched by a counter-gift creates a lasting bond, restricting the debtor's freedom and forcing him to adopt a peaceful, co-operative, prudent attitude); because in the absence of any juridical guarantee, or any coercive force, one of the few ways of "holding" someone is to *keep up* a lasting asymmetrical relationship such as indebtedness; and because the only recognized, legitimate form of possession is that achieved by dispossessing oneself – i.e. obligation, gratitude, prestige, or personal loyalty. Wealth, the ultimate basis of power, can exert power, and exert it durably, only in the form of symbolic capital; in other words, economic capital can be accumulated only in the form of symbolic capital, the unrecognizable, and hence socially recognizable, form of the other kinds of capital. The chief is indeed, in Malinowski's phrase, a "tribal banker", amassing food only to lavish it on others, in order to build up a capital of obligations and debts which will be repaid in the form of homage, respect, loyalty, and, when the opportunity arises, work and services, which may be the bases of a new accumulation of material goods.[60] Processes of circular circulation, such as the levying of a tribute followed by hierarchical redistribution, would appear absurd but for the effect they have of transmuting the nature of the social relation between the agents or groups involved. Wherever they are observed, these *consecration cycles* perform the fundamental operation of social alchemy, the transformation of arbitrary relations into legitimate relations, *de facto* differences into officially recognized distinctions. Distinctions and lasting associations are founded in the circular circulation from which the legitimation of power arises as a symbolic surplus value. If, like Lévi-Strauss, one considers only the *particular case* of exchanges of material and/or symbolic goods intended to legitimate relations of reciprocity, one is in danger of forgetting that all structures of inseparably material and symbolic exchange (i.e. involving both circulation and communication) function as ideological machines whenever the *de facto* state of affairs which they tend to legitimate by transforming a contingent social relationship into a recognized relationship is an unequal balance of power.

The endless reconversion of economic capital into symbolic capital, at the cost of a wastage of social energy which is the condition for the permanence of domination, cannot succeed without the complicity of the whole group: the work of denial which is the source of social alchemy is, like magic, a collective undertaking. As Mauss puts it, the whole society pays itself in the false coin of its dream. The collective misrecognition which is the basis of the ethic of honour, a collective denial of the economic reality of exchange, is only possible because, when the group lies to itself in this way, there is neither deceiver nor deceived: the peasant who treats his *khammes* as an associate, because that is the custom and because honour requires him to do so, deceives himself as much as he deceives his *khammes*, since the *only* form in which he can serve his interest is the euphemistic form presented by the ethic of honour; and nothing suits the *khammes* better than to play his part in an interested fiction which offers him an honourable representation of his condition. Thus the mechanisms responsible for reproducing the appropriate habitus are here an integral part of an apparatus of production which could not function without them. Agents lastingly "bind" each other, not only as parents and children, but also as creditor and debtor, master and *khammes*, only through the dispositions which the group inculcates in them and continuously reinforces, and which render *unthinkable* practices which would appear as legitimate and even be taken for granted in the disenchanted economy of "naked self-interest".[61]

The official truth produced by the collective work of euphemization, an elementary form of the labour of objectification which eventually leads to the juridical definition of acceptable behaviour, is not simply the group's means of saving its "spiritualistic point of honour"; it also has a practical efficacy, for, even if it were contradicted by everyone's behaviour, like a rule to which every case proved an exception, it would still remain a true description of such behaviour as is intended to be acceptable. The code of honour weighs on each agent with the weight of all the other agents, and the disenchantment which leads to the progressive unveiling of repressed meanings and functions can only result from a collapse of the social conditions of the *cross-censorship* to which each agent submits with impatience but which he imposes on all the others.[62]

If it be true that symbolic violence is the gentle, hidden form which violence takes when overt violence is impossible, it is understandable why symbolic forms of domination should have progressively withered away as objective mechanisms came to be constituted which, in rendering superfluous the work of euphemization, tended to produce the "disenchanted" dispositions their development demanded. It is equally clear why the progressive uncovering and neutralization of the ideological and practical effects of the mechanisms assuring the reproduction of the relations of domination should determine a return to forms of symbolic violence again based on dissimulation of the mechanisms of reproduction through the conversion of economic into symbolic capital: it is through legitimacy-giving redistribution, public ("social" policies) and private (financing of "disinterested" foundations, grants to hospitals and to academic and cultural institutions), which they make possible, that the efficacy of the mechanisms of reproduction is exerted.

To these forms of legitimate accumulation, through which the dominant groups or classes secure a capital of "credit" which seems to owe nothing to the logic of exploitation,[63] must be added another form of accumulation of symbolic capital, the collection of luxury goods attesting the taste and distinction of their owner. The denial of economy and of economic interest, which in pre-capitalist societies at first took place on a ground from which it had to be expelled in order for economy to be constituted as such, thus finds its favourite refuge in the domain of art and culture, the site of pure consumption – of money, of course, but also of time convertible into money. The world of art, a sacred island systematically and ostentatiously opposed to the profane, everyday world of production, a sanctuary for gratuitous, disinterested activity in a universe given over to money and self-interest, offers, like theology in a past epoch, an imaginary anthropology obtained by denial of all the negations really brought about by the economy.

Notes

CHAPTER 1. THE OBJECTIVE LIMITS OF OBJECTIVISM

1 C. Bally, *Le langage et la vie* (Geneva: Droz, 1965), pp. 58, 72, 102.

2 See E. Durkheim, *Education et sociologie* (Paris: PUF, 1968; 1st ed., 1922), pp. 68–9; English trans. *Education and Sociology* (New York: Free Press, 1956), p. 101.

3 Consider, for example, in very different fields, the petty bourgeoisie with its avid consumption of manuals of etiquette, and all academicisms, with their treatises on style.

4 Objectivism posits that immediate communication is possible if and only if the agents are objectively harmonized so as to associate the same meaning with the same sign (utterance, practice, or work), or, to put it another way, so as to refer in their coding and decoding operations, i.e. in their practices and interpretations, to one and the same system of constant relations, independent of individual consciousnesses and wills and irreducible to their *execution* in practices or works (e.g. Saussurian "*langue*" as code or cipher). In so doing, objectivist analysis does not, strictly speaking, contradict phenomenological analysis of primary experience of the social world and of the immediate comprehension of the utterances, acts, or works of others. It merely defines the limits of its validity by establishing the particular conditions within which it is possible, conditions which phenomenological analysis ignores.

5 See C. Lévi-Strauss, "Introduction à l'oeuvre de Marcel Mauss", in *Sociologie et anthropologie* (Paris: PUF, 1950), p. xxxviii.

6 *Ibid.* p. xxxvi.

7 Sayings which exalt generosity, the supreme virtue of the man of honour, coexist with proverbs betraying the temptation of the spirit of calculation: "A gift is a misfortune", says one of them; and another: "A present is a hen and the recompense is a camel." And, playing on the word *lahna*, which means both a gift and peace, and the word *lahdia*, meaning a gift, they say: "You who bring us peace [a gift], leave us in peace", or "Leave us in peace [*lahna*] with your gift [*lahdia*], or "The best gift is peace." [These examples, and those which follow, draw on the author's fieldwork in Kabylia, Algeria. Translator.]

8 The language of *form*, taken in the sense of "*structure of becoming*" which it has in musical theory (e.g. the suite, or sonata form) would no doubt be more appropriate than the language of logical structure, to describe the logically but also chronologically articulated sequences of a musical composition, a dance, or any temporally structured practice. It is significant that the only way which R. Jakobson and C. Lévi-Strauss ("'Les chats' de Charles Baudelaire", *L'Homme*, 2, 1 (Jan.–April 1962), pp. 5–21) find to explain the movement from structure to form, and the experience of form, that is to say, to poetic and musical pleasure, is to invoke *frustrated expectation*, which objectivist analysis can describe only by bringing together in simultaneity, in the form of a set of themes linked by relations of logical transformation (e.g. the movement from the metaphorical form, the scientist, the lover, the cat, to metonymic form, the cat), the essentially

[198]

polythetic (in Husserl's sense) structure of a poetic discourse which *in practice* is communicated only in and through time. In reality, as temporal structures, musical or poetical forms can only be understood inasmuch as they perform *expressive functions* of various types.

9 "Don't be offended at me for making this offer. I am so thoroughly conscious of counting for nothing in your eyes, that you can even take money from me. You can't take offence at a gift from me" (see F. Dostoyevsky, *The Gambler, Bobok, A Nasty Story*, trans. J. Coulson (London: Penguin, 1966), p. 44).

10 *Mind, Self and Society* (Chicago: University of Chicago Press, 1962), pp. 42–3.

11 R. Jakobson, *Fundamentals of Language* (The Hague: Mouton, 1956), p. 58.

12 Three case studies illustrating these analyses are to be found in P. Bourdieu, "The Sentiment of Honour in Kabyle Society", in J. Peristiany (ed.), *Honour and Shame* (London: Weidenfeld and Nicholson, 1965), pp. 191–241.

13 G. Marcy, "Les vestiges de la parenté maternelle en droit coutumier berbère et le régime des successions touraègues", *Revue Africaine*, no. 85 (1941), pp. 187–211.

14 In the case of the *offence* which, unlike the simple challenge, is an attack on the sacred (*haram*) and in particular on the honour of the women, the room for manoeuvre is considerably reduced, the sole alternatives being the riposte which restores honour or the retreat which condemns the offended to social death or exile.

15 The *qanun*, a collection of customs peculiar to each village, essentially consists of an enumeration of particular offences, followed by the corresponding fine. Thus, for example, the *qanun* of Agouni-n-Tesellent, a village of the Ath Akbil tribe, includes, in a total of 249 articles, 219 "repressive" laws (in Durkheim's sense), i.e. 88 per cent, as against 25 "restitutory" laws, i.e. 10 per cent, and only 5 articles concerning the foundations of the political system. The customary rule, the product of a jurisprudence directly applied to the particular case and not of the application to the particular of a universal rule, is based not on formal, rational, explicit principles but on the "sense" of honour and equity. Its essence – that is to say, the totality of the values and principles that the community affirms by its very existence – remains implicit because unquestioned and unquestionable.

16 The statements contained in the customs of any particular group represent only a very small part of the universe of possible acts of jurisprudence (and even if one adds to them the statements produced from the same principles to be found in the customs of other groups one still has only a very limited idea of the full possibilities). Comparison of the *quanuns* of different groups (villages or tribes) brings out differences in the weight of the punishment inflicted for the same offence; these differences are understandable if it is a question of the same implicit schemes being put into practice, but would not be found if it were a matter of the application of a single explicit code expressly produced to serve as a basis for homogeneous and constant (i.e. predictable and calculable) acts of jurisprudence.

17 A. Hanoteau and A. Letourneux, *La Kabylie et les coutumes kabyles* (Paris: Imprimerie Nationale, 1873), vol. III, p. 338 (my italics).

18 A. Hanoteau (a brigadier) and A. Letourneux (an Appeal Court Judge), who present their analysis of Kabyle customs along the lines of the French "Code Civil", attribute the rôle of judge to the village assembly (see Hanoteau and Letourneux, *La Kabylie et les coutumes kabyles*, p. 2), while Dean M. Morand (see M. Morand, *Etude de droit musulman algérien*, Algiers: A. Jourdan, 1910, and "Le statut de la femme kabyle et la réforme des coutumes berbères", *Revue des*

Etudes Islamiques, 1927, part 1, pp. 47–94) regards the *qanun* as a set of provisions in the form of rules, based on conventions and contractual agreements. In reality the assembly operates not as a court pronouncing judgement by reference to a pre-existing code, but as a council which endeavours to reconcile the adversaries' points of view and persuade them to accept a compromise. This means that the functioning of the system presupposes the *orchestration of habitus*, since the mediator's decision can be applied only with the consent of the "convicted" party (without which the plaintiff has no alternative to resorting to force) and will not be accepted unless it is consistent with the "sense of justice" and imposed in a manner recognized by the "sense of honour".

19 G. W. F. Hegel, *Reason in History: A General Introduction to the Philosophy of History*, trans. with an introduction by R. S. Hartmann (Indianapolis: Bobbs-Merrill, 1953), p. 3.

20 As is suggested by a reading of the *Meno*, the emergence of institutionalized education is accompanied by a crisis in diffuse education, which goes directly from practice to practice without passing through discourse. Excellence has ceased to exist once people start asking whether it can be taught, i.e. as soon as the objective confrontation of different styles of excellence makes it necessary to say what goes without saying, justify what is taken for granted, make an ought-to-be and an ought-to-do out of what had up to then been regarded as the only way to be and do; hence to apprehend what had formerly seemed to be part of the nature of things (*phusei*) as in fact based on the arbitrary institution of law (*nomo*). The upholders of old-style education have no difficulty in devaluing a knowledge which, like that of the *mathontes*, bears the marks of apprenticeship; but the new masters can safely challenge the *kaloi kagathoi*, who are unable to bring to the level of discourse what they learned *apo tou automatou*, no one knows how, and possess only "insofar as they are what they are"; who, because they *are* what they know, do not *have* what they know, nor what they are.

21 M. Merleau-Ponty, *The Structure of Behaviour*, trans. Alden L. Fisher (London: Methuen, 1965), p. 124.

22 For example, the meanings agents give to rites, myths, or decorative motifs are much less stable in space, and doubtless over time, than the structures of the corresponding practices (see F. Boas, *Anthropology and Modern Life* (New York: Norton, 1962; 1st ed., 1928), pp. 164–6).

23 See A. Schutz, *Collected Papers. I: The Problem of Social Reality*, edited and introduced by Maurice Nathanson (The Hague: Martinus Nijhoff, 1962), p. 59. Schutz seeks to show that the contradiction which he himself observes between what he calls the postulate of subjective interpretation and the method of the most advanced sciences, such as economics, is only an apparent contradiction (see pp. 34–5).

24 H. Garfinkel, *Studies in Ethnomethodology*, Englewood Cliffs, N.J.: Prentice-Hall, 1967.

25 Thus it is the objectivist construction of the structure of the statistical chances objectively attached to an economic or social condition (that of a simple-reproduction economy, or a sub-proletariat, for example) which makes it possible to give a complete explanation of the form of temporal experience which phenomenological analysis brings to light.

26 The effect of symbolic imposition which official representation intrinsically produces is overlaid by a more profound effect when semi-learned grammar, a normative description, is made the object of teaching (differentially) dispensed by a specific institution and becomes thereby the principle of a *cultivated habitus*.

Thus, the legitimate linguistic habitus, in a class society, presupposes objectification (and, more precisely, compilation into a "treasury" and formalization by a body of grammarians) and inculcation by the family and the educational system, of the product of that objectification, grammar. In this case no in the domain of art, and of learned culture in general, it is the semi-learned norm which is internalized to become the principle of the production and comprehension of practices and discourses. Relations to learned culture (including learned language) are objectively defined by the degree of internalization of the linguistic norm. Broadly speaking, they range from excellence, the rule converted into a habitus capable of playing with the rule of the game, through the strict conformity of those condemned merely to *execute*, to the dispossession of the layman.

27 Ritual denunciation of the reassuring half-truths of legalism (to which some may be tempted to reduce a number of the analyses set out here) has doubtless played a part in discouraging any serious consideration of the relationship between practice and the rule, and, more precisely, of the strategies employed in the games (and tricks) played with the rules of the game, which give the rule a practical efficacy quite different from the efficacy naively attributed to it by the "legalistic approach", as Malinowski termed it (B. Malinowski, *Coral Gardens and Their Magic*, vol. 1 (London: Allen and Unwin, 1966; 1st ed., 1935), p. 379).

28 F. de Saussure, *Cours de linguistique générale* (Paris: Payot, 1960), pp. 37–8; trans. W. Baskin as *Course in General Linguistics*, New York: Philosophical Library, 1959.

29 "Neither is the psychological part wholly involved: the executive side is left outside, for execution is never the work of the mass; it is always individual, and the individual is always the master of it; we shall call it speech" (*ibid.* p. 30; see English translation, p. 13). The most explicit formulation of the theory of speech as execution is doubtless found in the work of Hjelmslev, who clearly brings out the various dimensions of the Saussurian opposition between language and speech – institution, social, "fixed", and execution, individual, non-fixed (L. Hjelmslev, *Essais linguistiques* (Copenhagen: Nordisk Sprog-og Kulturforlag, 1959), esp. p. 79).

30 The most violent opponents of the notion of "culture", such as Radcliffe-Brown, have nothing better than a naive realism to offer against the realism of the intelligible which presents "culture" as a transcendent reality endowed with an autonomous existence and obeying its internal laws even in its history. This apart, "culture" is opposed to concepts as different in their epistemological status as society, the individual, or conduct. If we except the rare authors who give the notion of conduct a significance rigorously defined by the operation which sets it up in opposition to "culture" (e.g. H. D. Lasswell, who posits that "if an act conforms to culture, then it is conduct, if not, it is behaviour" – "Collective Autism as a Consequence of Culture Contact", *Zeitschrift für Sozialforschung*, 4 (1935), pp. 232–47), most users of the opposition put forward epistemologically discordant definitions of culture or conduct, which oppose a constructed object to a preconstructed datum, leaving empty the place of the second constructed object, namely practice as execution. Thus – and this is far from being the worst example – Harris opposes "cultural patterns" to "culturally patterned behaviours", as respectively, "what is constructed by the anthropologist" and "what members of the society observe or impose upon others" (M. Harris, "Review of Selected Writings of Edward Sapir, Language, Culture and Personality", *Language*, 27, 3 (1951), pp. 288–333). The imaginary dialogue on the notion of culture presented by Clyde Kluckhohn and William H. Kelly (see "The Concept

of Culture ", in R. Linton (ed.), *The Science of Man in the World Crisis* (New York: Columbia University Press, 1945), pp. 78–105) gives a more summary, though livelier, picture of this debate than A. L. Kroeber and C. Kluckhohn in their *Culture: A Critical Review of Concepts and Definitions* (Papers of the Peabody Museum of American Archaeology and Ethnology, XLVII, 1, Cambridge, Mass.: Harvard University Press, 1952). It has not escaped Leach that despite their apparent opposition, Malinowski and Radcliffe-Brown at least agree in considering each "society" or each "culture" (in their respective vocabularies) as a "totality made up of a number of discrete, empirical 'things', of rather diverse kinds, e.g. groups of people, 'institutions', customs" or again as "an empirical whole made up of a limited number of readily identifiable parts", comparison of different societies consisting of examining whether "the same kinds of parts" are to be found in all cases (E. R. Leach, *Rethinking Anthropology* (London: Athlone Press, 1961), p. 6).

31 L. J. Prieto, *Principes de noölogie*, Paris: Mouton, 1964; and J. C. Pariente, "Vers un nouvel esprit linguistique", *Critique*, April 1966, pp. 334–58. Oswald Ducrot makes the same point when he indicates that *presupposition* is part of language use itself and that every speech act entails assumptions which may or may not be satisfied or accepted by the interlocutor.

32 Bally, *Le langage et la vie*, p. 21.

33 J. Van Velsen, *The Politics of Kinship: A Study in Social Manipulation among the Lakeside Tonga*, Manchester: Manchester University Press, 1964; new ed., 1971.

34 See M. Gluckman, "Ethnographic Data in British Social Anthropology", *Sociological Review*, 9, 1 (March 1961), pp. 5–17.

35 E. R. Leach, "On Certain Unconsidered Aspects of Double Descent Systems," *Man*, 62 (1962), p. 133.

36 Van Velsen, *The Politics of Kinship*, p. xxvi.

37 Despite this point of disagreement, Van Velsen's analyses are essentially consistent with my own analysis of the strategic uses made of kin relations (which I wrote before *The Politics of Kinship* came to my notice): cf., for example, on pp. 73–4; the selection of "practical" kinsmen among the nominal kinsmen; on p. 182, *matrilineal descent* seen as a privileged rationalization of action in fact determined by other factors, and the function of the idealization of cross-cousin marriage as "a means of counteracting the fissiparous tendencies in the marriage and thus the village".

38 In a typical statement of a highly eclectic philosophy, Lévi-Strauss explicitly evacuates individual and collective history (and everything covered by the concept of the habitus) by establishing a direct, unmediated identity between the mind and nature: "As the mind too *is a thing*, the functioning of this thing teaches us something about the nature of things: even pure reflexion is in the last analysis an *internalization of the cosmos*" (C. Lévi-Strauss, *The Savage Mind* (London: Weidenfeld and Nicolson, 1966), p. 248; my italics to emphasize the oscillation, in the same sentence, between two contradictory explanations of the declared identity of the mind and nature, first an essential identity – the mind is a thing – then identity acquired through learning – internalization of the cosmos – two theses which merge in the ambiguity of another formulation – "an image of the world inscribed in the architecture of the mind": *Le cru et le cuit* (Paris: Plon, 1964), p. 346). Beneath its airs of radical materialism, this philosophy of mind returns to a form of idealism affirming the universality and eternity of the logical categories, while ignoring the dialectic of the social structures and structured, structuring dispositions – or, in a more eighteenth-century language, of mind and

nature – within which the schemes of thought are formed and transformed, and in particular the logical categories, *principles of division* which through the intermediary of the principles of the *division of labour,* correspond to the structure of the social world and not the natural world.

39 E. Durkheim, *Les règles de la méthode sociologique,* 18th ed. (Paris: PUF, 1973; 1st ed., Alcan, 1895), p. 9; English translation, *The Rules of Sociological Method* (New York: Free Press, 1964), p. 7.

40 The hypnotic power of the notion of the unconscious has the effect of blotting out the question of the relationship between the practice-generating schemes and the representations – themselves more or less sanctioned by the collectivity – they give of their practice to themselves or others. It thereby discourages analysis of the theoretical or practical alterations that the various forms of discourse about practice impose on practice.

41 "A person who knows a language has represented in his brain some very abstract system of underlying structures along with an abstract system of rules that determine, by free iteration, an infinite range of sound–meaning correspondence" (see N. Chomsky, "General Properties of Language", in I. L. Darley (ed.) *Brain Mechanism Underlying Speech and Language* (New York and London: Grune and Straton, 1967), pp. 73–88).

42 C. Lévi-Strauss, *The Elementary Structures of Kinship,* rev. ed. (London: Social Science Paperbacks, 1969), p. 33 (my italics).

43 *Ibid.*

44 Lévi-Strauss, *Structural Anthropology* (London: Allen Lane, 1968), p. 34.

45 *Elementary Structures,* p. 32.

46 *Ibid.*

47 It is an unwarranted transfer of the same type which, according to Merleau-Ponty, engenders the intellectualist and empiricist errors in psychology (see *The Structure of Behaviour,* esp. pp. 114 and 124).

48 L. Wittgenstein, *Philosophical Investigations* (Oxford: Blackwell, 1963), pp. 38–9.

49 If it is the case that making practice explicit subjects it to an essential alteration, by speaking of what goes without saying or by naming regularities by definition unremarked, it follows that any scientific objectification ought to be preceded by a sign indicating "everything takes place as if . . .", which, functioning in the same way as quantifiers in logic, would constantly remind us of the epistemological status of the constructed concepts of objective science. Everything conspires to encourage the reifying of concepts and of theoretical constructs, starting with the logic of ordinary language, which inclines us to infer the substance from the substantive or to confer on concepts the power to act in history as the words designating them act in the sentences of historical discourse, i.e. as historical *subjects.* It is clear what theoretical (and political) effects arise from the *personification of collectives* (in sentences like "the bourgeoisie thinks that . . ." or "the working class refuses to accept . . ."), which leads, as surely as Durkheim's professions of faith, to postulating the existence of a group or class "collective consciousness": by crediting groups or institutions with dispositions which can be constituted only in individual consciousnesses, even when they are the product of collective conditions such as the awakening of awareness (*prise de conscience*) of class interests, one gets out of having to analyse these conditions, in particular those determining the degree of objective and subjective homogeneity of the group in question and the degree of consciousness of its members.

50 P. Ziff, *Semantic Analysis* (New York: Cornell University Press, 1960), p. 38.

51 W. V. Quine, "Methodological Reflections on Current Linguistic Theory", in D. Harman and G. Davidson (eds.), *Semantics of Natural Language* (Dordrecht: Reidel, 1972), pp. 442–54.

52 L. Wittgenstein, *Tractatus Logico-philosophicus*, 2nd ed. (London: Routledge and Kegan Paul, 1971), p. 49.

53 For another application of the analyses in section I, see P. Bourdieu, "Marriage Strategies as Strategies of Social Reproduction", in R. Forster and O. Ranum (eds.), *Family and Society: Selections from the Annales* (Baltimore: Johns Hopkins University Press, 1976), pp. 117–44.

54 The research leading up this study was carried out with other projects between 1960 and 1970. In the context of an analysis of economic and social structures carried out first in various villages in Kabylia, then in the Collo region, and finally in the Chélif valley and Ouarsenis, I collected genealogies which attempted to situate in a rough way the relative economic positions of groups brought together by marriage. Statistical analysis of these genealogies, carried out between 1962 and 1964, established certain extremely obvious relationships such as the higher rate of endogamy among marabout families or the dyssymmetry of matrimonial exchanges between groups separated by economic inequalities. But it was impossible not to feel the artificial and abstract nature of the distributions and groupings which it was necessary to carry out in order to calculate rates of parallel-cousin marriage. Having abandoned the study of genealogies, which had yielded only negative information, for the analysis of ritual, I soon realized that the *variations* observable in the unfolding of sequences of ritual actions, which I had initially been led to treat as simple "variants", corresponded, in the case of marriage, to unions which were structurally and functionally different, the ritual deployed in full for marriages between great families from different tribes being reduced to its simplest form for marriage between parallel cousins: thus each marriage (and each form which the rite takes) appeared as a moment of a strategy the principle of which lies in objective conditions of a particular type and not in a norm explicitly posited and obeyed, or in an unconscious "model". So it was not possible to give an account of matrimonial exchanges unless, in addition to the purely genealogical relationship between the spouses, one established the objective relationship between the positions in the social structure of the groups brought together by the marriage, the history of the economic and symbolic exchanges which had occurred between them, and the state of those transactions at the moment when matrimonial negotiation was undertaken, the history of that negotiation, the moment at which it took place in the lives of the spouses (childhood or adolescence), its length, the agents responsible for it, the exchanges to which it gave rise, and in particular the value of the bridewealth, etc. In other words, the study of matrimonial exchanges cannot be separated from the families' economic and social history, of which a genealogical diagram gives only a skeleton. This is why I undertook to reconstitute a family's social history, without really being able to complete the task, which would in fact be interminable: this work, which made it possible to measure in concrete terms all that the ordinary genealogist neglects, also provided most of the illustrations for the theoretical analyses set out here.

55 See Claude Lévi-Strauss, "Le problème des relations de parenté", in J. Berque (ed.), *Systèmes de parenté* (Contributions to the interdisciplinary conference on Moslem societies; Paris, Ecole Pratique des Hautes Etudes, 1959), pp. 13–14.

56 *Introduction à deux théories d'anthropologie sociale* (Paris: Mouton, 1971), p. 119.

57 R. Needham, "The Formal Analysis of Prescriptive Patrilateral Cross-cousin Marriage", *Southwestern Journal of Anthropology*, 14 (1958), pp. 199–219.

58 On the deductive relationship between kinship terminology and kinship attitudes, see A. R. Radcliffe-Brown, *Structure and Function in Primitive Society* (London: Cohen and West, 1952), p. 62, and *African Systems of Kinship and Marriage* (London: Oxford University Press, 1960), introduction, p. 25; Lévi-Strauss, *Structural Anthropology*, p. 38. On the term *jural* and the use which Radcliffe-Brown makes of it see Dumont, *Introduction à deux théories*, p. 41: "jural" relationships are those "which are subject to precise, binding prescriptions, whether concerning people or things".

59 "Principles of Social Organization in Southern Kurdistan", *Universitetets Ethnografiske Museum Bulletin*, no. 7, Oslo, 1953.

60 R. F. Murphy and L. Kasdan, "The Structure of Parallel Cousin Marriage", *American Anthropologist*, 61 (February 1959), pp. 17–29.

61 The majority of earlier investigators accepted the native explanation that endogamous marriage had the function of keeping the property in the family, advancing as evidence – and with some reason – the closeness of the relationship between marriage and inheritance practices. Against this explanation Murphy and Kasdan very rightly object that the Koranic law which gives to a woman half of a son's share is rarely observed, and that the family can in any case count on the inheritance contributed by in-marrying women (H. Granqvist, "Marriage Conditions in a Palestinian Village", *Commentationes Humanarum, Societas Scientiarium Fennica* 3 (1931); H. Rosenfeld, "An Analysis of Marriage Statistics for a Moslem and Christian Arab Village", *International Archives of Ethnography*, 48 (1957), pp. 32–62).

62 Both these theories accept an undifferentiated definition of function, which reduces it to the function *for the group as a whole*. For example, Murphy and Kasdan write, "Most explanations of patrilateral parallel cousin marriage are of a causal-motivational kind, in which the institution is explained through reference to the consciously felt goals of the individual role players. We have not attempted to explain the origin of the custom in this paper but have taken it as a given factor and then proceeded to analyze its function, i.e. its operation within Bedouin social structure. It was found that parallel cousin marriage contributes to the extreme fission of agnatic lines in Arab society, and, through in-marriage, encysts the patrilineal segments" ("Structure of Parallel Cousin Marriage", p. 27).

63 J. Cuisenier, "Endogamie et exogamie dans le mariage arabe", *L'Homme*, 2, 2 (May–August 1962), pp. 80–105.

64 "It has long been known that societies which advocate marriage between certain types of kin adhere to the norm only in a small number of cases, as demonstrated by Kunstadter and his team through the use of computer simulations. Fertility and reproduction rates, the demographic balance of the sexes and the age pyramid never show the perfect harmony necessary for every individual, when the time comes for him to marry, to be assured of finding a suitable spouse in the prescribed degree, even if the kinship nomenclature is broad enough to confuse degrees of the same type but unequally distant, often so much so that the notion of a common descent becomes merely theoretical" (Lévi-Strauss, *Elementary Structures of Kinship*, p. xxx).

65 The calculation of "rates of endogamy" by genealogical level, an unreal intersection of abstract "categories", leads one to treat as identical, by a second-order abstraction, individuals who, although on the same level of the genealogical tree, may be of widely differing ages and whose marriages for this very reason may have been arranged in different circumstances corresponding to different states of the matrimonial market. Or, conversely, it may lead one to treat genealogically

separate but chronologically simultaneous marriages as different – it being possible, for example, for a man to marry at the same time as one of his uncles.

66 "Some Structural Aspects of the Feud among the Camel-herding Bedouin of Cyrenaica", *Africa*, 37, 3 (July 1967), pp. 261–82. Murphy was saying the same thing but without drawing conclusions when he remarked that genealogies and the manipulation of genealogies have as their main function the encouragement of the vertical integration of social units which parallel-cousin marriage tends to divide and close in upon themselves.

67 The most rigorously checked genealogies do indeed contain systematic lacunae: since the strength of the group's memory of an individual depends on the value they attach to him or her at the moment of data-collecting, genealogies are better at recording men (and men's marriages), especially when they have produced many male descendants, than at recording women (except, of course, when the latter married within the lineage); they record close marriages better than distant marriages, single marriages rather than much-married individuals' complete series of marriages (polygamy; multiple marriages after divorce or the partner's death). And there is every reason to believe that entire lineages may be left unmentioned by informants when the last representative has died without leaving any descendants or (which amounts to the same thing) without male descendants.

68 It is as instruments of knowledge and construction of the social world that kinship structures fulfil a political function (in the same way as religion and all other ideologies). What are terms of address and reference, if not *categories* of kinship, in the etymological sense of collective, public imputations? (*Kategoreisthai*: to accuse publicly, to impute a thing to someone in front of everyone). The constituting power of these designations, pregnant with a universe of prescriptions and taboos, is brought home when one considers all that is contained in a phrase like "She's your sister" – an *imperative declaration* which is the sole practical statement of the incest taboo. But, though every social relationship is organized in terms of a representation of the social universe, structured in accordance with kinship categories, it would be naive to suppose that social practices, even in relationships with kinsmen, are implied in their genealogical definition.

69 The error is that of all academicisms, which subject the production to the rules they have retrospectively derived from the product.

70 A new-born child is not normally given the name of a living relative; this is avoided, because it would mean "bringing him back to life" before he was dead, thereby throwing down an insulting challenge, and, worse, casting a curse on him; this is true even when the breakup of the undivided patrimony is consecrated by a formal sharing out or when the family splits up on moving to the city or emigrating to France. A father cannot give his son his own first name, and when a son does bear his father's name it is because the father died "leaving him in his mother's womb". But, here as elsewhere, there is no lack of subterfuges and loopholes. Sometimes the name the child was first given is changed so as to give him a name made available by the death of his father or grandfather (the original name is then reserved for private use, by his mother and the women of the family). Sometimes the same first name is given in slightly different forms to several children, with an element added or suppressed (e.g. Mohand Ourabah instead of Rabah, and vice versa; Akli instead of Mohand Akli, and vice versa) or with a slight alteration (Beza instead of Mohand Ameziane, Hamimi or Dahmane instead of Ahmed, Ouali or Alilou instead of Ali, or again, Seghir or Mohand Seghir – arabicized forms – instead of Meziane or Mohand Ameziane). Similarly, although giving a child the same name as his elder brother is avoided, certain

associations of names which are very close to one another or derived from the same name are much appreciated (Ahcène and Elhocine, Ahmed and Mohamed, Seghir or Meziane and Moqrane, etc.), especially if one of them is the name of an ancestor. Since the more integrated the family is, the greater the range of unusable first-names, the choice of first names actually made gives an indication of the "strength of feeling" in the lineage. The same name, or whole series composed of the same names, may coexist in a genealogy, running down parallel lines: the more remote the common origin (or the weaker the unity between the sub-groups), the more it seems legitimate to use the same names, thus perpetuating the memory of the same ancestors in increasingly autonomous lineages.

71 To make completely explicit the implicit demand which lies behind genealogical inquiry, as it lies behind all inquiries, one would first have to study the social history of the genealogical tool, paying particular attention to the functions which, in the traditions of which anthropologists are the product, have produced and reproduced the need for this instrument, viz. the problems of inheritance and succession. This social genealogy of genealogy would have to extend into a social history of the relationship between the "scientific" uses and the social uses of the instrument. But the most important thing would be to carry out an epistemological study of the mode of investigation which is the precondition for production of the genealogical diagram. This would aim to determine the full significance of the ontological transmutation which learned inquiry brings about simply by virtue of the fact that it demands a quasi-theoretical relation to kinship, implying a break with the practical relation directly oriented towards functions.

72 Under the network of genealogical relationships is dissimulated the network of practical relationships, which are the product of the history of the economic and symbolic exchanges. It can be shown in a particular case (P. Bourdieu, *Esquisse d'une théorie de la pratique, précédé de trois études d'ethnologie kabyle* (Paris and Geneva: Librairie Droz, 1972), pp. 85–8) that the agents organize their practice in relation to the useful divisions, finding in the genealogical representation an instrument of legitimation.

73 Dumont, *Introduction à deux théories d'anthropologie sociale*, pp. 122–3.

74 The ritualization of violence in fighting is doubtless one of the most typical manifestations of the dialectic of strategy and ritual: although the battles were almost always motivated by harm done to economic or symbolic interests – the theft of an animal or an insult to members of the group, e.g. the shepherds – their limits were set by the ritualized model of the war of honour, which applied even more strictly in the seasonal games, also endowed with a ritual function, such as the ball games played in autumn and spring (see Bourdieu, *Esquisse*, pp. 21–3). It is possible to understand in terms of this logic, i.e. as the symbolic manipulation of violence aimed at resolving the tensions arising from contact between alien and sometimes traditionally hostile groups, all the particularly strict rites to which marriage between distant groups gives rise. Rules and ritual become increasingly necessary as it ceases to be possible to count on the automatic orchestration of practices that is ensured by homogeneity of habitus and interests (which explains, in a general way, why the ritualization of interactions rises with the distance between the individuals or groups and hence with the size of the groups).

75 Thus, the seemingly most ritualized acts in the marriage negotiation and in the ceremonials accompanying the wedding – which by their degree of solemnity have the secondary function of declaring the social significance of the marriage (the

solemnity of the ceremony tending to rise with the families' position in the social hierarchy and with the genealogical distance between them) – constitute so many opportunities to deploy strategies aimed at manipulating the objective meaning of a relationship which is never entirely unequivocal, whether by choosing the inevitable and – making a virtue of necessity – scrupulously conforming to the proprieties, or by disguising the objective significance of the marriage under the ritual intended to celebrate it.

76 This explains in part the early age of marriage; the unmarried girl is the very incarnation of the group's vulnerability; "the straightest of them is twisted as a sickle", says the proverb. So the father's chief concern is to get rid of this danger as quickly as possible by putting her under the protection of another man.

77 J. Chelhod, who reports that "in the low language of Aleppo, prostitutes are called 'daughters of the maternal aunt'", also quotes a Syrian proverb which expresses the same disapproval of marriage with the mother's sister's daughter: "Because of his impure character, he married his maternal aunt's daughter" ("Le mariage avec la cousine parallèle dans le système arabe", *L'Homme*, 4, 3–4 (July–December 1964), pp. 113–73). Similarly, in Kabylia, to express the total lack of any genealogical relationship, men will say, "What are you to me? Not even the son of the daughter of my mother's sister [*mis illis khalti*]."

78 An indirect confirmation of the meaning given to marriage between parallel cousins may be seen in the fact that the person responsible for the solemn opening of the ploughing, the action homologous with inaugural marriage, had *no political rôle* to play and that his duties were purely *honorary*, or, one might say, *symbolic*, i.e. at once undemanding and respected. This *baraka*-endowed person is referred to by the names *amezwar* (the first), *aneflus* (the man of trust) or *aqdhim* (the elder), *amghar* (the old man), *amas'ud* (the man of luck), or, more precisely, *amezwar, aneflus, amghar nat-yuga* (the first, the man of trust, the old man of the team of oxen or of the plough). The most significant term, because it explicitly states the ploughing–marriage homology manifested by countless other indications, is unquestionably *boula'ras* (the man of the wedding). The same connotation is found in another designation – *mefthah n ss'ad* (the key of good luck, he who *opens*) (see E. Laoust, *Mots et choses berbères: notes de linguistique et d'ethnographie*, Paris: Challamel, 1920).

79 "You must marry your paternal uncle's daughter, even if she has fallen into neglect." And various other proverbs point in the same direction: "Turn with the road if it turns. Marry the daughter of your *'amm* if she has been abandoned [is lying fallow]"; "The daughter of your *'amm* even if she has been abandoned; the road of peace even if it twists." As the metaphor shows (the twisted road as opposed to the straight way), parallel-cousin marriage (like marriage to a brother's widow) is seen more than often not as a forced sacrifice which it is desirable to turn into a voluntary submission to the call of honour. "If you do not marry the daughter of your *'amm*, who will take her? You are the one who must take her, whether you want to or not." "Even if she be ugly and worthless, her paternal uncle is expected to take her for his son; if he seeks a wife for his son elsewhere, people will laugh at him, and say: 'He has gone and found a stranger for his son, and left his brother's daughter.'"

80 But here, too, every sort of compromise and, of course, strategy, is to be found: although in the case of land, the best-placed relative may be aware that more distant kin would willingly steal a march on him and win the symbolic and material advantage accruing from such a meritorious purchase, or, in the case of the vengeance of honour, that a rival avenger is ready to step in and take over

the revenge and the ensuing honour, nothing similar occurs in the case of marriage, and there may be many ways of backing out: sometimes the son takes flight, with his parents' connivance, thereby providing them with the only acceptable excuse that a brother can be given. Short of this extreme solution, it is not uncommon for the obligation to marry leftover daughters to devolve upon the "poor relations", who are bound by all sorts of "obligations" to the richer members of the group. And there is no better proof of the *ideological function* of marriage to the parallel cousin (or to any female cousin in the paternal lineage, however distant) than the use that may be made, in such cases, of the exalted representation of this ideal marriage.

81 Physical and mental infirmity presents an extremely difficult problem for a group which rigorously denies social status to a woman without a husband or even to a man without a wife (even a widower is obliged to rush into a new marriage). All the more so when these infirmities are seen and interpreted through the mythico-ritual categories: one can imagine the sacrifice it represents – in a universe in which a wife can be repudiated because she has a reputation for bringing bad luck – to marry a woman who is left-handed, half-blind, lame, or hunchbacked (this deformity representing an inversion of pregnancy) or who is simply sick and weak, all omens of barrenness and wickedness.

82 "You give wheat, but take barley." "You give wheat to bad teeth." "Make your offspring out of clay; if you don't get a cooking pot you will get a couscous dish." Among the eulogies of parallel-cousin marriage I have collected, the following are typical: "She will not ask you for much for herself, and there will be no need to spend a great deal on the wedding." "He may do what he will with his brother's daughter and no evil will come from her. Thereafter he will live in greater unity with his brother, doing as their father recommended for the sake of brotherhood [*thaymats*]: 'Do not listen to your women!'" "The woman who is a stranger will despise you, she will be an insult to your ancestors, believing that hers are more noble than yours. Whereas with the daughter of your *'amm*, your grandfather and hers are one; she will never say 'a curse on your father's father'. The daughter of your *'amm* will not abandon you. If you have no tea she will not demand any from you, and even if she should die of hunger in your house, she will bear it all and never complain about you."

83 A. Hanoteau, *Poésies populaires de la Kabylie du Djurdjura* (Paris: Imprimerie Impériale, 1867), p. 475.

84 Jurists' fascination with what *survives* of matrilineal kinship has led them to take an interest in the case of the *awrith*, which they see, to use their own terminology, as a "contract for the adoption of an adult male" (for Algeria, see G. H. Bousquet, "Note sur le mariage mechrouth dans la région de Gouraya", *Revue Algérienne*, January–February 1934, pp. 9–11, and L. Lefèvre, *Recherches sur la condition de la femme kabyle*, Algiers: Carbonel, 1939; for Morocco, G. Marcy, "Le mariage en droit coutumier zemmoûr", *Revue Algérienne, Tunisienne et Marocaine de Législation et Jurisprudence*, July 1930, and "Les vestiges de la parenté maternelle en droit coutumier berbère", *Revue Africaine*, no. 85 (1941), pp. 187–211: Capitaine Bendaoud, "L'adoption des adultes par contrat mixte de mariage et de travail chez les Beni Mguild", *Revue Marocaine de Législation, Doctrine, Jurisprudence Chérifiennes*, no. 2 (1935), pp. 34–40; Capitaine Turbet, "L'adoption des adultes chez les Ighezrane", *ibid.* p. 40, and no. 3 (1935), p. 41).

85 For example, in a large family in the village of Aghbala in Lesser Kabylia, of 218 male marriages (each man's first) 34% were with families outside the limits of the tribe; only 8%, those with the spatially and socially most distant groups,

present all the features of prestige marriages: they are all the work of one family which wants to distinguish itself from the other lineages by original matrimonial practices. The other distant marriages (26%) merely renew established relationships (relationships "through the women" or "through the maternal uncles", constantly maintained on the occasion of marriages, departures and returns, funerals and sometimes even large work projects). Two thirds of the marriages (66%) were made within the tribe (made up of nine villages): apart from marriages with the opposing clan, which are very rare (4%) and always have a political significance (especially for the older generations) on account of the traditional antagonism between the two groups, all the other unions fall within the class of ordinary marriages. Only 6% of the marriages were made within the lineage (as against 17% in the other lineages and 39% in the field of practical relationships): 4% *with the parallel cousin* and 2% with another cousin (and it must be added that in two-thirds of these cases the families which make this marriage have abandoned undivided ownership).

86 The following testimony is particularly significant: "As soon as her first son was born, Fatima set about finding his future wife. She never missed an opportunity – she kept her eyes open on all occasions, in her neighbour's houses, among her own family, in the village, when visiting friends, at weddings, on pilgrimages, at the fountain, far from home, and even when she had to go and present her condolences. In this way she married off all her children without difficulty and almost without noticing it" (Yamina Aït Amar Ou Saïd, *Le mariage en Kabylie* (Fichier de Documentation Berbère), 1960, p. 10).

87 As I have shown elsewhere (cf. *Esquisse*, pp. 110–12), the frequency and solemnity of ritual acts increase as one moves from marriages contracted within the undivided family or practical kinship, through marriages within close and then distant practical relationships, and finally to extra-ordinary marriages. Everything takes place as if extra-ordinary marriages gave us the opportunity to grasp in its achieved form a ceremonial which is reduced to its simplest expression when the marriage is situated in the ordinary universe.

88 If we leave aside the mythical idealization (blood, purity, the inside) and ethical exaltation (honour, virtue, etc.) surrounding purely agnatic marriage, we find that these ordinary marriages are described no differently from parallel-cousin marriage. For example, marriage with the father's sister's daughter is regarded, like marriage with the parallel cousin, as capable of securing agreement among the women and the wife's respect for her husband's relatives (her *khal* and her *khalt*) at the lowest cost, since the tension resulting from the rivalry implicitly triggered off by any marriage between different groups over the status and living conditions offered to the young wife has no reason to occur at this degree of familiarity.

89 These extra-ordinary marriages are not subject to the constraints and proprieties which apply to ordinary marriages (partly because they have no "sequel"): apart from the cases in which the defeated group (clan or tribe) would give the victorious group a woman, or, to show that there was neither winner nor loser, the two groups exchanged women, it also sometimes happened that the victorious group would give the other group a woman without taking anything in return, but then the marriage took place not between the most powerful families, but between families asymmetrically situated: a small family in the victorious group gave a woman to a great family in the other group. The victorious group intended to show, by the very inequality of the union, that the least of its own members was superior to the greatest of its opponents.

90 "Marriage afar is exile" (*azwaj lab'adh d'anfi*): "Marriage outside, marriage into
    exile" (*azwaj ibarra, azwaj elghurba*), a mother often says when her daughter has
    been given to another group in which she has no acquaintances (*thamusni*) and
    not even distant kin (*arriha*, a scent – of her native land). It is also the song of
    the wife who has been married into exile· "O mountain, open your door to the
    exile. Let her see her native land. Foreign soil is the sister of death, for man as
    for woman."

91 The generalization of monetary exchanges and of the associated calculative dispo-
    sitions has brought about a decline of this tradition (which was kept up longer
    in more profane exchanges such as the sale of a yoke of oxen) by destroying the
    ambiguities which characterized it and reducing it to a shameful and ridiculous
    haggling over the amount of the bridewealth.

92 In such a system, the failures of the reproduction mechanisms – matrimonial
    misalliance, sterility leading to disappearance of the lineage, the *break-up of
    undivided ownership* – are undoubtedly the principal factors responsible for trans-
    formations of the economic and social hierarchy.

93 The countless *chikayat*, some of which come before the courts, are motivated not
    by a spirit of "quibbling" but by the intent of throwing down or taking up a
    challenge: the same is true of the (very rare) lawsuits which have been conducted
    in the hope of obtaining the annulment of a land sale in the name of the right
    of pre-emption.

94 The simple challenge to the point of honour (*thirzi nennif*, the act of challenging;
    sennif "by *nif*, I challenge you! I dare you!") is not the same thing as the offence
    which calls *hurma* into question. There is derision for the attitude of the nouveau
    riche who, ignorant of the rules of honour and attempting to redress a slur upon
    hurma, riposted by challenging his offender to beat him in a race or to lay out
    more thousand-franc notes. He was confusing two totally different orders, the
    order of the challenge and the order of the offence which involves the most sacred
    values. An attack on *hurma* tends to exclude evasions and settlements such as *diya*,
    compensation paid to the victim's family by the murderer's family. Of the man
    who accepts, people say, "He's a man who's agreed to eat his brother's blood;
    for him, only the belly counts." In the case of a slur upon *hurma*, albeit indirectly
    or thoughtlessly, the pressure of opinion is such as to rule out any outcome other
    than vengeance: if vengeance is not forthcoming, the coward lacking in *nif* can
    only choose between dishonour and exile.

95 Honour in the sense of esteem is termed *sar: essar* is the secret, prestige,
    radiance, "glory", "presence". It is said of a man that "*essar* follows him and
    shines about him", or that he is protected by "the fence of *essar*" (*zarb nessar*):
    the holder of *essar* is exempt from challenge and the would-be offender is
    paralysed by its mysterious influence, by the fear (*alhiba*) it inspires. To put a
    man to shame is "to take away his *essar*" (or "to take away his *lahya*", respect):
    essar, the indefinable attribute of the man of honour, is as fragile and vulnerable
    as it is imponderable. "The burnous of *essar*", say the Kabyles, "lies lightly on
    a man's shoulders."

96 And indeed the customary laws, which all, without exception, provide for
    sanctions against the person who murders the man from whom he is to inherit,
    are evidence that overt conflicts were frequent: "If a man kills a relative (whose
    heir he is) unjustly and so as to inherit from him, the *djemâa* shall take all the
    murderer's goods" (*qanun* of the Iouadhien tribe, reported in Hanoteau and
    Letourneux, *La Kabylie et les coutumes kabyles*, vol. III, p. 432; see also pp. 356,
    358, 368, etc.).

97 Here is just one typical testimony relating to the breaking up of undivided ownership: "You can't find two brothers who live together (*zaddi*) now, still less we who are not sprung from the same womb. I swear that I can't even remember what relation I am to *dadda* Braham. Sooner or later it's bound to happen, and everyone in his heart wants it to, everyone thinks he does too much for the others, 'If I only had my wife and children, I wouldn't have to work so hard', or 'I would have reached the "divine throne" [the seventh heaven].' Once people start thinking like that, there's nothing for it, it's all over. It's like a canker. The women already thought that way, and when the men join in and start saying the same things, it's finished. That's what all the women want; they are the enemies of *zaddi*, because the devil is in them: they do all they can to contaminate the men. With their determination, they never fail."

98 The weakening of the cohesive forces (correlative with the slump in symbolic values) and the strengthening of the disruptive forces (linked to the appearance of sources of monetary income and to the ensuing crisis of the peasant economy) lead to refusal of the elders' authority and of the austere, frugal aspects of peasant existence; the younger generation demand the right to dispose of the profit of their labour, in order to spend it on consumer goods rather than on the symbolic goods which would increase the family's prestige and influence. "In the past, no one dared to ask for the heritage to be broken up. There was the authority of the elders. If anyone had tried, he'd have been beaten, cast out, and cursed: 'He is a cause of bankruptcy [*lakhla ukham*, the fallow of the house].' 'He wants it all shared out' [*itsabib ibbatu*]': the elders refuse to 'give him the share-out'. Now everybody insists on their rights. Once it was 'eat your piece of wheatcake and keep quiet': once, being head of the family, going to market, sitting in *thajma'th*, meant something. Now, everyone knows that widows' houses are more prosperous than those of men [of honour]. 'Those who were children only yesterday want to run things now!'"

99 Without speculating as to the causal link between these facts, it may be noted that "illnesses of acute *jealousy*" (*atan an-tsismin thissamamin*, the sickness of bitter jealousy) receive great attention from relatives, especially mothers, who wield a whole arsenal of curative and prophylactic rites (to suggest an insurmountable hatred, reference is made to the feeling of the little boy who, suddenly deprived of his mother's affection by the arrival of a new baby, grew thin and pale like someone moribund, *am'ut*, or "constipated", *bubran*).

100 It is significant that customary law, which only exceptionally intervenes in domestic life, explicitly favours undivided ownership (*thidukli bukham* or *zaddi*): "People living in a family association pay no fine if they fight. If they separate, they pay like other people" (Hanoteau and Letourneux, *La Kabylie*, vol. III, p. 423).

101 A female informant gives a typical account of how this sort of marriage is arranged: "Before he had leant to walk, his father found him a bride. One evening, after supper, Arab went to call on his elder brother (*dadda*). They chatted. His brother's wife had her daughter on her lap; the little girl stretched out her arms towards her uncle, who picked her up, saying 'May God make her Idir's wife! That's so, isn't it, *dadda*? You won't say no?' Arab's brother replied: 'What does a blind man want? Light! If you relieve me of the care she gives me, may God take your cares from you. I give her to you, with her grain and her chaff, for nothing!'" (Yamina Aït Amar Ou Saïd, *Le mariage en Kabylie*, p. 10).

102 As J. Chelhod rightly points out, all observations confirm that the tendency to

marry endogamously, which is more marked in nomadic tribes in a constant state of war than in settled tribes, tends to reappear or to be accentuated when there are threats of war or conflict ("Le mariage avec la cousine parallèle dans le système arabe", pp. 113–73). Those who perpetuate undivided ownership – or the appearances of it – often invoke the danger of separating so long as rival families remain united.

103 It follows from this axiom that the dominant are functionalists, because function so defined – that is, in the sense of the structural-functionalist school – is simply the interest of the dominant, or more precisely, the interest the dominant have in the perpetuation of a system consistent with their interests. Those who explain matrimonial strategies by their effects – for example, the "fission and fusion" of Murphy and Kasden are effects which one gains nothing by terming functions – are no less remote from the reality of practices than those who invoke the efficacy of the rule. To say that parallel-cousin marriage has the function of fission and/or fusion without inquiring *for whom*, *for what*, to what (measurable) extent, and under what conditions, is to resort, shamefacedly of course, to explanation by *final causes* instead of inquiring how the economic and social conditions characteristic of a social formation impose the pursuit of the satisfaction of a determinate type of interests which itself leads to the production of a determinate type of collective effect.

104 By means of secret negotiations, *thamgharth* sometimes manages to interfere in a marriage being arranged entirely by the men, and to make *thislith* promise to leave her complete authority in the house, warning her that otherwise she will prevent the marriage. The sons have some justification in suspecting their mothers of giving them for wives girls they – the mothers – will be able to dominate without difficulty.

105 The marriages of the poor (especially those poor in symbolic capital) are to those of the rich, *mutatis mutandis*, what female marriages are to male marriages. The poor cannot afford to be too demanding in matters of honour. "The only thing the poor man can do is show he is jealous." This means that, like women, the poor are less concerned with the symbolic and political functions of a marriage than with its *practical* functions, attaching, for example, much more importance to the personal qualities of the spouses.

106 The girl's value on the marriage market is in a sense a direct projection of the value socially attributed to the two lineages of which she is the product. This can be seen clearly when the father has had children by several marriages: whereas the boys' value is unrelated to their mothers' value, the girl's value depends on the social status of their mothers' lineages and the strength of their mothers' positions in the family.

107 The relevant genealogy is to be found in Bourdieu, *Esquisse*, p. 149.

108 "Spontaneous psychology" perfectly describes the "girls' boy" (*aqchich bu thaqchichin*), coddled and cosseted by the women of the family who are always inclined to keep him with them longer than the other boys; he eventually identifies with the social rôle created for him, and becomes a sickly, puny child, "eaten up by his many long-haired sisters". The same reasons which lead the family to lavish care on a product too rare and precious to be allowed to run the slightest risk – to spare him agricultural work and to prolong his education, thus setting him apart from his friends by his more refined speech, cleaner clothes, and more elaborate food – also lead them to arrange an early marriage for him.

109 A girl's value rises with the number of her brothers, the guardians of her honour (in particular of her virginity) and potential allies of her future husband. Tales

express the jealousy inspired by the girl with seven brothers, protected sevenfold like "a fig among the leaves": "A girl who was lucky enough to have seven brothers could be proud, and *there was no lack of suitors*. She was *sure of being sought after and appreciated*. When she was married, her husband, her husband's parents, the whole family, and even the neighbours and their wives *respected* her: had she not seven men on her side, was she not the sister of seven brothers, seven *protectors*? If there was the slightest argument, they came and set things right, and if their sister committed a fault, or ever came to be repudiated, they would have taken her back *home with them, respected by everyone. No dishonour could touch them*. No one would dare to enter *the lions' den*."

110 Particularly skilful strategies can make the most of the limited capital available, through bluff (difficult when one is operating in the area of familiar relationships) or, more simply, through shrewd exploitation of the ambiguities of the symbolic patrimony or discrepancies between different components of the patrimony. Although it may be regarded as part of symbolic capital, which is itself relatively autonomous of strictly economic capital, the skill which enables one to make the best use of the patrimony through shrewd investments, such as successful marriages, is relatively independent of it. Thus the poor, who have nothing to sell but their virtue, can take advantage of their daughter's marriage to gain prestigious allies or at least powerful protectors, by purveying honour to highly placed buyers.

111 Inasmuch as they belong to the class of reproduction strategies, matrimonial strategies differ in no way in their logic from those strategies designed to preserve or increase symbolic capital which conform to the dialectic of honour, whether they involve the buying back of land or the paying back of insults, rape, or murder; in each case, the same dialectical relationship can be observed between vulnerability (through land, women, the house, in short, *ḥurma*) and the protection (through men, rifles, the point of honour; in short, *nif*) which preserves or increases symbolic capital (prestige, honour; in short, *ḥurma*).

CHAPTER 2. STRUCTURES AND THE HABITUS

1 The word *disposition* seems particularly suited to express what is covered by the concept of habitus (defined as a system of dispositions). It expresses first the *result of an organizing action*, with a meaning close to that of words such as structure; it also designates a *way of being*, a *habitual state* (especially of the body) and, in particular, a *predisposition, tendency, propensity*, or *inclination*. [The semantic cluster of "disposition" is rather wider in French than in English, but as this note – translated literally – shows, the equivalence is adequate. Translator.]

2 The most profitable strategies are usually those produced, on the hither side of all calculation and in the illusion of the most "authentic" sincerity, by a habitus objectively fitted to the objective structures. These strategies without strategic calculation procure an important secondary advantage for those who can scarcely be called their authors – the social approval accruing from apparent disinterestedness.

3 "Here we confront the distressing fact that the sample episode chain under analysis is a fragment of a larger segment of behavior which in the complete record contains some 480 separate episodes. Moreover, it took only twenty minutes for these 480 behavior stream events to occur. If my wife's rate of behavior is roughly representative of that of other actors, we must be prepared to deal with

an inventory of episodes produced at the rate of some 20,000 per sixteen-hour day per actor... In a population consisting of several hundred actor-types, the number of different episodes in the total repertory must amount to many millions during the course of an annual cycle" (M. Harris, *The Nature of Cultural Things* (New York: Random House, 1964), pp. 74–5).

4 See A. Touraine, *Sociologie de l'action*, Paris: Seuil, 1965, and "La raison d'être d'une sociologie de l'action", *Revue Française de Sociologie*, 7 (October–December 1966), pp. 518–27.

5 J.-P. Sartre, *L'etre et le néant* (Paris: Gallimard, 1943), p. 510 (*Being and Nothingness* (London: Methuen, 1957), pp. 434–5 [translation emended]); see also Sartre, "Répose à Lefort", *Les Temps Modernes*, no. 89 (April 1963), pp. 1571–1629.

6 *L'être et le néant*, p. 669; *Being and Nothingness*, p. 580.

7 *L'être et le néant*, p. 521; *Being and Nothingness*, p. 445.

8 E. Durkheim, *Les règles de la méthode sociologique*, 18th ed. (Paris: PUF, 1973), p. 18; English trans. *The Rules of Sociological Method* (New York: Free Press, 1964), p. 17.

9 *L'être et le néant*, p. 543; *Being and Nothingness*, p. 465.

10 *Critique de la raison dialectique* (Paris: Gallimard, 1960), p. 161.

11 *Critique*, p. 305.

12 *Critique*, p. 357.

13 *Règles*, p. 19; *Rules*, p. 18.

14 *Critique*, p. 133.

15 *Critique*, pp. 234 and 281.

16 *Critique*, p. 294.

17 *Critique*, p. 179.

18 Can one avoid attributing to the permanence of a habitus the constancy with which the objective intention of the Sartrian philosophy (despite its language) asserts itself against the subjective intentions of its author, that is, against a permanent project of "conversion", a project never more manifest and manifestly sincere than in certain anathemas which would perhaps be less violent if they were not redolent of conscious or unconscious self-critique? (Thus, for example, one needs to bear in mind the famous analysis of the café waiter for a full appreciation of a sentence such as this: "To all those who take themselves for angels, their neighbour's activities seem absurd, because such people presume to transcend the human enterprise by refusing to take part in it": *Critique*, pp. 182–3). And when, in his analysis of the relationship between Flaubert and the bourgeoisie, Sartre makes the awakening of consciousness the basis of an existence and an oeuvre, he testifies that it is not sufficient to become aware of class condition in order to be liberated from the lasting dispositions it produces (see P. Bourdieu, "Champ du pouvoir, champ intellectuel et habitus de classe", *Scolies*, 1 (1971), pp. 7–26, esp. pp. 12–14).

19 See the whole chapter entitled "Rechtsordnung, Konvention und Sitte", in which Max Weber analyses the differences and transitions between custom, convention, and law (*Wirtschaft und Gesellschaft* (Cologne and Berlin: Kiepenhauer und Witsch, 1964), vol. 1, pp. 240–50, esp. pp. 246–9; English trans. "Law, Convention and Custom", *Economy and Society*, ed. G. Roth and C. Wittich (New York: Bedminster Press, 1968), 1, pp. 319–33).

20 "We call this subjective, variable probability – which sometimes excludes doubt and engenders a certainty *sui generis* and which at other times appears as no more than a vague glimmer – *philosophical probability*, because it refers to the exercise of the higher faculty whereby we comprehend the order and the rationality of

things. All reasonable men have a confused notion of similar probabilities; this then determines, or at least justifies, those unshakable beliefs we call *common sense*" (A. Cournot, *Essai sur les fondements de la connaissance et sur les caractères de la critique philosophique* (Paris: Hachette, 1922; 1st ed., 1851), p. 70).

21 E. Durkheim, *L'évolution pedagogique en France* (Paris: Alcan, 1938), p. 16.

22 R. Ruyer, *Paradoxes de la conscience et limites de l'automatisme* (Paris: Albin Michel, 1966), p. 136.

23 This universalization has the same limits as the objective conditions of which the principle generating practices and works is the product. The objective conditions exercise simultaneously a universalizing effect and a particularizing effect, because they cannot homogenize the agents whom they determine and whom they constitute into an objective group, without distinguishing them from all the agents produced in different conditions.

24 One of the merits of subjectivism and moralism is that the analyses in which it condemns, as inauthentic, actions subject to the objective solicitations of the world (e.g. Heidegger on everyday existence and "*das Man*" or Sartre on the "spirit of seriousness") demonstrate, *per absurdum*, the impossibility of the authentic existence that would gather up all pregiven significations and objective determinations into a project of freedom. The *purely ethical* pursuit of authenticity is the privilege of the leisured thinker who can afford to dispense with the economy of thought which "inauthentic" conduct allows.

25 G. W. Leibniz, "Second éclaircissement du système de la communication des substances" (1696), in *Oeuvres philosophiques*, ed. P. Janet (Paris: de Lagrange, 1866), vol. II, p. 548.

26 Thus, ignorance of the surest but best-hidden foundation of group or class integration leads some (e.g. Aron, Dahl, etc.) to deny the unity of the dominant class with no other proof than the impossibility of establishing empirically that the members of the dominant class have an explicit *policy*, expressly imposed by explicit co-ordination, and others (Sartre, for example) to see the awakening of class consciousness – a sort of revolutionary cogito bringing the class into existence by constituting it as a "class for itself" – as the only possible foundation of the unity of the dominated class.

27 Leibniz, "Second éclaircissement", p. 548.

28 Were such language not dangerous in another way, one would be tempted to say, against all forms of subjectivist voluntarism, that class unity rests fundamentally on the "class unconscious". The awakening of "class consciousness" is not a primal act constituting the class in a blaze of freedom; its sole efficacy, as with all actions of symbolic reduplication, lies in the extent to which it brings to consciousness all that is implicitly assumed in the unconscious mode in the class habitus.

29 This takes us beyond the false opposition in which the theories of acculturation have allowed themselves to be trapped, with, on the one hand, the *realism of the structure* which represents cultural or linguistic contacts as contacts between cultures or languages, subject to generic laws (e.g. the law of the restructuring of borrowings) and specific laws (those established by analysis of the structures specific to the languages or cultures in contact) and on the other hand the *realism of the element*, which emphasizes the contacts between the *societies* (regarded as populations) involved or, at best, the structures of the relations between those societies (domination, etc.).

30 *The People of Alor*, Minneapolis: University of Minnesota Press, 1944.

31 *Culture and Personality* (New York: Random House, 1965), p. 86.

32 If illiterate societies seem to have a particular bent for the structural games which fascinate the anthropologist, their purpose is often quite simply mnemonic: the remarkable homology to be observed in Kabylia between the structure of the distribution of the families in the village and the structure of the distribution of graves in the cemetery (Aït Hichem, Tizi Hibel) clearly makes it easier to locate the traditionally anonymous graves (with expressly transmitted landmarks added to the structural principles).

33 B. Berelson and G. A. Steiner, *Human Behavior* (New York: Harcourt, Brace and World, 1964), p. 193.

34 *The Singer of the Tales* (Cambridge, Mass.: Harvard University Press, 1960), p. 30.

35 *Ibid.* p. 32.

36 *Ibid.* p. 24.

37 Thus, in the game of *qochra*, which the children play in early spring, the cork ball (the *qochra*) which is fought for, passed and defended, is the practical equivalent of woman. In the course of the game the players must both defend themselves against it and, possessing it, defend it against those trying to take it away. At the start of the match, the leader of the game repeatedly asks, "Whose daughter is she?" but no one will volunteer to be her father and protect her: a daughter is always a liability for men. And so lots have to be drawn for her, and the unlucky player who gets her must accept his fate. He now has to protect the ball against the attacks of all the others, while at the same time trying to pass it on to another player; but he can only do so in an honourable, approved way. A player whom the "father" manages to touch with his stick, telling him "She's your daughter", has to acknowledge defeat, like a man temporarily obliged to a socially inferior family from whom he has taken a wife. For the suitors the temptation is to take the prestigious course of abduction, whereas the father wants a marriage that will free him from guardianship and allow him to re-enter the game. The loser of the game is excluded from the world of men; the ball is tied under his shirt so that he looks like a girl who has been got pregnant.

38 It is said that formerly the women used to go to market alone; but they are so talkative that the market went on until the market time of the following week. So the men turned up one day with sticks and put an end to their wives' gossiping... It can be seen that the "myth" "explains" the present division of space and work by invoking the "evil nature" of women. When a man wants to say that the world is topsy-turvy, he says that "the women are going to market".

39 A full presentation of the analysis of the internal structure of the Kabyle house, of which it has only been possible to give the indispensable outline here, can be found in P. Bourdieu, *Esquisse d'une théorie de la pratique* (Paris and Geneva: Librairie Droz, 1972), pp. 45–69.

40 This means to say that the "learning by doing" hypothesis, associated with the name of Arrow (see K. J. Arrow, "The Economic Implications of Learning by Doing", *Review of Economic Studies*, 29, 3, no. 80 (June 1962), pp. 155–73) is a particular case (whose particularity needs to be specified) of a very general law: every made product – including symbolic products such as works of art, games, myths, etc. – exerts by its very functioning, particularly by the use made of it, an educative effect which helps to make it easier to acquire the dispositions necessary for its adequate use.

41 Erikson's analyses of the Yoruk might be interpreted in the same light (see E. H. Erikson, "Observations on the Yoruk: Childhood and World Image" (University of California Publications in American Archaeology and Ethnology, vol. 35, no. 10, Berkeley: University of California Press, 1943), pp. 257–302).

42 E. H. Erikson, "Childhood and Tradition in Two American Tribes", in *The Psychoanalytic Study of the Child* (New York: International Universities Press, 1945), vol. i, pp. 319–50.

43 *Contributions to Psycho-analysis 1921–1945* (London: Hogarth Press, 1948), p. 109n1 and p. 260n1.

44 Every group entrusts to bodily automatisms those principles most basic to it and most indispensable to its conservation. In societies which lack any other recording and objectifying instrument, inherited knowledge can survive only in its embodied state. Among other consequences, it follows that it is never detached from the body which bears it and which – as Plato noted – can deliver it only at the price of a sort of gymnastics intended to evoke it: *mimesis*. The body is thus continuously mingled with all the knowledge it reproduces, which can never have the objectivity and distance stemming from objectification in writing.

45 A. Matheron, *Individu et société chez Spinoza* (Paris: Editions de Minuit, 1969), p. 349.

46 Thus, practical mastery of what are called the rules of politeness, and in particular the art of adjusting each of the available formulae (e.g. at the end of a letter) to the different classes of possible addressees, presupposes the implicit mastery, hence the recognition, of a set of oppositions constituting the implicit axiomatics of a determinate political order: in the example considered these are (in France) the opposition between men and women, the former requiring "homage", the latter "salutations" or "sentiments"; the opposition between the older and the younger; the opposition between the personal, or private, and the impersonal – with administrative or business letters; and finally the hierarchical opposition between superiors, equals, and inferiors, which governs the subtle grading of marks of respect.

47 One of the reasons for the use of the term habitus is the wish to set aside the common conception of habit as a mechanical assembly or preformed programme, as Hegel does when in the *Phenomenology of Mind* he speaks of "habit as dexterity".

48 For a sociological application of these analyses, see P. Bourdieu, "Avenir de classe et causalité du probable", *Revue Française de Sociologie*, 15, (January–March 1974), pp. 3–42. English translation forthcoming.

CHAPTER 3. GENERATIVE SCHEMES AND PRACTICAL LOGIC

1 The antigenetic prejudice leading to unconscious or overt refusal to seek the genesis of objective structures and internalized structures in individual or collective history combines with the antifunctionalist prejudice, which refuses to take account of the practical functions which symbolic systems may perform; and together they reinforce the tendency of structuralist anthropology to credit historical systems with more coherence than they have or need to have in order to function. In reality these systems remain, like culture as described by Lowie, "things of shreds and patches", even if these patches are constantly undergoing unconscious and intentional restructurings and reworkings tending to integrate them into the system.

2 The history of perspective offered by Panofsky (E. Panofsky, "Die Perspektive als 'symbolische Form'", *Vorträge der Bibliothek Warburg*, Leipzig and Berlin, 1924–5, pp. 258–330) is an exemplary contribution to a social history of conventional modes of cognition and expression; doubtless, in order to make a radical break with the idealist tradition of "symbolic forms" one would have to relate

historical forms of perception and representation more systematically to the social conditions in which they are produced and reproduced (by express or diffuse education), i.e. to the structure of the groups producing and reproducing them and the position of those groups in the social structure.

3 The degree to which the principles of the habitus are objectified in knowledges fixed and taught as such varies considerably from one area of activity to another: a rough count indicates that the relative frequency of highly codified sayings, proverbs, and rites declines as one moves from the agrarian calendar (and the calendars closely associated with it, which are already less codified, such as the women's weaving and pottery calendar, and the cooking calendar) to the divisions of the day or the ages of human life, not to mention areas apparently given over to arbitrariness, such as the organization of the space inside the house, the parts of the body, colours, or animals. Striking evidence of the connivance between the anthropologist and his informant in legalist formalism may be found in the fact that the hierarchy of domains, in terms of their degree of objectification, more or less matches their relative prominence in anthropologists' data-collecting. Because its social function puts it into competition with the Moslem calendar and the learned or semi-learned traditions associated with it – those which are conveyed by the ephemerides and almanacs and have long been diffused through the intermediary of the literate – the agrarian calendar is, of all the different domains of the tradition, the one which most directly bears the mark of Islamic contributions.

4 This capital of knowledge is not distributed uniformly among all members of the group (although the disparities are never so great as those found in literate societies with educational systems): the division of labour between the sexes or the age-groups and (albeit in a rudimentary form) between the professions (with the oppositions between the peasant, the scholar, and the smith or the butcher) inclines the different categories of agents (whose practical calendars, though different, are objectively orchestrated) to practise very different degrees of accumulation of the various instruments handed on by the cultural tradition and, in particular, predisposes and prepares them in very different ways to memorize those instruments which are objectified in the form of codified (and sometimes written) knowledge. It is among the old women and the smiths, both of whom occupy an ambiguous position in the group, that one generally finds the greatest competence in *private magic*, minor, optional rites, intended to serve private ends, such as the rites of curative or love magic, which generally make use of transparent symbolism and simple ritual strategies, such as the transference of good or evil on to a person or an object; whereas it is the most influential members of the group, the oldest men of the most respected families, who are generally the most adept in the rites of collective magic, official, obligatory rites which, like the agrarian rites, involve the whole group because they fulfil the same function for every member of the group.

5 This sort of homogenization and unification was successfully undertaken by the great priestly bureaucracies of antiquity, which wielded sufficient authority to impose a genuine *religious code*, with its rites performed on *fixed dates* regardless of fluctuations in the climate and the diversity of economic and social conditions.

6 The (arbitrary) mode of representation which has been adopted here to reconstitute the logic immanent in representations and practices (and which runs the risk of encouraging a "structuralist" reading through the effect of a synoptic diagram) highlights the turning-points or *thresholds* (spring, autumn), while presenting the marked moments of the agrarian year as the ordinate points of a linear, oriented

sequence (running from autumn to summer, i.e. from west to east, evening to morning, etc.) or as the points on a circle which may be obtained by folding the diagram along the axis XY.

7 Other informants even say it is impossible to know which is the first day of winter.

8 These names refer to the legend of the borrowed days, which tells how winter (or January, or February, etc.) borrowed a few days from the next period so as to punish an old woman (or a goat, or a Negro) who had issued a challenge.

9 Although it must not be forgotten that to bring together, in the form of a series, a set of features present in a particular region is itself an entirely artificial syncretic operation, the three main series are indicated in the diagram, viz. *imirghane, amerdil, thamgharth, ahgan* or *thiftirine, nisan*; *thimgharine, hayan, nisan*; *el mwalah, el qwarah, el swalah, el fwatah, husum, natah, nisan*. These series could (for the sake of simplicity) be said to correspond to the Djurdjura region, to Lesser Kabylia, and, in the last case, to the most Islamized areas or to literate informants.

10 This was how an informant spoke of *la'didal*, a period of dreadful cold whose coming can never be predicted. It is mentioned in a song which the women sing while working at the flour mill: "If *la'didal* are like the nights of *hayan* for me, tell the shepherds to flee to the village." And according to informants in the Djurdjura region, one night in the month of *bujember* (no one knows which one) water turns to blood.

11 This semi-scholarly series is sometimes called *ma, qa, sa, fin*, by a mnemonic device used by the marabouts, in which each name is represented by its initial. Similarly, it is thanks to its mnemonic qualities that informants almost always cite the series of the divisions of the beginning of summer (*izegzawen, iwraghen, imellalen, iquranen*); the series is also sometimes designated by the first consonants of the roots of the Berber names for the divisions: *za, ra, ma, qin*.

12 Other taboos of *hayan* and *husum*: ploughing, weddings, sex; working at night; making and firing pottery; preparing wool; weaving. At Aïn Aghbel, during *husum*, all work on the land is forbidden – it is *el faragh*, emptiness. It is inauspicious "to start any building work, celebrate a marriage, hold a feast, or buy an animal". In a general way, people refrain from any activity involving the future.

13 *Thafsuth*, spring, is related to *efsu*, to undo, untie, to draw wool, and in the passive, to open out, burgeon, flower.

14 Marriages take place either in autumn, like the marriage of the earth and the sky, or in spring, in mid-April, when, according to a scholarly tradition, all the beings *on* the earth marry. Sterile women are recommended to eat boiled herbs picked during *natah*.

15 *Azal* denotes the daytime, broad daylight (as opposed to night and morning), and more especially the hottest moment of the summer day, devoted to rest. The "return of *azal*" is essentially marked by a change in the rhythm of daily activity, which is analysed below.

16 Just as acts of fecundation are excluded from the month of May, so sleep is excluded from the first day of summer: people take care not to sleep that day for fear of falling ill or losing their courage or their sense of honour (the seat of which is the liver, the place of *ruh*, the male soul). Doubtless for the same reason, earth dug up on that day is used in the magic rites intended to reveal the weakening or disappearance of the point of honour (*nif*) in men, and the stubbornness in animals which makes them resist training.

17 Smoke is sometimes credited with fertilizing powers, which, at the time of *in sla*,

mainly act on the fig-trees (whose cycle is relatively independent of that of the cereals, and accompanied by a relatively small number of rites, owing to the fact that it involves no intervention "against nature"). Smoke, a synthesis of the moist and the dry obtained by burning moist things (green plants brawlies, and vegetation gathered from damp spots, such as poplars or oleander), is believed to have the power to "feminidate the fig-trees; fumigation is identified with canrification.

18 A number of proverbs explicitly link the two periods: for example, it is often said that if there is a severe sirocco in *smaïm* there will be cold weather and snow in *lyali*.

19 The word *lakhrif* is related to the verb *kherref*, meaning "to pick and eat fresh figs", and also "to joke, to tell funny and often obscene stories, in the style of the wandering singers", and sometimes "to talk nonsense" (*itskherrif* "he's rambling"; *akherraf*, joker, buffoon).

20 A similar effect may be observed in any social formation in which there coexist unequally legitimate practices and knowledges: when members of the working classes are questioned about their cultural practices and preferences, they select those which they regard as closest to the dominant definition of legitimate practice.

21 E. Husserl, *Ideas: General Introduction to Pure Phenomenology*, trans. W. R. Boyce Gibson (New York and London: Collier, 1972), pp. 309–11.

22 In a sort of commentary on Saussure's second principle ("the signifier unfolds in time and has the characteristics it gets from time": F. de Saussure, *Cours de linguistique générale* (Paris: Payot, 1960), p. 103; trans. W. Baskin as *Course in General Linguistics* (New York: Philosophical Library, 1959), p. 70), Cournot contrasts the properties of spoken or written discourse, "an essentially linear series" whose "mode of construction obliges us to use a successive, linear series of signs to express relationships which the mind perceives, or ought to perceive, simultaneously and in a different order", with "synoptic tables, family trees, historical atlases, mathematical tables, in which the surface expanse is more or less successfully exploited to represent systematic relations and links which it would be difficult to make out in the flow of discourse" (A. Cournot). *Essai sur les fondements de la connaissance et sur les caractères de la critique philosophique* (Paris: Hachette, 1922), p. 364).

23 See J. Favret, "La segmentarité au Maghreb", *L'Homme*, 6, 2 (1966), pp. 105–11, and "Relations de dépendance et manipulation de la violence en Kabylie", *L'Homme*, 8, 4 (1968), pp. 18–44.

24 Set out in greater detail in P. Bourdieu, *The Algerians* (Boston: Beacon Press, 1962), pp. 14–20.

25 The logic of rite and myth belongs to the class of natural logics, which logic, linguistics, and the philosophy of language are beginning to explore, with very different assumptions and methods. For example, according to George Lakoff, one of the founders of "generative semantics", the "fuzzy logic" of ordinary language is characterized by its use of "fuzzy concepts" and "hedges", such as *sort of, pretty much, rather, loosely speaking*, etc., which subject truth-values to a deformation which classical logic cannot account for.

26 The logic of practice owes a number of its properties to the fact that what logic calls the "universe of discourse" there remains implicit, in its practical state. One must never lose sight of the conditions which have to be fulfilled for a genuine universe of discourse to appear: the intellectual and material equipment needed for the successive operations of methodical recording; the leisure required to carry

out these operations and analyse their products; an "interest" in such activities, which, even if not experienced as such, cannot be dissociated from a reasonable expectation of material and/or symbolic profit, i.e. from the existence of a market for discourse and metadiscourse, etc.

27 It can be seen, in passing, that the points of view adopted on the house are opposed in accordance with the very logic (male/female) which they apply: this sort of reduplication, founded on the correspondence between social divisions and logical divisions, results in a circular reinforcement which no doubt makes an important contribution towards confining agents in a closed, finite world and a doxic experience of that world.

28 J. Nicod, *La géometrie dans le monde sensible*, with a preface by Bertrand Russell (Paris: PUF, 1962), pp. 43–4.

29 For similar observations, see M. Granet, *La civilisation chinoise* (Paris: A. Colin, 1929), *passim* and esp. p. 332. Another modulation technique is association by assonance; it may lead to connections with no mythico-ritual significance (*aman d laman*, water is trust) or, on the other hand, to connections which are symbolically overdetermined (*azka d azqa*, tomorrow is the grave). As in poetry, the practical logic of ritual exploits the duality of sound and sense (and, in other cases, the plurality of meanings of the same sound); the double link, by sound and by meaning, offers a crossroads, a choice between two paths, either of which may be taken, without contradiction, at different times and in different contexts.

30 Certain informants proceed in just this way when, avoiding mere recitation of the semi-scholarly series, they reconstruct the calendar by means of successive dichotomies.

31 In another tale, the snake which a sterile woman had brought up as her son is rejected by its first wife: it *draws itself up, swells*, and breathes out *a jet of poisonous flame* (*asqi*, the tempering of iron, also means poisoning) which reduces her to ashes.

32 The agrarian calendar reproduces, in a transfigured form, the rhythms of the farming year, or more precisely, the climatic rhythms as seen when translated into the alternation of labour periods and production periods which structures the farming year. (The pattern of rainfall is characterized by the opposition between the cold, wet season, from November to April – with the maximum rain or snow coming in November and December, followed by a drier period in January and more rain in February and March – and the hot, dry season, from May to October – the driest months being June, July, and August. The farmers' dependence on the climate was obviously exacerbated by the limited traction power available – for ploughing – and the inefficiency of the techniques used – swingplough and sickle – though some are more dependent than others, since the owners of the best land and the best oxen can plough immediately after the first rains, even if the soil is sticky, whereas the poorest farmers often have to wait until they can borrow or hire a yoke of oxen; and the same is true of reaping – those richest in symbolic capital can assemble the labour force required for a quick harvest.) In the same way, the symbolic equipment the rites can use naturally depends on what is in season (although in some cases reserves are set aside specially for ritual use); but the generative schemes make it possible to find substitutes and to turn external necessities and constraints to good account within the logic of the rite itself (and this explains the perfect harmony between technical reason and mythic reason to be found in more than one case, e.g. in the orientation of the house).

33 These schemes can be grasped only in the objective coherence of the ritual

actions to which they give rise, although they can sometimes be almost directly apprehended in discourse, when for no apparent reason an informant "associates" two ritual practices which have nothing in common except a scheme (e.g. the scheme of swelling, in one case in which an informant "related", by describing them one after the other, the meal eaten on the first day of spring – with *adhris* – and the wedding meal – with *ufthyen*).

34 Workmen who use a wooden roller and an iron bar to raise a stone are applying the rule of the composition of parallel forces in the same direction; they know how to vary the position of the fulcrum depending on their exact purpose and the weight or volume of the load, *as if they were not unaware* of the rule (which they would not be capable of formulating expressly) that the greater the ratio between the two arms of the lever, the less force is needed to counterbalance a resistance – or more generally, the rule that a loss in displacement is a gain in force. There is no reason to invoke the mysteries of an unconscious versed in physics, or the arcana of a philosophy of nature postulating a mysterious harmony between the structure of the human brain and the structure of the physical world. It might be interesting to know why the fact that the manipulation of language presupposes the acquisition of abstract structures and of rules for the carrying out of those operations (such as, according to Chomsky, the non-recursive nature of inversion) should arouse such wonderment.

35 This section owes much to Jean Nicod. Cf. *La géometrie dans le monde sensible*.

36 Quoted in G. Bachelard, *La poétique de l'espace* (Paris: PUF, 1961), p. 201.

37 *Ibid.*

38 Cf. J. F. Le Ny, *Apprentissage et activités psychologiques* (Paris: PUF, 1967), p. 137.

39 "Modern sociologists and psychologists resolve such problems by appealing to the unconscious activity of the mind; but when Durkheim was writing, psychology and modern linguistics had not yet reached their main conclusions. This explains why Durkheim foundered in what he regarded as an irreducible antinomy...: the blindness of history and the purposiveness of consciousness. Between the two obviously stands the unconscious finality of the mind... It is... at these intermediate or lower levels – such as that of unconscious thought – that the apparent opposition between the individual and society disappears, and it becomes possible to move from one point of view to the other." (C. Lévi-Strauss, "La sociologie française", in *La sociologie au XXe siècle*, ed. G. Gurvich and W. E. Moore (Paris: PUF, 1947), vol. II, p. 527).

40 This is why I cannot help feeling a certain unease at writing and describing in words what, after a learning process analogous (*mutatis mutandis*) to that of the native agent, I first mastered practically: the concept of "resurrection" is what the outsider, lacking practical mastery of the schemes of "opening" and "swelling" and of the objective intent to which they are subordinate, needs in order to "understand" rites generated practically from these schemes. But then he runs the risk of giving a false "understanding" both of the "understanding" which such a concept makes possible, and of the practical "understanding" which does not need concepts.

41 The most accomplished proverbs are those which manage to combine the necessity of a linguistic connection (which may range from mere assonance to a common root) with the necessity of a mythical connection (paronomasia, and in particular the highest variety, the word-play of philosophy, has no other basis).

42 Most of these meanings are expressed through euphemisms: e.g. the sense "extinguish" is conveyed by *ferrah*, to gladden.

43 Basic senses: heavy/light, hot/cold, dull/brilliant.

44 To cast behind is also, at a more superficial level, to neglect, despise ("to put behind one's ear"), or more simply, not to face up to, not to confront.

45 Even in ordinary language, it would not be difficult to find the elements of a description of this approximate logic, which "gets by" in a "rough and ready" way, "playing it by ear" and "following its nose": all is grist that comes to this mill. A few specimens: I'll be back in a second... just a tick... only a short step... any moment now... much the same... something like... sort of... once in a blue moon... never in a thousand years... taking an eternity... to some extent... all but... at a rough guess... a stone's throw... spitting distance... so to speak... the average is in the region of... a small minority of trouble-makers... not to put too fine a point upon it... umpteen... within a hair's breadth... most of the time... not entirely... virtually... tolerably... etc.

46 This is exactly Plato's complaint against the mythologists and poets: that they are incapable of re-producing a practice other than by "identifying themselves with someone else" *dia mimeseos*, through mime (cf. for example, *Republic* 392d).

47 Aristotle, *Metaphysics*, A 5, 986a–22sq.

48 It is significant that Empedocles, who of all the pre-Socratic thinkers is the closest to the *objective truth* of rite, and hence the furthest removed from rite, uses terms as manifestly social as *philia* and *neikos* to name these two principles of ritual action.

49 On the identification of the opposition between, on the one hand, *synkrisis* and *diakrisis*, and on the other hand, *genesis* and *phthora*, see J. Bollack, *Empédocle*, vol. 1 (Paris: Editions de Minuit, 1965), p. 191n1 and p. 25n3.

50 The preponderance assigned to the male principle, which enables it to impose its effects in every union, means that the opposition between the female-male (the male tempered by union) and the male-male, is never overtly recognized or declared, despite the disapproval of certain forms of excess of the male virtues, such as "the Devil's point of honour [*nif*]". But it is nonetheless possible to set in this class the *amengur*, the man without male descendants, the redhead (*azegway*) who sows discord everywhere, who has no moustache, whom nobody wants as a companion in the market, and who refuses indulgence at the last judgment, when everyone forgives offences; etc.

51 The duality of woman is retranslated into the logic of kinship in the form of the opposition between the patrilateral cross cousin and the matrilateral cross cousin.

52 The path (*abridh*) and "companionship" (*elwans*) are opposed to emptiness (*lakhla*), to "solitude, the wilderness" (*elwahch*). *Thajma'th* is that which can be empty within fullness; the path (and the crossroads) are fullness within emptiness.

53 The way to get abundant butter is to go unseen to a crossroads used by the flocks, and there find a small stone and a few sticks; the stone is put in the dish in which the milk is kept and the sticks are burnt so that the smoke impregnates it (Westermarck).

54 Measuring operations, which impose limitation, finiteness, breakage, are hedged with euphemisms and magical precautions: the master of the land refrains from measuring his own crop and entrusts the task to a *khammes* or a neighbour (who does it in his absence); ritual expressions are used to avoid certain numbers; ritual formulae are uttered (as they are every time anything is measured or weighed), such as "May God not measure out his bounty to us!" Praise of beauty, health (a child's, for example), or wealth is an implicit numbering, hence a cutting, and so it must be avoided and replaced with euphemisms or neutralized with ritual formulae. *Cutting* operations (extinguishing, closing, leaving, finishing, stopping,

breaking, overturning, etc.) are named by means of euphemisms: for example, to say that the stores, the harvest, or the milk are all gone, an expression meaning "There is abundance" is used.

55 It is also known that the harvesters wear a leather apron similar to the uunlui s (*thabanda*).

56 Circumcision (*khatn* or *ihara* – often replaced by euphemisms based on *dher*, to be clean, neat) is a purificatory cut which, as Durkheim suggests, is supposed to confer the immunity needed in order to confront the fearful forces enclosed in the vagina (cf. the use of the cauris, a symbol of the vulva, as a magical protection; the destructive power attributed to menstrual blood; the sexual abstinence imposed on important occasions) and especially those which sexual intercourse unleashes by effecting the union of contraries (E. Durkheim, *The Elementary Forms of the Religious Life* (London: Allen and Unwin, 1915), pp. 314–15).

57 Divination practices are particularly frequent on the first day of *ennayer* (in the middle of *lyali*, when the "black" nights give way to the "white" nights) and at the time of the renewal rites which mark the start of the new year and are centred on the house and the *kanun* (replacing the three hearthstones, whitewashing the houses); for example, at dawn, the sheep and goats are called out, and it is regarded as unlucky if it is a goat that comes first, lucky if it is a sheep (cf. the days of the goat – or of the old woman); the hearthstones are coated with a paste of wet clay, and it is reckoned that the year will be wet if the clay is wet in the morning, dry if the clay is dry. This is explained not only by the *inaugural* rôle of the first day of *ennayer* but also by the fact that it comes in a period of *waiting* and uncertainty, when there is nothing to be done but try to anticipate the future. This is why the prognostication rites concerning family life and especially the coming harvest are similar to those applied to pregnant women.

58 Winter, homologous with night, is the time when the oxen sleep in the *stable* (the night and the north of the house); the time of sexual intercourse (the partridge, whose eggs are symbols of fecundity, mates during *lyali*).

59 "Chchetwa telsemlaqab netsat d yiwen werğaz", *Fichier d'Archives Berbères*, no. 19 (January 1947). "I shall kill your cattle, says winter. When I arise, the knives will set to work."

60 The return of bad weather is sometimes explicitly attributed to the maleficent action of the "old women" of this or that village of the tribe or the neighbouring tribes, i.e. witches, each of whom has her particular day of the week.

61 In the tale called "the jackal's marriage", the jackal marries outside his own species; he marries the camel and, moreover, holds no wedding-feast. The sky shows its disapproval by sending hail and storms.

62 May marriages suffer every sort of calamity and will not last. "The cursed broom of May" is the exact opposite of the blessed broom of the "first day of spring": it brings ruin, emptiness, and sterility to the house or stable in which it is used.

63 These various instruments – especially the sickle – are used in the prophylactic rites against the malignant powers of the wet, such as the *djnun*.

64 Salt has strong links with the dry and with sterility: the words meaning to be hot, scorching, also mean to be spiced, strong (virile), as opposed to insipid, without bite, without intelligence (salt is sprinkled on babies so they will not be insipid, stupid, witless). The man who acts frivolously is said to "think he is scattering salt"; he thinks his acts are of no consequence. Oil shares these connotations: "The sun is as scorching as oil."

65 The scheme of turning round and turning over is set to work in all the rites

intended to bring about a radical change, particularly an abrupt passage from the dry to the wet and especially from the wet to the dry: the threshold, which is in itself a point of reversal, is one of the favourite spots for such rites. It is also in terms of this scheme that any reversal or inversion of facts is conceived: an unabashed liar is said to have "put the east in the west".

66 Hoeing, the only agrarian activity exclusively reserved for women, is opposed both to ploughing and to harvesting, operations which may not be entrusted to a woman except in case of absolute necessity, when they require a whole series of ritual precautions: she wears a dagger at her girdle, puts *arkasen* on her feet, etc.

67 The corresponding period in the cycle of life, i.e. childhood, is also marked by a whole series of ritual operations which aim to separate the boy from his mother and the female world, causing him at the same time to be reborn in his father and his male relatives – in particular all the ceremonies marking his first entry into the male world, such as his first visit to the market, his first haircut, and the culminating ceremony of circumcision.

68 *Azegzaw* denotes blue, green, and grey; it can qualify fruit (green), meat (raw), corn (unripe), a rainy sky (grey, like the ox sacrificed in autumn). *Azegzaw* brings good fortune: to make a present of something green, especially in the morning, brings good luck. Spring is the season for *asafruri*, i.e. leguminous plants, especially beans, a certain proportion of which are set aside to be eaten green. The women gather wild herbs in the course of their hoeing in the cultivated fields, and these are eaten raw (*waghzaz*, a raw, green plant the leaves of which can be nibbled, e.g. dandelions; *thizazwath*, greenery). The cattle, fed on green fodder in the stable or near the house, yield abundant milk, which is consumed in every form (whey, curd, butter, cheese).

69 K. Marx, *Capital*, ed. F. Engels (Moscow: Progress Publishers, 1956), vol. II, part II, ch. XIII "The time of production", pp. 242–51.

70 Circumcision and tree-pruning, like scarification and tattooing, partake of the logic of purification, in which the instruments made with fire have a beneficent function, like the *in sla* fires, rather than the logic of murder.

71 In this way the Negro or the smith, who are known to be the very opposite of the "bringer of good fortune" (*elfal*), may fulfil a beneficent function as "takers-away of ill fortune". The position of the family responsible for inaugurating the ploughing is no less ambiguous than that of the smith (*elfal* is never mentioned in relation to him), and their rôle as a lightning conductor does not entitle them to a high place in the hierarchy of prestige and honour.

72 J. G. Frazer, *The Golden Bough*, 3rd ed. (London: Macmillan, 1912), vol. I, part v, "The Spirits of the Corn and the Wild", ch. VII, pp. 214–69.

73 The miraculous properties of the meat of the sacrificed animal are appropriated in a communal meal. In several cases, the tail of the animal receives special treatment (it is hung up in the mosque) as if, like the last sheaf, sometimes known as "the tail of the field", it concentrated the vital potency of the whole.

74 The frequency of large- and small-scale fighting in the fig season used to lead some observers, encouraged by native remarks (an overexcited person is said to have "eaten too many figs"), to wonder if the source of the ebullience reigning at that time of year did not lie in the figs themselves: "There is one season in particular when it really seems that men's minds are more heated than any other time... when they speak of the fig season, which they call *kherif*, autumn, it seems to be agreed that everyone shall be agitated at that time, just as it is customary to be merry at carnival times" (C. Devaux, *Les Kebaïles de Djerdjera* (Marseilles: Carnion, and Paris: Challamel, 1859), pp. 85–6).

75 The men who encircle the boy comprise all the male members of the clan and sub-clan, together with the mother's male kinsmen and their guests (the *affines*, to whom the boy has been presented the previous week, by a delegation of rifle-bearing men from the sub-clan, in a rite called *aghrum* which imtcake, the dry and therefore male food par excellence, which also takes place before a marriage). The symbolism of the second, purely male birth, obeys the same logic as marriage with the parallel cousin, the most masculine of women.

76 Brahim Zellal, "Le roman de chacal, contes d'animaux", *Fichier d'Archives Berbères*, no. 81 (Fort National, Algeria), 1964.

77 Breach of the taboo of *lahlal* is a *haram* act (sacrilege) which gives rise to a *haram* product (cf. the legend of *yum chendul* – 18 September – the wise ploughman who, despite the heavy rain on that day, refused to plough before *lahlal*). In what is known as *el haq* (e.g. *el haq lakhrif*, the ban on fig-picking), the magical element is again present, since the assembly which pronounces the edict calls down a curse on all who break it; at the same time, the social-convention aspect of the interdict appears in the fact that the penalty for transgression is a fine (also called *el haq*). Although in the case of marriage the term *lahlal* is only used to denote the sum of money which the bridegroom gives the bride (in addition to the bride-wealth and the presents) before the marriage is consummated, the sanctioning function of the marriage ceremony is underlined by a number of features (e.g. *imensi lahlal*). Thus, as we have seen, the marriage season often used to open with a parallel-cousin marriage, a union predisposed to play this inaugural role by its conformity to the principles of the mythical world-view.

78 Or "the key of good luck".

79 The primordial union is represented, in the very place of procreation, in the form of the union of *asalas*, the central beam, and *thigejdith*, the pillar, a symbol of the marriage of sky and earth.

80 The ploughing ceremony, like the marriage ceremony, being a reunion of the divided and separate, *syncrisis*, is placed under the sign of the figure two: everything which comes in pairs – starting with the yoke of oxen (*thayuga* or *thazwijth*, formed from the Arabic *zwidja*), the symbol par excellence – is likely to favour coupling (the man who opens the ploughing is sometimes called "the old man of the yoke of oxen" – *amghar may-yuga*). In contrast, that which is singular and solitary, the bachelor for example, a symbol of division and separateness, is systematically excluded.

81 The seed corn, which always includes the grains of the last sheaf reaped (sometimes the grains of the last sheaf threshed or dust from the last plot of land harvested, or taken from the threshing floor as the last sheaf was threshed; or again, dust from the mausoleum of a saint, salt, etc.), is kept in the house itself, in sheepskins or chests stored in the damp part of the house and sometimes even under the bed of the master of the field; it is prepared in accordance with rites and taboos intended to preserve its properties.

82 The *snake*, a symbol of resurrection (see above) is often represented on the hand-made earthenware jars used to store grain for cooking or sowing.

83 The interdicts surrounding ploughing (or weaving, its female homologue) and marriage all bear on acts of *cutting* (shaving, cutting the hair or nails), *closing* (tying up the hair), *purifying* (sweeping, whitewashing the house), and contact with objects that are dry or associated with *the dry* (darkening the eyelids with kohl, dying the hands with henna, or, in the order of food, the use of spices).

84 The swollen part of the lamp, which represents woman's belly, is called "the pomegranate".

85 The action of *tying* is a typical example of the ambiguities which give practical logic its efficacy. Tying is in a sense doubly forbidden because it is opposed both to the male action of *opening* and to the female action of *swelling*. All forms of *tying* (crossing the arms or the legs, wearing knots or girdles, rings, etc.) or *closing* (of doors, chests, locks, etc.) are forbidden at the moment of childbirth, and the opposite actions recommended. The rites intended to render a man or woman incapable of sexual intercourse apply the scheme of closing (or its equivalent, cutting), again exploiting the coincidence (well expressed by the ambiguity of the verbs referring to state) of *opening* and *being opened*. It is natural that ritual, which always seeks to put all the odds on its own side, should in a sense kill two birds with one stone in recommending actions likely to favour (or not likely to hinder) *opening*, an operation male in its active form and female in its passive form.

86 I say "treated practically as" to avoid putting into the consciousness of the agents (with expressions like "seen as" or "conceived as") the representation which we must construct in order to understand scientifically the practices objectively oriented by the scheme of "resurrection" and in order to communicate that understanding.

87 The meaning of the rite is clearly shown in the rope game described by Laoust, a sort of tug-of-war between the men and the women, in the course of which the rope is suddenly cut and the women fall on their backs, inviting the sky to rain its fecundating seed upon them.

88 The snake, a symbol of the power of erection and resurrection which belongs to the male principle, is undoubtedly the *dry* which shoots out the dry: in the tale related above (p. 222), the aggrieved snake rises, swells, and spits out a poisonous flame.

89 All the evidence suggests that the usefulness of the *almost empty notion* of *baraka* (which has occupied a disproportionate place in the writings of anthropologists from Westermarck to the present day) lies in the fact that it makes it possible to name both the male principle of fecundity and the female principle of fertility without distinguishing between them. This also means that, though useful in social practice, it does not play a very important part in the economy of the symbolic system.

90 The familiarity with this mode of thought that is acquired in the course of scientific practice gives one an idea (though still a very abstract one) of the subjective feeling of necessity which it gives to those it possesses: there is no way in which this laxist logic of overdetermined, fuzzy relations, protected as it is by its very weakness against contradiction or error, could encounter within itself any obstacle or resistance capable of determining a reflexive return or a questioning of it. History can therefore only come to it from outside, through the contradictions generated by synchronization (favoured by literacy) and the systematizing intent that synchronization expresses and makes possible.

91 This function is sometimes explicitly formulated. It is said, for example, that when cereals, a soft food, are being sown, one must "eat soft".

92 The opposition between the cooking-pot (*achukth*) and the griddle (*bufrah*) sums up the series of oppositions between the two seasons and the two styles of cooking: cooking indoors, boiling, evening meal, unspiced; cooking outdoors, roasting, morning meal, spiced. With rare exceptions (when an animal has been slaughtered or when someone is ill) meat is regarded as too precious to be cooked on the fire. In summer, sweet peppers and tomatoes are cooked on the *kanun*. However, meat is always boiled in autumn whereas it can be roasted in spring.

93 Winter food is overall more female, summer food more male. In every season, female food, as one might expect, is a moist form of the corresponding male food: the men's food is based on wheatcake (*aghrum*) and couscous; the guest one wants to honour, the male par excellence, is offered at least one *sauous*, even if it has to be made with barley and if possible, a meat couscous; never soup, not even wheat soup, or boiled semolina. The women's food is liquid, less nourishing, less highly spiced, based on boiled cereals, broths, and sauces (*asqi*, which also denotes tempering and poisoning); their couscous is made with barley or even bran and flour (*abulbul*). In fact things are not so simple: semolina dumplings, which may appear as female because they are boiled in water, are also the most male of female foods, hence sometimes eaten by men, because they can be accompanied by meat; conversely, *berkukes*, a male food, can be eaten by women, because it is boiled, unlike couscous, which is simply sprinkled. A boy eats with the men as soon as he starts to walk and to go to the fields. Once he is old enough to take the goats to pasture, he has a right to the afternoon snack (a handful of figs, half a pint of milk).

94 Other direct indications of the homology: the weaving is done upwards, i.e. from west to east. The weft is called *thadrafth*; the warp *l'alam*. *'Allam* is to separate the strands of the warp into two strips and to mark out the field with the first furrow which divides it into plots, the even-numbered ones running eastward and the odd ones westward.

95 To tie a thread so that it cannot be untied is to "tie its soul".

96 For the same reason, weaving begun elsewhere is not brought into the house (unless a chicken is sacrificed first). This belief is also invoked at harvest time to justifying sacrificing an animal.

97 These various tasks are only part of the women's activities, which partake of all the more or less abstract series that can be constructed, thereby underlining the fact that practical unity lies not in the series (of farming tasks or the rites of passage) but in practice generating similarly structured behaviour in all domains.

98 The divisions of the year, particularly the most important one, "the return of *azal*", which marks the separation between the dry season and the wet season, are (relatively) independent of climatic conditions: thus the characteristic rhythm of the winter day is kept up both at the coldest moments and in the warmer and already "springlike" days of the wet season. The autonomy of the logic of ritual with respect to objective conditions is even clearer in the case of clothing, which as a symbol of *social status* cannot vary according to the season: how could the burnous be taken off in summer, if a man without a burnous is dishonoured? How could anyone fail to put on winter moccasins before reaping or undertaking a long mountain journey, when everyone knows that they are the footwear which characterizes the genuine peasant and the strong walker? How could the mistress of the house give up the traditional pair of blankets, worn pinned in front, which symbolize her authority, her ascendancy over her daughters-in-law, and her power over the running of the household, as does the belt on which she hangs the keys to the household stores?

99 For example, a man who is late in the morning is told, "All the shepherds are out." And to indicate a late hour in the afternoon: "All the shepherds have already 'given back' *azal*." In fact the return to the village at the time of *azal* is not absolutely obligatory, and some shepherds spend *azal* in the shade on the grazing land.

100 For example, a man who does not get up early on the first day of spring is likely to die in the course of the year; a man who gets up early on the first day of summer will get up early all through the year.

101 On this notion, see T. Vogel, *Théorie des systèmes evolutifs* (Paris: Gautier-Villars, 1965), pp. 8–10.

102 This future already present is the future of the emotion which speaks the future in the present ("I am dead", "I am done for") because it reads the future in the present as a potentiality objectively inscribed in the directly perceived present (and not, as Sartre would have it, as a *possible*, explicitly posited in a project, i.e. in an act of freedom – the consequence of this view being that emotion becomes bad faith).

103 People must particularly watch their language in the presence of young children, recently circumcised boys, and newly wed husbands, all of these being categories whose future, i.e. growth, virility, or fertility, is in question. Similarly, a number of the taboos and interdicts of spring can be seen as practical euphemisms intended to avoid compromising the fecundity of nature's labour.

104 For the feast called *tharurit wazal* (the return of *azal*), a distinction is made between lesser *azal*, the moment at which the women and children come back from the fields (about 10 a.m.) and great *azal*, about 11 a.m., when the men come back.

105 Thus in a rite performed to hasten a girl's marriage, the sorceress lights the lamp (*mesbah*), the symbol of the hoped-for man, at *azal*.

106 One could go on to draw a parallel between prophylactic rites such as "the dissociation from the month" and the separation from *ennayer*, or between the first haircut and the expulsion of *maras*, or again between all the curative practices applied to the child and the sacrifice of sparrows at the time of *asifedh*, etc.

107 In each village cemetery there is a grave covered with potsherds, sometimes euphemistically called "the last grave" (even if it is very old). It is the outsider's grave, on to which the evil afflicting babies or animals is transferred: the women go there taking a pot of water and an egg, which they eat, leaving the shells and the pot behind after burying or burning the sacrificed object or victim on which the evil has been "fixed". To "send the baby to sleep" in its mother's womb, the trivet (*elkanun wuzal*, the iron *kanun*) is turned seven times one way, seven times the other, around the pregnant woman's girdle, and then it is buried in the grave of the outsider, the man who is truly dead.

108 For example, depending on the needs and occasions of ritual practice, birth, as an opening and a beginning, can be linked either to the birth of the year – itself situated at different moments according to the occasion – or to the birth of spring, in the order of the year, or again, to dawn, in the order of the day, or to the appearance of the new moon, in the order of the month, or to the sprouting of the corn, in the order of the grain cycle; none of these relationships prevents death, to which birth is opposed, from being identified either with the harvest, within the cycle of the life of the field, or with fecundation treated as resurrection, i.e. with the birth of the year, within the grain cycle, etc.

109 Granet gives some striking examples of the would-be impeccable, but merely fantastic, constructs produced by the effort to resolve the contradictions arising from the hopeless ambition of giving the objectively systematic products of analogical reason an intentionally systematic form. E.g. the theory of the five elements, a scholarly elaboration (third to second centuries B.C.) of the mythical system, establishes homologies between the cardinal points (plus the centre), the seasons, the substances (earth, fire, wood, metal), and the musical notes (*La civilisation chinoise*, pp. 304–9).

110 Having failed to see in mythico-ritual logic a particular case of practical logic, of which ancient societies have no monopoly, and which must be analysed as such,

without any normative reference to logical logic, anthropology has become locked in the insoluble antinomy of otherness and identity, the "primitive mentality" and the "savage mind". The principle of this antinomy was indicated by Kant in the Appendix to the Transcendental Dialectic: depending on the interests which inspire it, "reason" obeys either the "principle of specification" which leads it to seek and accentuate differences, or the "principle of aggregation" or "homogeneity", which leads it to observe similarities, and, through an illusion which characterizes it, "reason" situates the principle of these judgments not in itself but in the *nature* of its objects.

111 An internal analysis of the structure of a system of symbolic relations is soundly based only if it is subordinated to a sociological analysis of the structure of the system of social relations of symbolic production, circulation, and consumption in which these relations are set up and in which the social functions that they objectively fulfil at any given moment are defined: the rites and myths of the Greek tradition tend to receive entirely different functions and meanings depending, for example, on whether they give rise to rationalizing, "routinizing" "readings", with corps of scholars, to inspired reinterpretations, with the magi and their initiatory teachings, or to rhetorical exercises, with the first professional professors, the Sophists. It follows that, as a point of method, any attempt to reconstruct the original meaning of a mythical tradition must include analysis of the laws of the deformation to which the various successive interpreters subject it on the basis of their systems of interests.

112 As G. Bateson shows (*Naven* (Stanford, Cal.: Stanford University Press, 1958; 1st ed., 1936), mythological culture can become the tool, and in some cases the object, of extremely complex strategies (which explains, among other things, why agents undertake the immense mnemonic effort needed to acquire mastery of it) even in societies which do not have a highly developed and differentiated religious apparatus. It follows that it is impossible fully to account for the structure of the mythical corpus and the transformations which affect it in the course of time, by means of a strictly internal analysis ignoring the functions that the corpus fulfils in the relations of competition or conflict for economic or symbolic power.

113 It goes without saying that the *regressive* use which Heidegger and the gnostic tradition that he has introduced into university philosophy make of the most "archaic" devices of language, out of a taste for the *primal* which is the reconversion of the conservative intent into the logic of the philosophical field, has nothing in common with the practice of the pre-Socratic thinkers, who mobilize all the resources of a language fraught with mythic resonances to reproduce in their discourse the objective systematicity of mythic practice or resolve the logical contradictions springing from that ambition.

114 R. Carnap, "Überwindung der Metaphysik durch logische Analyse der Sprache", *Erkenntnis*, 4 (1931), pp. 219–41.

CHAPTER 4. STRUCTURES, HABITUS, POWER

1 The wet season is the time for *oral* instruction through which the group memory is forged. In the dry season, that memory is acted out and enriched through participation in the acts and ceremonies which set the seal on group unity: it is in summer that the children undergo practical training in their future tasks as peasants and their obligations as men of honour.

2 The "shepherds" are the small boys of the village. (Translator.)

3 A principle which, as we have seen, belongs as much to magic as to morality.

For example, there is a saying *leftar n-esbah d-esbuḥ erbaḥ*, breakfast in the morning is the first well-omened encounter (*erbaḥ*, to succeed, prosper).

4 Early rising to let out the animals, to go to Koran school, or simply to be outside with the men, at the same time as the men, is an element of the conduct of honour which boys are taught to respect from an early age. On the first day of spring, the mistress of the house, who alone has a right to wake the daughters and daughters-in-law, calls the children: "Wake up, children! The longer you walk before sunrise, the longer you will live!" The women, for their part, set their point of honour on getting up at the same time as the men, if not earlier (the only way they can get all the time they want to attend to their appearance without being watched by the men, who pretend to be ignorant of the women's behaviour on this point).

5 The young incur even greater disapproval when they try to set up a power struggle between the generations, jeopardizing an order based on the maintenance of temporal distance; the generations are separated only by time, which is as much as to say by nothing, for one only has to wait and the difference will disappear; but the gap maintaining and maintained by the gerontocratic order is in fact unbridgeable, since the only way to cross it, short of refusing the game, is to wait.

6 It follows that disorganization of its temporal rhythms and spatial framework is one of the basic factors in the disorganization of the group; thus the concentrations of population imposed by the French Army during the war of liberation led to a profound (and often lasting) change in the status of the women, who, when deprived of the autonomy they derived from access to a separate place and time, were condemned either to be cloistered or to wear the veil, which, after the concentration, made its appearance among Berber populations where it was previously unknown.

7 It is understandable that collective dancing or singing, particularly spectacular cases of the synchronization of the homogeneous and the orchestration of the heterogeneous, are everywhere predisposed to symbolize group integration and, by symbolizing it, to strengthen it.

8 It goes without saying that logical integration is never total, though always sufficient to ensure the more-or-less-perfect predictability of all members of the group (setting aside the *amahbul* who takes it upon himself to break with the collective rhythms).

9 Brutal reduction of this twofold, two-faced discourse to its objective (or at least, objectivist) truth neglects the fact that it only produces its specifically symbolic effects inasmuch as it never directly imparts that truth; the enchanted relationship which scientific objectification has to destroy in order to constitute itself is an integral part of the full truth of practice. Science must integrate the objectivist truth of practice and the equally objective misrecognition of that truth into a higher definition of objectivity.

10 Whether through the intermediary of their control over inheritance, which lends itself to all sorts of strategic manipulation, from sheer delay in the effective transmission of powers to the threat of disinheritance, or through the intermediary of the various strategic uses to which they can put their officially recognized monopoly of matrimonial negotiations, the elders have the means of taking advantage of the socially recognized limits of youth. An analysis of the strategies used by the heads of noble houses to keep their heirs in a subordinate position, forcing them to go out on dangerous adventures far from home, is to be found in G. Duby, *Hommes et structures du Moyen-Age* (Paris and The Hague: Mouton, 1973), pp. 213–25, esp. p. 219.

11 Love, not immune to such ritualization, also conforms to this logic, as is well illustrated by the words of a young Kabyle woman: "A girl doesn't know her husband beforehand and she looks to him for everything. She loves him even before they marry, because she must; she has to love him, there is no other 'door'."

12 The full text of this conversation can be found in P. Bourdieu and A. Sayad, *Le déracinement* (Paris: Minuit, 1964), pp. 215–20.

13 M. Proust, *Contre Sainte-Beuve* (Paris: Gallimard, 1965), pp. 74–5.

14 Cf. J. M. W. Whiting, *Becoming a Kwoma* (New Haven, Conn: Yale University Press, 1941), p. 215.

15 The phenomenologists systematically forget to carry out an ultimate "reduction", the one which would reveal to them the social conditions of the possibility of the "reduction" and the *epoche*. What is radically excluded from phenomenological analysis of the "general thesis of the natural standpoint" which is constitutive of "primary experience" of the social world is the question of the economic and social conditions of the *belief* which consists in "taking the 'factworld' (*Wirklichkeit*) just as it gives itself" (E. Husserl, *Ideas* (New York: Collier-Macmillan, 1962), p. 96), a belief which the reduction subsequently causes to appear as a "thesis", or, more precisely, as an *epoche* of the *epoche*, a suspension of doubt as to the possibility that the world of the natural standpoint could be otherwise.

16 If the emergence of a field of discussion is historically linked to the development of cities, this is because the concentration of different ethnic and/or professional groups in the same space, with in particular the overthrow of spatial and temporal frameworks, favours the confrontation of different cultural traditions, which tends to expose their arbitrariness *practically*, through first-hand experience, in the very heart of the routine of the everyday order, of the possibility of doing the same things differently, or, no less important, of doing something different at the same time; and also because it permits and requires the development of a body of specialists charged with raising to the level of discourse, so as to rationalize and systematize them, the presuppositions of the traditional world-view, hitherto mastered in their practical state.

17 A whole aspect of what is nowadays referred to as sociology (or anthropology) partakes of this logic.

18 *Formal Logic: Or, the Calculus of Inference, Necessary and Probable* (London: Taylor and Walton, 1847), p. 41.

19 J.-P. Sartre, *L'idiot de la famille* (Paris: Gallimard, 1971), vol. 1, p. 783.

20 On belief as individual bad faith maintained and supported by collective bad faith, see P. Bourdieu, "Genèse et structure du champ religeux", *Revue Française de Sociologie*, 12, 3 (1971), p. 318.

21 To convince oneself that this is so, one only has to remember the tradition of "confraternity" within the medical profession. No doctor ever pays a fellow doctor a fee; instead he has to find him a present – without knowing what he wants or needs – not costing too much more or too much less than the consultation, but also not coming too close, because that would amount to stating the price of the consultation, thereby giving away the interested fiction that it was free.

22 "You've saved me from having to sell" is what is said in such cases to the lender who prevents land falling into the hands of a stranger, by means of a sort of fictitious sale (he gives the money while allowing the owner the continued use of his property).

23 M. Mauss, "Essai sur le don", in *Sociologie et anthropologie* (Paris: PUF, 1950), p. 239; trans. I. Cunnison as *The Gift* (London, 1966), p. 52.

24 The sacred character of the meal appears in the formulae used in swearing an

oath: "By the food and the salt before us" or "By the food and the salt we have shared". A pact sealed by eating together would become a curse for the man who betrayed it: "I do not curse him, the broth and the salt curse him." To invite one's guest to take a second helping, one says: "There's no need to swear, the food does it [for you]"; "The food will settle its score with you [if you leave it]." A shared meal is also a ceremony of reconciliation, leading to the abandonment of vengeance. Similarly, an offering of food to a patron saint or the group's ancestor implies a contract of alliance. The *thiwizi* is inconceivable without the final meal: and thus it usually only brings together people of the same *adhrum* or the same *thakharubth*.

25 There is strong disapproval of individuals who are no use to their family or the group, "dead men whom God has drawn from living men", in the words of the verse of the Koran often applied to them: they are incapable of "pulling any weight". To remain idle, especially when one belongs to a great family, is to shirk the duties and tasks which are an inseparable part of belonging to the group. And so a man who has been out of farming for some time, because he has been away or been ill, is quickly found a place in the cycle of work and the circuit of the exchange of services. The group has the right to demand of each of its members that he should have an occupation, however unproductive, and it must therefore make sure that everyone is found an occupation, even a purely symbolic one: the peasant who provides idlers with an opportunity to work on his land is universally approved, because he is giving marginal individuals a chance to integrate themselves into the group by doing their duty as men.

26 The cost of time rises with rising productivity (i.e. the quantity of goods offered for consumption, and hence consumption itself, which also takes time); time thus tends to become scarcer, while the scarcity of goods diminishes. Squandering of goods may even become the only way of saving time, which is now more valuable than the products which could be saved if time were devoted to maintenance and repair, etc. (cf. G. S. Becker, "A Theory of the Allocation of Time", *Economic Journal*, 75, no. 289 (September 1965), pp. 493–517). This is no doubt the objective basis of the contrast in attitudes to time which has often been described.

27 A variant of this contradiction is expressed in the saying "When the year is bad, there are always too many bellies to be filled; when it is good, there are never enough hands to do the work."

28 It would not be difficult to show that debates about Berber (and more generally, ancient) "democracy" similarly oppose first-degree naivety to second-degree naivety; the latter is perhaps the more pernicious, because the satisfaction derived from false lucidity makes it impossible to attain the adequate knowledge which simultaneously transcends and conserves the two forms of naivety: "*ancient democracy*" owes its specificity to the fact that it leaves implicit and unquestioned (doxa) the principles which liberal "democracy" can and must profess (orthodoxy) because they have ceased to govern conduct in the practical state.

29 The man who "gives others no more than the time he owes them" is reproached in terms like these: "You've only just arrived, and now you're off again." "Are you leaving us? We've only just sat down...We've hardly spoken." The analogy between a man's relationships with others and his relationship to the land leads to condemnation of the man who thoughtlessly hurries in his work and, like the guest who leaves almost as soon as he arrives, does not give it the care and time, i.e. the respect, which are its due.

30 R. Maunier, *Mélanges de sociologie nord-africaine* (Paris: Alcan, 1930), p. 68.

31 Such tactics are, as far as possible, kept out of transactions between kinsmen,

and there is disapproval of the man who takes advantage of the destitution of the person forced to sell.

32 The trap is all the more infallible when, as in marriage, the circulation of immediately perceptible material goods, such as the bridewealth, the apparent issue at stake in matrimonial negotiations, conceals the total circulation, actual or potential, of goods that are indissociably material and symbolic, of which they are only the aspect most visible to the eye of the capitalist *homo economicus*. The amount of the payment, always of small value in relative and absolute terms, would not justify the hard bargaining to which it gives rise, did it not take on a symbolic value of the highest importance as the unequivocal demonstration of the worth of a family's products on the matrimonial exchange market, and of the capacity of the heads of the family to obtain the best price for their products through their negotiating skills. The best proof of the irreducibility of the stakes of matrimonial strategy to the amount of the bridewealth is provided by history, which here too has dissociated the symbolic and material aspects of transactions: once reduced to its purely monetary value, the bridewealth lost its significance as a symbolic rating, and the bargains of honour, thus reduced to the level of mere haggling, were from then on considered shameful.

33 Although he fails to draw any real conclusions from it, in a work which proves disappointing, Bertrand Russell admirably expresses an insight into the analogy between energy and power which could serve as the basis for a unification of social science: "Like energy, power has many forms, such as wealth, armaments, civil authority, influence or opinion. No one of these can be regarded as subordinate to any other, and there is no one form from which the others are derivative. The attempt to treat one form of power, say wealth, in isolation, can only be partially successful, just as the study of one form of energy will be defective at certain points, unless other forms are taken into account. Wealth may result from military power or from influence over opinion, just as either of these may result from wealth" (*Power: A New Social Analysis* (London: Allen and Unwin, 1938), pp. 12–13). And he goes on to define the programme for this unified science of social energy: "Power, like energy, must be regarded as continually passing from any one of its forms into any other, and it should be the business of social science to seek the laws of such transformations" (pp. 13–14).

34 It has often been pointed out that the logic which makes the redistribution of goods the *sine qua non* of the continuation of power tends to reduce or prevent the primitive accumulation of economic capital and the development of class division (cf. for example E. Wolf, *Sons of the Shaking Earth* (Chicago: University of Chicago Press, 1959), p. 216).

35 M. I. Finley, "Technical Innovation and Economic Progress in the Ancient World", *Economic History Review*, 18, 1 (August 1965), pp. 29–45, esp. p. 37; and see "Land Debt and the Man of Property in Classical Athens", *Political Science Quarterly*, 68 (1953), pp. 249–68.

36 See P. Bohannan, "Some Principles of Exchange and Investment among the Tiv", *American Anthropologist*, 57, 1 (1955), pp. 60–70.

37 K. Polyani, *Primitive Archaic and Modern Economics*, ed. George Dalton, New York: Doubleday, 1968, and *The Great Transformation*, New York: Rinehart, 1944. It is rather paradoxical that in his contribution to a collection of essays edited by Karl Polyani, Francisco Benet pays so much attention to the contrast between the market and the village and scarcely mentions the factors which keep the local *ṣuq* under the control of the values of the good-faith economy (see F. Benet, "Explosive Markets: The Berber Highlands", in K. Polyani, C. M. Arensberg,

and H. W. Pearson (eds.), *Trade and Market in the Early Empires*, New York: Free Press, 1957).

38 The shady dealer cannot find anyone to answer for him (or his wares) and so he cannot demand guarantees from the buyer.

39 The belief, often held in gnostic religions, that knowledge may be transmitted through various forms of magical contact – most typically, through a kiss – may be seen as an attempt to transcend the limits of this mode of preservation: "Whatever it is that the practitioner learns, he learns from another *dukun*, who is his *guru* (teacher); and whatever he learns, he and others call his *ilmu* (science). *Ilmu* is generally considered to be a kind of abstract knowledge or supernormal skill, but by the more concrete-minded and 'old-fashioned', it is sometimes viewed as a kind of substantive magical power, in which case its transmission may be more direct than through teaching" (C. Geertz, *The Religion of Java* (London: Collier-Macmillan, 1960), p. 88).

40 See in particular J. Goody and I. Watt, "The Consequences of Literacy", *Comparative Studies in Society and History*, 5, (1962–3), pp. 304ff., and J. Goody (ed.), *Literacy in Traditional Societies*, Cambridge: University Press, 1968.

41 "The poet is the incarnate book of the oral people" (J. A. Notopoulos, "Mnemosyme in Oral Literature", *Transactions and Proceedings of the American Philological Association*, 69 (1938), pp. 465–93, esp. p. 469). In a very impressive article, William C. Greene shows how a change in the mode of accumulation, circulation, and reproduction of culture results in a change in the function it is made to perform, together with a change in the structure of cultural products ("The Spoken and the Written Word", *Harvard Studies in Classical Philology*, 9 (1951), pp. 24–58). And Eric A. Havelock similarly shows that even the content of cultural resources is transformed by the transformation of "the technology of preserved communication", and in particular, by the abandonment of *mimesis*, a practical reactivation mobilizing all the resources of a "pattern of organized actions" – music, rhythm, words – for mnemonic purposes in an act of affective identification, in favour of written discourse, which, because it exists as a text, is repeatable, reversible, detached from the situation, and predisposed by its permanence to become the object of analysis, comparison, contrast, and reflexion (*Preface to Plato*, Cambridge, Mass.: Harvard University Press, 1963). Until language is objectified in the written text, speech is inseparable from the speaker's whole person, and in his absence it can be manipulated only in the mode of *mimesis*, which is not open to analysis or criticism.

42 A social history of all forms of *distinction* (of which the *title* is a particular case) would have to show the social conditions and the consequences of the transition from a personal authority which can neither be delegated nor inherited (e.g. the *gratia*, esteem, influence, of the Romans) to the *title* – from honour to the *jus honorum*. In Rome, for example, the use of titles (e.g. *eques Romanus*) defining a *dignitas*, an officially recognized position in the State (as distinct from a purely personal quality), was, like the use of *insignia*, progressively subjected to detailed control by custom or law (cf. C. Nicolet, *L'ordre équestre à l'époque républicaine*, vol. 1: *Définitions juridiques et structures sociales* (Paris, 1966), pp. 236–41).

43 On this point see P. Bourdieu and L. Boltanksi, "Le titre et le poste: rapports entre le système de production et le système de reproduction", *Actes de la Recherche en Sciences Sociales*, no. 2, March 1975; trans. "Qualifications and Jobs", *CCCS Stencilled Paper 46* (University of Birmingham, 1977).

44 This is true, for example, of the charismatic (or meritocratic) ideology which explains the differential probability of access to academic qualifications by reference to the inequality of innate talent, thus reproducing the effect of the

mechanisms which dissimulate the relationship between academic attainment and inherited cultural capital.

45 E. Durkheim, *Montesquieu et Rousseau précurseurs de la sociologie* (Paris: Rivière 1953), p. 197.

46 *Ibid.* p. 195. The analogy with the Cartesian theory of continuous creation is perfect. And when Leibniz criticized a conception of God condemned to move the world "as a carpenter moves his axe or as a miller drives his millstone by directing the water towards the wheel" (G. W. Leibniz, "De ipsa natura", *Opuscula philosophica selecta*, ed. P. Shrecker (Paris: Boivin, 1939), p. 92), and put forward in place of the Cartesian universe, which cannot exist without unremitting divine attention, a physical universe endowed with a *vis propria*, he was initiating the critique, which did not find expression until much later (i.e. in Hegel's introduction to the *Philosophy of Right*), of all forms of the refusal to acknowledge that the social world has a nature, i.e. an immanent necessity.

47 If acts of communication – exchanges of gifts, challenges, or words – always bear within them a potential conflict, it is because they always contain the possibility of domination. *Symbolic violence* is that form of domination which, transcending the opposition usually drawn between sense relations and power relations, communication and domination, is only exerted *through* the communication in which it is disguised.

48 It can be seen that if one is trying to account for the *specific* form in which domination is realized in the pre-capitalist economy, it is not sufficient to observe, as Marshall D. Sahlins does, that the pre-capitalist economy does not provide the conditions necessary for an indirect, impersonal mode of domination, in which the worker's dependence on the employer is the quasi-automatic product of the mechanisms of the labour market (cf. "Political Power and the Economy in Primitive Society", in G. E. Dole and R. L. Carneiro (eds.), *Essays in the Science of Culture* (New York: Crowell, 1960), pp. 390–415; "Poor Man, Rich Man, Big Man, Chief: Political Types in Melanesia and Polynesia", *Comparative Studies in Society and History*, 5 (1962–3), pp. 285–303; "On the Sociology of Primitive Exchange", in M. Banton (ed.), *The Relevance of Models for Social Anthropology* (London: Tavistock, 1965), pp. 139–236). These *negative conditions* (which one is amply justified in pointing to when it is a question of countering any form of idealism or idealization) do not account for the internal logic of symbolic violence, any more than the absence of the lightning rod and the electric telegraph, which Marx refers to in a famous passage in the introduction to the *Grundrisse*, can be used to explain Jupiter and Hermes, i.e. the internal logic of Greek mythology and art.

49 The interactionist "gaze", which ignores the objective mechanisms and their operation, in order to look into the direct interactions between agents, would find an ideal terrain in this sort of society, i.e. precisely in the case in which, because of the relationship normally existing between the anthropologist and his object, it is least likely to be possible. Another paradox appears in the fact that structuralism, in the strict sense of the word, i.e. the sciences of the objective structures of the social world (and not simply of agents' images of them), is least adequate and least fruitful when applied to societies in which relations of domination and dependence are the product of continuous creation. (Unless one chooses to posit, as the structuralism of Lévi-Strauss implicitly does, that in such cases the structure lies in the ideology, and that power lies in the possession of the instrument of appropriation of these structures, i.e. in a form of cultural capital.)

50 Emile Benveniste's history of the vocabulary of Indo-European institutions charts the linguistic milestones in the process of *unveiling* and *disenchantment* which runs from physical or symbolic violence to law and order, from ransom to purchase, from the prize for a notable action to the rate for the job, from recognition of services to recognition of debts, from moral worth to creditworthiness, and from moral obligation to the court order (*Indo-European Language and Society* (London: Faber, 1973), esp. pp. 101–62). And similarly, Moses Finley shows how debts which were sometimes contrived so as to produce situations of enslavement could also serve to create relations of solidarity between equals ("La servitude pour dettes", *Revue d'Histoire du Droit Français et Etranger*, 4th series, 43, 2 (April–June 1965), pp. 159–84).

51 The question of the relative worth of the different modes of domination – a question raised, implicitly at least, by Rousseauistic accounts of primitive paradises and disquisitions on "modernization" – is totally meaningless and can only give rise to necessarily interminable debates on *the advantages and disadvantages of the situations before and after*, the only interest of which lies in the revelation of the researcher's social phantasms, i.e. his unanalysed relationship with his own society. As in all comparisons of one system with another, it is possible *ad infinitum* to contrast representations of the two systems (e.g. enchantment versus disenchantment) differing in their affective colouring and ethical connotations depending on which of the two is taken as a standpoint. The only legitimate object of comparison is each system considered *as* a system, and this precludes any evaluation other than that implied in the immanent logic of its evolution.

52 Certain usurers, fearing dishonour and ostracism by the group, prefer to grant their debtors new time-limits for repayment (e.g. until the olive harvest) to save them from having to sell land in order to pay. Many of those who had been prepared to flout public opinion paid the price of their defiance, sometimes with their lives, during the war of liberation.

54 E. Benveniste, *Indo-European Language and Society*, pp. 84ff.

55 The marabouts are in a different position, because they wield an institutionally delegated authority as members of a respected body of "religious officials" and because they keep up a separate status – in particular, through fairly strict endogamy and a whole set of traditions, such as the practice of confining their women to the house. The fact remains that the only occasions on which men who "like the mountain torrents grow greater in stormy times" can, as the proverb suggests, take advantage of their quasi-institutionalized rôle as mediators, are when their knowledge of the traditions and acquaintance with the persons involved enable them to exercise a symbolic authority which can only exist through direct delegation by the group: the marabouts are most often simply the loophole, the "door", as the Kabyles say, which enables groups in conflict to reach an agreement without losing face.

56 Conversely, whereas institutionalized delegation of authority, which is accompanied by an explicit definition of responsibilities, tends to limit the consequences of individual shortcomings, diffuse delegation, which comes as the corollary of membership of the group, underwrites all members of the group, without distinction, with the guarantee of the collectively owned capital, but does not cover the group against the discredit which it may incur from the conduct of any member; this accounts for the importance which the "great" attach to defending the collective honour in the honour of the weakest member of their group.

57 See S. Freud, "Negation", *Complete Psychological Works* (standard ed.), ed. J. Strachey, vol. xix (London: Hogarth Press, 1961), pp. 235–6.

58 See S. B. Linder, *The Harried Leisure Class*, New York and London: Columbia University Press, 1970.

59 "Lord, give to me that I may give" (only the saint can give without possessing). Wealth is God's gift to man to enable him to relieve the poverty of others. "A generous man is the friend of Allah." Both worlds belong to him. He who wishes to keep his wealth must show he is worthy of it, by showing that he is generous; otherwise his wealth will be taken from him.

60 It would be a mistake to overemphasize the contrast between the symmetry of gift-exchange and the asymmetry of the ostentatious distribution which is the basis of the constitution of political authority. It is possible to move by successive degrees from one pattern to the other: as one moves away from perfect reciprocity, so an increasing proportion of the counter-prestations come to be made up of homage, respect, obligations, and moral debts. Those who, like Polyani and Sahlins, have seen clearly the determining function of redistribution in the constitution of political authority and in the operation of tribal economy (with the circuit of accumulation and redistribution functioning in a similar way to a State's budget) have not analysed the way in which this process, the device par excellence for conversion of economic capital into symbolic capital, creates lasting relations of dependence which, though economically based, are disguised under the veil of moral relations.

61 It follows that the objectivist error – in particular the mistake of ignoring the effects of objectifying the non-objectified – is more far-reaching in its consequences in a world in which, as here, reproduction of the social order depends more on the unceasing reproduction of concordant habitus than on the automatic reproduction of structures capable of producing or selecting concordant habitus.

62 Urbanization, which brings together groups with different traditions and weakens reciprocal controls (and, even before urbanization, the generalization of monetary exchanges and the introduction of wage labour), results in the collapse of the collectively maintained collective fiction of the religion of honour. *Trust* is replaced by *credit* (*talq*), which was formerly cursed or despised (as is shown by the insult "Face of credit!" – the face of the man who has ceased to feel dishonour – and by the fact that repudiation without restitution, the greatest offence imaginable, is called *berru natalq*). "In the age of credit", said an informant, "wretched indeed are those who can only appeal to the trust in which their parents were held. All that counts now is the goods you have immediately to hand. Everyone wants to be a market man. Everyone thinks he has a right to trust, so that there's no trust anywhere now."

63 It was not a sociologist but a group of American industrialists who conceived the "bank-account" theory of public relations: "It necessitates making *regular and frequent* deposits in the Bank of Public Good-Will, so that valid checks can be drawn on this account when it is desirable" (quoted in Dayton MacKean, *Party and Pressure Politics*, New York: Houghton Mifflin, 1944). See also R. W. Gable, "N.A.M.: Influential Lobby or Kiss of Death?", *Journal of Politics*, 15, 2 (May 1953), p. 262 (on the different ways in which the National Association of Manufacturers tries to influence the general public, educators, churchmen, women's club leaders, farmers' leaders, etc.), and H. A. Turner, "How Pressure Groups Operate", *Annals of the American Academy of Political and Social Science*, 319 (September 1958), pp. 63–72 (on the way in which "an organization elevates itself in the esteem of the general public and conditions their attitudes so that a state of public opinion will be created in which the public will almost automatically respond with favor to the programs desired by the group").

Index

abstraction, *see* genealogy, objectivism
academicism, 19, 206 n.69
accomplished, *see* excellence, honour
accounts, 21
acculturation, 216 n.29
accumulation, 162, 179–80, 195
age classes, 165; *see also* generation
alliances (*nesba*), 65, 178; *see also* capital: symbolic
amahbul, 12, 40, 232 n.8
amengur, 47, 48, 224 n.50
analogical transfer, 83, 119
analogy, 112–13, 119, 123, 156; sense of, 112, 223 n.33
anthropologist, 18, 36, 43, 49, 108, 117, 118, 219 n.3; point of view of, 1–2, 17, 37, 96, 116–17, 237 n.49, 238 n.51
anthropology, 22, 156, 233 n.17; colonial, 115; cultural, 24–5; participant, 115; social, 24; structural, 26–9, *and see* structuralism
arbitrariness, 189, 195; cultural, 76, 89, 94–5, 141, 142, 163, 164, 166, 168, 200 n.20, 219 n.3; and urbanization, 233 n.16
Aristotle, 96, 224 n.47
Aron, R., 216 n.26
Arrow, K. J., 217 n.40
art, 1–2, 23, 88, 167, 178, 187, 201 n.26; for art's sake, 194; history, 1; of living, *see* excellence; as symbolic capital, 197
"articulation of instances", 83
artificialism, 80, 189
assembly, 46, 63, 159, 199 n.18, 213 n.98; place of (*thajma'th*), 89, 94, 111, 224 n.52
authority, 21, 167, 170–1, 192–3, 236 n.42; *see also* delegation, language
autonomy, relative, 184
awrith, 47, 50–1, 53, 209 n.84
azegzaw, 145, 226 n.68

Bachelard, G., 223 n.36
Bally, C., 1, 25, 198 n.1, 202 n.32
baraka, 228 n.89
bard, 88, 187, 236 n.41
barley, origin of, 162–3
Barth, F., 32
Bateson, G., 231 n.112

Becker, G. S., 234 n.26
behaviourism, 95
behind/in front, 122–3
belief, 164, 167, 233 n.15
Benet, F., 235 n.37
bent'amm, *see* cousin
Benveniste, E., 176, 193, 238 nn.50 & 54
Berelson, B., 217 n.33
bilingualism, 26, 81
biography, 86–7
Bloomfield, L., 95
bluff, 10, 181, 185, 214 n.110; *see also* strategy
Boas, F., 200 n.22
body, and cultural arbitrariness, 89, 91–2, 94–5; and knowledge, 96, 218 n.44; male and female, techniques of, 94; and mimesis, 2, 116, 218 n.44; as practical operator, 116–19; relation to, 92–4; socially informed, 124; *see also* embodiment, emotion, hexis, inversion, mimesis, sexuality, space, symbolism, virility
Bollack, J., 224 n.49
bottom/top, 15, 53, 90, 94, 110, 113, 118, 121
break, epistemological and social, 1–2, 216 n.24, 221–2 n.26
bridewealth, 54–5, 56, 211 n.91, 235 n.32
brothers, relation between, 39, 47, 57–8, 63–5, 173
bureaucracy, priestly, 219 n.5; *see also* specialists
butcher, 127, 163, 219 n.4

calculation, 62–3, 105, 171, 172–83, 198 n.7, 211 n.91
calendar, 97–109; agrarian, 100–4, 131, 219 n.3, 222 n.32; cooking, 143–6; homology of calendars, 143; mythical and climatic, 130; practical, 219 n.4; ritual, 7, 44, 136; unreality of, 107; women's, 146–8
capital, cultural, 89, 183–4, 236 n.41, (competence and) 186, (primitive accumulation of) 187; of land and livestock, 49; of men, 49, 61, 69; symbolic, 6, 36, 40, 41, 47, 54, 55, 59, 60, 65, 70, 171–83, 214 n.111, 222 n.32, *and see* honour, name, (and early